Understanding Stamp Duty Land Tax

Eighth edition

Related titles available from Law Society Publishing:

Commonhold
Gary Cowen, James Driscoll and Laurence Target

Conveyancing Handbook
General Editor: Frances Silverman

Environmental Law Handbook (6th edn)
Trevor Hellawell

Licensing for Conveyancers
Tim Hayden and Jane Hanney

Planning and Compulsory Purchase Act 2004
Stephen Tromans, Martin Edwards, Richard Harwood, Justine Thornton

Profitable Conveyancing
Stephanie Dale

Trust Practitioner's Handbook
Gill Steel with contributions by Robert Mowbray and Charles Christian

All books from Law Society Publishing can be ordered from good bookshops or direct from our distributors, Marston Book Services, by telephone 01235 465656 or email law.society@marston.co.uk. Please confirm the price before ordering.

For further information or a catalogue, please email our editorial and marketing office: publishing@lawsociety.co.uk.

UNDERSTANDING STAMP DUTY LAND TAX

Eighth edition

Reg Nock

The Law Society

All rights reserved. No part of this publication may be reproduced in any material form, whether by photocopying, scanning, downloading onto computer or otherwise without the written permission of the Law Society and the author except in accordance with the provisions of the Copyright, Designs and Patents Act 1988. Applications should be addressed in the first instance, in writing, to Law Society Publishing.

Whilst all reasonable care has been taken in the preparation of this publication, neither the publisher nor the author can accept any responsibility for any loss occasioned to any person acting or refraining from action as a result of relying upon its contents.

The views expressed in this publication should be taken as those of the authors only unless it is specifically indicated that the Law Society has given its endorsement.

The author has asserted the right under the Copyright, Designs and Patents Act 1988 to be identified as the author of this work.

© Reg Nock 2006

ISBN-10: 1–85328–982–5
ISBN-13: 978–1–85328–982–8

Published in 2006 by Law Society Publishing
113 Chancery Lane, London WC2A 1PL

Typeset by J&L Composition, Filey, North Yorkshire
Printed by TJ International Ltd, Padstow, Cornwall

Contents

Table of cases	x
Table of statutes	xv
Table of statutory instruments	xxii
Budget 2006	xxiii

1	**Introduction and general principles**		**1**
	1.1	Background	1
	1.2	General principles	5
	1.3	Sources	30
	1.4	Jurisdiction	31
	1.5	Form or substance – tax avoidance	32
2	**Chargeable transactions**		**37**
	2.1	Basic charging provisions	37
	2.2	Specific chargeable transactions	41
	2.3	Chargeable interests	44
3	**Taxable events – effective date**		**48**
	3.1	Actions not documents	48
	3.2	Basic position	50
	3.3	Special rules	51
4	**Computation of tax**		**59**
	4.1	Rates	59
	4.2	Disadvantaged land	61
	4.3	'Residential property'	61
	4.4	Special situations	63
	4.5	Linked transactions	66

CONTENTS

	4.6	Chargeable consideration	72
	4.7	'Provisional tax'	75
	4.8	Global consideration and apportionment	77
	4.9	Consideration in kind and market value	82
	4.10	'Costs'	86
	4.11	Theory and practice	87
	4.12	Particular items of consideration	89
5	**Exemptions and reliefs**		**111**
	5.1	Exemptions	111
	5.2	Types of relief	116
6	**Options and rights of pre-emption**		**125**
	6.1	Options and exchanges	125
	6.2	Linked transactions	127
	6.3	Sales of options	128
	6.4	Due diligence	128
	6.5	Compliance issue	129
7	**Exchanges and partitions**		**130**
	7.1	General	130
	7.2	Partition	134
8	**Leases**		**136**
	8.1	General	136
	8.2	Leases and nominees	138
	8.3	'Lease'	139
	8.4	Leases and compliance	142
	8.5	'Double charge'	143
	8.6	Grant of leases to third parties	146
	8.7	The charge to tax on leases	147
	8.8	Rents	148
	8.9	Linked transactions and renewals of leases	163
	8.10	The term of the lease	164
	8.11	The premium	167
	8.12	Exclusions from the charge on premiums	172
	8.13	Variations of leases	174
	8.14	Assignment of leases	176

	8.15	Termination of leases	179
	8.16	Exemptions from lease duty	181
	8.17	Reliefs not available for leases	185
9	**Construction, fitting out and other 'works'**	**186**
	9.1	Background	186
	9.2	Works	190
	9.3	Site assembly	191
	9.4	Calculation and payment	194
10	**Trusts, wills and intestate estates**	**196**
	10.1	Creation of trusts	196
	10.2	Resulting and other similar trusts	198
	10.3	Trusts: general	199
	10.4	Trusts and SDLT	202
	10.5	Property into trust	203
	10.6	Purchase of land	203
	10.7	Initial vesting of trust assets	203
	10.8	Appointment and retirement of trustees	205
	10.9	Dispositions of trust property – dealings in equitable interests	206
	10.10	Interests of beneficiaries	207
	10.11	Severing joint tenancies	208
	10.12	Computational issues	210
	10.13	Discretionary trusts	211
	10.14	Creation of derivative trusts	212
	10.15	Internal rearrangement of beneficial interests	213
	10.16	Powers of appointment and advancement	214
	10.17	Reservation of benefit	215
	10.18	Estates of deceased persons	216
	10.19	Wills and intestacies	218
	10.20	Testamentary trusts	219
	10.21	Assents and appropriations	219
	10.22	Variation of estates of deceased persons	220
	10.23	Purchasers of land from personal representatives	222
11	**Partnerships**	**223**
	11.1	General	223
	11.2	Stamp duty	224

CONTENTS

11.3	Stamp duty land tax	225
11.4	Acquisitions of chargeable interests from connected persons	231
11.5	Actual consideration	232
11.6	Sum of the lower proportions	233
11.7	Removal of land from partnership	234
11.8	Transfers of partnership interests	237

12 Corporate transactions — 242

12.1	Background	242
12.2	'Company'	242
12.3	Acquisitions by companies	243
12.4	Purchases from companies	246
12.5	'Time bombs'	246
12.6	Corporate reorganisations	247
12.7	Procedure	248
12.8	Partitions and reorganisations of companies – reduced rate	251
12.9	Relief for intra-group transactions	254
12.10	Arrangements	256
12.11	Clawback of intra-group relief	256
12.12	Share sales, warranties, indemnities and due diligence	258
12.13	Compliance situation	258
12.14	Deferred or provisional tax	259

13 Liability for the tax — 261

13.1	General	261
13.2	The taxable person – 'the purchaser'	261
13.3	The issues – a moving target	262
13.4	'Vendor'	265
13.5	Land Registry issues	265
13.6	Connected parties	266
13.7	Accountability for the tax	275
13.8	Registration of title	276
13.9	Notifiable transactions	278
13.10	The two certificates	279
13.11	Self-assessment	281

14 HMRC powers and enforcement — 282

14.1	General	282
14.2	Enquiries	282

14.3	Assessments by HMRC	283
14.4	Enquiries into land transaction returns (SDLT 1)	286
14.5	Enquiries into self-certificate (SDLT 60)	286
14.6	Post-transaction rulings	286
14.7	Scope of Enquiries	286
14.8	Appeals	287
14.9	Completion of Enquiry	287
14.10	Information powers	288
14.11	Other information powers	288
14.12	Record-keeping obligations	288
14.13	Powers to call for information	289

Appendices — **294**

A	Land areas for investigation	294
B	Particular problems for the vendor	300
C	Share purchase issues for investigation	302
D	Completing the tax return	304

Index — 317

Table of cases

Addiscombe Garden Estates *v.* Crabbe [1958] 1 QB 513; [1957] 3 All ER
    563, CA 18, 34, 139, 193
Akasuc Enterprise Ltd *v.* Farmar & Shirreff [2003] EWHC 1275; [2003]
    PL SCS 127, ChD 85, 106
Alan Estates Ltd *v.* WG Stores Ltd [1982] Ch 511; [1981] 3 All ER 481,
    CA (Civ Div) 164
Archer Shee *v.* Baker *See* Baker *v.* Archer Shee
Archer Shee *v.* Garland [1931] AC 212; 15 TC 693, HL 32, 207
Att-Gen *v.* Brown (1849) 3 Exch 662 .... 73, 146
Att-Gen *v.* Cohen [1937] KB 478; [1937] 1 All ER 17, CA 67–8
Baker *v.* Archer Shee [1927] AC 844; 15 TC 1, HL 32, 207
Baker *v.* Merckel [1960] 1 QB 657, CA 165–6, 175
Banning *v.* Wright [1972] 1 WLR 972; 48 TC 421, HL 174–5
Barrett *v.* Morgan [2000] 2 AC 264; [2000] 1 All ER 481, HL 38, 180
Baytrust Holdings Ltd *v.* IRC [1971] 1 WLR 1333, ChD 251
Belaney *v.* Belaney (1867) 2 Ch App 138, Lord Chancellor 138
Binions *v.* Evans [1972] Ch 359; [1972] 2 All ER 70, CA (Civ Div) 19, 74, 197
Blendett *v.* IRC [1984] STC 95, CA (Civ Div) 93
British India Steam Navigation Co *v.* IRC [1891] 2 QB 165, QBD 34
Brown and Root Technology Ltd *v.* Sun Life and London Assurance Co
    Ltd [2001] Ch 733; [2000] 2 WLR 566, CA (Civ Div) 69
Carreras Group Ltd *v.* Stamp Commissioner [2004] UKPC 16; [2004]
    STC 1377, PC (Jam) 5
Central and District Properties *v.* IRC [1966] 1 WLR 1015; [1966] 2 All
    ER 433, HL 80, 249, 251
City Permanent Building Society *v.* Miller [1952] Ch 840, CA 137
Clarke-Chapman John Thompson Ltd *v.* IRC [1976] Ch 91; [1975] STC
    567, CA (Civ Div) 183, 249
Commissioners of Inland Revenue *v.* Mitsubishi Motors New Zealand
    Ltd. [1996] AC 315; [1995] STC 989, PC (NZ) 5
Collector of Stamp Revenue *v.* Arrowtown Assets Ltd 6 ITL Rep. 454;
    HKCFA 46, CFA (HK) 5
Commissioner of Stamp Duty (Queensland) *v.* Livingston [1965] AC 694;
    [1964] 3 All ER 692, PC (Aus) 45, 218
Cook's Settlement Trusts, *Re* [1965] Ch 902, ChD 197
Cooper *v.* Critchley [1955] Ch 431, CA 213

Coren v. Keighley [1972] 1 WLR 1556, ChD 93
Cowan de Groot Properties Ltd v. Eagle Trust plc [1992] 4 All ER 700;
　[1991] BCLC 1045, ChD 82, 132, 202
Crane-Fruehauf v. IRC [1975] 1 All ER 429; [1975] STC 51, CA
　(Civ Div) 80, 105, 249, 251
Curzon Offices v. IRC [1944] 1 All ER 163 100
Dearle v. Hall (1828) 3 Russ 1 211
Duke of Westminster's Settled Estates, Re (No. 2) [1921] 1 Ch 585, ChD 180
E Gomme Ltd v. IRC [1964] 1 WLR 1348, ChD 251
ER Ives Investment Ltd v. High [1967] 2 QB 379, CA 19
Eastham v. Leigh, London and Provincial Properties Ltd [1971] Ch 871;
　[1971] 2 All ER 887, CA (Civ Div) 19, 74, 99, 167, 170, 188–9, 194
Eilbeck v. Rawling See WT Ramsay Ltd v. IRC
Errington v. Errington and Woods [1952] 1 KB 290, CA 19, 74
Escoigne Properties Ltd v. IRC [1958] AC 549, HL 255
Facchini v. Bryson [1952] 1 TLR 1386, CA 19, 139, 196
Faith Construction v. Customs and Excise Commissioners [1989] QB 179;
　[1988] STC 35, QBD; *affirmed* [1990] 1 QB 905, CA (Civ Div) 54
Firstpost Homes Ltd v. Johnson [1995] 1 WLR 1567; [1995] 4 All ER 355,
　CA (Civ Div) 3, 18, 74
Forster v. Hale (1798) 3 Ves 696 197
Furniss v. Dawson [1984] AC 474; [1984] STC 153, HL; *reversing* [1982]
　STC 267, ChD 33, 36, 170
GUS Merchandise Corp Ltd v. Customs and Excise Commissioners [1981]
　1 WLR 1309; [1981] STC 569, CA (Civ Div) 19–20, 74
Gable Construction Co v. IRC [1968] 1 WLR 1426, ChD; *affirmed* (1970)
　49 ATC 244, CA (Civ Div) 151, 175
Gage v. King [1961] 1 QB 188, QBD 74
Garland v. Archer Shee See Archer Shee v. Garland
Gartside v. IRC [1968] AC 553, HL 211
George Wimpey & Co v. IRC [1975] 1 WLR 995; [1975] STC 248, CA
　(Civ Div) 127–8
Giambrone v. JMC Holidays (No. 2) [2004] EWCA Civ 158; [2004] 2 All
　ER 891, CA (Civ Div) 100
Glenrothes Development Corp v. IRC 1994 SC 169; [1993] STC 74, IH
　(1 Div) 89, 92
Great Western Railway Ltd v. IRC [1894] 1 QB 507, CA 34
Grey v. IRC [1960] AC 1, HL 206
Halsall v. Brizell [1957] Ch 169, ChD 97
Henneker v. Henneker (1852) 1 E&B 54 ....200, 213
Higher Education Statistics Agency Ltd v. Customs and Excise [2000]
　STC 332, QBD 91
Hill v. Booth [1930] 1 KB 381, CA 151
Hodge, Re [1940] Ch 260, ChD 204
Hollebone's Agreement, Re [1959] 1 WLR 536; [1959] 2 All ER 152, CA 43, 79
Holmden v. IRC [1968] AC 685, HL 211
Hurlingham Estates Ltd v. Wilde & Partners [1997] 1 Lloyd's Rep 525;
　[1997] STC 627, ChD 36

TABLE OF CASES

Ingram v. IRC [1986] Ch 585; [1985] STC 835, ChD 34
Ingram v. IRC (No. 2) [2000] 1 AC 293; [1999] STC 37, HL 138, 216
Ingle v. Vaughan Jenkins [1900] 2 Ch 368, ChD 139
IRC v. Duke of Westminster [1936] AC 1, HL 33
IRC v. Henry Ansbacher & Co [1963] AC 191, HL 113
IRC v. Tyre Investment Ltd [1924] 12 TC 646 251
J & P Coats Ltd v. IRC [1897] 2 QB 423, CA; affirming [1897] 1 QB 778,
    QBD 34
J Rothschild Holdings plc v. IRC [1989] STC 435, CA (Civ Div); affirming
    [1988] STC 645, ChD 31, 304
Johnstone v. Holdway [1963] 1 QB 601; [1963] 1 All ER 432, CA 40, 131, 189
Jopling v. IRC [1940] 2 KB 282, KBD 219
Kay's Settlement Trusts, Re [1939] Ch 329, ChD 197
Kildrummy (Jersey) Ltd v. IRC [1990] STC 657, IH (1 Div) 138, 216
Kimbers & Co v. IRC [1936] 1 KB 132, KBD 187
King's Will Trusts, Re [1964] Ch 542, ChD 204
LM Tenancies (No.1) plc v. IRC [1998] 1 WLR 1269; [1998] STC 326,
    CA (Civ Div), affirming [1996] STC 880, ChD 5, 21, 32
Lace v. Chantler [1944] KB 368, CA 138, 153, 166
Lady Ingram v. IRC See Ingram v. IRC (No. 2)
Langham v. Veltema [2004] EWCA Civ 193; [2004] STC 544, CA
    (Civ Div) 26, 76, 88, 115, 282–3, 304
Lap Shun Textiles Industrial Co v. Collector of Stamp Revenue [1976]
    AC 530; [1976] 1 All ER 833, PC (HK) 76, 82, 132
Letts v. IRC [1957] 1 WLR 201, ChD 206
Littlewoods Mail Order Stores v. IRC [1961] Ch 597, CA; affirmed [1963]
    AC 135, HL 35
Lloyds and Scottish Finance v. Cyril Lord Carpet Sales [1992] BCLC 609, HL ...34
Lloyds and Scottish Finance v. Prentice 121 SJ 847, CA (Civ Div) 77
Lloyds Private Banking Ltd v. IRC [1998] STC 559, ChD 19
McGuckian v. IRC [1997] 1 WLR 991; [1997] STC 908. HL (NI) 4–5
Macleod v. IRC (1885) 22 SLR 674 187
MacNiven v. Westmoreland Investments Ltd [2001] UKHL 6; [2003]
    1 AC 311; [2001] STC 237, HL 5
Massey v. Crown Life Insurance Co [1978] 1 WLR 676; [1978] 2 All
    ER 576, CA (Civ Div) 140
Matrix Securities Ltd v. IRC [1994] 1 WLR 334; [1994] STC 272, HL 284
Metal Box Plastic Films Ltd v. IRC [1969] 1 WLR 1620, ChD 98
Michaels v. Harley House (Marylebone) Ltd [2000] Ch 104; [1999]
    3 WLR 229, CA (Civ Div) 39, 206
Milmo v. Carreras [1946] KB 306, CA 138
Milroy v. Lord (1862) 4 De GF & J 264 197
Ministre des Finances v. Weidert (Case C-242/03) [2005] STC 1241,
    ECJ (1st Chamber) 243
Morley v. Hall (1834) 2 Dowl 494 32
Mullins v. Wessex Motors Ltd [1947] 2 All ER 727, CA 44, 177
Neville v. Wilson [1997] Ch 144, CA (Civ Div) 19, 199, 206, 212
Neville Estates Ltd v. Madden [1962] Ch 832, ChD 270

TABLE OF CASES

Nichols v. IRC [1975] 1 WLR 534; [1975] STC 278, CA (Civ Div);
  affirming [1974] 1 WLR 296; [1973] STC 497, ChD 216
Nokes v. Doncaster Amalgamated Collieries Ltd [1940] AC 1014, HL 81
O'Brien v. Benson's Hosiery (Holdings) Ltd [1980] AC 562; [1979] STC
  735, HL 81
Ogwr BC v. Dykes [1989] 1 WLR 295; [1989] 2 All ER 880, CA
  (Civ Div) 19, 34, 139, 193
Oswald Tillotson Ltd v. IRC [1933] 1 KB 134, CA 249
Oughtred v. IRC [1960] AC 206, HL 4, 199, 206, 213
Parinv (Hatfield) Ltd v. IRC [1998] STC 305, CA (Civ Div) 285
Park v. IRC [1970] 1 WLR 626, ChD; reversed [1970] 2 All ER 248, CA
  (Civ Div) 216
Park v. IRC (No. 2) [1972] Ch 385, CA (Civ Div) 216
Paul v. Constance [1977] 1 WLR 527, CA (Civ Div) 196
Paul v. IRC 1936 SC 443, IH (1 Div) 187
Pauling's Settlement, Re [1962] 1 WLR 86, ChD; affirmed [1964]
  Ch 303, CA 213
Penrose, Re [1933] Ch 793, ChD 221
Perry v. IRC [2005] STC (SpCD) 474, Sp Comm 19
Peter Bone Ltd v. IRC [1995] STC 921, Ch D 34
Platt's Trustees v. IRC 46 R & IT 605; (1953) 34 ATC 292 213
Ponder, Re [1921] 2 Ch 59, ChD 204
Pritchard v. Briggs [1980] Ch 338, CA (Civ Div) 125
Prudential Assurance Co Ltd v. IRC [1993] 1 WLR 211; [1992] STC
  863, ChD 91, 187
Quietlece Ltd v. IRC [1984] STC 95 94
R. v. Industrial Disputes Tribunal, ex p. Courage and Co Ltd [1956]
  1 WLR 1062, DC 251
Ralli's Will Trusts, Re [1964] Ch 288, ChD 197
Ramsay v. IRC See WT Ramsay Ltd v. IRC
Ready Mixed Concrete (South East) Ltd v. Minister of Pensions and
  National Insurance [1968] 2 QB 497; [1968] 1 All ER 433, QBD 140
Richards v. Delbridge (1874) LR 18 Eq 11, Ct of Chancery 204
Ridgeons Bulk v. Customs and Excise Commissioners [1994] STC 427, QBD 21
Rochefoucauld v. Boustead [1897] 1 Ch 196, CA 197
Rose, Re [1949] Ch 78, ChD 197
Rye v. Rye [1962] AC 496; [1961] 1 All ER 146, HL 138, 216
St Edmundsbury and Ipswich Diocesan Board of Finance v. Clark (No. 2)
  [1975] 1 WLR 468; [1975] 1 All ER 772, CA (Civ Div); affirming
  [1973] 1 WLR 1572; [1973] 2 All ER 903, ChD 131, 189
Saunders v. Edwards [1987] 1 WLR 1116; [1987] 2 All ER 651, CA
  (Civ Div) 43, 62, 68, 78–9, 187, 301
Saunders v. Vautier (1841) 4 Beav 115 202
Saywell v. Pope [1979] STC 824, ChD 98
Secretan v. Hart [1969] 1 WLR 1599; [1969] 3 All ER 1196; 45 TC 701,
  ChD 79–81, 86
Shannon, The v. Venner [1965] Ch 682; [1965] 1 All ER 590, CA 189
Shepherd v. Lyntress [1989] STC 617, DC 35

TABLE OF CASES

Sherdley v. Sherdley [1986] 1 WLR 732; [1987] STC 266; CA (Civ Div);
  reversed [1988] AC 213, HL 35
Shop and Store Developments v. IRC [1967] 1 AC 472, HL 80
Skipton Building Society v. Clayton (1993) 66 P&CR 223, CA (Civ Div) ...138, 216
Snook v. London and West Riding Investments Ltd [1967] 2 QB 786, CA
  (Civ Div) 34
Spiro v. Glencrown Properties Ltd [1991] Ch 537; [1991] 2 WLR 931,
  ChD 3, 19, 137
Stanton Ltd v. Drayton Commercial Investment Co Ltd [1983] 1 AC
  501; [1982] STC 585, HL 82
Stekel v. Ellice [1973] 1 WLR 191; [1973] 1 All ER 465, ChD 224
Street v. Mountford [1985] 1 AC 809; [1985] 2 WLR 877, HL 19, 139–40, 193
Strong v. Bird (1874) LR Eq 315, Ct of Chancery 197
Swayne v. IRC [1900] 1 QB 172, CA 97
Swithland Investmens v. IRC [1990] STC 448, ChD 250
T & E Homes Ltd v. Robinson [1976] 1 WLR 1150; [1976] STC 462,
  ChDm reversed [1979] 1 WLR 452; [1979] STC 351, CA (Civ Div) 44, 151
T Choithram International SA v. Pagarani [2001] 1 WLR 1; [2001] 2 All
  ER 492, PC (BVI)..196
Tootal Clothing Ltd v. Guinea Properties Management Ltd (1992) 674
  P&CR 452, CA (Civ Div) 3, 20
Tower Cabinet Co v. Ingram [1949] 2 KB 397, DC 224
Tyler, Re [1967] 1 WLR 1269; [1967] 3 All ER 367, ChD 206
Vandervell v. IRC [1967] 2 AC 291; [1967] 1 All ER 1, HL 198, 204
Veltema v. Langham See Langham v. Veltema
WT Ramsay Ltd v. IRC [1982] AC 300; [1981] 2 WLR 449; [1981]
  STC 174, HL; affirming [1979] 1 WLR 974, CA 5, 33, 36, 66, 170
Wachtel v. IRC [1971] Ch 573; 46 TC 543, ChD 100
Walsh v. Lonsdale (1882) 21 Ch D 9, CA 206
Warmington v. Miller [1973] QB 877; [1973] 2 All ER 372, CA (Civ Div) 18, 39
Wasdale, Re [1899] 1 Ch 163, ChD 212
West London Syndicate Ltd v. IRC [1898] 2 QB 507, CA 34
Western United Investment Co Ltd v. IRC [1951] Ch 392, ChD 90, 94, 99
Whiteman Smith Motor Co Ltd v. Chaplin [1934] 2 KB 35, KBD 177
William Brandt's Sons & Co v. Dunlop Rubber Co Ltd [1905] AC 454, HL 211
Williams & Glyn's Bank Ltd v. Boland [1981] AC 487, HL 207
Willoughby v. IRC [1995] STC 143, CA (Civ Div); affirmed [1997] 1 WLR
  1071, HL 35
Workers Trust & Merchant Bank Ltd v. Dojap Investments Ltd [1993]
  AC 573; [1993] 2 All ER 370, PC (Jam) 54
Wragg Ltd, Re [1897] 1 Ch 796, CA 43, 78
Wynn Realisations Ltd v. Vogue Holdings Inc [1999] STC 524, CA
  (Civ Div) 21
Yaxley v. Gotts [2000] Ch 162; [1999] 2 WLR 1217, CA (Civ Div) 3, 19, 100,
                                                              197, 199, 206

Table of statutes

Administration of Estates Act 1925
   s.36(4), (7) 204
Building Societies Act 1986 123
Capital Allowances Act 2000
   s.546 24
Companies Act 1985 315
Family Law (Scotland) Act 1985
   s.8(2) 119
   s.14(1) 119
Finance Act 1930
   s.42 ....247, 254
Finance Act 1965
   s.90 96
Finance Act 1982
   ss.75, 77 247
Finance Act 1986
   s.75 257
   s.76(3A) 252
      (6A)(a), (b) 252
   s.77 254
   s.87 ....1, 200, 204
   s.99 ....113, 200
Finance Act 1999
   Sched. 13, para. 7 ....212, 224
Finance Act 2000
   s.120 214
Finance Act 2002
   s.77 132
Finance Act 2003 ....30, 35, 79,
                 111, 137, 143
   Pt 1 256
   s.4 40
   s.42(2) 31
      (a) 40
   s.43 ....2–3, 17, 80, 132, 229
      (1) 37, 116

      (2) 40, 180
      (3)(a), (b) 38
        (c) 38, 174
        (d) .38, 59, 142, 148, 161, 174
      (4) 264
      (5) 265
      (6) 77
   s.44 ....20, 51, 143, 193
      (1)(c) 51
      (2) 50, 52, 164, 277
      (4) 278
      (5)(a) 77
      (6) 53, 55
        (a) 53
        (b) 47, 53
      (7) 39
        (a)–(c) 53
      (8) 17–18, 48–9, 52, 165
      (9) 39, 57, 212, 307
   s.44A 42, 45, 47, 51, 77,
               80, 100, 140, 147,
               186, 192–3, 279
      (2) 50
      (3) 278
      (6) 186
   s.45 ....12, 45, 51, 146–7,
            184, 192, 215, 264,
            266, 277–8, 297
      (2) 50, 277
      (3) 263
      (5)(a) 255
   s.45A 42, 45, 47, 51,
          140, 147, 186, 192, 263
      (2) 50
   ss.45B, 45C 116
   s.46 ....17, 50–2, 66, 127, 278

TABLE OF STATUTES

Finance Act 2003 (*cont.*)
   (1) 23, 56, 70, 126, 163
      (b) 125
   (2) 126
   (3) 58, 126
  s.47 . . . . .39, 50, 81, 126,
                130, 170, 175,
             192, 198, 208–10,
                215–16, 220,
                  263, 310
  s.48 . . . . .139, 214
   (1) 44
      (a) 32
      (b) 153
      (c)(i) 153
   (2) 44
      (a), (b) 116
      (c) 116
        (i) 141, 167
   (3)(a) 44, 116
  s.49(1) .37
  s.51 . . . . .22, 85, 87, 89–90,
               93, 95, 101–3, 153,
             155, 158, 160, 169,
             176, 188, 217, 311
   (2) 156
   (3) 103
   (4) 109
  s.52 . . . . .17, 20, 23, 59, 91,
            93, 141, 151–2, 169
   (1), (2) 94, 169
   (3) 169
   (4) 95
   (6) 93, 152, 169
  s.53 . . . . .46, 73, 118, 139,
            168, 171, 182, 200–1,
             203, 205, 213–14,
                243, 253
  s.54 . . . . .46, 73, 118, 139, 205,
             213–14, 244–5, 315
  s.55 . . . . .60, 167
   (2) 65
   (4) 66
  s.56 151
  s.57 76
  s.57A 84, 123, 141, 155, 171,
             178, 183, 216, 246
  s.59 122

  s.60 . . . . .132, 185, 191
  s.61 . . . . .122, 185
  s.60(2)–(4) 122
  s.64A .264
  s.66 . . . . .122, 141, 178, 185
  s.67 . . . . .122, 185
  s.69 123
  s.71 44
   (2), (4) 121
  s.71A 44
  s.72 . . . . .44, 185
   (6), (9) 124
  s.73 185
   (4) 124
   (5)(b) 124
   (6) 124
  s.75 2
  s.76 . . . . .10, 27, 113, 136, 263
   (2) 3
   (3)(a) 114
  s.77 . . . . .10, 37, 41, 65, 112,
             134, 164–5, 176, 181,
                  184, 229
   (2) 141
      (b)(ii) 153
  s.79 277
   (1) 276–7
   (2)(a), (b) 277
   (3) 276
      (a), (b) 276
  s.80 . . . . .22, 52, 76, 87, 90,
            101–3, 105, 156, 169,
             177, 188, 217, 275
   (2)(c) 150
   (4) 158
  s.81A 67, 70, 76, 163,
                177, 262, 311
  s.81B 263, 273
  s.82 . . . . .87, 307
  s.85 263
  s.87(5) 101
  s.90 . . . . .87, 90, 101, 103,
           108–9, 168–9, 218, 311
  s.91 101–4
  s.95 . . . . .8, 68, 79, 96, 117,
                 129, 200, 296
  s.96 . . . . .8, 68, 79, 96, 117,
                 200, 292, 296

s.100 243	para. 3 . . . . .77, 93, 95
(4) 270	(a), (c) 97
(7)(a), (b) 270	para. 4 . . . . .61, 151, 187, 210
s.101 268	(1), (2) 77
s.103(2)(a), (c) 267	(3) 155
(4) 267	(4) 43
s.106 . . . . .273, 275	para. 5 . . . . . . .39–40, 50, 81, 133, 170, 176, 180, 192, 209, 220, 235
(1) 267, 273	
(2) 273	
(3) 217, 274	
(4) 272	(3) 220
s.108 . . . . .16, 65, 67, 127, 163, 275	(4) . . .126, 134, 221
(1) .67	(a), (b) . .210–11
s.110 249	para. 6 . . . . .134, 214, 235
s.116 62	para. 7 . . . . .49, 81, 84
(2), (3) 64	para. 8 . . . . . .84, 96, 118, 205, 214, 245
(5)(a), (b) 63	
(6) .64	(1), (2) 97
(7) .65	para. 8A 98, 118, 219
(8)(a) 64	(1) 120
s.117 . . . . .132, 136, 141, 198, 210, 220	para. 9 99
	para. 10 . . . .20–1, 49, 54, 81, 86, 89, 92, 99, 137, 144–5, 169, 186–7, 192–3
s.118 84	
s.119 . . . . .20, 22, 48, 50, 143, 205	
s.120 134	
(2)(a) 165	
(b) 167	(2) 170, 264
s.121 . . . . . . .42, 202, 208, 214, 267	(2A) 170
s.123(3) 141	(3) 194
Sched. 3 . . . . .112, 220, 279–80	(b) 99
para. 1 . . . .10, 19, 37, 72, 118, 176, 178, 182, 200, 205, 214, 233, 262, 265	para. 11 . . .19, 49, 74, 81, 86, 88–9, 92, 173
	para. 12 153
	para. 13 . . . . .172, 179
	(2) 174
	para. 14 134
para. 2 . . . . .118, 184	para. 15 . . . . .109, 180
para. 3 . . . .119, 182, 221, 254, 273	(1) 177
	(2)(b) 177
para. 3A 46, 98, 120, 219, 273	para. 16 . . . . . .97–8, 172, 176, 188
para. 4 . . . . . .46, 98, 119, 183, 221, 254	para. 17 . . . . . . .132, 171, 185, 188
Sched. 4 . . . . .20, 80, 130, 167	(4A) 112
para. 1 . . . . . . .79–80, 86, 100, 132, 173, 192, 262	Sched. 5 . . . . .59, 71, 164, 172, 312
(1) 263	
para. 2 . . . . .152, 155, 190	para. 1A . . .148, 153, 313

TABLE OF STATUTES

Finance Act 2003 (*cont.*)
    para. 2 . . . .16, 23, 60, 148
        (5), (6) 67, 163
    para. 4(1) 172
    para. 6(2) 164
        (5) 163, 165
    para. 9(1) 167
        (2) 65
        (4) 148
        (5) 70, 167
    para. 12 70
Sched. 6 65
    para. 5 148
    para. 6 65
    para. 7(2) 61
    para. 8 280
    para. 9 148
        (5) 148
    para. 11 42
    para. 13 . . . .112, 205, 220
Sched. 6A 62, 121, 185, 279
    paras. 1, 2 134
    paras. 3, 8 222
    para. 11(3) 222
Sched. 7 . . . . .35, 111, 115
    Pt 1 26, 141, 144, 178, 183,
        244, 246
    Pt 2 . . .116, 141, 178, 183,
        244, 246
    para. 1 . . . . .249, 257
    para. 3 . . . . . . .37, 42, 46
        (2) 49
    para. 4 248
        (2), (4), (5) 257
        (6) 248, 257
        (7) 248
    para. 5 172
    para. 7 . . . . .249, 253
        (4) 251
    para. 8 . . . . . .42, 249, 253
    para. 9 . . . . . . .37, 46, 253
        (2) 49
        (3) 254
        (4) 256
        (5)(a) 253
Sched. 8 . . .141, 178, 182, 188, 246
    para. 2 . . . . .42, 89
        (2) 49

Sched. 9 . . . . .120, 184
    para. 6 184
Sched. 10 2
    para. 1A . .267, 305, 316
    para. 1B 273
    paras. 3, 4 268
    para. 5 . . . . . . .129, 268
    para. 6 . . . .57, 304, 308
        (3) 76
    para. 7 . . . . .27, 76,
        288, 308
    para. 8 . . . . .2, 25–8, 79,
        218, 264,
        268, 282
    para. 9 . . . . . .264, 289
    para. 12(2) 26
        (3) 286
    para. 13 287
        (2) 287
    paras. 14–16 288
    paras. 19, 23 287
    para. 24 . . . . .283, 287
    para. 25 283
    paras. 27, 28 284
    para. 30 283–4
        (3)(b) 283
        (4) . . .4, 28, 285
    para. 31 129
        (2) 160
        (4) 274
    para. 34 . . . .13, 90, 304
Sched. 11 276
    para. 4 289
    para. 7(2) 26
        (3) 286
    para. 8 287
    paras. 9–11 288
    paras. 12, 16, 17 287
Sched. 11A 304, 307–8
Sched. 13, para. 1 289
    paras. 2, 4, 6 290
    paras. 7, 9–11 291
    paras. 14–16 292
    para. 20 290–2
    para. 21 291
        (1) 290
        (2) 291
        (3) 292

para. 22	.292
para. 23	.290, 292
para. 24	.291
para. 25	.291–2
para. 26(1)(a), (b)	.291
(2), (3)	.291
para. 27	.292
paras. 28, 31	.290
paras. 32–34	.293
para. 35	.291
paras. 36, 40, 43, 45, 48	.293
Sched. 15	.32, 42, 223–4, 227, 270
Pt 1	.243
Pt 3	.171, 182, 264
Pt 7	.171
para. 1	.227
(1)	.42, 46
para. 2	.223
para. 6	.225
(2)	.271
para. 7	.225–6
(1), (1A)	.271
para. 8	.226, 271
para. 9	.229
(2)	.229
(c)	.38
para. 13	.214, 236
para. 14	.46, 227–8, 237
(4)	.239
para. 15	.46, 230, 240
para. 16	.134, 214, 235
para. 17	.239–40
para. 17A	.229, 234, 239, 241
para. 20	.236
para. 24	.214
para. 25	.203
para. 27	.240
para. 30	.238
para. 32	.237
para. 33	.224
para. 34	.230
(1)	.230
(2)	.233
para. 35	.229–30

para. 36	.228, 230, 238–9
(2)	.238
para. 37	.229–30
(a)	.230
para. 38	.231
Sched. 16, para. 1	.219, 226, 268
(2), (3)	.202
para. 2	.32, 207
para. 3	.118, 137, 139, 178, 204, 226, 266, 268
(1)	.201
(3)	.201, 204
para. 5	.203
(2)	.273
(3)	.272
(4)	.273
para. 6	.203
para. 7	.45, 211, 213–14, 280
Sched. 17A	.59, 158, 166
para. 1	.44, 140, 151
para. 1A	.312
para. 2(b)	.166
para. 3	.42, 138, 154, 275
para. 4	.42, 138, 177, 275
(1)	.167
(2)	.166
(5)(c)	.166
para. 5	.17, 23, 66, 127, 163, 166, 275
para. 6	.44, 174
(1)	.151–2
para. 7	.23, 41, 76, 107, 144, 177, 179
para. 7A	.155, 157, 164
(c)	.145
para. 8	.23, 41, 76, 107, 144, 177, 179, 275

TABLE OF STATUTES

Finance Act 2003 (cont.)
 para. 9 ...10, 83, 148, 154, 162, 165, 171, 175, 182
  (1)(d) 173
 para. 10 .....99, 152, 274
 para. 11 ......26, 38, 41, 67, 107–8, 110, 124, 139, 141, 148, 168, 169, 183, 201, 244–6, 256, 262, 265, 268
  (1)(b) 118
 para. 12 ......16, 22, 76, 143, 149, 163, 177, 217, 262, 311
  (1)(b)–(d) ..275
 para. 12A 17–18, 22, 42, 48–9, 52, 57–8, 89, 107, 137, 142, 144–5, 147, 152, 157, 170, 182, 243, 309, 312, 314
  (2) 278
 para. 12B 4, 8, 12, 24, 45, 51, 73, 116, 146, 184, 191, 192, 275, 278, 297
 para. 13 .....41, 142, 154, 160, 169, 278
  (1) 154
 para. 14 ......16, 23, 37–8, 107, 142–3, 154–5, 159, 163, 178
  (3) 154
  (5) 71, 159
  (6) 142
 para. 15 ...16, 23, 37, 107, 142–3, 155, 159, 163, 178
 para. 15A 38, 142, 148, 161, 174–5, 278
 para. 16 ......10, 83, 171, 175, 180
 para. 17 .....99, 174, 176, 188, 274
 para. 18 172
 para. 19 17
  (3) 278
 Sched. 19 ....1, 13, 49, 295
 para. 6 248
 para. 7 13
 para. 9 .....13, 71, 295
 Sched. 20 1
Finance Act 2004 ....139, 141–2, 186, 245
 Pt 7......................36
Finance Act 2005 ....22, 49, 60–1, 245
Finance (No. 2) Act 2005 ....139, 141, 175, 178
 s.47 3
 Sched. 10, para. 21 224
Finance (Northern Ireland) Act 1954
 s.11 254
Housing Act 1988
 Pt III 121
Housing Act 1996
 s.18 121
Housing Grants, Construction and Regeneration Act 1996
 s.126 121
Housing (Scotland) Act 1988
 s.2 121
Income and Capital Taxes Act 1984
 ss.767, 788 294
Income and Corporation Taxes Act 1988
 s.416 252
 s.703 250

TABLE OF STATUTES

Income and Corporation Taxes Act 1988 (*cont.*)
   s.839(3) 244
   s.840A 123
Income Tax (Earnings and Pensions) Act 2003
   Pt 3, Ch. 5 153
Inheritance Tax Act 1984
   s.142 220
Interpretation Act 1989
   Sched. 1 42
Land Registration Act 2003
   s.34 278
Land Registration Act (Northern Ireland) 1970
   s.38 278
Landlord and Tenant Act 1954 .... 136, 166, 179, 182
   Pt II 154, 161
Law of Property Act 1925 ..... 18, 166
   s.2 207
   s.27 .... 245, 265, 267–8, 296
   s.36(2) 209
   s.40 .... 197, 213
      (1) 213
   s.52 .... 3, 18, 57, 137, 180
   s.53(1)(b) 196, 213
       (c) 199, 204, 206, 212
       (2) 3, 19, 197–9, 206
   s.54 138
   s.62 40
   s.136 197
   s.137 211
   s.149(6) 138, 166
   s.185 139
   s.205(1)(xxvii) 136
Law of Property (Miscellaneous Provisions) Act 1989 ...... 3, 18, 206

   s.1(6) 207
   s.2 .... 17, 74, 137, 199, 213
      (6) 197, 206–7
      (8) 197
Limited Partnerships Act 1907 223
Local Government Act 1972 ... 118, 121
Local Government (Scotland) Act 1994
   s.2 .... 118, 121
Matrimonial Causes Act 1973
   ss.22A, 23A, 24A 119
National Lottery Act 1993
   s.25 121
Partnership Act 1890 223
   s.14 224
Police and Criminal Evidence Act 1984
   ss.12, 13 290–2
Settled Land Act 1925 212
Stamp Act 1891 232
   s.14 .... 13, 285
   s.17 .... 6, 10
   s.56 .... 94, 152
   s.58(4), (5) 12, 116, 192
   s.122 1
Taxation of Chargeable Gains Act 1992
   s.62 220
   ss.137–139 294
   s.242(1) 84
   ss.272–274 84
Town and Country Planning Act 1990
   s.106 .... 98, 188
Trustee Act 1925
   s.32 213
Trusts of Land and Appointment of Trustees Act 1996 202
Value Added Tax Act 1994
   s.19 92

Table of statutory instruments

Housing (Northern Ireland) Order 1992, SI 1992/1725
    art. 33 121
Stamp Duty (Disadvantaged Areas) (Application of Exemptions) Regulations
    2003, SI 2003/1056 60
Stamp Duty (Disadvantaged Areas) Regulations 2001, SI 2001/3747 60
Stamp Duty (Exempt Instrument) Regulations 1987, SI 1987/516 307
Stamp Duty Land Tax (Administration) (Amendment) Regulations 2004,
    SI 2004/3124 306
Stamp Duty Land Tax (Administration) Regulations 2003, SI 2003/2837 ...87, 102,
                                                                        108, 168,
                                                                        218, 293
    Pt 4 ....49, 54, 86, 88, 92, 101,
                                                                   103, 109, 195, 311
    reg. 15(3) 307
    Scheds. 1, 2 305
Stamp Duty Land Tax (Amendments) Regulations 2003, SI 2003/2837 108
Stamp Duty Land Tax Avoidance Schemes (Prescribed Descriptions of
    Arrangements) Regulations 2005, SI 2005/1868 36
Stamp Duty Land Tax (Consequential Amendment of Enactments)
    Regulations 2003, SI 2003/2867 ....124, 141, 178
Stamp Duty and Stamp Duty Land Tax (Consequential Amendment of
    Enactments) Regulations 2003, SI 2003/2868 36
Value Added Tax (General) Regulations 1995, SI 1995/2518
    Pt XV 92

Budget 2006

The major change for stamp taxes effected by the Budget 2006 is indirect, although there are other significant direct changes, including yet another major revision of the taxation of partners and yet more tinkering with the taxation of leases.

0.1 TRUSTS AND ESTATES (CHAPTER 10)

There are no further revisions directly affecting the dealings involving trusts and estates. However, the major increase in inheritance tax charges in the area means that the limited period for the variation of trusts and estates will entail significant risks of such alterations, even where effected with the assistance of the court involving substantial charges to stamp taxes which can frequently be reduced by careful planning. It is clear that variations of estates are taxable, since there are limited reliefs from stamp duty land tax (SDLT) for such arrangements (Finance Act (FA) 2003, Sched. 3, paras. 3A and 4) (see p. 119) which would not be necessary if there were no charges to tax.

The issue will be whether the variations, releases and surrenders (which can be chargeable transactions (FA 2003, s.44)) are for chargeable consideration. This will frequently be the case since there will be mutual variations of rights (see, for example, *Oughtred* v. *IRC* [1960] AC 206), and since SDLT applies where there is consideration in money or money's worth, charges can arise. Fortunately, this may be slightly eased by Finance (No.2) Bill 2006, clause 166 which provides that where trustees of a settlement reallocate trust property so that a beneficiary acquires an interest in some property but ceases to be interested in other property, the fact that the beneficiary consents to the reallocation does not mean that there is chargeable consideration.

Regrettably, this does not cover all variations of trusts and estates since it applies only to the powers of the trustees, and the agreement of the beneficiaries; where there is consideration, the scope of the charge will depend upon the nature of the 'consideration' for the variation, release or surrender of the chargeable interest. Where this is another chargeable interest there is likely to be a land exchange (FA 2003, s.47), but, fortunately, limited interests in land;

such life interests or remainders are minor interests so that upon an exchange only the value of the consideration provided by way of equality is taxable. However, where one or more of the chargeable interests in a major interest is involved, the exchanges are both taxable upon the market value of the interest received (FA 2003, Sched. 4, para. 5). Where the consideration does not include chargeable interests there will be an acquisition taxable upon the market value of the consideration provided upon normal principles. Where the variation involves a mixture of land and other property, it will be necessary to apportion the consideration between the land and the other property.

This need to consider other property raises a difficulty where the interest concerned consists of or includes shares or marketable interests or equitable interests therein. This brings into play stamp duty and the principal charge to stamp duty reserve tax (FA 1986, s.86), which are outside the scope of the current work. However, it can be noted that an agreement for the transfer of an interest in securities for a consideration in money or money's worth is *prima facie* subject to SDLT at 0.5 per cent. This can include an agreement to transfer an interest in shares for an interest in land. The land is subject to SDLT on the market value of the shares at 4 per cent; the shares are subject to stamp duty reserve tax at 0.5 per cent. Whilst there are limited exemptions from SDLT there are no reliefs from the principal charge to stamp duty reserve tax. Fortunately, payment of stamp duty can cancel the liability to stamp duty reserve tax (FA 1986, s.92 (as amended)) and this applies where the stamp duty is nil because of an exemption (such as FA 1985, s.84) or is the fixed duty because the instrument is not a transfer on sale.

In consequence, it will be necessary to organise variations of trusts and estates in such a way as to fall within the limited range of exemptions, or exercising powers of apportionment or advancement so that there is no chargeable consideration (FA 2003, Sched. 3, para. 1) and within self-certification (SDLT 60) (FA 2003, s.77 (as amended)) and the anti-avoidance rules of FA 2003, Sched. 16, para. 7 do not apply.

0.2 UNIT TRUST SCHEMES

The seeding relief for unit trusts (FA 2003, s.64A) is withdrawn (Finance (No.2) Bill 2006, clause 167).

0.3 ALTERNATIVE FINANCING

The relief for financing transactions designed to apply to Islamic banking and similar arrangements (FA 2003, ss.71A–73; see p. 123) does not apply where corporate reconstruction relief applies (FA 2003, Sched. 7; Finance (No.2) Bill 2006, clause 169). This amendment is necessary because the relief is extended to acquisitions by persons other than individuals such as alternative financing of land acquisitions.

0.4 INTRA-GROUP RELIEF

Intra-group relief (FA 2003, Sched. 7; see p. 254) is not available for the demutualisation of insurance companies (Finance (No.2) Bill 2006, clause 168).

0.5 LEASES (CHAPTER 8)

Notifiable transactions (p. 278)

The assignment of a lease is notifiable if there is chargeable consideration for the assignment and either:

- the lease is for seven years or longer; or
- the consideration exceeds the nil rate threshold regardless of whether the assignment is exempt (Finance (No.2) Bill 2006, clause 165(1)).

Rent formula – Sched. 5 (p. 149)

The term 'in the year i' is altered to 'in respect of year i' to catch arrangements where rent is payable in respect of a year but is not payable in that year (Finance (No.2) Bill 2006, clause 165(2)).

Agricultural tenancies

The possibility that rent may be varied pursuant to the agricultural holdings and tenancies legislation brings the tenancy into the variable rent provisions.

Holding over (p.161)

Where a tenant is holding over and is granted a new lease of substantially the same premises which is backdated to the termination of the original lease, there is a credit for the rent subject to tax during the overlap period, i.e. the period from the termination of the lease to the grant of the new lease (Finance (No.2) Bill 2006, Sched. 25, para. 3).

0.6 EFFECTIVE DATE FOR LEASES

There are, in the view of HMRC Stamp Taxes, two effective dates for new leases (FA 2003, Sched. 17A, para. 12A), namely substantial performance of the agreement for lease and the subsequent grant (p. 58; see also linked transactions). It is provided (Finance (No.2) Bill 2006, Sched. 25, para. 4) that the grant of the lease is not linked with the deemed lease on substantial performance. This removes the potential double charge upon the future rent and gives full effect to the rent credit. It is essentially a technical amendment to deal with certain drafting errors, but does not appear to be retrospective.

Abnormal increases in rent

Increases of rent other than pursuant to a term of the lease (see p. 160), such as where the landlord buys the tenant's improvements, do not give rise to a chargeable transaction unless entered into before the end of the fifth year of the term (FA 2003, Sched. 17A, para. 13; Finance (No.2) Bill 2006, Sched. 25, para. 6).

However, such variations after the fifth year of the term may be chargeable as 'abnormal increases' of the rent (FA 2003, Sched. 17A, paras. 14 and 15). Fortunately the test for determining whether there is an abnormal increase (see p. 159) is simplified. Broadly, in the current proposal (Finance (No.2) Bill 2006, Sched. 15, para. 8) the increase is 'abnormal' if it exceeds 20 per cent of the 'assumed rent', i.e. the rent taken into account as the rent for the term of the lease after the fifth year of the term.

0.7 PARTNERSHIPS (CHAPTER 11)

Finance (No.2) Bill 2006, Sched. 24 makes substantial and technical amendments to the taxation of transactions involving partnerships.

The most important of these is the re-writing of the formula for calculating the tax upon transfers of land by partners into the partnership and by partnerships to partners (FA 2003, Sched. 15, paras. 10, 18 and 23). The references to actual consideration (AC) are removed and the charges are linked to the market value of the property as reduced by the sum of the lower proportions (i.e. the proportion of the land treated as still belonging to the partner and the persons connected with him). The payment of cash by the partners to the transferor is ignored. These are, however, potentially applicable anti-avoidance provisions where cash subsequently changes hands (FA 2003, Sched. 15, paras. 17 and 17A) which may also involve deemed transfers of partnership interests (FA 2003, Sched. 15 paras. 14 and 36). These provisions have given rise to technical problems which have been dealt with so as to avoid potential double charges to tax.

Transfers of partnership interests

The charge to tax upon transfers of partnership interests (FA 2003, Sched. 15, para. 14) is restricted. It is to apply only to transfers of interests in 'property investment partnerships', i.e. partnerships whose sole or main activity is investing or dealing in chargeable interests whether or not that involves construction operations on the land (Finance (No.2) Bill 2006, Sched. 25, para. 9). This will take changes of partners in professional firms such as solicitors out of the tax.

CHAPTER 1

Introduction and general principles

1.1 BACKGROUND

Stamp duty land tax (SDLT) replaces stamp duty upon land transactions with effect from 1 December 2003 subject to certain complex transitional provisions in Sched. 19 to the Finance Act (FA) 2003[1] largely designed to exclude from the new tax transactions entered into before 11 July 2003, but subsequent amendments, some retrospective, are intended to bring into charge to SDLT transactions entered into between 10 July and 1 December 2003 which are 'completed' or performed on or after the latter date.

In addition to such transitional reliefs, stamp duty remains applicable to:

- transactions relating to shares and marketable securities (Stamp Act 1891, s.122) where stamp duty reserve tax also applies (Finance Act 1986, s.87). The attempt to apply land rich company rules[2] have temporarily been abandoned;[3]
- 'transfers' in writing of partnership interests where the partnership owns stock or marketable securities to the extent that the consideration or deemed consideration for the transfer is apportioned to shares and marketable securities where the 0.5 per cent rate will apply (FA 2003, Sched. 20 (as amended)).

---

[1] It is usually significantly better for the taxpayer to remain within the former stamp duty regime because the amount of tax, timing of payment, penalties and interest and the compliance obligations, including being audited by Her Majesty's Revenue and Customs (HMRC) Stamp Taxes, are less onerous than in the new regime. It is important, therefore, to avoid any transaction which may cancel the transitional benefits such as variations of contracts, sub-sales and assignments or, importantly, surrenders and regrants of leases because many of the charges in the new regime do not apply to 'stamp duty leases' such as holding over but any variation that amounts to a surrender and regrant will bring the new regime into operation immediately.
[2] Recently abandoned in Australia.
[3] The inevitable attack has been focused upon attempts to convert land into shares by imposing charges upon routine commercial transactions such as business incorporations or clawback of reliefs on an arbitrary basis not concerned with tax avoidance motives.

It is important to note that stamp duty land tax, although introduced as a panic measure after a defective so-called consultation process intended to block certain very simple stamp duty mitigation techniques, such as the need for writing of a particular type, is very different from stamp duty not merely as regards enforcement and compliance but also as regards its nature and scope. It is, therefore, a fundamental error to regard SDLT as simply stamp duty with SDLT 1 and related forms replacing the old 'PD' form. It differs from stamp duty in that:

- it is a transaction-based tax not a document-based tax, i.e. a tax charge can arise even where there is no document (FA 2003, s.43);
- the charging provisions apply to a wider range of transactions than stamp duty;
- the principles for the computation and payment are completely different;
- there is no real finality so that the tax liability for a purchase with a clawback provision remains open for at least a century after the initial transaction on current conveyancing practice. There is no equivalent to adjudication and an Enquiry does not end the taxpayer's exposure to the tax;
- it arises at totally different stages in the sale or lease process;
- it is directly enforceable (FA 2003, s.75 and Sched. 10);
- there is a limited form of wait-and-see dealing with the areas formerly within the contingency principle for stamp duty such as variable or deferred consideration such as overage and clawback payments and rent reviews. This together with certain compliance provisions (such as FA 2003, Sched. 10, para. 8 which has no limitation period) produces a lack of finality which is creating problems for persons such as personal representatives of deceased persons and liquidators of companies which may prevent the early termination of their administration of the assets and raises considerable difficulty for all parties when negotiating rent reviews, overage and clawback provisions where the 'costs' involved in the calculation of the payment include stamp tax liabilities which may never be finalised, particularly given the current practice of Her Majesty's Revenue and Customs (HMRC) Stamp Taxes of enacting retrospective legislation under the pretence of 'clarifying' earlier defective drafting;
- it raises fundamentally different issues in relation to registration of title and the investigation of the vendor's title;
- a wholly new set of warranties and indemnities for routine land transactions is required;
- the warranties and indemnities required in relation to the acquisition of shares in companies, including companies incorporated outside the UK are totally different;
- major changes are required in relation to the valuation of shares because of the nature of the tax and its lack of finality;

INTRODUCTION AND GENERAL PRINCIPLES

- significant practical problems arise when purchasing interests in land from companies; and
- it has a different jurisdictional basis.

These issues are considered at various places in this book but the comments, whilst covering a wide range of routine transactions where there are serious traps for the unwary practitioner, do not necessarily indicate all of the problem areas where difficulties exist, especially where the parties' advisers seek by unorthodox means to provide commercial protection against minimal commercial risks whilst considering the enormous increase in the SDLT charges.

The most important practical change is the non-documentary nature of the tax. In consequence, liability to the tax and obligations to report and pay can arise notwithstanding there is no document (FA 2003, s.43), and this transaction basis affects the time at which the tax arises.[4] Although many transactions can be effective only if in writing[5] there are many situations where informal or oral arrangements can be effective to pass title (see, e.g. Law of Property Act 1925, ss.52 and 53(2); *Yaxley* v. *Gotts* [1999] 2 WLR 1217), and completion of an ineffective arrangement will be effective to pass title (*Tootal* v. *Guinea Properties Management* (1992) 64 P&CR 452) and give rise to a charge to the tax. Although intended to deal with the problems of electronic conveyancing (see, e.g. amendment in Finance (No.2) Act 2005, s.47) even to the extent of creating the possibility of instant payment of the tax at the time of electronic completion (FA 2003, s.76(2)), with significant implications for the structuring of payment at completion and risks of personal accountability for client tax for solicitors, there are still unresolved issues of the legal effectiveness of electronic or telephone arrangements and the impact of the new regime.

Moreover, this impression of the new tax as simply stamp duty is reinforced by the initial reading of the legislation: notwithstanding the attempt at a plain English style of drafting, many of the old stamp duty provisions, or something that looks like the old legislation, appear in FA 2003. However, it is rarely obvious whether a word is used in its traditional technical sense or in a new 'plain English' meaning. This causes difficulties in a subject as technical as land law and conveyancing, which is not only beset with technical terms that have acquired specialised meanings, but is also based upon legislation drafted in the old practice of technical wording or provisions in

---

4 But note that in some cases, but not all, the charge is linked to the date of the documentation. This currently gives rise to significant problems in relation to agreements for lease and leases – see Chapter 8.
5 See, for example, Law of Property (Miscellaneous Provisions) Act 1989 and that writing is in proper form and content (*First Post Homes* v. *Johnson* [1995] 4 All ER 355); but the contract may be contained in more than one instrument (see, e.g. *Spiro* v. *Glencrown Properties* [1991] 2 WLR 931).

identical terms to the old stamp duty provisions. For example, difficulties have emerged whereby 'excepting and reserving interests' is now attacked by HMRC Stamp Taxes as a land exchange.

Yet these long-standing stamp duty terms do not necessarily continue to bear their former stamp duty meaning when construed in the context of the new legislation. Although it seems that, in practice, HMRC Stamp Taxes will tend to carry forward the former interpretations, this presumption cannot be acted upon as a general principle since they are given, directly or indirectly, somewhat unusual meanings either expressly or impliedly. Even the new plain English provisions have to be given very unplain meanings if the legislation is to work: for example, 'conveyance' must include leases, thereby providing a trap for the unwary. To approach the legislation upon the basis of stamp duty interpretations and practices is something that must be resisted.

At present much of the baggage of stamp duty continues to influence the practice of both HMRC Stamp Taxes and professionals in this area, such as the conduct of Enquiries which operate as though they were adjudications and are, in consequence, not conducted in accordance with the legislative requirements. This is deceptive since both the charging provisions and the compliance obligations of both the taxpayer and HMRC Stamp Taxes are fundamentally different from stamp duty but only the taxpayer is exposed to the risk of penalties and the costs of the Enquiries; badly conducted Enquiries do not expose HMRC Stamp Taxes to financial sanctions although it may be a ground for applying to the Special Commissioners for an order that the Enquiry be terminated. In addition, the restrictions upon the power of HMRC Stamp Taxes to issue a 'discovery assessment' is protected notwithstanding an ineptly conducted Enquiry since there are extremely helpful provisions limiting the knowledge of the transaction which it is deemed to have (FA 2003, Sched. 10, para. 30(4)) which might otherwise preclude it from effectively reopening the Enquiry.

In some cases, the special 'plain English' meaning is made clear by a specific definition such as 'acquisition', although even here the definition frequently states that the word being defined 'includes' rather than 'means' various matters so that it is not exhaustive (*Oughtred* v. *IRC* [1960] AC 206) and remains capable of expansion or modification by HMRC Stamp Taxes. In other cases the meaning of plain English words such as 'purchaser', 'completion' and 'conveyance' have to bear bizarre meanings such as 'purchaser' being a lessee or landlord depending upon context; and 'conveyance' and 'transfer' and 'assignment' (FA 2003, Sched. 17A, para. 12B) have to bear some very unusual meanings since 'conveyance' includes 'lease' but 'transfer' does not. The special meanings for routine words have to be discovered from the overall context of the legislation. Moreover, as it is a transaction-based tax the interpretation of the legislation may be affected by the judicial adoption of a purposive construction principle (*McGuckian* v.

INTRODUCTION AND GENERAL PRINCIPLES

IRC [1997] STC 908) such as the comments of Carnworth J.[6] in relation to stamp duty that in an area as technical as this the judge should not pay too much attention to the wording of the legislation but should seek to apply the 'spirit' of the Acts! Moreover, as a transaction tax, SDLT will almost certainly be subject to the fluctuating principles of the *Ramsay*[7] approach.

1.2 GENERAL PRINCIPLES

Although rushed into legislation after several previous failures in legislation to block certain simple stamp duty mitigation arrangements, the tax is not a stamp duty upon documents, it is a transaction-based tax governed by totally different principles and enforced in a totally different way. Unfortunately the background of attempting to block so-called loopholes, which has dominated the drafting of the legislation and regulations, including attacks upon the basic sub-sale relief which was considered essential to the fair application of stamp duty for over 200 years, means that it is difficult, if not impossible, to find anything approaching a coherent and consistent structure for the new tax. The following comments are, therefore, somewhat tentative and are merely intended to provide a limited tool for approaching the construction of the legislation, but the detailed applications and modifications of these principles are considered in later chapters.

(a) Title issues

The fundamental change in the nature of the tax has considerable practical implications for routine conveyancing. Some of these are beneficial such as the fact that the landlord's counterpart is no longer taxable and can be

---

6 See the nonsense judgment in *L.M. Tenancies (No.1)* v. *IRC* [1996] STC 880 (on appeal [1998] STC 326) where interestingly the Court of Appeal did not adopt the so-called reasons for the decision of first instance in refusing the appeal and decided this case on equally intellectually indefensible grounds.

7 *Ramsay* v. *IRC* [1982] AC 300, which, astonishingly, has been applied to stamp duty in overseas jurisdictions see *Collector* v. *Arrowtown* [2003] HKCFA 46; *Carreras Group Limited* v. *The Stamp Commissioner* (Privy Council Appeal No.24 of 2003) [2004] STC 1377, notwithstanding that the judge in the latter case repudiated his own comments in *MacNiven* v. *Westmoreland* [2001] STC 237, which indicated a reasonable but not totally accurate appreciation of the unique nature of stamp taxes as a cost falling upon the purchaser without relief which marks it out as totally different from other taxes. It was also the same judge who in *Commissioners of Inland Revenue* v. *Mitsubishi Motors New Zealand Ltd* [1995] STC 989 laid out the superior policy that no matter how effective the arguments of the taxpayer might be the judiciary should follow the arguments of the Inland Revenue because the judges could not foresee all of the implications of their decisions and were not prepared to leave an issue of imposing restrictions upon their decision to Parliament or subsequent tribunals.

utilised in court to enforce payment of the rent or other provisions in the lease. Others are not so beneficial and require major changes in practice, particularly in relation to completion arrangements. Not only will the provisions of contracts dealing with situations where the vendor has not yet obtained registration of the title, including but not limited to sub-sale situations (see Chapter 5), require modification, such as requiring the vendor to produce a land transaction return certificate (SDLT 5) or a self-certificate (SDLT 60) since there will be no duly stamped transfer to produce, but also fundamental changes are required in relation to investigations of title and the warranties, indemnities and undertakings required to be included in the contract.[8]

Security arrangements

For example, the practice of retaining money pending the registration of title has been fundamentally altered. Mortgagees concerned about their security pending registration and perfection of their security no longer need to retain substantial sums for a significant period pending HMRC challenges. They will need to retain only the amount shown as tax payable in Box 15 of SDLT 1 and can release those funds once the SDLT 5 or, where appropriate, SDLT 60 has been produced and acted upon by the Land Registry. Essentially the Land Registry no longer has the power to investigate the stamping of the documentation and cannot challenge the certificate presented to it simply because it believes that insufficient tax has been paid.[9] Moreover, once the title has been registered the registration cannot be challenged notwithstanding that the SDLT originally paid was insufficient or a relief claimed is subsequently rejected by HMRC Stamp Taxes. This follows because there is, as considered later in this chapter, no real finality in relation to many areas of SDLT and without unchallengeable registration rights titles would become extremely uncertain.

However, the security issues are not all so straightforward. Since the tax charge can arise before completion and even when the rights of the purchaser remain conditional because of the complexities of 'substantial performance' (see Chapter 3), taxpayers such as developers who need to raise money in order to fund the new tax charges[10] that arise at an early stage in the trans-

---

[8] Additionally, major changes in relation to the warranties and indemnities and valuations on share purchase are required.

[9] In practice, certain offices of the Land Registry wrongly believe that their powers pursuant to Stamp Act 1891, s.17 etc. have survived. They are, however, gradually becoming aware of their new limited role in this area.

[10] And which, together with the related funding costs represents a new and additional item of cost of a cascade nature that has to be factored into their selling price or development costs. However, the absence of finality in the new tax means that there may be other difficulties; see below in this chapter.

action will find that the security which they can offer, such as a conditional agreement for lease, will frequently not be entirely satisfactory to potential funders.

Payment of tax and title – third party problems

Although to some extent the payment of SDLT is essential in many routine situations in order to obtain registration of title so as to make certain entries in the Land Register in the relevant jurisdiction, the evidence and title issues of stamp duty do not apply. They have, however, been replaced with completely different and more complex problems, including:

- obtaining registration of title, including the change where the seller or landlord has not been registered at the time when he is required to complete and deliver legal title;
- investigating the title of the seller since in many cases the SDLT obligations of the seller in relation to his previous acquisition or later dealings in relation to the property are dealt with initially only on a provisional basis. In consequence there may be either a statutory passing of the outstanding tax obligations from the seller to the purchaser or special charges may apply, in effect, counteracting or cancelling any relief obtained by the seller by taxing the transaction on a totally artificial basis so that the purchaser's tax liability is totally different from the actual transaction. His tax charge is influenced by the tax payable upon the original acquisition of the seller or even his predecessors in title. The assignee of a lease is liable not merely for the filing of land transactions returns for the immediate transaction but also for any additional SDLT arising, for example, in respect of the vendor's acquisition. Moreover, the assignee may be entitled to a tax refund if the original tax estimate should prove to be excessive. In consequence, appropriate undertakings, warranties or indemnities as regards making the necessary returns, paying over underpaid or overpaid tax, dealing with late payment, interest and penalties and providing the necessary information to enable these and future obligations to be performed properly will be required in addition to the warranties that all land transaction returns relevant to the chargeable interest have been prepared on a proper basis and have been filed;
- the purchaser's or lessee's tax position may be affected by subsequent actions of the seller or landlord or even other persons not parties to the transaction such as other tenants of the landlord which may require undertakings by the relevant party to produce full disclosure of the SDLT history of the chargeable interest concerned including potentially commercially sensitive information and, in certain cases, the purchaser or lessee may be required to supply information to the vendor or lessor in order to enable the latter to deal with his outstanding tax position. The

assignee may also require information to be supplied by the seller because certain obligations to notify HMRC Stamp Taxes and to recalculate and pay the tax pass to him.

Investigations of title

As a transaction-based rather than a document-based tax, SDLT is not a title issue nor an issue for the rules of evidence in quite the same way as was the case with stamp duty. The fact that a person has not paid SDLT or may have paid an incorrect amount does not affect the validity of his title and any registration of that title remains effective. For example, the fact that a transfer was registered on the basis that the transfer was exempt because of intra-group relief, which is subsequently successfully challenged by HMRC Stamp Taxes or is clawed back by subsequent de-grouping, does not affect the validity of the original registration and any charge over that title remains effective. Neither the Land Registry nor HMRC Stamp Taxes have power either to challenge the application for registration or to alter the register once the title has been changed.[11] This alleviates the problems surrounding the quality of the title offered to purchasers and lessees and provides better security for mortgagees and an easier situation for dealing with retentions for stamp taxes at completion.[12]

However, where the vendor has not been registered in respect of his acquisition, such as in a sub-sale situation, the question of whether he has paid or is in the process of paying the tax is an issue and appropriate undertakings as to the delivery of the land transaction return and payment of the tax and prompt procedure with the registration process will be required. Until the vendor has become registered or can produce a land transaction certificate (SDLT 5) or a covering letter setting out a claim to sub-sale or similar relief, he cannot deliver an instrument of transfer or lease that will be recognised as effective by the Land Registry since it will not be executed by a person whose name appears on the register.[13] The charge upon third parties who receive the directed grant of a lease depends upon the history of the transaction and, in particular, the state of substantial performance of any contract (FA 2003, Sched. 17A, para. 12B; see Chapter 8).

---

11 However, it is probable that HMRC Stamp Taxes will seek to develop the common law crimes of forgery and fraud by seeking to prosecute for obtaining registration by deception where incorrect returns or self-certificates are produced. This is in addition to the special sanction imposed by FA 2003, ss.95 and 96.

12 The same principles will apply in relation to unregistered titles; the non-payment of the correct amount of SDLT is not generally a title issue.

13 But see Chapter 5 on the machinery to be adopted in certain sub-sale situations.

INTRODUCTION AND GENERAL PRINCIPLES

Registration can only be achieved by production of an appropriate certificate, namely either an SDLT 5 certificate to the effect that a land transaction has been returned and any tax shown by that return has been paid, or a self-certificate (SDLT 60) in certain circumstances where no tax is payable (see Chapter 13). Non-payment of tax may in consequence in many, but not all cases, provide a title issue for purchasers. It is not sufficient that the purchaser can produce an executed Land Registry transfer and an appropriate certificate if the unregistered person executing the transfer as transferor cannot produce the necessary documentation to enable his registration so that the transfer can be recognised by the Land Registry.[14] In consequence, it is important for solicitors to ensure that the SDLT 1 is properly completed and ready by completion in order to ensure prompt registration. The contractual provisions relating to completion should, therefore, require production of the necessary certificate at some stage and a prudent purchaser may prefer not to make payment until the paper chain is completed. It is no longer possible simply to retain a sum equal to the vendor's stamp tax liability because if the vendor has not completed, signed and delivered the necessary land transaction returns it is not possible for the purchaser to rectify the situation by paying the tax. In the absence of the correctly signed and completed return (SDLT 1) HMRC Stamp Taxes will refuse to accept the payment and to issue the appropriate certificate (SDLT 5). Where it is necessary to deal with the Land Registry an unregistered vendor should, it seems, be required to establish that he has delivered the appropriate returns, if any are needed, to HMRC Stamp Taxes together with payment and an undertaking to pursue such notification expeditiously so that the purchaser will be in a position to produce his complete documentation to the Land Registry within the registration time limits (not the SDLT timetable which is different and not necessarily compatible with the registration regime). These issues do, however, raise practical problems even in routine conveyancing since there has been no attempt to harmonise the SDLT compliance requirements with the Land Registry requirements, particularly where the SDLT documentation differs from the Land Registry documentation such as where the registered owners or applicants for registration are nominees so that the names on the Land Registry transfer and SDLT 5 certificate differ. Notwithstanding the detailed code for tax, the real timetable is dictated by Land Registry requirements so that it is necessary to send in the land transaction return (SDLT 1) in sufficient time for the SDLT 5 to be issued so that the Land Registry application can be filed in accordance with the registration deadlines.

---

14 These issues seem to be less of a problem in Scotland where it is possible to deal with the tax 'over the counter' in Edinburgh producing the necessary certificate in a few minutes, unlike England where the target of HMRC Stamp Taxes is a turnaround time of five days.

Timetable – completion and other problems

The land transaction return (SDLT 1) has to be filed with HMRC Stamp Taxes within 30 days after the effective date; but this timetable is misleading. The deadline means that the cheque has to be received by HMRC Stamp Taxes by that date (FA 2003, s.76) so that earlier positing is required. The major practical problem is that the timetable pays no regard to the requirements of the land registration regime with its own timetables which have shorter deadlines. It will be noted that it is necessary to file the land transaction return and cheque in time for it to be processed and the SDLT 5 certificate (SDLT 5) to be returned in time for the documents to be submitted to the Land Registry on time. This puts great pressure on HMRC Stamp Taxes to process documents speedily which, of course, restricts the scope for scrutiny of the land transaction return and any covering letter or application for a post-transaction ruling. The initial undertaking was to turn all returns around within a maximum of five days. However, to cover the possibility that this time limit might not be achieved the Land Registry has continued its practice of provisional registration. If 20 days have elapsed from the filing of the land transaction return and nothing has been received from HMRC Stamp Taxes the application for registration can be processed in order to protect priorities and timetables.

Fundamental issues of principle underlie the above comments. One of these is the power of the Land Registry to challenge the certificate produced by the parties. There is no equivalent to the stamp duty provisions of s.17 of the Stamp Act 1891 which imposed penalties for registering an insufficiently stamped document. In consequence, the Land Registry has no general power to refuse to act upon a document that appears to be correct, even though subsequently it may prove to be incorrect. For example, an SDLT 5 certificate based upon the intra-group relief has to be accepted and the Land Registry cannot require the person presenting the documents to justify the claim in support of that exemption. Similarly, where the taxpayer produces a self-certificate (SDLT 60) this cannot be challenged by the Land Registry upon the basis that the person producing the certificate may have made an error. A frequent abuse in this area by the Land Registry concerns surrenders and regrants of leases where it is provided that the new lease is not consideration for the surrender of the existing lease (FA 2003, Sched. 17A, paras. 9 and 16). This means that normally the surrender will be for no chargeable consideration and will fall within the exemption contained in para. 1 of Sched. 3 to FA 2003. As a result, it is not a notifiable transaction requiring SDLT 1 and SDLT 5 for registration (FA 2003, s.77 (as amended)). The Land Registry has not always acted upon this analysis. It may, perhaps, charitably be explained upon the basis that the officials in the Land Registry do not understand the tax and compliance principles involved rather than a misguided attempt to make themselves fiscal police having power to enforce the tax as agents of

INTRODUCTION AND GENERAL PRINCIPLES

HMRC Stamp Taxes. It will almost certainly take time before the Land Registry is brought up to speed on the principles of the tax and recognises its non-existent role in the enforcement of tax.

The fact that the incorrect amount of SDLT has been paid does not affect title. For example, the taxpayer may form the opinion that he is entitled to an exemption from the tax or that the market value or estimated rent upon which he calculates the tax is correct and file the land transaction return (SDLT 1) on that basis and pay the tax shown in Box 15 on that return. Since the powers and resources available to HMRC Stamp Taxes to challenge the return other than for minor errors such as incorrect arithmetic or, as seems popular at present, its habit of challenging for non-errors such as the fact that there is no reference to a national insurance number for a body corporate or second purchaser, it is highly probable that eventually[15] an SDLT 5 certificate will be issued which can be acted upon. The taxpayer will then make the appropriate change to the Land Register supported by the SDLT 5 certificate. Alternatively, he may form the opinion that the transaction does not require a land transaction return and submit an SDLT 60 ('self-certification') to the Land Registry which will be required to act on the basis of the certificate since it no longer has any obligations or power to challenge applications for registration by reason of the insufficiency of the stamp tax paid. Legal title will pass to the taxpayer, and the mortgagee will obtain good security, upon registration; the fact that subsequently HMRC Stamp Taxes on an Enquiry establishes that insufficient tax has been paid because, for example, the exemption claimed in SDLT 1 is not available or the market value included in Box 10 thereof was too low, does not affect the validity of the legal title of the taxpayer and his mortgagees and tenants. There is no power for HMRC or the Land Registry to remove the entry from the register in such circumstances.

Moreover, it is not always necessary to require the immediate vendor to produce an SDLT 5 certificate (see Chapter 5). This will apply in cases where the registration of the vendor, or his nominee, is not required because he will not be a person executing the Land Registry transfer in favour of the purchaser such as where there is a routine sub-sale pursuant to a previous uncompleted contract or where there is an assignment of the benefit of a contract for sale or agreement for lease, where the relevant documentation will be executed by the original vendor who may be the registered owner of

---

15 Currently HMRC Stamp Taxes is maintaining a campaign to blame solicitors for the delays in the system (see, e.g. *Daily Telegraph* 15 August 2005), although many of the problems are its own errors, or arise because of incorrect advice provided by the so-called helpline which cannot be relied upon to bind HMRC Stamp Taxes or even to support an application for a mitigation of penalties. Moreover, many of the rejected returns are rejected in error by HMRC Stamp Taxes.

the property (FA 2003, s.45 (as amended) and Sched. 17A, para. 12B). As there will be no transfer or grant by the immediate seller there will be no need to produce an SDLT 5 certificate for the intermediate vendor who is not seeking registration. An explanatory letter to the Land Registry may be required because the SDLT 5 will have a different vendor from the transferor identified in the Land Registry documentation.

This situation can also arise in relation to certain cases where the intermediate vendor has received a Land Registry transfer since there is a limited relief for sub-sales (FA 2003, s.45 (as amended); see Chapter 5). This relief for SDLT is not linked to the absence of transfers as was the case with the equivalent relief from stamp duty (Stamp Act 1891, s.58(4) and (5)). The relief is available notwithstanding that the first purchaser has received a Land Registry transfer from the original seller. If the conditions for the relief are met there is no chargeable transaction, notwithstanding that the transfer has been delivered. In this situation it is sufficient to obtain title by producing the two transfers so that the names of the parties match the Land Register, together with an SDLT 5 in relation to the sale of the ultimate purchaser/transferee together with a covering letter explaining that no SDLT 5 is required in respect of the transfer from the original vendor to the first purchaser because the conditions of s.45 of FA 2003 are believed to have been satisfied. The fact that subsequently, upon an Enquiry, HMRC Stamp Taxes establishes that the sub-sale relief was not available is irrelevant to the Land Registry entries and cannot affect the validity of the entry of the ultimate purchaser.

It is assumed that similar practices will apply to the equivalent provision for leases in para. 12B of Sched. 17A to FA 2003 where no charge arises upon the original tenant where there has been an assignment of the right to call for the lease (whatever that may mean) before the agreement for lease is substantially performed.[16] In this case the liability for the original SDLT passes to the assignee and is added to any other chargeable consideration that he may be providing directly or indirectly. It is expected that no SDLT 5 will be requested by the Land Registry in relation to the original tenant and that it will be satisfied by a covering letter explaining that no charge has arisen in respect of the original tenant pursuant to para. 12B.

---

16 There are many technical problems with the drafting of these provisions which, if taken strictly, do not always match conveyancing practice in this area. Until the law is clarified, parties may be making errors but this should not affect the title registered for the new lease.

INTRODUCTION AND GENERAL PRINCIPLES

Transitional titles

For many years to come, vendors and, particularly, landlords, will be relying upon title based on the stamp duty regime.[17] This will apply not merely to titles acquired before 1 December 2003 but also to titles vested after that date pursuant to transactions entered into prior to that date which, although completed on or after that date, remain subject to stamp duty pursuant to the provisions of Sched. 19 to FA 2003 (as amended, in some cases retrospectively so as to transfer transactions from stamp duty to stamp duty land tax). Since incorrect payment of SDLT will not produce a duly stamped instrument sufficient to satisfy the title and admissible evidence rules (Stamp Act 1891, s.14), this will leave the purchaser and others vulnerable to attack upon their titles[18] and the need to pay stamp duty. HMRC Stamp Taxes is receiving land transaction returns (SDLT 1) and payment without investigating whether the transitional provisions apply and the document is strictly chargeable with stamp duty. This means that where it is a stamp duty transaction, professional advisers need to be aware of the transitional arrangements not merely for the completion of outstanding contracts because of the residual risk that the wrong tax may be paid, but also because the vendor may have paid the wrong tax or insufficient stamp duty or because the Land Registry is still obliged to challenge stamp duty payments but cannot challenge SDLT certificates.

Title investigation and due diligence

Title investigation and the new stamp taxes, unfortunately, create a wide area of new problems for purchasers, particularly in the area of the acquisition of existing leases, but problems can apply in other areas and a wide range of new warranties and indemnities are needed and there should be changes in valuation practices in relation to shares and company acquisition (see Chapter 12 for further discussion of these issues). These new problem areas arise because of the general lack of finality for many areas of SDLT even though the return has been the subject-matter of an Enquiry. Whilst there appears to be no general wait-and-see principle there are many situations such as reviewable rents where the initial tax self-assessment is provisional and further returns

---

17 This issue will also have substantive consequences. For example, holding over a lease is potentially a chargeable transaction for the purposes of SDLT but it is currently accepted by HMRC Stamp Taxes that, notwithstanding the technical issues in this area, no charge to tax arises where the lease being held over is one that was within the former stamp duty regime. There may also be issues for linked transactions and other transactions, see FA 2003, Sched. 19, paras. 7 and 9.
18 It may also mean that the SDLT has been paid unnecessarily so that it may be necessary for the purchaser to make an error or mistake repayment claim pursuant to FA 2003, Sched. 10, para. 34, which is subject to time limits.

and payments of tax will be required. Prospective purchasers have at least two new areas to investigate because:

- in certain cases the obligation to deal with the outstanding provisional tax position such as variable premiums for lease and linked transactions and their wide-ranging implications is, by statute, passed to the purchaser; and
- although in certain cases the liabilities for the outstanding tax position remain with the original taxpayer, the future tax position of the purchaser such as upon second or subsequent rent reviews is based upon the tax position of the vendor.

In addition, for conveyancers, these areas requiring investigation will now require undertakings by the relevant party to produce full disclosure of the SDLT history of the chargeable interest concerned and, in certain cases, the purchaser or lessee may be required to supply information to the vendor or lessor in order to enable the latter to deal with his outstanding tax position. The assignee may require information to be supplied by the seller because certain obligations to notify HMRC Stamp Taxes and to recalculate the tax pass to him.

It must be noted that certain areas may require disclosure of highly confidential personal or business information such as details of business turnover or profits where the rent reserved by a lease is linked to such matters. This imposes an obligation upon advisers to ensure that appropriate provisions are contained in the contract since there is no statutory power to demand the information; it is the taxpayer's own obligation to negotiate a contractual right to call for or to require disclosure of the information. It is not possible to obtain the information from HMRC Stamp Taxes because much of the information will not be notifiable to it otherwise than by the taxpayer. HMRC Stamp Taxes will be dependent upon the taxpayer to supply the information notwithstanding that he is not a party to the transaction which gives rise to the notification obligation, i.e. the person who is under the obligation to produce the information is the very person who is dependent upon other persons to notify him of the relevant subsequent events to which he is not necessarily a party. Additionally, HMRC Stamp Taxes will not disclose the information because of taxpayer confidentiality and data protection. Moreover, since each notifiable event requires a separate land transaction return with its unique bar code reference number, rather than a transaction or property reference, any person seeking information upon the optimistic assumptions that HMRC Stamp Taxes will be prepared to help and, even more optimistically at present, can find the records, will have to produce a complete list of all such bar code references.

INTRODUCTION AND GENERAL PRINCIPLES

Warranties and indemnities

Also, the parties to the particular transaction may find it necessary to require indemnities relating to the tax liability. For example, as so much of the initial assessment of SDLT is made on a provisional estimated basis there will be crucial questions of initial overpayment or underpayment of tax, together with related questions of interest and penalties for inadequate payment or inaccurate returns to be dealt with and liabilities and refunds to be allocated between the parties arising for subsequent retrospective adjustments in the overall tax position.

Investigations and requisitions

The areas for investigation and/or requiring the production of information and indemnities include:

1. Transactions where the vendor acquired his interest in the land, whether the whole or only part of which is being sold or leased in the current transaction, for a variable consideration such as an overage payment or a long-term clawback arrangement (see Chapter 4). In such cases the vendor's tax position will have been dealt with on a provisional estimated basis until the variable consideration position is finally resolved, with consequent problems for executors, liquidators and others who may not be in a position to complete their administration of the estate or business because there are outstanding tax liabilities which are passed over by the legislation to the successor in title to the chargeable interest in question. This open tax position remains with the vendor notwithstanding the disposal of all or part of the chargeable interest in question. Insofar as the parties do not renegotiate the position with the original seller or landlord, the vendor will require undertakings from the purchaser to provide information as to any dealings by himself or his successors in title that may have a bearing on the vendor's open tax position. Obviously the terms of any such renegotiation will have their own SDLT implications particularly if the purchaser in that transaction is, effectively, taking over the original purchaser's liability for the additional consideration. However, there are important practical issues if the legislation provides for the liabilities to pass to a person acquiring the chargeable interest. The personal representative, liquidator or other party will in theory cease to have any involvement with the tax. However, in practice, the person acquiring the chargeable interest may impose contractual obligations for notification and/or indemnities from the vendor which may be outstanding for many years so that the administration or liquidation cannot be concluded because of the possibilities of a claim under the contract.
2. Where the variable payment arose in connection with the grant of a new lease, whether in the form of a variable premium or variable rent (including

UNDERSTANDING SDLT

rent reviews as well as turnover rents; see Chapter 8), the position differs. It is provided that the assignee takes over the outstanding tax position of the original tenant to deal with the variable premium or rent (FA 2003, Sched. 17A, para. 12). A full SDLT history will be required as well as provisions to deal with any overpayment or underpayment of tax made on the initial self-assessment by the original tenant and with any interest or penalties arising.

3. Since there is a deemed new lease liable to tax arising where there is an abnormal increase in the rent after the expiration of the fifth year of the term of the lease (FA 2003, Sched. 17A, paras. 14 and 15), assignees of leases will require a full SDLT history of the lease since the starting point for testing whether the increase is abnormal is not the passing rent immediately before the increase but the highest rent paid in any 12 consecutive calendar months during the first five years of the term of the lease. This is the assumed rent taken into account when calculating the tax due in respect of the grant of the lease.

4. A similar need for a full SDLT history is required by an assignee who may hold over a tenancy after the expiration of the contractual term or who becomes entitled to a periodic tenancy which continues beyond the current period, because the holding over or continuation of the tenancy is treated as an extension of the original lease or tenancy for a period of one year. This requires the current tenant to revisit the original self-assessment or any amended or subsequent adjustment of the tax relating to the grant of the lease or tenancy and to reassess the original or latest tax return upon the basis of a lease for the deemed longer term. The current tenant is liable to pay any additional tax arising. As this requires a retrospective adjustment of the previous assessments the assignee will need full details of these.

5. It is specifically provided that the assignee of a lease is responsible to make a return and presumably pay any additional tax arising in connection with a later linked transaction. This will require complicated mutual contractual obligations because of what appears to be HMRC Stamp Taxes's view that assignees can enter into linked transactions notwithstanding that the legislation (FA 2003, s.108) requires the transaction to be between the same parties or persons connected with them (see Chapter 4). Each party will require disclosure from the other of details of any transaction which may be linked, particularly as the later linked transaction does not have to relate to the same property or chargeable interest. For example, where there are linked leases the nil rate slice, applicable to the aggregate net present value of the rents of the linked lease, has to be allocated between the various linked leases in the proportion that the levels of the individual rent values bear to the aggregate rents (FA 2003, Sched. 5, para. 2 (as amended)). This allocation of the proportionate part of the nil rate slice will, of course, be relevant in

calculating the tax due in respect of the lease such as on the first rent review or holding over as well as retrospectively in relation to the original grant. The assignee will require disclosure of the relevant amount.
6. Since subsequent events may affect the tax calculation retrospectively, such as linked successive leases arising pursuant to the exercise of an option to renew (FA 2003, Sched. 17A, para. 5), this would require a re-allocation of the nil rate slice between that and any other linked leases which may affect, for example, the position of an assignee. The same consequences would also appear to follow from any holding over of any one or more of the linked leases. The parties to an assignment will, in consequence, require notification of any transaction that might have an impact on this allocation of the nil rate slice.

(b) Transaction tax not documents

Unlike stamp duty, SDLT is based upon transactions and not documentation. It is specifically provided that the tax arises notwithstanding that there is no document (FA 2003, s.43), and a charge will frequently be triggered by events prior to formal completion in the sense of the delivery of the written conveyance or lease.[19] This is reinforced by statutory provisions that the tax applies to transactions taking effect pursuant to statute, court order or by operation of law (FA 2003, s.43). In many cases without written instruments in the appropriate form, whether deed, written contract or memorandum, there will be no valid and enforceable transaction (Law of Property (Miscellaneous Provisions) Act 1989, s.2), but this is not an invariable principle. The cases indicate that unwritten arrangements can be effective to pass title to land. This is not to state that documentation is irrelevant for the purposes of stamp duty land tax. In certain cases, 'completion' by a written instrument may be the event giving rise to the charge to tax (FA 2003, s.44(8)) or to reporting obligations or even, as in the case of new leases, a second chargeable event in respect of the same transaction (FA 2003, Sched. 17A, para. 12A). In addition, the drafting of the documentation may influence whether there is a charge to tax such as whether this is a lease or a licence (FA 2003, Sched. 17A, para. 19 (as amended)) or the extent of the charge such as whether there is a payment by instalments or a periodical payment (FA 2003, s.52).

This transaction basis of SDLT means that:

- although apart from options and pre-emption rights (FA 2003, s.46) the making of the contract is not, of itself, a chargeable transaction the liability

---

19 There are many potential problems arising from the gap between the effective date and completion such as it will be possible to prove that the conditions for relief have been satisfied since these actions have yet to be performed. HMRC Stamp Taxes has not yet addressed these issues.

to notify the transaction and pay the tax may arise early in the transaction and before completion. This can occur where the contract is still conditional such as where a prospective tenant goes into possession of the land to be demised in order to fit out the premises before the landlord has consented to the assignment or grant of the sub-lease (*Warmington* v. *Miller* [1973] 2 All ER 372);
- it may be necessary to file at least two full land transaction returns, namely on the effective date and at 'completion' when the documentation is executed (FA 2003, s.44(8));[20]
- since land transactions may continue over time and many initial returns are filed and tax paid only on a provisional basis (see below), it may be necessary to file several land transaction returns for the same transaction and the outstanding provisional obligations of the initial taxpayer may by law pass to third parties.

This acceleration of the obligation to pay the tax before legal title has been obtained can give rise to funding problems because at that time the security which the taxpayer can offer may not be acceptable to the lender, especially where the contract is still conditional or there are substantial obligations to be performed before he can obtain legal title to the property or outstanding interests such as restrictive covenants have still to be cleared off the title.

Non-documentary arrangements

Notwithstanding the numerous provisions in the Law of Property Act 1925 and the Law of Property (Miscellaneous Provisions) Act 1989 (see, e.g. *First Post Homes* v. *Johnson* [1995] 4 All ER 355) there are many situations where oral or informal arrangements are binding upon the parties and can pass interests in land. This is reinforced by the provision that the tax can apply to transactions taking effect without writing or 'by operation of law'. These unwritten transactions which are valid can include:
- certain leases and tenancies for less than three years (Law of Property Act 1925, s.52). Informal arrangements for the occupation of premises are a major problem for SDLT in practice. There is, of course, the basic issue of whether the relationship created is by way of a lease or a licence (see Chapter 8) since only the former is within the charge to stamp duty land tax. Since this is a matter of construing the right and duties created (*Addiscombe Garden Estates* v. *Crabbe* [1958] 1 QB 513) and, apart from perhaps residential property where the excessive statements of Lord

---

20 This has become an acute problem in relation to agreements for lease where pursuant to FA 2003, Sched. 17A, para. 12A there may be two separate chargeable events with only limited credit being available; see Chapter 8 below.

Templeman in *Street* v. *Mountford* [1958] 1 AC 809[21] that the sole test is exclusive possession may retain some slight credibility, the absence of a written record of the detailed arrangements between the parties makes an analysis of their relationship in legal terms extremely difficult[22] and matters may ultimately turn upon assumptions and presumptions which seem, in practice, to be a matter of judicial whimsy and, therefore, a risky strategy. There is also the question of the terms upon which a person is allowed into occupation, albeit as licensee, since these rights of entry may amount to taking possession and so constitute substantial performance of another agreement triggering a tax charge and reporting obligations (see Chapter 3);

- oral exercise of an option (which appears to be effective see, e.g. *Spiro* v. *Glencrown Properties Ltd* [1991] 2 WLR 931 on the oral exercise of options over land);
- surrenders of leases and tenancies by operation of law which will frequently arise in practice particularly where the tenancy is for a short term or periodic nature or terminated by notice to quit;
- implied, resulting and constructive trusts (Law of Property Act 1925, s.53(2); see *Neville* v. *Wilson* [1997] Ch 144). The area of constructive and similar trusts is likely to cause problems in practice since this will catch many informal arrangements. For example, the principles of proprietary estoppel may prevent parties from refusing to act upon their oral promises where these have been acted upon by other persons who have substantially changed their position (*Binions* v. *Evans* [1972] Ch 359; *E.R. Ives (Investments)* v. *High* [1967] 2 QB 379; *Perry* v. *IRC* [2005] STC (SpCD) 474)). Thus an oral statement by parents that their house will belong to the daughter if she pays off the balance of the mortgage or cares for them in their old age[23] may bind the parties and equitable title may pass eventually (*Errington* v. *Errington & Woods* [1952] 1 KB 290; *Yaxley* v. *Gotts* [1999] 2 WLR 1217). It will not be possible to regard these as conditional gifts exempt from the charge to SDLT (FA 2003, Sched. 3, para. 1) because the 'condition' is really the performance of the consideration for the 'gift' making it contractual (*Eastham* v. *Leigh, London and Provincial Properties Limited* [1971] 2 All ER 887; *G.U.S. Merchandise* v. *HM*

---

21 A more realistic approach has been taken in relation to commercial property. However, even in relation to residential property, domestic or family arrangements that are not normally intended to create legal relationships may produce licence rather than lease; see, e.g. *Facchini* v. *Bryson* [1952] 1 TLR 1386; *Perry* v. *IRC* [2005] STC (SpCD) 474; but the parties' intention to have some form of protected interest may produce more significant legal consequences; see, e.g. *Lloyds Bank* v. *IRC* [1998] STC 559.

22 Note especially *Ogwr* v. *Dykes* [1989] 2 All ER 880 on the possible importance of a written provision that the arrangements are not intended to create a tenancy.

23 Such services would be chargeable consideration: FA 2003, Sched. 4, para. 11.

Customs & Excise [1981] STC 569). This transaction basis of the tax linked with the width of the types of consideration that are subject to tax (FA 2003, Sched. 4; see Chapter 4) means that many transactions not subject to stamp duty are now taxable such as extensions of options, variations of rights to light and release of restrictive covenants;
- situations where a tax charge arises in respect of certain transactions that do not necessarily relate to the land in question notwithstanding the absence of writing, such as clawback of certain reliefs for charities or intra-group transactions where there is a sale of shares in a company or even a subsidiary company owning the land.

Significance of documents and drafting issues

HMRC Stamp Taxes made confident statements that the drafting and structuring of documentation would no longer be effective to reduce the tax liability. It is, however, potentially misleading to regard the tax as a totally transaction-bound tax, since documentation does have a significant impact on whether and when the charge arises. Drafting may have an important effect upon the nature of the rights or interests involved in the transaction, and have a significant impact upon the tax charge. For example:

- whether the effective date is completion or substantial performance of the contract depends upon whether the contract is to be completed by a 'conveyance' so that the drafting of the completion arrangements may affect the timing of the tax charge. For example, a provision in the contract that the seller will, as from payment of the purchase price, hold the property as a bare trustee for the purchaser may in certain types of contract defer the time for paying the tax giving a cash flow/interest saving benefit for the taxpayer notwithstanding the taking of possession;[24]
- the execution of documents may be the 'transaction' which triggers the tax charge, such as where the parties perform a legally ineffective oral agreement by a formal conveyance (*Tootal* v. *Guinea Properties* (1992) 64 P&CR 452) because in general 'completion' by writing is the basic effective date (see Chapter 3);
- the drafting of the document may affect the nature of the transaction such as whether there is a lease or a licence or whether there is payment by instalments or a periodical payment (FA 2003, s.52);
- whether fitting-out arrangements are chargeable consideration, i.e. a form of premium being provided by the tenant, depends upon the terms of the agreement for lease (FA 2003, Sched. 4, para. 10);

---

24 FA 2003, s.119; s.44 thereof applies only where there is a contract to be completed by a 'conveyance' and does not override the basic provision where there is no 'conveyance' contemplated by the contract.

- whether entry upon the land involves taking possession, operating as substantial performance of the contract depends upon the terms upon which such entry is made. The nature of the arrangements for fitting out and rent-free periods can affect whether the tenant's ability to enter on to the premises to fit out is part of the chargeable non-rent consideration for the grant of the lease taxable upon the open market cost (FA 2003, Sched. 4, para. 10). It may be important whether the tenant is obliged to fit out so as to earn the rent-free period (*Ridgeons Bulk* v. *Customs & Excise* [1994] STC 427) or because the landlord is anxious to ensure that the tenant begins trading as soon as possible or whether the agreement merely permits the tenant to enter to fit out if he so wishes. Also, the terms upon which the tenant enters may affect whether he is a licensee taking possession of the whole or substantially the whole of the chargeable interest or merely has limited access to the premises; the former may be taxable events, the latter may not be taxable;
- the availability of various reliefs may depend upon drafting, particularly where VAT is involved. Since this is the vendor's risk the contract will usually provide for the payment of the tax (*Wynn Realisations Ltd* v. *Vogue Holdings Inc* [1999] STC 524). For example, although the parties believe that they have a transfer of a going concern, the contract may provide that should the transaction not qualify as a transfer of a going concern the transferee company acquiring the assets will pay the VAT to the transferor company. Clearly, if any such VAT is paid, even where there is a proper wait-and-see, relief will be lost. However, since it appears that the tax is assessed as at the effective date the relief would not be available because the possibility that cash might be paid means that the conditions relating to the issue of shares cannot be satisfied. An attempt to deal with the problem by providing that the VAT liability will be satisfied by the issue of further shares will not solve the problem if the SDLT follows stamp duty principles as a once-for-all tax. The possibility of the VAT charge would create a contractual right to be allotted shares which is a separate chose-in-action and is not the 'issue' of shares. The conditions as to the consideration would, in consequence, not be satisfied as at the effective date. However, a true wait-and-see might make the relief available, but this is debatable since the consideration is the right to be allotted shares and is not the shares issued later.[25] The only safe procedure in such a situation is to provide that the initial issue of consideration is inclusive of

---

25 However, the taxpayer may be able to use the bizarre decision of Carnworth J. in *L.M. Tenancies (No.1) plc* v. *IRC* [1996] STC 880 that in relation to the stamp duty contingency principle the consideration was the cash that might ultimately be payable and not the contingent right to receive such cash. Although manifestly wrong in terms of a rational analysis of stamp duty principles, this decision could prove a considerable embarrassment for HMRC Stamp Taxes.

VAT and avoid creating any right to a contingent or deferred consideration (see Chapter 4).

Documentation and multiple reporting

The basic rule is that the tax arises at 'completion' (FA 2003, s.119; but note the amendments in FA 2005) which is not defined, but there are many special rules. The most important special rule, in practice, is that when there is a contract which is to be completed by a 'conveyance' which is defined but only for these purposes in effect, as being any written instrument, the tax event is the earlier of substantial performance of the contract and completion, i.e. delivery of the written instrument. Moreover, even if substantial performance precedes 'completion' there is an obligation following such completion to complete and file a full land transaction return (SDLT 1) bearing a different transaction number (bar code) from the original return even though no further tax is payable. As the principle will apply to virtually every contract relating to land, the execution of the final documentation will produce an obligation to notify the tax charge. This time lapse between substantial performance of the contract and completion is particularly important in relation to leases, since in attempting to deal with certain inconveniences in the compliance system (FA 2003, Sched. 17A, para. 12A; see Chapter 8) HMRC Stamp Taxes claims to have created two separate chargeable transactions for the same legal/commercial transaction. The timing of the execution of the actual lease, which is frequently arbitrary, now has major taxation consequences.

(c) Provisional tax and wait-and-see

Stamp duty land tax, unlike stamp duty is not a once-for-all tax producing finality and certainty as to stamp tax costs shortly after the relevant event. However, much of SDLT is of a provisional nature being dealt with initially on the basis of 'reasonable estimates' and having to be reviewed from time to time and, as described above, the obligations to deal with such reviews and pay any tax arising (or recover tax provisionally overpaid) may pass to subsequent owners of the land (see, e.g. FA 2003, s.80 and Sched. 17A, para. 12). There is, therefore, an aspect of wait-and-see at least as regards the computation of the tax, but there is no statutory guidance upon the other more significant aspect of wait-and-see principles, namely whether there is a general principle that events arising after the effective date can affect the liability to the tax. The many occasions in practice when a provisional return is required include:

- variable consideration and lease premiums such as overage payments or clawback arrangements (FA 2003, s.51), but not variable annuities and

INTRODUCTION AND GENERAL PRINCIPLES

periodical payments (FA 2003, s.52). Since these arrangements can extend over a long period, including up to 80 years for clawback provisions, the initial tax position can remain open for many years, until the final payments have been agreed;
- variable rents, including virtually all forms of rent reviews, remain open for up to five years (FA 2003, Sched. 17A, paras. 7 and 8), with implication for a longer period because of the charge arising where there is a subsequent abnormal increase in the rent (FA 2003, Sched. 17A, paras. 14 and 15);
- certain reliefs are subject to clawback and the transaction becomes retrospectively taxable should certain events occur within a specified period;
- where there is or may be a linked transaction the particular transaction is vulnerable to retrospective adjustment. Thus the initial assessment of SDLT in respect of the premium paid for the grant of an option will require adjustment if the option is exercised because the option premium and the purchase price may have to be aggregated (FA 2003, s.46(1) using the word 'may') which is likely to have the effect of increasing the rate of SDLT applied to the option premium;
- where there is a lease with options for one or more renewals the lease or leases arising pursuant to the exercise of the option may be a linked transaction with the original lease so that the original lease is retrospectively treated as a single lease for a term for the aggregate terms of the original lease and all renewals thereof (FA 2003, Sched. 17A, para. 5 (as amended)), and the original application of the formula for the net present value of the rent has to be revisited on the basis of a longer term with additional years of rent to be included in the revised calculation (see Chapter 8). This will, at first sight, increase the SDLT payable over the sum originally paid, but without interest and penalty. The uncertainty extends beyond such simple situations because where there are linked leases the nil rate slice of the net present value of the rent has to be allocated between the various linked leases pro rata to the net present value of the rent (FA 2003, Sched. 5, para. 2 (as amended)). In consequence, if there is a later linked lease including a later lease arising pursuant to the exercise of an option to renew another lease with a consequent increase in the net present value of the rent for that lease, there will have to be an adjustment of the allocation of the nil rate slice for all of the current linked leases. This reduction in the nil rate slice will, it seems, have to be separately notified since it will affect the initial self-assessment of the net present value subject to the 1 per cent rate, so it will affect the computation of SDLT in relation to that lease after the initial calculation including rent reviews that have taken place and been taxed between the original effective date and the effective date for the linked transaction.

These are, however, merely specific provisions dealing with a more general problem, i.e. is the whole of SDLT underpinned by a wait-and-see principle, and is there a general principle that all tax returns can be revisited in the light of the later events such as where there is a claim for breach of contract and the purchase price is effectively reduced. The problem for the relief for corporate reconstructions set out above is another illustration of whether the relief can be claimed retrospectively if the VAT is not payable. Similarly, there is a question of whether such relief can be claimed because the consideration shares will frequently not have been issued, i.e. registered at the effective date or at the time when the land transaction return is filed because the parties may take a relaxed approach to tidying up the paperwork. At that time the conditions have not been satisfied. In practice, this latter point was not taken by HMRC Stamp Taxes for the purposes of the equivalent stamp duty reliefs but the whole timing and structure of SDLT raises different problems and there are expected to be significant problems in this area if there is not instant completion and all paperwork properly completed at that time.

The position is at present uncertain and there is a risk that because there are numerous specific provisions dealing with timing issues there cannot be a general wait-and-see principle since this would render many of the particular provisions redundant. In consequence, notwithstanding the extended nature of the time over which the SDLT has to be computed, it is unclear whether there is a fully developed wait-and-see principle or whether there is a degree of a once-for-all tax retained and brought over from stamp duty. It seems to be the view of HMRC Stamp Taxes that the wait-and-see aspects of SDLT are limited to dealing with the calculation only and are intended solely to deal with the problems of the stamp duty contingency principle whereby, with suitable drafting, certain parts of the consideration could escape tax. In its apparent view because there is, in general, only one effective date (but see FA 2003, Sched. 17A, para. 12B), the question of liability to tax and the availability of exemptions or reliefs is answered once and for all as at that date and subsequent events, although relevant for computing the stamp duty land tax, cannot affect the liability to the tax or eligibility to any reliefs.

No finality

This problem of the limited set of wait-and-see principles produces outstanding tax positions with the related uncertainty as to the costs of the acquisition.[26]

---

26 Which will, of course, affect the purchaser's overall tax position such as the base cost for capital gains tax and the sums paid for capital allowances. Whilst the SDLT is unresolved or open to challenge, it may prove difficult to determine the amount upon which capital allowances may be claimed or what is the base cost for capital gains. There will also be issues as to whether there is a potential liability for SDLT against the estate of the deceased for the purposes of inheritance tax. These are complex issues (see, e.g. the extremely difficult legislation for VAT and the capital goods scheme contained in Capital Allowances Act 2000, ss.546 *et seq.*).

There are other situations where, unlike stamp duty and adjudication, the new regime does not produce a situation where the tax position can be regarded as closed without the risk of having to file further returns and pay additional tax. This may affect third parties such as grantees and assignees of leases (see Chapter 8). However, since personal representatives and liquidators and certain receivers take over responsibility for the unresolved SDLT position of the deceased or company in addition to possibly becoming liable for exercising options entered into by the deceased or the company prior to their taking office, they will have an obligation to investigate whether there is an outstanding position, including warranties and indemnities given where the chargeable interest has been transferred to or acquired by a third party. It will in many cases be a potential obstacle to the final administration of the estate or conclusion of the liquidation since the circumstances where the SDLT can be finalised may not have occurred and may not occur for many years in the future.

Other arrangements may be affected by the lack of finality. For example, there may be a purchase price for land linked to the profits or earnings from the development of the land. The calculation is likely to involve a deduction for any stamp tax costs. Unfortunately, these costs can never, in theory, be finally determined because of the potential 21-year period for discovery notices and the eternal obligation of the taxpayer to rectify the situation if an error in the return emerges (FA 2003, Sched. 10, para. 8). Parties will have to take their chances on this by providing for an arbitrary cut-off date when the provisional tax computation will be deemed to be conclusive for the purposes of the calculation. At present, it is uncertain which is the appropriate cut-off date to select but it seems likely that a period of seven years (i.e. one year after the expiration of the basic period for discovery assessments) could be the most convenient in practice for the time being until this legislative mess is sorted out by HMRC Stamp Taxes.

Fortunately, as indicated above, this open-ended nature of SDLT does not affect title issues, but it has the potential for producing considerable difficulties in practice. There are, however, important points to note such as the fact that a land transaction return (SDLT 1) and the enclosed payment have been accepted by HMRC Stamp Taxes and an SDLT 5 certificate has been issued does not mean that the return is accepted as correct because the powers of HMRC Stamp Taxes to investigate returns at this stage are severely limited so as to offer the possibility of a rapid turnaround of the return in order not to cause severe difficulties to taxpayers because of the different timetables applicable to land registration.[27]

---

[27] Even where there has been an Enquiry into a land transaction return or a self-certificate HMRC Stamp Taxes is empowered to issue an assessment if it makes a discovery.

It might be thought that this problem of uncertainty as to tax costs and of the long-term possibility of a challenge by HMRC Stamp Taxes should end after the expiration of the nine months during which an Enquiry can be launched (FA 2003, Sched. 10, para. 12(2): land transaction returns (SDLT 1); Sched. 11, para. 7(2): SDLT 60 – self-certificate). However, where HMRC Stamp Taxes makes a 'discovery', which is relatively easy given the deficiencies in the self-assessment regime and the design of the forms (see *Langham v. Veltema* [2004] STC 544), it may issue an assessment at any time up to six years after the effective date for the transaction. However, where there is evidence of fraud or negligence the discovery assessment may be made up to 21 years after the effective date of the transaction. Since fraud is widely defined and includes wrongful allocation of the consideration between chattels and land and 'negligence' includes not merely an error of law in deciding how the SDLT regime applies to the transaction such as whether there is an arrangement within the anti-avoidance provisions for the intra-group relief pursuant to Part 1 of Sched. 7 to FA 2003, but also applies to errors in the completion of the return such as not taking proper steps to determine the market value of the property or to obtain reasonable evidence as to future variable payments of contingent sums and rent reviews, there will be ample opportunity for HMRC Stamp Taxes to extend the discovery assessment time limit to 21 years.

Moreover, even if this were not enough of a problem, it is provided that where a taxpayer discovers that an error was made in the completion of the land transaction, including an error made innocently, without fraud or negligence, he is under an obligation under a tax-related penalty to remedy the defect within a reasonable time after discovering the error (FA 2003, Sched. 10, para. 8). There will be interesting questions as to what constitutes appropriate knowledge of such an error, particularly where it arises out of litigation to which the taxpayer is not a party and which does not relate to SDLT but the construction of documents relating to land. This obligation is unlimited in time, and it is not clear how it affects persons other than the taxpayer such as his personal representatives and his professional advisers, nor is it clear whether they have a continuing obligation to notify clients of developments possibly affecting their tax return for a chargeable transaction filed many years previously.

Side effects

This lack of finality also affects transactions indirectly. For example, a company may be a tenant of a lease with variable rents, or a lease that was exempt when granted but which may have a negative value because of the special charge upon assignment being taxed as a new lease (FA 2003, Sched. 17A, para. 11 (as amended)), or there are clawback risks (see further Chapter 6). There are crucial issues in the pricing of the shares. Similarly, the valuation of interests in trusts may be influenced by open SDLT assessments such as where land has been acquired for a consideration including an overage payment.

(d) Self-assessment

Unlike stamp duty where the obligation to assess the tax lies with HMRC Stamp Taxes, SDLT is initially and subsequently calculated by the taxpayer as part of the process of completing the land transaction return (FA 2003, s.76). This assessment may be challenged by HMRC Stamp Taxes upon initial filing but this can occur only where there is a manifest omission or error in the arithmetic (FA 2003, Sched. 10, para. 7). The issue of an SDLT 5 certificate is, therefore, not conclusive that the correct amount of tax has been paid and any additional tax can be assessed by HMRC Stamp Taxes by means of a 'discovery assessment' for up to 21 years after the effective date of the transaction where negligence is involved and the taxpayer is exposed in perpetuity to an obligation to rectify any errors in the return including payment of additional tax, interest and penalties should he become aware of errors such as by way of subsequent litigation between parties with whom he is not associated concerning the valuation techniques adopted.[28]

The obligation of the taxpayer is to provide an accurate assessment of his tax liability. This requires an appreciation of:

- whether a land transaction return (SDLT 1) is required, which requires:
  - an appreciation of when an initial return is required;
  - an understanding of when a further return is required for the same transaction, including situations where the taxpayer although not a party to the transaction is nevertheless required to file a return and pay additional tax such as the linked transaction charges; and
  - when amendments or corrective returns are required (such as FA 2003, Sched. 10, para. 8);
- when the tax charge arises since the effective date will be crucial for a variety of issues such as the date for determining market values or whether the option to charge VAT has been exercised;
- the nature of the transaction;
- the precise conditions for the availability of any exemptions and whether they are satisfied;
- the details relating to chargeable consideration which is not the same as the actual consideration in many cases such as where connected

---

28 The responsibility of professional advisers to keep the clients informed of such developments long after the association has ceased remains to be explored and should be expressly provided for in any retainer letter.

companies or partnerships are involved, or works or services provide all or part of the consideration;
- whether the correct procedures for determining the market value or reasonable estimates of future payments or rents have been adopted or whether other 'guestimates' that are required when completing the return have been correctly determined.

It will be clear from the above list of potential areas of difficulty that a whole new area of negligence has been created. It will also be clear that such new negligence is important in relation to the client since it may extend the discovery assessment period from six to 21 years and leave the client exposed for a theoretical eternity to the need to rectify the erroneous tax return which, however, applies even where the return was not prepared negligently (FA 2003, Sched. 10, para. 8).

In broad terms, self-assessment creates three areas of potential negligence; namely:

- negligence in relation to the charging or relieving provisions;
- negligence in computing the tax because, for example, the correct consideration was not utilised; and
- negligence in relation to the methodology adopted for the preparation of the land transaction return,[29] for example, no proper evidence as to market value was obtained.

The first two areas are the traditional area of the quality of the advice relating to the transaction such as whether the taxpayer is entitled to a relief or exemption. The last area is totally new and has to be approached with circumspection since, because the amount of information contained in the land transaction returns is limited and does not permit disclosure of the calculation or valuations or assumptions behind the final entry,[30] it is unbelievably easy for the HMRC Stamp Taxes to issue a discovery assessment.

In consequence of this new compliance regime, the question of completing the forms (SDLT 1 to 4 and 60) is now of major significance with real conse-

---

29 There is also a possible issue of whether, should the client refuse to accept advice as to the proper procedures for preparing the land transaction return and may in consequence be acting fraudulently, i.e. knowingly submitting a return prepared on an incorrect basis, the professional adviser is exposing himself to criminal penalties for 'knowingly' (whatever that may ultimately be held to mean in this context) assisting in the preparation of an incorrect return.

30 The situation is unlike the old-fashioned mathematics examinations where the candidate is advised to show his workings so that errors of arithmetic can be dealt with and credit given if the principles adopted are correct. The self-assessment system does not permit such 'workings' to be disclosed, only the final answer; see also FA 2003, Sched. 10, para. 30(4).

quences for errors in the form of tax-related penalties and extended periods for discovery assessments (see Chapter 14 and Appendix D). There is a need to give careful thought not only to the analysis of the transaction such as lease or a licence, conditional gift or contract for consideration but also to the methodology to be adopted in gathering the data and producing the information required by the land transaction returns such as the correct method for apportioning the consideration between the land and fixtures and chattels as required by the amended SDLT 4, or determining the market value or for making reasonable estimates of future rents and future overage or clawback payments.

Negligence

There will be an important area of law to be developed in this context concerning the difference between errors that are negligent and mistakes that are not negligent. Simply because a conclusion whether of law or the methodology adopted for preparing the return is not accepted by HMRC Stamp Taxes or is rejected by the court on appeal does not necessarily mean that the decision was negligent. If the taxpayer and/or his advisers have prepared contemporaneous records of the decision-making process and can establish that all relevant issues have been properly investigated and that nothing has been overlooked, it will be extremely difficult for HMRC Stamp Taxes to establish 'negligence'.

Since many of the difficulties for taxpayers and self-assessment arise because of the problems of lack of space to set out the background, particularly to explain entries that appear on the forms described as 'other', this renders taxpayers vulnerable to discovery assessments. Attempts have been made to cover the deficiencies in the forms by submitting covering letters setting out the background to the form. However, it seems that such attempts are not likely to be successful, although these letters may be helpful in combating allegations of fraud which will be difficult for HMRC Stamp Taxes to maintain because the taxpayer has sought from the beginning to make full disclosure to it. Since fraud may require a degree of concealment, covering letters may be helpful.

However, they will not produce 'finality'. HMRC Stamp Taxes has indicated that it will not take notice of such letters and that the employees processing the land transaction return have no authority to consider or act upon such letters. In consequence, such letters will not bind HMRC Stamp Taxes because it will be beyond the authority of the recipients to deal with them.

UNDERSTANDING SDLT

Post-transaction rulings

It is theoretically possible to apply for a ruling after the transaction so as to reduce the risk of errors attracting substantial penalties and interest.[31] Unfortunately, this is of little benefit in practice since there can be no such post-transaction ruling to provide a speedy answer where a land transaction return has been filed. As mentioned above, the 30-day time limit is irrelevant because it ignores the Land Registry time limits so that it is potentially imprudent to delay filing to obtain a ruling. At this stage the request for a ruling is converted into a full-blown expensive and time-consuming Enquiry.

Compliance

Unlike stamp duty which was in many respects described as a voluntary tax, SDLT is a directly enforceable tax with obligations under penalty to notify HMRC (see Chapter 14).

1.3 SOURCES

The main provisions at present are contained in FA 2003, but these have been substantially amended by later legislation and statutory instruments. HMRC has an exceedingly large number of powers to issue regulations on a wide range of issues and these can change the tax by altering the charging and relieving provisions and the compliance requirements, including prescribing the land transaction return forms and arrangements for postponing tax payments.

HMRC Stamp Taxes has begun to publish a draft Manual, but at present this is far from complete and is little more than a précis of the legislation. Moreover, it is uncertain how far the Manual can be relied upon at present because it is only a 'draft' and HMRC generally is, it seems, seeking to limit the ability of taxpayers to rely upon statements in Manuals which it claims are not binding because they are intended purely for internal guidance and not as the equivalent of Statements of Practice. They are published merely as a courtesy to assist taxpayers as to the broad lines of the approach of HMRC and not intended to be exhaustive or definitive nor to restrict HMRC in any particular case. It remains to be seen how far this view is developed in practice.

HMRC Stamp Taxes has begun a practice of issuing bulletins or notices setting out its views and possible practices in certain areas, but since none of these has been formally issued as a Statement of Practice it may lack any

---

31 Reliance upon the so-called helpline is not regarded as being non-negligent. HMRC Stamp Taxes does not regard itself as bound by the helpline and refuses to mitigate penalties where its advice is wrong.

INTRODUCTION AND GENERAL PRINCIPLES

binding power to prevent these views not being applied in practice where they prove to be inconvenient.

There is a so-called 'helpline' but at present this has high records of incorrect and inconsistent advice. Moreover, advice given over the telephone does not bind HMRC (*J Rothschild Holdings Ltd* v. *IRC* [1988] STC 645 (on appeal on other grounds [1989] STC 435)) and it seems that relying upon the helpline will not even be regarded as a reason for the mitigation of penalties.

Past practice or previous dealings are not regarded as binding since it has been stated to the editor by a senior officer of HMRC Stamp Taxes on several occasions that they do not have practices; they have been making mistakes which are not practices and they cannot be bound by their past mistakes. Additionally, it will be difficult to establish practice in particular areas (*J Rothschild Holdings Ltd* v. *IRC* [1988] STC 645) since HMRC can refuse to disclose details of previous dealings with taxpayers on the ground of confidentiality so that it is virtually impossible to produce evidence of the treatment of previous transactions that will convince the current judiciary.

It might be thought that as much of the legislation is in the same or similar terms to the old stamp duty that the former case law and Statements of Practice will be relevant in relation to the new tax. In certain cases this may be a correct assumption but it is one that has to be approached with caution. The 'one-size-fits-all' and plain English style of the drafting and structuring of the legislation mean that words have to be given unusual meanings in order to make the tax even vaguely workable and their new meanings or the subtle effects of the 'one-size-fits-all' drafting, which can work against as well as for HMRC Stamp Taxes, may alter the meaning of both stamp duty and conveyancing terms. Nevertheless as there are some indications in practice that a certain amount of stamp duty baggage is being brought across the old stamp duty position may be a potential source for guidance.

1.4 JURISDICTION

SDLT is a global tax in that it applies in cases where there is an instrument effecting the transaction when it is irrelevant whether the instrument is executed in the UK or abroad. More importantly, it applies whether or not any party to the transaction is present or resident in the UK. Thus non-residents such as foreign trustees and beneficiaries of such trusts and foreign estates will be subject to the tax (FA 2003, s.42(2)). This gives rise to problems because of the need for personal signature by the taxpayer on the SDLT 1 where it may be necessary to arrange for the return to be sent to several different countries for signature. Even where it is possible for a person holding a power of attorney or other authority to sign on behalf of the taxpayer, it may be necessary to obtain the appropriate power of attorney or company resolution for the representative to act for the party overseas.

SDLT is limited to chargeable interests in land situate in the UK; foreign land is not subject to stamp taxes. Although the tax is limited to interests in land in the UK (FA 2003, s.48(1)(a)), it is clear that certain interests that appear to be foreign are to be regarded as interests in or over land in the UK. These are interests in trusts and estates of deceased persons which arise because of the rules providing for a look through where a beneficiary is 'absolutely entitled' as against the trustee (FA 2003, Sched. 16, para. 2; see Chapter 10) and deeming foreign trusts as being the same as English trusts where the draftsman took the view that beneficiaries have a proprietary interest in the assets held by the trustees (*Baker* v. *Archer Shee* 15 TC 1; *Archer Shee* v. *Garland* 15 TC 693). Two main areas in practice will be involved, namely:

- foreign fixed interest (as opposed to discretionary) trusts because of the rules equating these with English trusts where the legislation works upon the basis that beneficiaries under such trusts have an equitable interest in the underlying assets (as a separate interest in the land held by the trustees this interest will be a chargeable interest; FA 2003, Sched. 16, para 2). Consequently, where a foreign trust holds land in the UK the equitable interests will be within the charge to tax even where the settlor is non-domiciled. Such trustees should consider holding land through a body corporate; and
- foreign partnerships where, although it is now accepted by HMRC Stamp Taxes that a share in a partnership wherever established is not itself a chargeable interest, there are provisions in Sched. 15 (as amended) to FA 2003 imposing a charge upon dealings in partnership interests. Participants in such arrangements should consider how either the land in the UK and/or the partnership share should be held to side-step these problems.

1.5 FORM OR SUBSTANCE – TAX AVOIDANCE

To what extent can a potential payer of SDLT arrange his affairs so as to minimise his liability for the charge? There was a weaker presumption in the case of stamp duties than in other fields of taxation that there is a rational and coherent system of taxation. It was observed by Taunton J. in *Morley* v. *Hall* (1834) 2 Dowl 494 that stamp duty 'involves nothing of the principle or reason but depends altogether on the language of the legislature' although more recently Carnworth J. stated that in stamp duty he should not pay too much attention to the wording of the legislation (*L.M. Tenancies* v. *IRC* [1996] STC 880 (on appeal [1998] STC 326)). However, the peculiar nature of stamp duty as a documentary tax gave rise to numerous issues as to how far HMRC Stamp Taxes can go behind the documents and restructure the transaction and/or rewrite the documents where these have been designed to minimise stamp duty. The principle long held of general application to all taxing statutes was that avoidance used to be acceptable in that it was perfectly permissible deliberately to arrange one's affairs with a view to minimising the payment of tax (*IRC* v. *Duke of Westminster* [1936] AC 1). The resultant mushrooming of tax avoidance in other spheres of taxation by the use of highly complex and artificial schemes resulted in a severe curtailment of the operation of the *Westminster* principle by the House of Lords (*WT Ramsay Ltd* v. *IRC* [1979] 1 WLR 974; *Eilbeck* v. *Rawling* [1981] 2 WLR 449; *Furniss* v. *Dawson* [1984] STC 153) in the leading cases since, but this principle has undergone significant revision in later cases. It does, however, permit the courts to take a more robust approach to the legal form of the transaction when analysing matters as regards the tax consequences.

To what extent can these principles be held applicable to stamp duty land tax? Historically stamp taxes have been regarded as a tax of wholly different nature from other taxes. A key issue is that the tax falls upon the purchaser. Most taxes fall upon the vendor. It is, in consequence, a cost of the transaction rather than a tax upon the disposal proceeds. Additionally, it is a tax upon the gross price whereas most taxes are upon the profits or gains of the taxpayer. Stamp taxes are imposed upon individual transactions whereas most taxes fall upon the annual profits or gains of the vendor. It might be said that similar issues apply to VAT; but in regard to that tax the purchaser may be entitled to recover the input tax on his transaction. If he cannot recover the input tax, it will be unlikely that the purchaser will be required to charge tax on his onward sale so that the cascade effect of transaction-based taxes is avoided to a significant extent. Unfortunately, there is no such relief for stamp taxes against this cascade effect of tax upon the same tax since sub-sale relief which was designed to deal with such problems has been severely truncated. These issues applied to stamp duty as well as SDLT but the current judiciary have shown themselves to be out of their depth, unable to tackle these cascade tax problems and have failed to appreciate the simple basic distinction between tax avoidance and cost reduction. Moreover, since SDLT is a transaction-based tax this judicial inability to understand the basic issues makes it likely that the tax avoidance cases will be applied to the new tax regardless of the issues and consequences. There are, therefore, major points of principle that can be made but the current judiciary will not be able to cope with these issues on a reasonable basis. The main issue is whether HMRC Stamp Taxes having traditionally not pursued the point in practice in relation to stamp duty will bring this practice forward as part of the inevitable baggage of previous law carried over with the new tax. Previous cases have shown that the courts were only too ready in this field to tax the legal substance of the transaction rather than the form but in this context of a highly technical land law regime 'legal substance' has a particular meaning, namely the true legal effect of the transaction rather than any 'label' which the parties may attach to their document. Thus a transfer of assets to a company may be described as an amalgamation but in stamp tax terms it is an acquisition (*Great Western Railways* v. *IRC* [1894] 1 QB 507; *J&P Coats Ltd* v. *IRC* [1897] 1 QB 778, on appeal [1897] 2 QB 423).

In the same way, the grant of some rights over land will be stampable as a lease regardless of the fact that the parties term the instrument a licence, if the legal relationship which the instrument creates is one of lessor and lessee (see *Addiscombe Garden Estates Ltd* v. *Crabbe* [1958] 1 QB 513). However, on occasion the label used by the parties to describe their document may tip the balance when interpreting its effect (*British India Steam Navigation* v. *IRC* [1891] 2 QB 165; *Ogwr* v. *Dykes* [1989] 2 All ER 880) but, in general, the parties' intention is irrelevant in arriving at the legal effect or construction of the document (*Peter Bone* v. *IRC* [1995] STC 921). Hence, the substance of an instrument has traditionally meant strict legal effect looking at all the circumstances rather than an alternative economic or commercial arrangement.

Two concepts are involved here, as discussed below.

(a) Sham

These examples, however, concerned the artificial nature of the end result of the transactions, and provided that they were genuine in themselves it was considered allowable to arrive at their conclusion by a circuitous route provided that the steps taken genuinely had the effect intended. As Lord Wilberforce observed in *Ramsay*, a sham transaction is one which 'while professing to be one thing, is in fact something different'. This raises the question of whether the documentation setting out the various steps represents the true bargain between the parties. The normal principles of construction involve only the words in the instrument so that extrinsic materials such as the parties' intentions are irrelevant (*West London Syndicate Ltd* v. *IRC* [1898] 2 QB 507). This can work both for and against the parties since they are not allowed to contradict their written words (*Peter Bone* v. *IRC* [1995] STC 921). In consequence the nature of the transaction and its SDLT consequences depend upon the drafting and the parties' conduct is not relevant to the analysis unless such conduct shows that the drafting was misleading and intended to produce a tax result different from that which would have applied had the transaction been accurately described (*Lloyds and Scottish* v. *Cyril Lord* [1992] BCLC 609; *Snook* v. *London and West Riding* [1967] 2 QB 783; *Ingram* v. *IRC* [1985] STC 835).

(b) Form and substance

There are the questions of whether HMRC Stamp Taxes can go behind the legal structure adopted by the parties and investigate whether the parties have

INTRODUCTION AND GENERAL PRINCIPLES

correctly and accurately set this out in the documentation and whether they can charge SDLT upon the basis that the same economic and commercial result could have been achieved by other means attracting a higher liability to tax. It is clear that in SDLT no such power exists. A taxpayer is entitled to choose between alternative routes to reach the same commercial end (*Sherdley* v. *Sherdley* [1987] STC 266) and it is permissible for that choice to be made upon the basis of a better post-tax result (*Willoughby* v. *IRC* [1995] STC 143). Tax efficiency in choice of routes is not tax avoidance. This is important in the context of certain reliefs from SDLT for company reconstructions (FA 2003, Sched. 7) where one of the conditions for relief is the absence of a stamp duty avoidance motive.[32]

Forward planning

In the light of the above judicial observations there would seem to be no objection, for example, to transferring land to an offshore company with a view to finding a purchaser at a later date, even though by passing it out in this way a stamp duty liability may be avoided: a series of transactions is not 'pre-ordained' unless it involves a degree of certainty and control over the end result at the time when the intermediate steps are taken (*Shepherd* v. *Lyntress* [1989] STC 617; *Littlewoods Mail Order Stores* v. *IRC* [1961] Ch 597). Preparatory steps such as these cannot be attacked as tax avoidance, because at this stage no tax charge has arisen; the parties have merely put themselves in a position whereby at a later date a transaction may escape a tax charge that might have arisen had not the steps been taken. In such situations the question is how the current judiciary will develop the need for a cut-and-dried or pre-arranged scheme as an integral part of the tax avoidance principle and if such a scheme rather than a hope or expectation[33] is required for these principles to apply, how this concept of a scheme is to be interpreted. This could be important where the parties take steps to convert land into shares by vesting it in a company but the importance of such forward planning has been substantially diminished by the three-year clawback provisions introduced by FA 2003 and subsequently as a long-term antiavoidance measure of an extremely crude nature.

Sophisticated schemes were never within the scope of this book, but other straightforward – and hopefully still recognised – side-steps which can be legitimately and safely employed to avoid major pitfalls or to minimise or

---

32 Thus, for example, it has been accepted by the Special Commissioners that deciding upon a transaction and seeking to implement it with the minimum stamp duty is not a tax avoidance motive for these purposes.
33 See the attempt by HMRC Stamp Taxes to introduce such a concept in the effectively abortive Statement of Practice SP3/98 in relation to stamp duty.

avoid tax, are dealt with as and when appropriate in the following chapters.[34] A key obligation owed to clients is to avoid pitfalls which lead to an unnecessary large charge to tax such as inappropriate drafting and to suggest a structure which produces a reasonably tax efficient implementation of the transaction and this duty applies notwithstanding that the adviser may have indicated that he does not advise on tax as such (*Hurlingham Estates* v. *Wilde* [1997] STC 627). Attempts are made in the following chapters to indicate such pitfalls and possible alternatives.

The linked transaction rules exist solely for the purposes of fixing the rates of tax and are not a general principle that enables HMRC Stamp Taxes to introduce some form of associated operations principle. The chargeable transaction has to be dealt with in accordance with its own terms; the fact that it is part of a larger transaction or arrangement cannot, of itself, affect the taxation consequences. Any such attack by HMRC Stamp Taxes must be based, if at all, on the 'tax avoidance cases' based upon *Ramsay* [1978] STC 253 and *Furniss* v. *Dawson* [1982] STC 267 and the issue of form over substance or the purposive construction or however the principle is developed by judicial whimsy and lack of consistency in the future. The issue is considered below, but there is a danger that the wait-and-see provision, if applicable to the particular chargeable transaction, might mean that later events could become relevant and there is the risk that the tax avoidance cases could mean that the later facts could be utilised by the current judiciary to make the relief unavailable because it was simply a stepping stone to some larger avoidance arrangement not covered by the relief.

---

34 Moreover, such planning may involve advance disclosure to HMRC pursuant to FA 2004, Part 7; Stamp Duty Land Tax Avoidance Schemes (Prescribed Descriptions of Arrangements) Regulations 2005, SI 2005/1868.

CHAPTER 2

Chargeable transactions

2.1 BASIC CHARGING PROVISIONS

A charge to SDLT arises upon 'land transactions' which includes the general charge to the tax plus a whole range of specifically chargeable transactions, i.e. transactions deemed to be chargeable transactions such as 'abnormal' increases in rent after the expiration of the fifth year of the term of the lease (FA 2003, Sched. 17A, paras. 14 and 15) or the clawback of previously taken reliefs (see, e.g. FA 2003, Sched. 7, paras. 3 and 9). However, there is not a total correlation between chargeable transactions and notifiable transactions so that although a transaction is not chargeable there are many situations where it is notifiable. The mere fact that tax is not payable does not mean that some form of notification is not required whether directly by means of a land transaction (SDLT 1) or indirectly through the Land Registry by means of the self-certificate (SDLT 60) required to support certain non-taxable transactions such as most gifts. However, there are numerous reasons why a transaction is not taxable and the reason why it is not a chargeable transaction is important for compliance purposes. Section 77 of FA 2003, for example, provides that a transaction that is not chargeable is notifiable unless it is exempt for certain purposes.

The effect of the interaction of the various definitions (FA 2003, ss.49(1) and 43(1)) is that a tax charge arises upon the acquisition of a chargeable interest in land in the UK which is not a transaction that is exempt from charge (FA 2003, s.49(1)). Although not expressly stated, chargeable consideration, which can include deemed consideration, is required since there is a general exemption for transactions where there is no chargeable consideration (FA 2003, Sched. 3, para. 1; see Chapter 5).

The definition of a chargeable transaction does not include a transaction which is 'exempt' which is a word of some ambiguity in stamp tax practice (see Chapter 5), but it seems that it includes cases where the transaction is not chargeable because it relates to an exempt interest or because the particular transaction qualifies for relief, such as a lease to a charity.

There are several aspects of the basic charge that require expansion and these will now be discussed in turn.

(a) 'Acquisition'

The 'plain English' meaning of 'acquisition' is artificially extended to include:

- the creation of a chargeable interest (FA 2003, s.43(3)(a));[1]
- the surrender of a chargeable interest (FA 2003, s.43(3)(b));
- the release[2] of a chargeable interest (FA 2003, s.43(3)(b));
- the variation of a chargeable interest other than variations of leases (FA 2003, s.43(3)(c));
- certain variations of leases (FA 2003, s.43(3)(d) (as amended) and Sched. 17A, para. 15A (as amended); see Chapter 8. There are issues around break clauses).

The basic charge will apply to sales of freeholds and leases and the grant of leases, although in some situations (FA 2003, Sched. 17A, paras. 11 and 14) there is an 'acquisition' producing a chargeable transaction, and that transaction may be taxed in a manner totally different from its correct legal analysis. For example, the assignment or variation of a lease may be taxed upon the basis that it is the grant of a new lease (FA 2003, Sched. 17A, para. 15A (as amended)).

In consequence, the inappropriateness of this use of 'acquisition' is likely to mislead taxpayers in cases such as where on surrender or release interests disappear so that there is no obvious 'acquisition'. It is difficult to see who 'acquires' what when an option is varied or the property interest involved 'disappears' such as upon the release of a restrictive covenant. However, since this definition merely 'includes' there is the potential for HMRC Stamp Taxes to seek to bring other types of transaction into charge. Problem areas could include disclaimers and waivers. However, the definition of 'renunciation' in relation to transfers involving partnerships (FA 2003, Sched. 15, para. 9(2)(c)) suggests that, because it was thought necessary to include it, renunciations, disclaimers and waivers are not acquisitions because these dispose of property not owned by the person entering into the transaction.

There is also a question of whether 'acquisition' requires a bi-lateral transaction so that a possible movement of an interest in land as a result of the actions of one person acting alone such as giving a notice to quit (*Barnett* v. *Morgan* [2000] 2 AC 264) which has the practical effect of returning the tenancy interest to the landlord may not be an 'acquisition'. It is, however, understood that HMRC Stamp Taxes is investigating the possibility of challenging notices to quit and break clauses as 'acquisitions' (see also FA 2003, s.43(3)(d) and Sched. 17A, para. 15A (as amended)). Fortunately, it seems

---

1 It remains to be seen whether 'creation' includes an interest arising by reason of 'exception and reservation' in a conveyance or grant.
2 It remains to be seen whether 'release' and 'surrender' includes actions such as 'waiver' or 'disclaimer'.

that there is no intention to treat 'mergers' of separate interests held by the same person as acquisitions because notwithstanding the change in the nature of the reversionary interest of the owner he does not 'acquire' any additional interest in the property.[3]

Notwithstanding that the SDLT is based upon 'acquisition' of chargeable interests the tax charge, i.e. the effective date, can arise before any interest is 'acquired' by the purchaser in the traditional sense of property vesting even in cases where property is transferred, such as sales. It is, therefore, essential to note that the rules apply by reference to artificial dates that are essentially unrelated to the passing of title whether legal or equitable. Any correspondence between the passing of title, whether legal or equitable, and the charge to tax will be essentially a matter of coincidence rather than a matter of principle. For example, the constructive trust in favour of purchasers arises and the equitable interest vests only where the purchase price is paid in full (*Michaels* v. *Harley House (Marylebone) Ltd* [1999] 3 WLR 229); but the charge arises when only 90 per cent of the purchase price is paid as substantial performance of the contract (FA 2003, s.44(7)).

The charge can also arise, i.e. an effective date can occur, where a purchaser goes into possession when the contract is still conditional such as where the assignment of a lease or the grant of an underlease is dependent upon the consent of the landlord where no equitable interest passes until the consent has been obtained (*Warmington* v. *Miller* [1973] 2 All ER 372). It is for this reason that it has proved essential to provide that if the contract is cancelled or rescinded the SDLT can be reclaimed (FA 2003, s.44(9)).

Types of 'acquisition'

This extended definition of 'acquisition' gives rise to several surprising consequences because of the implications derived from the legislation as to the construction of the various sub-aspects of acquisitions such as 'creation'. For example, the word 'creation', which is not itself defined, may convert what appears to be a straightforward 'sale' into a land exchange because of the extended meaning given to that term by FA 2003, s.47. It is not unusual for a developer of residential or industrial sites involving several properties to convey[4] each property subject to some form of 'estate covenant'. On occasion

---

3 However, this issue is less clear where there is a severance of a beneficial joint interest because the interests of the co-owners are 'enlarged' by the power to dispose of the property. It may also be a 'variation' taxable as a land exchange.

4 Different issues may arise where the developer grants leases which contain appropriate covenants. Although there is a question of whether the giving of covenants in a lease constitutes entering into a land contract within the terms of FA 2003, s.47, which would appear to be the case, it is understood that HMRC Stamp Taxes has not responded to an enquiry as to whether they will treat every lease as two taxable events within FA 2003, Sched. 4, para. 5. Fortunately, hitherto, no points have been taken in

this covenant or benefit may be retained by the developer by means of provisions relating to the 'exception and reservation' of rights from the conveyance when it may be arguable that there is no 'creation' of a new right, simply an exclusion from the property transferred. However, as expected, HMRC Stamp Taxes does not accept this analysis of routine transactions and claims that such exception and reservation involves the creation of a new right in exactly the same way as where there is an outright transfer with a regrant of the right back to the transferor by the transferee,[5] which represents the express creation of a new right rather than the retention of an existing right implicit in the ownership of the land. Wherever the arrangement 'creates' a new right there will be a land exchange, probably of a major interest for a minor interest, thereby leading to two transactions deemed to take place at market value (FA 2003, s.4 and Sched. 4, para. 5; see Chapter 4 on the vexed question of the market value of minor interests). There will be considerable debate as to what rights, if any, may be excepted and/or reserved without the need for a regrant. It seems at present that only minerals and already existing separate rights over the land are regarded by HMRC Stamp Taxes as being capable of retention not requiring a 'regrant'.

Acquisitions will include surrenders of leases by operation of law and releases of life interests in settlements and easements. Variations other than leases will include any modification of a chargeable interest such as the extension of an option, moving a right of way or changes in rights to light. Variations of leases have caused HMRC Stamp Taxes considerable problems and have produced numerous changes so that variations of leases must be regarded as an extremely fluid matter requiring constant inspection of the legislation and regulations (see for details Chapter 8).

Process of 'acquisition'

The charge to tax applies whether the 'acquisition' is effected by act of the parties, by order of the court or other authority by or under any statutory provision[6] or by operation of law (FA 2003, s.43(2)). These are the provisions that make the SDLT transaction-based since the charge applies whether or not there is any instrument effecting the transaction (FA 2003, s.42(2)(a)),

---

practice on this basis but in the absence of a formal statement, there are risks should HMRC Stamp Taxes form the impression that any particular case is one where 'tax avoidance' is involved.

5 Relying upon *Johnstone* v. *Holdway* [1963] 1 All ER 432; HMRC Stamp Taxes has failed to address the issue of rights arising pursuant to Law of Property 1925, s.62 but as the tax applies to transactions taking effect by operation of law it seems that such transactions may be taxable and fall within the land exchange head of charge.

6 The effect of rights created by provisions such as Law of Property Act 1925, s.62 remains an open question.

and bring into the charge to tax many transactions entered into informally and without professional advice but which are nonetheless effective to constitute 'acquisitions' exposing the lay taxpayer to considerable risks of penalties and interest, particular in family arrangements such as caring for elderly relatives.

Not exempt

In addition to the issue of those interests in or rights of land that are exempt, i.e. not chargeable interests so that their 'acquisition' cannot constitute chargeable land transactions, it is provided that transactions that are 'exempt'[7] are not chargeable transactions. However, because of the lack of consistency in the drafting not all transactions which are 'exempt' are not chargeable transactions. Certain 'exempt' transactions are effectively excluded from the charge to tax; but others are notifiable transactions although no charge arises. Since transactions are 'exempt' for a variety of reasons, it is important to note that there is a variety of exemptions and reliefs from SDLT and the manner in which the relief is given can have significant consequences for the compliance regime and for subsequent transactions relating to that property (see Chapter 5).

2.2 SPECIFIC CHARGEABLE TRANSACTIONS

The general charge to tax arising upon 'acquisitions' has been progressively enlarged by an ever-growing number of situations where a charge to tax arises but is not covered by the basic charging provisions, even in cases where there are no transfers of or modifications of titles or interests in land. These extensions of the tax base include:

- rent reviews during the first five years;
- increases of rent otherwise than pursuant to the terms of the lease (FA 2003, Sched. 17A, para. 13; see Chapter 8);
- abnormal increases in rent after the earlier of first review date or the expiration of the fifth year of the term of the lease (FA 2003, Sched. 17A, paras. 7 and 8; see Chapter 8);
- assignments of certain leases which were exempt when granted (FA 2003, Sched. 17A, para. 11; see Chapter 8);

---

[7] The restricted nature of this issue must be noted since not being liable to SDLT is based upon several different bases, not all of which qualify as 'exemption' within the peculiar terminology of stamp duty land tax. For example, a land transaction will remain a chargeable transaction for the purposes of deciding whether it is notifiable within FA 2003, s.77 notwithstanding that some provisions reduce the chargeable consideration to nil.

- the clawback of various reliefs as a consequence of subsequent transactions (FA 2003, Sched. 6, para. 11; Sched. 7, paras. 3 and 8; Sched. 8, para. 2; see Chapter 5);
- the formal grant of a lease subsequent to substantial performance of the agreement for lease (FA 2003, Sched. 17A, para. 12A; see Chapter 8). Although this provision was introduced to deal with drafting errors which created problems in relation to compliance, it is being treated by HMRC Stamp Taxes as a separate chargeable transaction not merely a second stage of a single transaction involving entry into possession and later grant, creating a wide range of problems for the conveyancer;
- holding over leases after the expiration of the contractual term or continuation of periodic tenancies or similar arrangements where the aggregate net present value of rent exceeds the chargeable threshold so that tax becomes initially payable or additional tax is payable by reason of the deemed extension of the lease or tenancy (FA 2003, Sched. 17A, paras. 3 and 4);
- contracts with a power to direct a conveyance (FA 2003, ss.44A and 45A). In order to combat mitigation arrangements such as where a developer rather than purchase the land enters into a building agreement whereby he is to receive a specified percentage of the sale proceeds of the development, it is provided that a charge to tax arises upon substantial performance of a contract whereby a person has the right to direct a conveyance (which will include power to direct the grant of a lease) to a third party or to the person himself or such a third party.

Chargeable interests in land

This part of the definition involves several factors, namely:

Land

The charge is limited to chargeable interests in land in the UK. Other forms of property such as shares and chattels are not subject to the tax but special rules apply to dealings in interests in partnerships which own interests in land (FA 2003, Sched. 15 (as amended)). 'Land' is defined (FA 2003, s.121; Interpretation Act 1989, Sched. 1) in standard terms but the legislation extends the definition of 'chargeable interest' to cases where land is not owned directly. Special rules apply to equitable and other interests in trusts and estates (see Chapter 10) notwithstanding that these involve non-resident, non-domiciled and non-national individuals and the special charges applying to partnerships (see Chapter 11) include partnerships established abroad (FA 2003, Sched. 15, para. 1(1)). The key issue is whether the trust, estate or partnership has a chargeable interest in land in the UK.

Fixtures

The charge to SDLT does not apply to chattels so that, subject to a proper apportionment of the consideration (FA 2003, Sched. 4, para. 4(4); *Saunders v. Edwards* [1987] 2 All ER 651) no charge will arise in respect of items other than land such as carpets and curtains. In consequence, the issue of 'fixtures' gives rise to two problem areas for the conveyancer; namely:

WHAT IS A FIXTURE?

Not everything that is fixed to land is a 'fixture'. The test for determining this is basic land law and turns upon two factors:

- the degree of affixation and whether it is possible to remove the chattel without substantial damage to the physical premises; and
- the purpose of the annexation, i.e. whether it is fixed simply for its better use as a chattel which may encompass industrial safety requirements and not with the intention of making it part of the land.

This latter test has become more relevant in the light of recent cases which look more to the purpose of the affixation and whether it was simply to permit the chattel to be used as a chattel rather than with the intention of making it part of the structure. This means that under the modern approach many items of equipment that are attached to land simply for the purposes of industrial safety are not tenants' fixtures but retain their character as chattels with the consequent SDLT advantages.

ALLOCATING THE PRICE

On occasion the parties may sell several assets for a single or global consideration. The question is how much freedom do the parties have in making the allocation between these various assets? As decisions such as *Saunders v. Edwards* [1987] 2 All ER 651 indicate, a totally artificial and unjustifiable allocation of the consideration between the assets in order to produce a particular taxation result may be a criminal fraud on HMRC (*Re Wragg* [1897] 1 Ch 796) and lead to an unenforceable illegal contract (see the discussion on *Saunders v. Edwards* [1987] 2 All ER 657). It may also be professional misconduct and conspiracy for the parties' advisers to assist in the exercise (*Saunders v. Edwards* [1987] 2 All ER 657).[8] This can cause practical problems of classification between chattels, intangibles such as goodwill and land. However, there is no general obligation to sell or apportion at market value which is useful for sales at 'cost' or 'book value'.

---

8 Such an exercise may also have unforeseen taxation or contractual consequences. See, e.g. *Re Hollebone* [1959] 2 All ER 52.

'Goodwill'

Although goodwill proper is free of stamp taxes, except to the extent that its value affects the price for shares in a company, what is described as goodwill may, in law, be a premium price for the land because of its location and planning permission (see, e.g. *Mullins* v. *Wessex Motors* [1947] 2 All ER 727). Proper advice should be sought when dealing with this issue, particularly on the sale of a business.

2.3 CHARGEABLE INTERESTS

A chargeable interest is defined (FA 2003, s.48(1)) as being:

- an estate, interest, right or power in or over land in the UK; or
- the benefit of an obligation, restriction or condition affecting the value of any such estate, interest, right or power;

other than an exempt interest, which is defined (FA 2003, s.48(2)) as:

- any security interest which means an interest or right, other than a rent charge, held for the purpose of securing the payment of money or the performance of any other obligation (FA 2003, s.48(3)(a)). This will include mortgages (on mortgages in general see Chapter 4) and special reliefs which apply to other forms of financing property transactions some of which are intended to assist persons who for religious reasons cannot be involved in borrowing at interest but the relief is not restricted to such persons (FA 2003, ss.71, 71A and 72);
- a licence to use or occupy land. Not all transactions described as 'licences' will be exempt. For example, a mineral licence is not a licence as such; it is a licence to enter upon land and remove minerals, i.e. it is a *profit à prendre* and a chargeable interest.[9] It remains to be seen what restrictions upon the exemption arise from the words 'use or occupy';
- in England and Wales and Northern Ireland a tenancy at will or an advowson, franchise[10] or manor.

In consequence, transactions involving the following interests in or rights over land are chargeable interests:

- options and pre-emption rights where various special rules apply;
- easements such as rights of way and rights to light;

---

9 On questions of whether it is deemed to be a lease and whether the royalty payments are 'rent' see FA 2003, s.52 and Sched. 17A, paras. 1 and 6; *T&E Homes Limited* v. *Robinson* [1979] STC 351; see Chapter 8.

10 Used in the technical sense and not including commercial arrangements to exploit a business name or concept.

- profits, where it must be noted that certain interests such as mineral licences may not be licences exempt from the tax but profits which are chargeable; and, possibly
- tenant's fixtures, i.e. those chattels which become part of the land but which the tenant may remove on the termination of the tenancy or which the tenant is obliged to maintain, repair and/or remove by the terms of the lease.

There are many problems with this definition since, as with so much of the legislation, it is not clear whether it is intended to be so-called 'plain English' or technical in order to deal with the highly technical land law and conveyancing underlying land transactions. 'Estate' and 'interest' in or over land are well known, but 'rights' or 'powers' in or over land are not explained. Clearly, rights of way or rights to light will be rights over land, but it seems that the definition is intended to apply on a wider basis. For example, powers of appointment or advancement whether of a general or a special nature will be regarded as chargeable interests. Contractual rights such as options and pre-emption rights as well as contracts to purchase or lease land are chargeable interests, although many dealings in contractual rights are expressly made non-chargeable (see, e.g. FA 2003, ss.45 and 45A and Sched. 17A, para. 12B).[11] Contractual rights restricting the use of land falling short of restrictive covenants because there is no dominant land to be benefited,[12] such as restrictions related to some form of overage or clawback arrangement, are intended to be chargeable interests.[13] Attempts to create derivative interests in land such as contracts to account for a sum equal to a specified share in the proceeds of sale or profits from the land may be chargeable interests where they affect the value of any estate or interest or right or power in or over land (see also FA 2003, ss.44A and 45A).

It must, however, be noted that the draftsman assumes that certain indirect interests may be chargeable interests. It is assumed that under English law persons entitled to interests in non-discretionary trusts have an interest in the underlying assets (FA 2003, Sched. 16, para. 7). There are certain technical problems in relation to estates (see further Chapter 10). Whilst it is well-settled law that, in certain cases, persons interested in unadministered estates have no equitable or beneficial interest in the assets for the time being held by the personal representatives of the deceased (see, e.g. *Commissioner of Stamp Duty* v. *Livingston* [1964] 3 All ER 692), this is regarded by HMRC Stamp Taxes as applying to all beneficiaries in an estate, including, it seems,

---

11 Different issues may arise in Scotland where contracts do not create equitable interests.
12 Which may mean that the retention of a ransom strip to support such an arrangement may not qualify as a restrictive covenant.
13 This may raise questions whether payment of the overage is an 'acquisition' of a chargeable interest.

specific devises of land where the estate is solvent and it regards devisees or persons entitled on intestacy as having no interest in the property. This will be important where any variation of the estate takes place which does not qualify for the exemptions contained in paras. 3A and 4 of Sched. 3 to FA 2003 (as amended) (see Chapter 10). It seems that the current official view would accept, for example, that no charge arises in relation to a variation outside the two-year period because the participants do not have 'chargeable interests' and the charge is restricted to cases where the deceased's estate has been fully administered. It is considered that the official view is incorrect and that it may be perilous to rely upon it so that the two-year time limit and other conditions should be carefully observed.

At present, shares in companies holding land in the UK are not chargeable interests but it is understood that HMRC Stamp Taxes is continuing to investigate the possibility of treating shares as land in order to counter planning opportunities whereby, for example, persons such as trustees hold their UK land through companies preferably incorporated offshore so that no stamp duty or stamp duty reserve tax should arise on the sale of such shares, representing a substantial tax saving which can be shared with the purchaser in the form of an increased purchase price. As part of the attack upon land-holding companies, there are numerous anti-avoidance provisions which are available for HMRC Stamp Taxes to attack attempts to 'convert' land into shares such as the charge upon market value when a chargeable interest is acquired by a company connected with the 'vendor' (FA 2003, ss.53 and 54), or the clawback provision for intra-group transfers and company reorganisations (FA 2003, Sched. 7, paras. 3 and 9). These rules do not require a tax avoidance purpose and so will apply to routine commercial transactions such as incorporating a family business or vesting land in a corporate trustee for the family unless it is an exempt trustee (FA 2003, s.54). There are, in addition, many special provisions producing traps where one of the parties to a transaction is a company.

Special rules apply to partnerships, including foreign partnerships, treating certain transactions in relation to partnership shares as chargeable transactions (FA 2003, Sched. 15, para. 14 (as amended)). Notwithstanding the look through provisions for all partnerships wherever established (FA 2003, Sched. 15, para. 1(1) (as amended)), which appear to apply only for the purposes of enforcing (see Chapter 11) the tax, a partnership interest is not as such a chargeable interest and dealings on such interests are taxable only in accordance with the special charging provisions (FA 2003, Sched. 15, paras. 14 and 15 (as amended)). Consequently, partnerships should consider the feasibility of holding UK land through appropriate corporate vehicles.

Special charging provisions

Licences and tenancies at will are exempt interests, but they do have tax implications. For example, taking possession of land as a licensee or tenant at will may amount to substantial performance of another contract and produce an effective date (FA 2003, s.44(6)(b)).

The FA 2003, ss.44A and 45A brings certain arrangements, possibly involving licences, into charge. These arise where a person has a contract which gives a power to direct a conveyance (which includes a lease) whether to himself or to another person who is not a party to the contract. This will apply, typically, to an agreement between A and B whereby B agrees to carry out works on A's land and A agrees to convey or lease the land either to B or to a third party at B's direction. If B substantially performs the contract with A there is a chargeable transaction even though B may not even have a licence to enter upon A's land.

CHAPTER 3

Taxable events – effective date

3.1 ACTIONS NOT DOCUMENTS

SDLT is a transaction-based tax and not a tax upon documentation. Consequently, the time or times at which the charge to tax arises is not necessarily linked to paperwork. This is particularly important since events both before and after 'completion' in the traditional conveyancing meaning of the term give rise to obligations to pay tax and to file returns and, as described elsewhere, much of the tax is of a provisional nature so that subsequent events unrelated to the paperwork give rise to retrospective adjustments. The one major charging area where paperwork matters is the possible double charge upon substantial performance of agreements for lease and the subsequent grant thereof (FA 2003, Sched. 17A, para. 12A; see Chapter 8) which in the opinion of HMRC produces two chargeable events. In other cases, paperwork may trigger a reporting obligation but it rarely triggers a separate chargeable transaction since it relates back to the effective date for the transaction. Whilst the basic charge is linked to 'completion' (FA 2003, s.119), i.e. paperwork, this is subject to numerous special provisions because one of the key policies behind the legislation is to prevent parties deferring the payment of tax simply by delaying the execution of documentation but otherwise carrying out their contract by taking possession of the land and paying the price. As a result, the actions of the parties between contract and 'completion' can operate to trigger a tax charge with a further charge and notification obligation on the subsequent completion (FA 2003, s.44(8)). Unfortunately there are no provisions dealing adequately with this time discrepancy between substantial performance and completion, although what happens at completion may be vital to the charge such as whether the condition for the relief can be satisfied early, and there may not be a general wait-and-see principle to deal with the problems arising.

How many effective dates – retrospection

As a basic principle there is only one effective date for each transaction, although the provisional nature of much SDLT means that the tax has to be

TAXABLE EVENTS – EFFECTIVE DATE

recalculated on several occasions and the transaction has to be notified on each such occasion but such reassessments relate back to the original effective date and the subsequent operative events which give rise to payment obligations are not separate effective dates (but see FA 2003, Sched.17A, para. 12A).

The key basic time point[1] for the purposes of SDLT is the 'effective date'. This is important for the following reasons:

- it establishes *inter alia* the time for assessing the tax;
- it is the date for determining whether the consideration is uncertain or unascertained;
- it is the date for determining the market value of chargeable interests or consideration *in specie* (FA 2003, Sched. 4, para. 7); but this does not apply necessarily to situations where the consideration consists of the carrying out of works (FA 2003, Sched. 4, para. 10) or the provision of services (FA 2003, Sched. 4, para. 11) when the question of 'cost' which HMRC Stamp Taxes seems to regard as actual cost (Stamp Duty Land Tax (Administration) Regulations 2003, SI 2003/2837, Part 4) may raise other issues;
- it is the date for determining whether the conditions for the potential exemption from tax are satisfied;
- it is the date for determining the rate of tax applicable to the transaction even for later stages of the same transaction such as:
  - formal completion following substantial performance of a contract (FA 2003, s.44(8));
  - the recalculation of SDLT upon a variable rent;
  - clawback of certain reliefs for corporate reorganisations, intra-group acquisitions and charities (FA 2003, Sched. 7, paras. 3(2) and 9(2) and Sched. 8, para. 2(2));
- it is the date from which the time for filing the initial land transaction return (SDLT 1) and for payment of the initial estimate of the tax begins to run;

---

1 Different timing issues apply to transitional provisions whether in relation to the change over from stamp duty to SDLT on 1 December 2003 (FA 2003, Sched. 19 (as amended)) or for changes to SDLT itself (see, e.g. Finance Act 2005 in relation to disadvantaged land) (relief for transactions entered into prior to Budget Date 2005). Although there are certain fundamental differences in the change over from stamp duty to SDLT the less extensive restrictions upon changes within the SDLT regime will be applied aggressively by HMRC Stamp Taxes against taxpayers who might benefit, such as the wider interpretation of the provisions cancelling transitional relief where a pre-changeover date contract is 'varied', i.e. all variations will cancel the relief unless it is totally trivial such as a change of colour scheme or a modification relating to pets on the premises. Moreover, HMRC Stamp Taxes has stated that the double charge upon leases has to be completely reassessed on 'grant' so that the transitional reliefs will be lost if the substantial performance and the grant straddle the change.

- it is the date from which the periods for the clawback of reliefs begin to run;
- it is the basis for fixing the date from which penalties and late payment interest commence, including the time when the penalties increase;
- it is the basis for fixing the start date for HMRC Stamp Taxes's powers to launch an Enquiry or issue a discovery assessment, but as this may extend for 21 years the start date is unlikely to have much real significance;
- it needs to be ascertained whether VAT arises after the effective date such as pursuant to the exercise of the option to tax or whether this is to be ignored in computing stamp duty land tax;
- it is the start of the period during which records must be maintained;
- it is the start of the limited period during which a taxpayer may 'amend' a land transaction return;
- works carried out upon the land being acquired after the effective date are excluded from charge;
- it is the date for the rate of conversion for foreign currency;
- it enables computation of the amount of liabilities assumed as part of the consideration and the amount of interest accrued since only debt and interest outstanding at the effective date are chargeable;
- it enables computation of the temporal discount rate for the calculation of the net present value of the rent for both the initial and any subsequent reassessments of the rent (see Chapter 8).

3.2 BASIC POSITION

The transaction-based nature of SDLT is emphasised by the fact that there are numerous provisions (FA 2003, ss.44(2), 44A(2), 45(2), 45A(2)) which state that simply entering into a contract (or agreement for lease) is not, of itself, a chargeable transaction; something more is required. In consequence, tax no longer arises upon contracts other than options and pre-emption rights (FA 2003, s.46; see Chapter 6) or agreements for lease and entries can be made at the relevant Land Registry to protect such contracts without the production of either form of certificate (SDLT 1 or 60).

The basic definition (FA 2003, s.119), which is made subject to special provision,[2] of 'effective date' is 'completion' which is not generally

---

[2] This may not be a problem where these various events are expressed to be simultaneous. There will be difficult problems where the contract provides for different payment dates and transfer dates. HMRC Stamp Taxes takes the view that an arrangement for postponing the delivery of vacant possession is a post-completion transaction involving a completion and regrant and has on occasion taken the point that the right to remain in occupation of the premises is the regrant of a lease producing a land exchange pursuant to FA 2003, s.47 and Sched. 4, para. 5; see further Chapter 7.

defined;[3] but which appears to mean the date when the parties perform their obligations pursuant to the terms of the contract such as payment of the purchase price in full and delivery of the title documentation and delivery up of the premises with vacant possession. The legislation on this point gives a totally misleading impression of the times at which the payment obligations arise in at least two ways; namely:

- it defines the effective date in terms of completion, but then subjects this definition to special rules which because they will apply in virtually every case that will occur in practice deprive this provision of any practical effect; and
- it does not make clear that other events give rise to those payment and/or notification obligations.

Other specific provision where the basic effective date is not 'completion' is made for:

- contracts to be completed by a 'conveyance' which is defined as any written instrument (FA 2003, s.44). Since standard form contracts provide for completion to require the delivery of an appropriate written instrument this special rule will apply in virtually every case in practice;
- options and pre-emption rights (FA 2003, s.46);
- agreements to direct conveyances to third parties and sub-sales thereof (FA 2003, ss.44A and 45A);
- agreements for lease and grants (FA 2003, Sched. 17A, para. 12A);
- assignments of agreements for lease (FA 2003, Sched. 17A, para. 12B).

Where there are specific charging arrangements such as clawback of reliefs these usually have their own arrangements for the 'effective date' for the arrangements.

3.3 SPECIAL RULES

Routine contracts

Where, as will usually be the case, there is a contract or an agreement for lease which provides for completion by a written instrument between the same parties, which will include contracts with the usual power to sub-sell which provides that one form of completion contemplates a transfer to the original purchaser the effective date is the earlier of substantial performance of the contract or agreement or 'completion' (FA 2003, s.45). Where these two events are not simultaneous, dual charges and notification obligations arise

---

3 FA 2003, s.44(1)(c) provides that for the purposes of that section 'completion' means in conformity with the contract between the same parties.

with extremely complex rules and problems for agreements for lease (FA 2003, Sched. 17A, para. 12A; see Chapter 8), although, in general, there remains only one effective date. In consequence:

- there is, in general, no charge to SDLT simply upon exchanges of contracts for sale or agreements for lease or contracts to create or terminate rights except options and pre-emption rights (FA 2003, s.46; see Chapter 6);
- there is a charge to tax upon substantial performance of the contract should this precede 'completion' such as where a tenant is allowed into possession early in order to fit out the premises;
- there is a charge to tax upon 'completion'. However, where there has been prior substantial performance (FA 2003, s.44(2)), completion may mean that there is a notification obligation and additional tax is payable (FA 2003, s.44(8)). Additional tax will be unusual except for problems arising in relation to the grant of leases because the SDLT is payable upon substantial performance in respect of the whole of the chargeable consideration including any relevant VAT and overage or similar payments or variable rents albeit on an estimated basis (FA 2003, Sched. 17A, para. 12A). It is unlikely that there will be any change of circumstances requiring a recalculation of the SDLT between substantial performance and completion in accordance with the principles governing variable payment. Moreover, should there be a charge after substantial performance and prior to completion this will normally require its own return and payment of tax (FA 2003, s.80). The obligation arises even where a land transaction return (SDLT 1) has been previously filed and tax paid by reference to substantial performance. It is important, particularly for smaller transactions, that this double notification if possible be avoided in order to keep costs to a reasonable amount. Otherwise these costs may be disproportionate since the second land transaction return requires a new[4] fully completed SDLT 1 (with any necessary SDLT 2, 3 or 4 forms) with a new bar code reference notwithstanding this is merely repeating the information already produced to HMRC Stamp Taxes on the original SDLT 1 filed at substantial performance.

Substantially performed

The rules for substantial performance depend upon whether the contract involves a grant of a new lease or any other transaction.

---

[4] It is essential that a completely new return is filed rather than the original form 'amended' even if this were possible.

TAXABLE EVENTS – EFFECTIVE DATE

SALES

Where the transaction is not one involving a grant or deemed grant of a lease such as a sale of a freehold or the sale or surrender of an existing lease, a lease or a release of an interest or variation of a restrictive covenant, then the contract is substantially performed on the earlier of:

- the purchaser taking possession of the whole or substantially the whole of the subject-matter of the contract. For these purposes the purchaser takes possession if he receives or becomes entitled to receive rents and profits (FA 2003, s.44(6)(a)). It is immaterial whether a purchaser takes possession under the contract or under a licence or lease of a temporary character (FA 2003, s.44(6)(b)); or
- a substantial amount of the consideration being paid or provided.[5]

NEW LEASES

Where the grant of a new lease is involved (see also Chapter 8 for special problems for leases), the agreement for lease is substantially performed on the earliest of:

- the purchaser taking possession of the whole or substantially the whole of the subject-matter of the contract. For these purposes a lessee takes possession if he receives or becomes entitled to receive rents and profits and it is immaterial whether the lessee takes possession under the contract or under a licence or lease of a temporary character (FA 2003, s.44(6)); or
- a substantial amount of the premium being paid or provided (FA 2003, s.44(7)(c)); or
- the first payment of rent being made (FA 2003, s.44(7)(b)). This refers to actual payment of the rent.

Substantial payment or provision of the consideration

Little guidance has been provided as to the official view upon when the consideration is substantially provided. It is stated in SDLT 6 (Notes for Guidance) that this is regarded as occurring when 90 per cent of the consideration is provided. This is a simple test where cash is involved although problems can arise as detailed below.

---

5 FA 2003, s.44(7)(a) provides, somewhat unnecessarily, that a substantial amount of consideration is provided or paid where the whole or substantially the whole of the consideration is paid or provided.

Deposits/stage payments

The payment of a normal deposit of 5 or 10 per cent[6] will not amount to substantial provision of the consideration. However, where there are building or other arrangements involving stage payments then this question will have to be considered more closely and payments for variations which may or may not be part of the land transaction may increase the amount paid towards the land price. Obviously, the first few stage payments will not amount to payment of 'substantially the whole' of the price but it is not unlikely that there will be anti-avoidance concepts developed. In consequence, where the developer enters into some form of pre-sale or pre-let as a means of financing the arrangement then the contract may have been substantially performed.[7]

Similarly, where a prospective purchaser or tenant as part of the financing arrangements and in order to reduce the costs agrees to make a loan to the developer on favourable terms,[8] there will be questions as to whether the provision of such a 'soft loan' or a guarantee of any loan taken out by the developer from a bank might amount to 'indirect provision of the consideration' within the view of HMRC Stamp Taxes. These may be quite rare in relation to single dwelling transactions but where the residential construction is part of a larger project involving, for example, social housing or affordable housing with a local authority or housing association such financing may be more common. The implications for the timing of any transactions will be an important part of the structuring of such arrangements.

Variable payments, consideration in kind and other problems

The 90 per cent test leaves open difficult issues where there is consideration in kind such as the issue of shares or the performance of services or building works. It seems that in the case of shares these are 'provided' when the board of directors resolves to allot the shares rather than when they are 'issued', i.e. entered in the register of members.

Other difficulties arise where the chargeable consideration is variable or is linked to open market cost.[9] Since the final figure may not be known for many years, it will be difficult to determine when the 90 per cent threshold has been crossed. It is unlikely that HMRC Stamp Taxes will be prepared to wait until

---

6 On whether larger payments are deposits or penalties see *Workers Trust and Merchant Bank Ltd* v. *Dojap Investments* [1993] 2 All ER 370.
7 Such arrangements also have to be viewed in the context of whether such arrangements might adversely affect the taxation of any related building contracts pursuant to FA 2003, Sched. 4, para. 10 (as amended); see Chapter 9.
8 Compare the VAT position of *Faith Construction* v. *Customs and Excise* [1988] STC 35.
9 For the treatment of such payments see SDLT (Administration) Regulations 2003, SI 2003/2837, Part 4.

the parties have made payments close to the commercially anticipated maximum since this would offer the opportunity to postpone the payment of the tax without interest and penalties. In consequence, it is probable that there will be an in-depth Enquiry as to whether there has been 'completion' in accordance with the contract notwithstanding that no transfer, lease or conveyance has been executed, such as whether the purchaser has taken 'possession' of substantially the whole of the land. For example, where there is a sale of land with a basic price plus additional consideration for overage or clawback with a clawback period of 80 years, it is probable that HMRC Stamp Taxes will in practice treat substantial performance as taking place when the purchaser has either paid 90 per cent of the basic price, or has taken possession or has received the 'conveyance'.

Taking possession

There is no statutory definition of what constitutes 'possession' other than an extension so that for these purposes a person takes possession if he receives or becomes entitled to receive rents and profits or, it would seem, moves into physical occupation of the land with some degree of exclusivity and territorial control otherwise than for some possibly limited purpose. It is immaterial whether he takes possession under the contract or under a licence or lease of a temporary character (FA 2003, s.44(6) (as amended)). Thus allowing a purchaser or tenant into 'possession' in whatever capacity may trigger an early tax charge and probably two reporting obligations. Therefore, there may be dangers for purchasers going on to the land prior to payment of the purchase price or conveyance. This may give rise to difficulties where there is a lease and the tenant is allowed into occupation of the land for the purpose of carrying out fitting out or repairs or redecoration prior to actual completion in the sense of payment, but sometimes early possession can avoid a charge upon building works and fitting out (see Chapter 9).

Apart from the above amended reference to receipt of rents there is no attempt to define what constitutes taking possession for these purposes. It is the view of HMRC Stamp Taxes that the obtaining of the key to the premises, is, of itself, sufficient to constitute taking possession even without physical entry. However, this ignores the fact that the key or access to the premises may be made available only upon a restricted basis such as for a limited time or for a limited purpose. Entry whilst at the same time the 'vendor' remains in physical occupation of the premises would not give sufficient control of the premises to constitute possession for that purpose. Permission to enter upon the land to investigate minerals or geological structures prior to development is unlikely to constitute taking possession, but entry for the purpose of preparing foundations will probably involve taking possession.

Moreover, given the extended definition of 'acquisition' it will be difficult to apply this test of possession in many cases other than sales and leases. For example, where there is an agreement to release or vary a restrictive covenant or right to light it is difficult to see when the purchaser can take possession of the varied covenant. In such a case notwithstanding that the contract will provide for the execution and delivery of a deed or other instrument it seems unlikely that the rules of substantial performance relating to possession will be appropriate and the effective date may be linked to the payment of a substantial part of the consideration.

Phased completion

The 'possession' must be of the whole or substantially the whole of the land within the contract. No guidance is provided as to the percentage of the land that amounts to substantially the whole, but it seems probable that this will require something like 90 per cent of the total area. This could be a problem where there is to be a phased completion with only parts of the land being made available to the purchaser from time to time. In such cases it would seem to be more efficient to have not a single contract with phased completion, but separate contracts each of which is separately completed in full. The fact that the contracts will be linked should not affect the question of whether each individual contract has been substantially performed or completed, since linking merely affects the rate and does not amalgamate the contracts for the purpose of substantial performance.

Conditional and similar arrangements

Substantial performance can occur notwithstanding that the contract in question is not binding. For example, where a person who has executed an agreement for lease which is subject to the consent of the superior landlord which is yet to be obtained[10] enters upon the premises to fit out this may amount to a taking of possession which triggers the tax charge upon the conditional agreement for lease.

However, there must be a contract or agreement for lease albeit conditional before this can occur. For example, where the parties have entered into an option arrangement there will have been a chargeable transaction on the grant of the option but taking possession before the option is exercised will not produce a tax charge but there will be a charge upon substantial performance and/or completion of the contract arising pursuant to the exercise of the option and thus 'may' be a linked transaction with the original grant (FA 2003, s.46(1)). Where there is an existing lease with an option to renew the lease, the exercise of that option during the currency of the original lease will

---

10 Such as where the landlord has indicated that he has no objections but the paperwork has yet to be completed.

not give rise to an immediate charge to SDLT because although the tenant is in possession of the demised premises this will be possession in his capacity as the existing tenant and not a fresh taking of possession as a new tenant pursuant to the renewed lease. In such a case the effective date will be the earlier of 'completion', i.e. the grant of the new lease or the first actual payment of rent thereunder.[11] As this illustrates, the mere fact of being in possession is not conclusive: it will be necessary to investigate the nature of the possession and the capacity of the occupier. Similarly, where a prospective tenant enters on to the land during the negotiations for a lease there will be no contract in place and so there is nothing to be substantially performed.[12] However, where the person is already in possession under a prior arrangement the subsequent exchange of a contract or the exercise of the option may mean that there is simultaneous substantial performance and an immediate tax charge. This will depend upon the precise circumstances of each individual case. For example, entry during the negotiations for a lease may lead to substantial performance when the agreement is executed, but it is arguable that since there was a prior right to occupy the land there is no 'taking possession of the subject matter of the contract' unless there is some alteration in the pre-existing relationship which creates a new licence to occupy.

Subsequent rescission or cancellation

Since 'substantial performance' can precede payment in full or 'completion' in the generally accepted sense of the word, it is provided that where the contract has been substantially performed and is, to any extent, afterwards rescinded or annulled or is for any other reason not carried into effect the tax paid in connection with the substantial performance is to the appropriate extent to be repaid by HMRC Stamp Taxes (FA 2003, s.44(9)). Repayment must be claimed by amendment of the land transaction return in respect of the contract (FA 2003, s.44(9)) and the contract must accompany the claim. The procedure for amending returns by a taxpayer is contained in para. 6 of Sched. 10 to FA 2003 (see Appendix D).

---

11 The complications of FA 2003, Sched. 17A, para. 12A should not arise in the former case, but there are likely to be two chargeable transactions in the latter case.
12 There may, however, be a question of whether the terms upon which he has entered constitute a potentially taxable tenancy which may be some form of periodic tenancy that can be effectively created without writing: Law of Property Act 1925, s.52.

Options and pre-emption rights

Special rules apply to options and pre-emption rights (see further Chapter 6).

The effective date of the transaction in the case of the acquisition of an option or pre-emption right is when the right is acquired as opposed to when it becomes exercisable (FA 2003, s.46(3)). For example, where there is an option to acquire land *if* planning permission is obtained not *when* the planning permission is obtained, the SDLT arises upon the grant of the option.

Agreements for lease

Paragraph 12A of Sched. 17A to FA 2003 raises many problems for leases where there is a delay between substantial performance and formal grant (see also Chapter 8). The substantial performance is treated as the grant of the lease and the subsequent grant of the lease is treated as some form of surrender and regrant but with only a credit in respect of the rent for the overlap period. HMRC Stamp Taxes regards this as not merely a compliance amendment but as creating a totally separate chargeable event for the same lease, i.e. there are two separate taxable events (see further Chapter 8). This may affect, *inter alia*:

- the availability of reliefs;
- VAT where the option to tax has been exercised;
- the five-year period for rent reviews;
- rent increases in the interim period;
- clawback periods;
- the computation formula in relation to the net present value of the rent when the lease is granted;
- the rent taken into account for the charge upon abnormal increases in rent after the expiration of the fifth year of the term of the lease;
- whether the relief for rent reviews and backdating to the previous quarter day is effective because the actual grant is more than three months after the term.

CHAPTER 4

Computation of tax

4.1 RATES

There are two basic regimes for the computation of SDLT, namely:

- the general regime for most 'acquisitions' such as sales, releases and variations other than variation of leases; and
- a special regime for leases including variations thereof (FA 2003, s.43(3)(d), Scheds. 5 and 17A (as amended)) whereby the rules for determining the tax charge upon premiums are generally calculated in accordance with the general regime, although the availability of the nil rate for premiums is restricted by reference to the level of rent, and there is a completely different regime for calculating the SDLT upon rents (see Chapter 8 on leases).

The two components of consideration and rates are interlinked since:

- the rate is, to a large extent, dependent upon the amount of the chargeable consideration as affected by the linked transaction rules; and
- the amount of the chargeable consideration itself involves many issues, namely:
  - what is consideration;
  - what types of consideration are chargeable;
  - is the transaction governed by special rules such as deemed chargeable consideration;
  - how is the amount or value of the consideration to be determined.

There is not a simple rate structure since the rate depends upon a variety of factors such as:

- the amount of a chargeable consideration;
- the provisional consideration as net present value of chargeable consideration or rent in many cases, although the estimates may have to be revised in the light of later events;[1]

---

[1] But not all cases require revision such as annuities and periodical payments: FA 2003, s.52.

UNDERSTANDING SDLT

- whether the property is residential or non-residential or 'mixed';
- whether it is wholly or partially in a disadvantaged area (FA 2003, Sched. 6 (as amended));[2] although the significance of this has been much reduced by Finance Act 2005;
- the net present value of the rent;
- the level of rent[3] in relation to the nil rate for leases with premiums; and
- whether there are 'linked transactions' either currently or in the future. It must be noted that the retrospective nature of the linked transaction rules means that the level of chargeable consideration can increase with a consequent increase in the rates;
- the impact of the linked transaction rules upon the nil rate slice for lease rents (FA 2003, Sched. 5, para. 2).

Residential property purchase price or premium[4]

Relevant consideration or premium	Percentage
Not more than £125,000	0%
More than £125,000 but not more than £250,000	1%
More than £250,000 but not more than £500,000	3%
More than £500,000	4%

Where only rent is involved in relation to residential property the position is:

Relevant rental value	Percentage
Not more than £125,000	0%
More than £125,000	1%

Special points on rate structure require notice:

- where the rent exceeds £600 per annum the nil rate is not available for premiums. This also affects the reporting obligations for certain leases where tax is or would but for an exemption be taxable at the 1% rate or higher since the absence of the nil rate for the premium will make even small leases at a rent notifiable;
- where the property is in a disadvantaged area the residential nil rate band is increased to £150,000 for price, premium and rent;
- in relation to rents it is only the excess over the relevant nil rate slice that is taxable.

---

2 To identify disadvantaged areas see Stamp Duty (Disadvantaged Areas) Regulations 2001, SI 2001/3747; Stamp Duty (Disadvantaged Areas) (Application of Exemptions) Regulations 2003, SI 2003/1056.
3 Whether greater than £600 per annum.
4 FA 2003, s.55 (as amended).

COMPUTATION OF TAX

Non-residential and mixed property

'Mixed property' is property that includes both residential and non-residential premises such as a shop and flat.

Purchase price and premium

Relevant consideration/premium	Percentage
Not more than £150,000	0%
More than £150,000 but not more than £250,000	1%
More than £250,000 but not more than £500,000	3%
More than £500,000	4%

Rents

Relevant rental value – net present value of rent	Percentage
Not more than £150,000	0%
More than £150,000	1%

4.2 DISADVANTAGED LAND

The scope of this relief has been severely restricted by the Finance Act 2005 which abolished the relief for non-residential property so that, in effect, the sole purpose of the relief is for a nil rate band of consideration not exceeding £150,000 as compared with the general nil rate of £125,000.

Where the conveyance or transfer includes land within a disadvantaged area and land not in such an area the consideration or rent must be apportioned between the various parts of the land on such basis as is 'just and reasonable' (FA 2003, Sched. 6, para. 7(2)).[5] If the consideration is not apportioned on a just and reasonable basis the allocation arrived at when HMRC Stamp Taxes has applied the 'correct approach' is to be the amount upon which the SDLT is to be charged and prevails over the parties' own allocation.

4.3 'RESIDENTIAL PROPERTY'

It was expected that there would be a separate and much simplified regime as regards both the taxation of residential property and the related compliance regime for land transaction returns and notification of transactions but there is, at present, no indication of any such separate or simplified regime (FA

---

[5] On apportionment of consideration generally, see FA 2003, Sched. 4, para. 4 which applies in this context.

UNDERSTANDING SDLT

2003, Sched. 6A) other than the general need not to file SDLT 4. There are several minor differences between residential and other property scattered throughout the legislation particularly in relation to reliefs (FA 2003, Sched. 6A). In consequence, the same charging provisions and the heavy compliance regime as applies to large-scale commercial transactions is applicable to single house purchases producing a disproportionate cost for the latter.

The intention of HMRC Stamp Taxes is for different percentages of transactions to be reviewed by means of Enquiries for residential property which is currently expected to be around 3 per cent of all residential property transactions, as opposed to up to 100 per cent of large commercial transactions. It is expected that a high proportion of the Enquiries in relation to residential property will be those where the purchase price or premium is close to the rate thresholds of £250,000 and £500,000 in order to test the propriety of the allocation of any consideration to carpets and curtains (*Saunders* v. *Edwards* [1987] 2 All ER 651).

'Residential property' defined

Residential property is defined (FA 2003, s.116) as meaning:

- a building that is suitable for use as a dwelling;
- a building that is in the process of being constructed or adapted for use as a dwelling;
- land that is or forms part of a garden or grounds of a building that is used or is intended for use or is being constructed or adapted for use as a dwelling; or
- an interest in or right over land that subsists for the benefit of a building or land suitable for use with a dwelling.

Actual use – not intentions

Actual use or suitability for use, not the proposed use, at the effective date for the chargeable transaction governs the status of the property as residential or non-residential. For example, where there is the acquisition of commercial property with a view to redevelopment as residential, such as the conversion of a hotel into flats, then its non-residential status will be the factor governing the liability or level of the nil rate for SDLT for that transaction; the future intended use will not be appropriate. On the other hand, if the property acquired consists of several dwellings and does not meet the relief for six or more dwellings acquired under a single transaction because there are different vendors[6] the fact that the dwellings are empty and about to be

---

6 Such acquisitions would be unlikely to be linked transactions because there are different parties.

demolished would indicate that the property is to be regarded as residential and the fact that the existing buildings are to be demolished and converted into non-residential property is irrelevant. This, of course, depends upon whether there is the acquisition of a block of seven or more flats, as the property will then be regarded as non-residential provided that acquisition from seven or more different vendors under potentially separate contracts can be regarded as a 'single transaction' (but see below). It is the nature of the land itself not the interest being acquired that matters. For example, where a management company is acquiring the landlord's interest in a block of flats this will be residential property even though the interest itself does not confer any power to dwell in the premises.[7]

Not in use at effective date

Where the building is not in use at the effective date but is suitable for a purpose that is to be treated as use as a dwelling and at least one of those purposes that is not to be regarded as use as a dwelling such as a hall of residence for students in further or higher education, then if there is one such use for which it is more or most suitable then when deciding whether it is a dwelling or not it is that use that is taken into account (FA 2003, s.116(5)(a)); but otherwise the building is to be treated as suitable for use as a dwelling (FA 2003, s.116(5)(b)).

4.4 SPECIAL SITUATIONS

Multiple occupancy

As the legislation is basically in terms of single occupancy, it is necessary to deal with situations of multiple occupancy such as old people's homes, hostels for asylum seekers and temporary accommodation for the homeless. Detailed provision is made but it does not appear to convert all of these arrangements into dwellings. A building is used as a dwelling when used as:

- residential accommodation for school pupils;
- residential accommodation for students other than accommodation as a hall of residence for students in further or higher education;
- residential accommodation for members of the armed forces;
- an institution that is the sole or main residence of at least 90 per cent of its residents and which is not used as:
    - a home or other institution providing residential accommodation for children;

---

7 This will require SDLT 4 to be filed.

- a hall of residence for students in further or higher education;
- a home or other institution providing residential accommodation with personal care for persons in need of personal care by reason of old age, disablement, past or present dependence on alcohol or drugs or past or present mental disorder. This it would seem would not necessarily cover the provision of hostel accommodation for unemployed or other homeless persons;
- a hospital or hospice. This would seem to be limited to hospices providing accommodation with some form of medical treatment;
- a prison or similar establishment;
- a hotel, inn or similar establishment (FA 2003, s.116(2) and (3); there is power to amend by statutory instrument in s.116(8)(a)), as hotels and inns are run for providing temporary accommodation[8] on a profit-making basis. It is considered that 'similar establishments' will not extend to hostels and similar accommodation for homeless and other persons because these are not likely to be operating on a profit-making basis in most cases.

Where at the effective date the building is actually being used for any of the institutional purposes that are not regarded as the provision of dwellings, it is that actual use that is taken into account and the fact that it is suitable for any other use is to be ignored.

Mixed property

For these purposes, building includes part of a building (FA 2003, s.116(6)) so that issues will arise where there is sale[9] or lease of a single structure with mixed use such as a shop with a flat above or a public house with accommodation for staff[10] or a house with a paddock, or a farm with housing occupied by agricultural works or a farmhouse. Particular rules apply.

---

8 There is an open question of whether the mixed property rule will apply to hotels and similar buildings which provide not only temporary accommodation for guests but also accommodation for members of the staff on a longer-term basis, even though the staff may be on short-term or temporary contracts of a seasonal nature. There is no exclusion for residential accommodation of an incidental nature. It seems that the main argument will be that although there is a 'long-term occupation' the structure or rooms involved are not in themselves suitable for use as a 'dwelling' because they may lack basic facilities for dwellings, but this test may prove difficult to define in practice because of problems with shared facilities in multiple occupancy buildings.

9 The rules as to linked transactions mean that it will be almost inevitable that such acquisitions are linked and aggregated. Separate rules each with their own lower rates will be extremely rare.

10 Rooms for hotel guests on a temporary basis will be governed by the exempting provisions.

Non-disadvantaged land

It would seem that where there is a single transaction that includes such a structure it will be treated as one that is for 'mixed property' where special tables of rates apply (FA 2003, s.55(2) Table B). In effect the property is treated as non-residential and the nil rate band extends to £150,000.[11]

Disadvantaged land[12]

The consideration which includes the purchase price and premium and rent for the entire building will have to be apportioned between the residential and non-residential parts on a just and reasonable basis and the nil rate band for the residential part extends to £150,000 (FA 2003, Sched. 6, para. 6).

Six or more properties

It is specifically provided that where there is a single transaction involving the transfer of major interests in or the grant of a lease over six or more separate dwellings, those dwellings are treated as not involving residential property (FA 2003, s.116(7)). Unfortunately there is no explanation of what is a 'single transaction' for these purposes. It is obviously not the same as a 'linked transaction' (FA 2003, s.108), and there is no provision that provides that linked transactions are to be single transactions. Although such transactions are aggregated for the purposes of determining the total chargeable consideration or the length of a lease, the transactions remain separate transactions and are *prima facie* separately reportable (FA 2003, ss.108 and 77) and have their own effective dates; they do not become a single contract or transaction. For example, a person proposing to redevelop by acquiring several adjacent properties with a view to demolition and construction of new premises or the refurbishment of existing premises will be dealing with separate vendors; technically, then, this would be several separate transactions and not a single transaction.[13] This consequence would also apply where the purchaser is acquiring numerous properties from connected vendors so that these transactions will be linked so as to attract the higher rate but would not qualify for the benefit of the non-residential property reliefs.

---

11 FA 2003, s.55(2) Table B, but note the restriction upon the availability of the nil rate band where the annual rent exceeds £600 such as FA 2003, Sched. 5, para. 9(2).
12 FA 2003, Sched. 6.
13 As there are separate vendors the transactions are *prima facie* not linked.

UNDERSTANDING SDLT

4.5 LINKED TRANSACTIONS

The question of linked transactions is important for:

- the availability of the lower rates of SDLT (FA 2003, s.55(4));
- determining the length of lease usually retrospectively in respect of the net present value of the rent.

In consequence, the rules will apply to determine whether the chargeable consideration for the related transactions or the lengths of the related leases has to be aggregated; but only chargeable consideration attributable to land transactions is to be aggregated. Where there is a sale of several parcels of land and chattels only the land prices are to be aggregated.

The rules which have the potential for great practical difficulties differ from certificates of value for stamp duty in that they are much wider in their scope; but they are subject to limitation in their application although attempts have been made by HMRC Stamp Taxes to put them to wider use than the legislation allows. It is important to note that, notwithstanding attempts by HMRC Stamp Taxes to apply the concept of linked transactions widely, it is not:

- a statutory equivalent of the anti-avoidance cases based upon *Ramsey* v. *IRC* [1981] STC 174; or
- a form of associated operation provisions providing power for HMRC Stamp Taxes to amalgamate, merge or separate transactions; or
- a power to recharacterise transactions. For example, it cannot convert legally separate contracts for building works and for the lease of the land into a single transaction for the lease of a completed building (see Chapter 9).

Problems arise because:

- the principles apply on a retrospective basis, unlike certificates of value for the purposes of stamp duty. In consequence, many transactions will to the surprise of taxpayers be initially dealt with only on a provisional basis and the initial land transaction return will have to be revised in the light of subsequent events. For example, the exercise of an option to renew a lease 'may' (see FA 2003, s.46) produce a successive linked lease (FA 2003, Sched. 17A, para. 5) so that the self-assessment of the tax upon the initial lease 'may'[14] have to be revised upon the basis that the initial lease must be treated retrospectively as a lease for a longer term, i.e. the aggregate of the terms of the original lease and of the renewed lease. Although retrospec-

---

14 It is initially for the taxpayer to decide under penalty whether the later lease is 'linked' with the original lease and any other previously renewed leases. Usually it will be beneficial for the taxpayer to argue for successive linked leases; see Chapter 8.

COMPUTATION OF TAX

tively affecting the initial calculation, this constitutes a separate transaction requiring its own return which will be separate from the land transaction return required for the subsequent transaction. The form (SDLT 1) requires the taxpayer to indicate whether the transaction is linked with another transaction. This question will be irrelevant for the first transaction which only becomes linked retrospectively so that it will not, as at the filing date, be a linked transaction but a separate return correcting the situation will, inevitably, be required when dealing with the later transaction;
- linked transactions may affect third parties such as assignees of leases (FA 2003, Sched. 5, para. 2(5) and (6));
- the principles have a significant impact upon rent reviews.

There is an open question, as far as HMRC Stamp Taxes is concerned, with third parties and linked transactions. Notwithstanding that the linked transaction rules apply only to transactions between the same parties (FA 2003, s.108), purchasers of chargeable interests whose liability to tax may depend not merely upon the immediate transaction but also future linked transactions retrospectively affecting them (see, e.g. FA 2003, s.81A and Sched. 17A, para. 11) and who may be affected by dealings involving other parties will need to insist not only upon appropriate disclosure of all relevant information relating to the history of the chargeable interest in land which they are acquiring, but also upon appropriate undertakings from the vendor or landlord to disclose all subsequent events which may be linked with their transaction, including full details of transactions with third parties which may be commercially sensitive. As in many cases in other key areas, the obtaining of the essential protection for clients may prove extremely difficult, if not impossible, particularly where the third parties sensibly require undertakings against the disclosure of information without their consent in order to protect their confidential business information.

Aggregating transactions – general principles

Transactions are linked if they form part of a single scheme, arrangement or series of transactions between the same vendor and purchaser or persons connected with either of them (FA 2003, s.108(1)). This definition leaves open many problems, particularly as the practice of HMRC Stamp Taxes is not supported by the legislation. For example, it is its automatic response that if the transaction involves the same parties it must be 'linked'. It seeks to apply this approach even where several separate lots have been purchased at an auction (note, however, *Att-Gen v. Cohen* [1937] 1 All ER 17). Clearly, there is no linkage but the official, erroneous, view is that they are linked. This view ignores the basic requirement that there must be 'a' scheme, arrangement or series of transactions. The utilisation of the word 'a' clearly indicates that two or more unrelated transactions cannot be linked because there are two schemes or arrangements. The fact that two or more transactions are more or less simultaneous is not sufficient to link transactions; there must be essentially a pre-arranged deal not a coincidental or fortuitous timing relationship between the various transactions.

It might be thought that it should be easy for HMRC Stamp Taxes to establish a 'series' from a succession of transactions. However, it has been held (*A-G* v. *Cohen* [1937] KB 478) that a series requires some form of contractual linkage such as a single option exercisable by instalments.

Since temporal coincidence is not sufficient, it is necessary for there to be some form of commercial linkage between the transactions. It is no longer sufficient to fragment the overall transaction into separate legally independent contracts if it can be established that the parties would not commercially have signed one agreement unless the others were also signed. What matters is the commercial agreement or understanding between the parties not the legal form into which it may be eventually reduced. If there is a commercial linkage the purchaser cannot escape from these provisions simply by arranging for separate contracts to be signed by associates or connected companies whether acting as nominees or beneficial owners in their own right. This need to deal with such 'commercial linkage' will be a matter of detailed contemporaneous evidence as to the manner in which the negotiation developed. Clearly, if there is a discount for the purchase of several properties the transactions will be linked because there will be 'a scheme' for a multiple sale at a reduced price. Professional advisers will find it appropriately prudent to have a full statement of the background to the transaction from their clients and ideally seek confirmation from the vendor or lessor that this understanding of the preliminary negotiations corresponds with the statement provided by the taxpayer since it would prove embarrassing in an Enquiry if the two versions diverge.[15]

The same parties

It is specifically provided that the transactions must be entered into between the same persons or persons connected with them.[16] Thus where there is a sub-sale of part of the property originally agreed to be purchased the sub-purchaser, if otherwise unconnected with the original purchaser, will not be

---

15 HMRC Stamp Taxes has the power to demand information and documents from the vendor and the vendor's advisers, and advisers are personally vulnerable to serious penalties involving imprisonment where fraud in the wide sense of *Saunders* v. *Edwards* [1987] 2 All ER 651 is involved. See, for example, FA 2003, ss.95 and 96 which include the vendor's advisers.
16 Difficult questions will no doubt arise in practice in due course where the original party has died and the option is exercised by a person interested in his estate or his personal representative. These do not appear to be 'connected persons', but the position is not entirely clear.

a party to a linked transaction since his agreement will be with the original purchaser.[17] He will be entitled to the lower rates.

It must be noted that the connected person rules apply to vendors. In general, where a single purchaser agrees to acquire several properties from different vendors these will not be linked transactions, notwithstanding that there may be a condition in each of the contracts that each of them will complete only if all of the other related contracts also complete simultaneously. However, where there is a contract to acquire a leasehold interest or a freehold interest from a company and as part of a single overall commercial arrangement, the reversion or an adjacent freehold is to be acquired from the shareholders the fact that the parties are connected will help to link the transactions even where they are in separate contracts.

The reference to the same persons or persons connected with them indicates quite clearly that transactions involving one or more different parties are not linked. However, it appears to be the view of HMRC Stamp Taxes that transactions involving third parties can be linked. For example, it is its view, almost certainly erroneous, that the exercise of an option, including an option to renew a lease, is linked with the initial grant of the option or lease notwithstanding that the option is exercised by the assignee of the option or the lease.[18] This view must be incorrect since the legislation requires the same persons to be involved and it is difficult to establish 'a scheme or arrangement' where third parties are involved who could not be parties to a cut-and-dried arrangement between the original parties and were not involved in the original contract. It seems, therefore, that assignees are not affected by the linked transaction rules which is crucial for assignees of leases with options to renew or extend the lease.

Side effects for assignees

However, although transactions entered into by assignees of chargeable interests are probably not linked transactions with transactions entered into by the assignor of the rights, this does not mean that the assignee will not be affected by transactions entered into by the assignor. The fact that the original taxpayer has sold on all or part of the originally acquired chargeable interests does not 'unlink' that transaction from subsequent transactions notwithstanding that this may adversely affect the overall tax position of the assignee. For example, a subsequent linked lease such as one created by the exercise of an option to renew another lease by the assignor will reduce the amount of the nil rate slice for the net present value of the rent of a lease

---

17 It is, of course, essential that none of the other sub-purchasers are connected with the particular sub-purchaser which may help to link the transactions.
18 Assuming that the correct party to exercise the option can be identified; see *Brown and Root Technology Ltd* v. *Sun Life and London Assurance Ltd* [2000] 2 WLR 566.

assigned to a third party in relation to the first rent review or a possible abnormal increase (FA 2003, Sched. 5, para. 12 (as amended)) in the rent after the expiration of the fifth year of the term of the original lease. Appropriate investigations of the SDLT history will be required together with appropriate undertakings from the vendor to supply detailed information of subsequent transactions which may affect the tax position of the purchaser of the chargeable interest so that he can comply with his obligations (FA 2003, s.81A) and/or compute his future tax correctly.

Lease premiums and rents

The double structure of taxation of lease premiums and lease rents provides for complexities. It appears that where any of the chargeable transactions includes a lease, any premium will be aggregated with any premiums for other leases and the chargeable consideration for other transactions.

However, where there is a lease at a rent which is a linked transaction no account is to be taken of rent in determining the relevant premium (FA 2003, Sched. 5, para. 9(5)). Where there are linked leases the nil rate slice has to be allocated between the linked leases in accordance with the proportion that the net present value of the rent for each individual lease bears to the total net present value of the rents reserved by all of the linked leases. Since the linked transaction rules can include later leases and renewals of leases the initial allocation of the relevant proportion of the nil rate slice for the rent will be on a provisional basis subject to review as each subsequent linked transaction occurs. In consequence, assignees will require the basic disclosure of the history of the lease and related transactions and of any subsequent potentially linked transactions.

Options and pre-emption rights

Special rules apply to link the grant of options with their exercise. It is provided that the grant of an option is a chargeable transaction in its own right distinct from any transaction resulting from the exercise of the optional right (FA 2003, s.46(1)). However, the provision goes on to indicate that the grant and the exercise of the option only 'may be' linked transactions. This word 'may' indicates that there is, at least in the view of the draftsmen, no automatic linkage between the grant of the option and the transaction arising pursuant to its exercise. This must be a matter of evidence in each case, i.e. whether there was an arrangement or understanding between the parties that the option would be exercised and possibly whether there is a realistic commercial possibility that it might not be exercised. The consideration for the option should be retrospectively aggregated with the consideration payable upon the exercise of the option so that, if appropriate, the higher rates of SDLT will be applicable to both the contract price and the option price. This means that it will be necessary to file a further land transaction return (SDLT 1) in respect of the initial grant of the option or pre-emption right because of an increase in the amount of tax payable by reason of a higher rate becoming applicable. This would seem to apply even where the premium for the option is a token sum of £1.[19] This return is in addition to the return on the grant of the option and the separate return required in respect of the contract or agreement for lease arising pursuant to the exercise of the option, i.e. at least three separate land transaction returns will be required.

Successive leases

It is not unusual for leases to contain an option to renew the lease. If there is a genuine commercial possibility that the option might not be exercised because of subsequent events, such as not renewing a lease because the trading activities at the demised premises might not have proved successful, it is an indication that the two stages are not linked.

Under the present regime relating to the calculation of SDLT upon rents by reason of the nil rate 'slice' of the net present value of the rent always being free of tax (FA 2003, Sched. 5), there may be opportunities to mitigate the tax by taking short agreements for lease with options to renew each of which may fall within the nil rates of SDLT. However, the legislation (FA 2003, Sched. 17A, para. 14(5)) indicates that the new lease may be linked with the original lease, and any previous renewals thereof.[20] This means that any premium for the new lease will be aggregated with the premium for any prior lease or leases, and the charge upon the rent reserved by the initial lease will have to be recalculated upon the basis that the original lease was for a term equal to the aggregate of the terms of the original lease and any linked renewals thereof. This, however, may in most cases be beneficial for tenants who will be arguing that their renewal is linked,[21] and a lease with options to renew will usually, to the discomfiture of HMRC Stamp Taxes who will find itself arguing for an unlinked transaction, be a more attractive proposition than a longer lease with break clauses (see Chapter 8).

The difficulty will be trying to predict when HMRC Stamp Taxes will accept that the original and the new leases are linked. It seems that if the lease has been assigned the exercise of the option will not be a linked transaction

---

19 But not, perhaps, a peppercorn.
20 See FA 2003, Sched. 19, para. 9 on the transitional position of the exercise of options to renew leases granted within the charge to stamp duty, which may include leases granted on or after 1 December 2004 but pursuant to an agreement entered into prior to that date.
21 This depends upon whether the nil rate slice is significant so that a second or third nil rate will outweigh the benefits of the rent being discounted over time.

UNDERSTANDING SDLT

since it is not between the same parties.[22] Where it is the original tenant who exercises the option the outcome will depend upon the original negotiations and whether there were 'side arrangements' relating to the renewal of the lease and whether these discussions were adequately documented at the time. In the absence of such direct contemporaneous evidence, the decision will depend largely upon inference from the facts. For example, where there is a long lease where much can happen the renewal is less likely to be a linked transaction than where the parties began by negotiating a seven-year lease and agreed a three-year lease with an option to renew. It is unclear whether the exercise of the option will be 'linked' with the original and any other prior agreements for lease so that the chargeable consideration has to be aggregated for these purposes, particularly where the lease has been assigned so that the person exercising the option is not the same person as the original tenant.

Deemed linked transactions

The legislation also deems certain transactions to be linked so that the deemed new lease arising upon an abnormal rent increase is deemed to be linked with the actual lease so that no nil rate slice will be available.

4.6 CHARGEABLE CONSIDERATION

Chargeable consideration which is required by the charging provisions (FA 2003, Sched. 3, para. 1), requires two elements, namely:

- the existence of actual consideration since, in general, the absence of actual consideration means that there is no chargeable transaction; although there are situations where there is a deemed consideration, most notably in relation to the connected company charge and the special regime for partnerships; and
- such actual or deemed consideration must be 'chargeable'. This is important since not all actual consideration is within the definition of chargeable consideration so that the transaction is 'exempt' or such actual consideration is to be 'ignored', treated as 'nil' or 'exempt'. These various concepts appear at various places in the legislation but it is unclear what, if any, are intended to be the general consequences of these differences in terminology

---

22 Provided that the assignee is not connected with the assignor. However, HMRC Stamp Taxes has previously acted upon the basis that since the contract between the original seller/landlord and the assignee is the same as that with the assignor, the assignor and the assignee are the same person. It is, however, difficult to justify this analysis as a matter of general principle, rather than a point depending upon the particular legislation.

although there are certain express differences in the compliance regime (see Chapter 1).

Chargeable consideration – general issues

This question of chargeable consideration raises some very fundamental issues affecting the scope of the tax and the computation thereof, namely:

- what is 'consideration';
- when is the actual consideration chargeable and so relevant for the purposes of the charge to tax;
- when is the actual consideration or absence of consideration replaced by a deemed amount of consideration;
- how is the chargeable amount to be calculated;
- where there is consideration in kind how is the chargeable amount to be determined, i.e. what are the valuation principles to be adopted; and
- how is variable consideration to be dealt with.

Unfortunately these are issues which those responsible for preparing the structure and drafting of the tax failed to appreciate and deal with adequately, leaving matters to general principles of highly technical law. As usual the taxpayer will have to bear the risk of interest, penalties of incorrect interpretations and may have to incur the cost of litigating to get a decision in his favour simply to avoid penalties and interest charges.

Consideration

There is no definition of what constitutes 'consideration' although there are certain general rules for determining the amount subject to charge in relation to certain situations. This clearly means that these situations must involve 'consideration' which is also chargeable and which is significantly wider than the categories of consideration that were required to create a charge to *ad valorem* stamp duty. There are also provisions such as the connected company charge (FA 2003, ss.53 and 54) which deem there to be a chargeable consideration.

However, subject to such specific provisions, 'consideration' must bear, at least, its general contractual meaning and all of the conditions relating thereto. Although it may be necessary for the consideration to move from the promisee (i.e. the 'purchaser' in SDLT parlance), it need not pass to the promisor (i.e. the 'vendor' for the purposes of SDLT), for example where a lease is granted by a landlord to a third party who pays a sum of money to a developer for building works which form part of the consideration.[23]

---

23 *Att-Gen* v. *Brown* (1849) 3 Exch 662; FA 2003, Sched. 17A, para. 12B; see Chapter 8.

This will require detailed understanding of the basic law of contract but certain provisions raise doubts as to whether 'consideration' is to be regarded as wider than its general meaning and includes 'benefits' or 'detriments' that would not rank as contractual consideration. This issue arises in relation to transactions 'taking effect by operation of law' where the passing of the property may be effected by the person suffering a detriment such as the performance of services rather than making a payment. For example, there are key issues as to whether acting upon oral statements so as to give rise to a constructive trust which arises by operation of law and are effective to pass or create property interests (see Chapter 1) constitutes 'consideration' or whether 'consideration' requires a 'contract' in the narrow sense of a valid, legally enforceable agreement arising solely from the agreement of the parties rather than from acting upon the basis of an otherwise unenforceable oral promise or statement. Since many arrangements, particularly those of a domestic nature, will be informal and not necessarily supported by any presumptions as to intention to enter into binding legal relationships,[24] but which are binding and enforceable simply because it would be 'inequitable' for the parties to insist or rely upon their strict legal position (*Binions* v. *Evans* [1972] Ch 359), there may not be sufficient consensual element to make contractual consideration out of the oral statements or promises which may fall short of formal 'offer'. It is probable that HMRC Stamp Taxes will take the view that such acts will be 'consideration' for the purpose of SDLT (relying upon FA 2003, Sched. 4, para. 11) notwithstanding that there cannot, in law, be a contract because there is not the degree of writing required by legislation (Law of Property (Miscellaneous Provisions) Act 1989, s.2; *First Post Homes* v. *Johnson* [1995] 4 All ER 355).

Similarly, what might appear to be a conditional gift (*G.U.S Merchandise* v. *Customs and Excise* [1981] 1 WLR 1309; *Errington* v. *Errington and Woods* [1952] 1 KB 290) or a conditional contract (*Eastham* v. *Leigh, London and Provincial Properties* [1971] 2 All ER 887) may be an offer for a consideration which is constituted by 'satisfying the condition', i.e. satisfying the condition constitutes the supplying of the consideration or part thereof which may be taxable as the supply of services (FA 2003, Sched. 4, para. 11). It may be, therefore, that undertakings by the parties such as to apply for planning permission or to carry out the fitting out of premises or to construct a building may be taxable consideration, particularly where one of the parties undertakes to use reasonable endeavours to procure the satisfaction of the conditions. Additionally, it remains to be seen how far HMRC Stamp Taxes will pursue the argument that undertakings to use reasonable endeavours to bring about the satisfaction of conditions precedent by themselves represent

---

24 See the presumptions in relation to domestic arrangements in cases such as *Gage* v. *King* [1961] 1 QB 188.

the provision of chargeable services which may have an open market cost. It is thought that there is no substance in the point but, from time to time, other divisions of HMRC have sought to argue that agreeing to procure the happening of an event or the completion of a transaction is the provision of services.

The draftsman also has a theory of 'reverse consideration'. He has provided that reverse payments such as sums paid by landlords as inducements for the grant of a lease or by assignors to assignees of leases where there are dilapidations are not to be taxable, and he assumes that where a tenant agrees to take a lease subject to the landlord constructing a building the landlord's building works (as opposed to the cash paid for them) are consideration provided by the tenant in return for the landlord granting the lease. Notwithstanding these bizarre provisions, it is considered that they do not affect the general proposition that there is no such reverse consideration; but the judiciary will be reluctant to strike them down as meaningless should there be an attempt by HMRC Stamp Taxes to develop this theory of a 'reverse consideration'.

Chargeable amount

Having determined that there is 'consideration', it is necessary to determine whether the consideration is 'chargeable' and then the next step in the self-assessment computation and compliance process is to determine the amount of the chargeable consideration for the transaction (including any linked transactions) to which the rate is applied.

4.7 'PROVISIONAL TAX'

It should be noted that in a significant number of cases the computation of the tax, for the first stage and possibly later stages of the same tax computation related to the effective date, will be provisional only being based upon certain assumptions or estimates and it will frequently be necessary to revisit the initial and later computations of the tax retrospectively and submit a fresh land transaction return with payments of any tax due.[25] It will not be appropriate to 'amend' the original land transaction return (SDLT 1) because the required re-self-assessment is a separate notifiable transaction (but not necessarily a separate chargeable transaction because usually, but not invariably, it relates back to the original effective date) and as such it requires a new land transaction return with a different bar code or transaction number.

---

25 There are also practical difficulties in that the amendment does not consist of altering the original form but submitting a written 'notice' in the prescribed form; see Appendix D.

Moreover, even if it were possible to deal with the situation as an 'amendment' the 'amendment' will usually be outside the maximum amendment period of 12 months from the filing date (FA 2003, Sched. 10, para. 6(3)), i.e. 30 days after the effective date.

Those areas where the initial computation is provisional include:

- transactions where there may be later linked transactions which operate retrospectively, such as leases with options to renew or transactions where there are numerous related options to purchase. It should be noted that the linked transaction rules, although expressed to be limited to transactions between the same parties or persons connected with them, may directly or indirectly affect purchasers and assignees of the chargeable interest and provision is made imposing obligations upon such third parties (see, e.g. FA 2003, s.81A) such as assignees of leases and for the allocation of the nil rate slice of rent;
- variable consideration such as overage or clawback arrangements (FA 2003, ss.57 and 80);
- variable premiums and rents (FA 2003, Sched. 17A, paras. 7 and 8), where the responsibility for dealing with the outstanding SDLT passes to the assignee of the lease (FA 2003, Sched. 17A, para. 12).

In a practical sense, all chargeable transactions where the chargeable consideration consists of or includes consideration in kind such as where market value or market costs are involved will be provisional since HMRC Stamp Taxes does not, in theory, regard itself as bound by the figures produced by the parties in the completion of the land transaction return (see, e.g. *Lap Shun Textiles* v. *Collector of Stamp Revenue* [1976] 1 All ER 833), and so can challenge the parties' figures during an Enquiry even where they are backed by independent professional advice. Moreover, owing to the deficiencies in the self-assessment system generally and the land transaction returns and related form in particular, as no background information can be produced upon the return, HMRC Stamp Taxes is free to make a discovery assessment at any time within six years because the officer processing the form did not have information as to the basis upon which the valuation was prepared.[26]

---

26 *Langham* v. *Veltema* [2004] STC 544. As the theory is that all land transaction returns should be processed by computer with the form scanned in, and not scrutinised by individual employees who in any event have only limited power to correct the land transaction returns in respect of 'obvious errors or omissions' (FA 2003, Sched. 10, para. 7), the subsequently shown to be incorrect choice of a basis for valuing the consideration in kind will not be an obvious error in relation to the original return, and there is no procedure for the forms to be rejected by the scanners, should they ever work, where, for example, consideration in kind is involved. Every return having been electronically processed will be open to challenge by a discovery assessment for at least six years not just nine months (see Chapter 14).

4.8 GLOBAL CONSIDERATION AND APPORTIONMENT

It may be that the land is not the only element of property being acquired by the transaction but there may be a single consideration expressed for the whole package such as where there is an acquisition of a business as a going concern where there may be land, chattels, goodwill[27] and so on,[28] being acquired for a single price (which may include general liabilities of the vendor which are not specifically charged upon the land) or the issue of shares. In this situation the chargeable consideration is that which is limited to the subject-matter of the land transaction,[29] which is the chargeable interest being acquired together with any interest or right appurtenant or pertaining to it that is acquired or with it.[30]

In such a case, the actual consideration has to be apportioned between consideration which is 'chargeable', i.e. relates to the subject-matter of the land transaction and other parts of the contract where the actual consideration is not 'chargeable' on a just and reasonable basis (FA 2003, Sched. 4, para. 4(1), this has to be done on the revised SDLT 4 in most cases). If the consideration is not apportioned the SDLT will apply as if it had been so apportioned (FA 2003, Sched. 4, para. 4(2)), and any consideration given for what is, in substance, one bargain is attributed to all the elements of the bargain even though separate consideration is or purports to be given for different elements of the bargain or there are or purport to be separate transactions in respect of different elements of the bargain (FA 2003, Sched. 4, para. 3), which seems to be intended to give HMRC Stamp Taxes power to reallocate consideration between what are technically legally independent contracts but which are part of a single overall commercial arrangement.[31]

No statutory guidance is provided as to what is a 'just and reasonable basis' and it is certain that the views of HMRC Stamp Taxes will differ significantly from those of taxpayers and their advisers, but arbitrary attempts to allocate consideration simply to mitigate the tax charge by obtaining the lower rates of tax (see, e.g. *Lloyds and Scottish* v. *Prentice* 121 SJ 847) will not

---

27 But note the problem of whether the 'goodwill' is really part of the land value.
28 In such case SDLT 4 (as amended) may have to be completed.
29 And any linked transactions; but the consideration for the non-land items does not have to be aggregated for the purposes of the lower rates of SDLT.
30 FA 2003, s.43(6). It will be noted that this definition differs from that applied for the purposes of determining substantial performance which relates to the subject-matter of the contract (FA 2003, s.44(5)(a)). It remains to be seen whether, in practice, HMRC Stamp Taxes will seek to exploit this difference which is important in relation to the scope of FA 2003, s.44A.
31 For example, this enables HMRC Stamp Taxes to reapportion the allocation of the consideration between the land price and any related building works but it has been advised that it does not enable it to make the two contracts into a single fully taxable contract.

be acceptable and will be attacked as attempts to defraud HMRC (*Saunders v. Edwards* [1987] 2 All ER 651). Seeking to reduce the tax by producing an artificially low consideration could be regarded as fraud (*Re Wragg* [1897] 1 Ch 796; *Saunders v. Edwards*) involving a conspiracy (*Saunders v. Edwards*) by those co-operating in the preparation of documentation or return forms on the basis of improper allocation so that the vendor and the various professional advisers could be conspirators. Any allocation of the consideration should, therefore, as a matter of prudence be supported by detailed contemporaneous documentation and failure to obtain such supporting independent evidence could be regarded as 'negligence' in the preparation of the land transaction return providing HMRC Stamp Taxes with the opportunity of issuing a discovery assessment for up to 21 years after the effective date, and to impose penalties upon the professional advisers for assisting in the preparation of a land transaction return which they knew to be incorrect because they knew that proper advice had not been obtained to support the data inserted into the SDLT 1. It should, however, be noted that the apportionment is not based upon market value. In other cases, of course, there may be situations where there is consideration in kind when the market value is the chargeable consideration. This market value has to be prepared on a proper basis and then suitably apportioned between the assets.[32] There will be situations where the land element in the transaction is deemed to be acquired at market value such as where the connected company charge applies, or the land exchange rules are relevant. In such a situation the market value rules will prevail over the apportionment obligation and the transaction will have to be returned as being for a market value consideration notwithstanding that this exceeds the actual consideration given for the totality of the assets.

A standard situation in practice is where the purchaser, without advice as to value, and without further thought, apportions the actual consideration on an arbitrary basis designed so that the land element falls below the relevant rate threshold. This will frequently arise in practice in residential conveyancing where parties, without advice, allocate the consideration to 'chattels', which is itself a difficult area requiring advice, so as to reduce the price for the land just below a rate change threshold or to remove as much as possible from the chargeable consideration. Such arbitrary allocation of the price will almost certainly be improper and the indications are that residential conveyancing in these areas is likely to be a high priority area for Enquiries or discovery assessments. Professional advisers may need to consider whether, having advised the taxpayer on the need to justify the allocation, it is prudent to continue to act if this advice is ignored because of the financial and criminal penalties potentially arising in relation to the comple-

---

[32] Possibly in accordance with SDLT 4 (as amended) which is required when there is the transfer of a business.

tion of the land transaction return in these circumstances, i.e. knowing that it has not been prepared on a proper basis. In addition to any general criminal sanctions that may be applicable for attempts to defraud HMRC Stamp Taxes or conspiracy to achieve the same (see *Saunders* v. *Edwards* [1987] 2 All ER 651), there is a tax-related penalty for any person who fraudulently delivers a land transaction return and fails to make a correction (FA 2003, s.95, Sched. 10, para. 8). In addition, a person who assists in or induces the preparation or delivery of any information, return or other document that he knows will be or is likely to be used for any purposes of SDLT and he knows to be incorrect is liable to a penalty not exceeding £3,000 (FA 2003, s.96). However, more significantly, a person who is knowingly concerned in fraudulent evasion of tax[33] by him or any other person[34] is guilty of an offence which carries with it:

- on summary conviction imprisonment for a term not exceeding six months or a fine not exceeding the statutory maximum, or both;
- on conviction on indictment imprisonment for a term not exceeding seven years or a fine or both (FA 2003, s.95).

'Chargeable consideration'

'Chargeable consideration' is defined (FA 2003, Sched. 4, para. 1) in addition to deemed consideration as any consideration:

- in money or money's worth (*Secretan* v. *Hart* 45 TC 701);
- that is given for the subject-matter of the transaction (i.e. the chargeable interest being acquired plus any interest or right pertaining or appurtenant to the interest being acquired) but not rights or assets other than 'land';
- directly or indirectly by the purchaser or a person connected with him;

---

[33] Such issues are not limited to SDLT but will apply to any attempt to produce a favourable result by an arbitrary allocation of the price, and it should be noted that a wrongful allocation may have other taxation consequences (see, e.g. *Re Hollebone* [1959] 2 All ER 152).

[34] As regards the new statutory sanctions in FA 2003, the liability here is likely to be limited to the purchaser's solicitor because the vendor is not involved in the preparation and submission of the land transaction return, but he and his advisers may be parties to a criminal conspiracy should they agree to an artificial apportionment of the consideration in the contract. Mortgagees may, in consequence, be adversely affected by these arrangements particularly where the same solicitor is acting for both the purchaser and the mortgagee so that it may be easy for the court to impute knowledge of the illegality to the mortgagee through his agent where knowledge of impropriety affects the rights or liabilities of the parties in the context. The criminal aspects of such arrangements for the contract would be subject to the restriction imposed upon illegal contracts so that they would be unenforceable.

but this is supplemented by various provisions in the legislation. For example, Sched. 4 contains provisions for calculating the amount of tax where the actual consideration is not money or money's worth which carries with it the clear implication that such consideration is chargeable.

Numerous problems arise upon this definition:

By the purchaser

It is necessary to identify the 'purchaser' which can include persons who do not provide consideration such as donees of gifts,[35] since consideration provided by other persons may not be chargeable (FA 2003, Sched. 4, para. 1; but note the provisions of FA 2003, s.44A). Inducement from third parties to enter into the contract may not be chargeable,[36] at least if the person providing the inducement is not connected with the purchaser.

In the context the word 'indirectly' will be significant in practice. No guidance as to HMRC Stamp Taxes's view has been given but it is likely to apply to situations other than where a person supplying the actual consideration is somehow reimbursed or indemnified by the person receiving the land. On the other hand, simply putting the person in funds such as by making a loan or purchasing part of the property or other assets from the taxpayer will not be the indirect provision of the consideration even though it puts cash into the taxpayer's hands.

However, although the consideration must be provided directly or indirectly by the 'purchaser', it seems that it is not necessary for it to pass to the 'vendor', i.e. the person disposing of the subject-matter of the transaction (FA 2003, s.43).

Money or money's worth

'Money's worth' has been judicially defined (*Secretan* v. *Hart* 45 TC 701) as being very familiar to lawyers, as being a way of expressing the price or consideration given for property where property is acquired in return for something other than money, such as services or other property, where the price or consideration which the acquirer gives for the property has to go to be turned into money before it can be expressed in terms of money. However, these limits on the concept of 'money's worth' have lost a lot of their significance since the provisions governing the amount of the chargeable consideration clearly indicate that its scope has been extended into areas where the

---

35 Such persons have to be treated as purchasers for the effectiveness of the compliance regimes, i.e. to identify the person to sign the relevant forms.
36 Cf. *Crane Fruehauf* v. *IRC* [1975] 1 All ER 429; *Central and District Properties* v. *IRC* [1966] 2 All ER 437; *Shop and Store Developments* v. *IRC* [1967] 1 AC 472.

actual consideration in question would not be 'money's worth' such as services[37] and certain building arrangements which cannot be sold in the open market.[38] In such cases the tax is calculated on the basis of open market cost (FA 2003, Sched. 4, paras. 10 and 11).

It is clear from these definitions that the item constituting or deemed to constitute the consideration must be something that is capable of being sold as a separate asset;[39] the fact that it is valuable does not of itself make it taxable. This will be important where many minor interests are involved such as where land is transferred in consideration of the grant of restrictive covenants which are valuable but which cannot be sold separately from that land except releases of them in favour of the servient land, the owner of which cannot be regarded as an open market.

Two issues arise where minor interests are involved as part of the consideration for the chargeable interest such as where interests are reserved to the seller. Since these may not be capable of separate sale, it might be thought that they are not money's worth, and can be ignored. This argument, however, is countered by the land exchange definition (FA 2003, s.47; see Chapter 7) which applies where one party as part of the consideration for one land transaction is to enter into another land transaction so that in the view of HMRC Stamp Taxes there are two separate land transactions with the chargeable consideration being determined pursuant to para. 5 of Sched. 4 to FA 2003; but it seems that as such minor interests are not capable of independent sale they do not have a market value. As the charge does not include the enhancement of the value of the dominant land, it is considered that the chargeable consideration, i.e. the market value of the restrictive covenant is nil.[40] As most minor interests cannot be separately sold as they exist only as rights for the benefit of the dominant land, it is considered that they do not have a market value. Similarly, where the transaction involves the release or surrender of an interest in circumstances where this is taxed by reference to the market value of that interest rather than the actual consideration,[41] it is considered that since there is nothing to sell there cannot be a market value in these terms.

---

37 Notwithstanding the comments in *Secretan* v. *Hart* 45 TC 701; see *Nokes* v. *Doncaster Amalgamated Collieries* [1940] AC 1014; *O'Brien* v. *Benson Hosiery* [1979] STC 735.
38 If these items were not intended to be chargeable consideration, it would not be necessary to include the computation rules.
39 This is supported by the definition of 'market value' which requires a sale in the open market (FA 2003, Sched. 4, para. 7).
40 This may mean that there is not a chargeable transaction at all. However, upon either view a self-certificate (SDLT 60) would support any change of the Land Register.
41 Such as where the land exchange rules or the connected company charges apply.

4.9 CONSIDERATION IN KIND AND MARKET VALUE

Unlike stamp duty which it replaces, SDLT applies to a wide range of types of non-cash consideration and numerous provisions exist for attributing a value to these situations. These issues apply not merely to land but to other property provided by way of consideration such as shares or even equipment where land is transferred in return for the transfer of assets.

The situations where the chargeable consideration is treated as being the market value of a chargeable interest include:

- the connected company charge;
- special dealings involving partnerships;
- consideration in kind;
- land exchanges.

There will be, initially at least, a question of whether it may be possible to avoid a valuation by inserting a cash amount into the documents. In *Stanton v. Drayton Commercial Investment Co. Ltd* [1982] STC 585 the consideration was expressed as a cash sum to be satisfied by the transfer of specified property. The House of Lords stated that, in the absence of any fraudulent or improper attempt to manipulate the tax position, the specified amount being bona fide was the taxable figure. However, that case was concerned with issues of 'value' rather than 'market value' and it was regarded as the price the parties put upon their bargain, but, notwithstanding that stamp duty was occasionally concerned with 'market value' the Inland Revenue Stamp Taxes Office in practice tended to act upon the basis of such figures inserted in the contract, largely because the costs of valuation in many transactions are disproportionate to the extra tax likely to be produced.

However, at the same time, the Inland Revenue Stamp Taxes Office continued with the contention based upon *Lap Shun Textiles v. Collector of Stamp Revenue* [1976] AC 530 that the parties' figures were not conclusive of market value even when the parties were at arm's length. The price may have been agreed for a quick sale and so not market value in accordance with the provision for fiscal valuations where the time of the sale is not a pressing factor relevant for consideration (see also *Cowan de Groot v. Eagle* [1991] BCLC 1045). This, of course, is likely to raise issues in relation to transactions where there is a discount; it is the official view that a discounted price whether for a quick sale or because several properties are involved is not a market price.

Nevertheless, whilst the parties' own figures are not necessarily conclusive they are likely to be important in practice, particularly in smaller transactions where the amount of tax is fairly small so that it is not economic for HMRC Stamp Taxes to mount a serious challenge. For example, in relation to exchanges or part exchanges, in practice, it is likely that the price at which the property was originally offered for sale will be taken by HMRC Stamp Taxes as the market value at least on a *prima facie* basis.[42] Figures supported by professional valuations are in many cases likely to be accepted as representing the market value, at least if the valuation is fairly close to the effective date. Such independent valuations will, moreover, be advisable, if not absolutely necessary, in practice since in the absence of such a valuation it is questionable whether the taxpayer will have complied with his obligation to make a correct return. Approximations as to value are not necessarily the correct way to complete the land transaction return (see Appendix D). The preparation of the return requires not merely the 'correct' market value but also the adoption of the current methodology for valuation, if allegations of negligent returns are to be avoided.

One area of difficulty affecting a wide range of transactions relates to transfer of interests in land subject to obligations to grant new rights back to the transferor, such as where a freehold is transferred subject to the obligation to grant a restrictive covenant and, if the current views of HMRC Stamp Taxes should prevail, virtually every case where the words 'excepting and reserving' appear as it contends that this can only operate as a regrant (see Chapter 2). This will produce a land exchange taxable by reference to the market values. The Inland Revenue Stamp Taxes Office has since 1994 consistently maintained that the hypothetical terms of sale must prevail over the actual terms of sale, and notwithstanding that the taxpayer acquires the chargeable interest already encumbered by a binding and specifically enforceable obligation to regrant interests to the 'vendor' or a third party the terms of the actual sale have to be ignored and the property valued freed from the regrant obligations ignoring the obligation to grant rights back. For example, where the tenants in a block of flats acquire the landlord's interest which they transfer to a management company in return for the grant of new leases at a token ground rent,[43] the freehold subject to such leases has negligible value; but HMRC Stamp Taxes contends that the market value of the reversionary interest has to be valued ignoring the leases back, i.e. the unencumbered freehold value which is significant. The leases back will also have a large value so that in effect the transaction will involve an 8 per cent charge upon the vacant possession value of the land.[44] These views are considered to be incorrect in

---

[42] It is possible to resist this depending upon the facts. For example, where the property had been on offer at that price but had not attracted any significant interest from prospective purchasers.
[43] Additionally, because this is connected with the transfer of the reversionary interests HMRC Stamp Taxes does not give the reliefs for surrenders and regrants.
[44] In these situations the tenants should seek to organise matters as a surrender and regrant for which substantial reliefs are available pursuant to FA 2003, Sched. 17A, paras. 9 and 16.

principle[45] and appear to be changing recently, but they are of considerable importance in the context of self-assessment since the taxpayer has to guess which approach HMRC Stamp Taxes may wish to take as to valuation upon an Enquiry at some time in the future.

Basic provisions

Subject to any specific provisions, the value of any chargeable consideration other than money, including foreign currency or 'debt' (defined in FA 2003, Sched. 4, para. 8), is its 'market value' at the effective date of the transaction (FA 2003, Sched. 4, para. 7). 'Market value' is to be determined in accordance with ss. 272–274 of the Taxation of Chargeable Gains Act 1992 (FA 2003, s.118).

'Market value' is the price which the relevant asset might reasonably be expected to fetch in a sale on the open market (Taxation of Chargeable Gains Act 1992, s.242(1)). Unfortunately this simple statement hides a multiplicity of problems, and although it is likely that in practice SDLT valuation will follow capital gains tax valuation practice, there are potential difficulties in applying the latter to SDLT so that special rules may have to be developed.

The issues include:

- identifying the property to be valued. Usually this will be the property being provided as consideration, but, for example, in relation to exchanges and part-exchanges involving major interests it is the value of the property being received by way of consideration;
- the meaning of 'open' market. Many interests in or rights over property cannot exist except in relation to other land. It is not possible to sell the benefit of a restrictive covenant to any person other than the owner of the servient land. It is considered that such non-saleable assets, although they are potentially valuable and enhance the value of the dominant land, do not have a 'market value'. Whilst the existence of special purchasers cannot be ignored and their possible presence on the open market if it should exist has to be taken into account, the fact that there is only one potential 'purchaser' cannot create an 'open' market;

---

45 Where there was a sale and leaseback qualifying for the relief in the original, now amended, s.57A, FA 2003 (as amended) the transfer of the reversionary interest was taxable upon not less than the market value of the interest, which was to be calculated as if it were not part of a sale and leaseback transaction. Presumably this meant that the reversionary interest is to be valued ignoring the obligation to grant the leaseback. This may be a useful argument should HMRC Stamp Taxes persist in its current views, i.e. a specific provision to ignore the reciprocal obligation suggests that upon general principles it should be included in the valuation process, but recently the official view seems to be changing to the correct principles of valuing subject to the regrant obligations.

- the terms of the sale. Fiscal valuations tend to work upon the basis of a willing buyer and a willing seller so that there is a hypothetical contract which may not be the same as the terms of the actual contract between the parties. A willing seller, for example, is under no pressure to sell so discounts are irrelevant. There are basic issues to be debated with HMRC Stamp Taxes as to the terms of the sale and how far these differ from the actual terms of any sale or lease between the parties. There are few legislative provisions setting out the detailed principles to be applied, such as the factors to be taken into account and the relative weight to be attached to the various factors. Where there is no sale but an exchange the terms of the sale will be largely hypothetical, but it is understood that HMRC Stamp Taxes takes the view that the market value includes VAT, but this is debatable particularly where the option to tax has not been exercised or the hypothetical sale could be a transfer of a going concern;
- unlike stamp duty, SDLT does not seek to impose a charge upon market rents because in the absence of detailed legislation HMRC Stamp Taxes appears to have realised there are many unanswerable questions. Where there is a lease issued on favourable terms and a market value charge arises this is usually taxed in the form of a deemed premium.

Future values and rents

The issue of future rents is not unique, there are many cases where future values are required such as overage and clawback arrangements (FA 2003, s.51; see below on such variable payments; *Akasuc Enterprises* v. *Farmar* [2003] PL SCS 127) or future rents such as rent reviews. Here the taxpayer has to make a reasonable estimate of future value, payments and rents. Interest and possibly penalties can be imposed if the estimate turns out to be incorrect (see below).

Practical issues

The practical difficulty is that professional advisers are justifiably reluctant to give advice that is essentially crystal-ball gazing and is not a valid professional exercise based upon valid data. Nevertheless, taxpayers are expected to make reasonable 'guestimates' of future values and future rents even though this can be a nonsensical exercise such as seeking to predict the likely effect of obtaining some form of planning permission in relation to the land some half-a-century or longer after the immediate sale. Nevertheless, these exercises have to be carried out and failure to obtain and preserve the details of proper advice exposes the taxpayer or his estate to the risk of significant penalties.

The HMRC Stamp Taxes helpline has been giving incorrect advice, such as simply to include only the current rent or current values knowing that this means there has been no attempt to make a reasonable estimate. This produces a negligent return enlarging the Enquiry period to 21 years. Taxpayers and their advisers cannot rely upon the advice given by the helpline which does not bind HMRC Stamp Taxes and so cannot use such bad advice as a negotiating counter in the mitigation of penalties.[46]

4.10 'COSTS'

The massive extension of the tax base means that many new detailed rules are required for calculating the chargeable consideration where money's worth or market value are inappropriate (FA 2003, Sched. 4, para. 1; *Secretan* v. *Hart* [1969] 3 All ER 1196) since they cannot be sold or otherwise turned into cash or if saleable their value would be insufficiently large to produce a 'worthwhile' tax yield. The main areas are works (FA 2003, Sched. 4, para. 10 (as amended); see Chapter 9) and services (FA 2003, Sched. 4, para. 11; see below). These are taxed upon an amount equal to the cost of such services or works on the open market (see Stamp Duty Land Tax (Administration) Regulations 2003, SI 2003/2837, Part 4), a novel concept in fiscal valuations in many respects.

Several basic issues arise in practice. First, as these are based upon the 'open market cost' it is clear that the actual costs incurred by the taxpayer are not necessarily the correct figure. In many cases there is likely to be no cost unless the loss of other income is regarded as a 'cost'; but since this offers HMRC Stamp Taxes a windfall bonus of desperately needed revenue in order to meet its promises to Government it may well wish to pursue this nonsense point. Moreover, even such lost income will not necessarily be open market cost, i.e. the price which the other party would pay for the services on a stand-alone basis with a third party seeking to make a profit on the transaction. For example, the cost to a builder employing his own labour force will almost certainly be different from the price which a third party seeking to make a profit might charge if the building work or other services were a separate transaction unrelated to the acquisition of an interest in land. The practical difficulty for taxpayers will be to obtain information from competitors as to their possible charges, particularly since this might reveal confidential business information; but, in the absence of such alternative quotations for the work or services on a stand-alone basis the land transaction return (SDLT 1) will not have been properly prepared pursuant to the rules relating to self-assessment with the consequences of extended Enquiry periods and the risk of discovery assessments plus interest and penalties.

---

46 The interest charge is mandatory and cannot be mitigated, a bonus for HMRC Stamp Taxes receipts!

Secondly, since works and services are supplied over a period of time they may be uncertain within the various categories of variable consideration. In this situation the taxpayer has to make a reasonable estimate of the open market cost (FA 2003, s.51) which has to be adjusted as the transaction proceeds (FA 2003, s.82). It is possible to apply to defer the payment of the tax upon the uncertain element provided that the transaction is likely to take more than six months to complete (FA 2003, s.90); but in certain cases the application to postpone the tax must be accompanied by a timetable indicating when HMRC Stamp Taxes may expect payments of tax pursuant to s.80 of FA 2003 (Stamp Duty Land Tax (Administration) Regulations 2003, SI 2003/2837).

Thirdly, the services in question may not be available on 'the open market'. There is at present no explanation of which 'services' HMRC Stamp Taxes regards as subject to the charge to tax. In consequence, 'services' supplied in the form of caring for elderly relatives are chargeable consideration but whilst the equivalent of certain of these services may be available through welfare and social services departments not every activity involved will be so covered. There may be issues as to whether supplying lunch has to be equated with meals on wheels, but other activities are not so clearly matched by outside suppliers. Moreover, there will be the need to report the chargeable transaction at some stage which will be very difficult to determine otherwise than retrospectively. Although many such transactions will be informal they will be effective as constructive trusts notwithstanding the absence of writing but the intention is that the relevant party will ultimately receive the legal title to the property so that the effective date will be substantial performance. But because this is potentially an open-ended arrangement, the final consideration will not be known and it is unlikely that, as the current owner remains in occupation of the premises, there will be taking of possession. (These issues are considered in detail elsewhere in this chapter.)

Finally, it seems that HMRC Stamp Taxes requires the costs to be determined upon the basis that they include VAT regardless of whether the taxpayer is able to recover all or any part of his input tax or would be so entitled if actual costs were incurred. There appears to be some statutory justification for this view since the charge is upon the price (i.e. total consideration) which would have to be paid on the open market.

4.11 THEORY AND PRACTICE

In basic fiscal valuation theory the open market concept requires a hypothetical transaction, largely because there is no actual transaction merely a deemed sale so that there is no real actual background. This means that much of the early negotiation with HMRC valuers involves debate as to the terms of the hypothetical sale or deemed transaction. In strict theory, these principles of the hypothetical sale or lease apply for the purposes of SDLT, but there will be an actual transaction which triggers the need for the valuation. This question of whether to look to a hypothetical or an actual transaction has produced a certain degree of confusion at HMRC Stamp Taxes as to how far the facts override the normal principles of hypothetical transactions involving different terms and conditions. Notwithstanding the basic valuation principles that, in general, actual dealings even more or less contemporaneous are of little assistance because such dealings might not be on truly 'open market' terms and conditions.

However, there is a tendency but not a consistent policy of taking into account the details of the actual transaction and, whilst in general valuation theory any contemporaneous sales are to be ignored because the actual terms may differ from the terms of a hypothetical sale, HMRC Stamp Taxes itself tends to look to the actual transaction and the prices and terms of sale adopted by the parties, and does not seek to substitute different terms and conditions even where these might in theory produce a higher price on the open market when dealing with a different buyer or tenant, which leaves open problems for them in relation to the existence of a possible special purchaser such as the owner of adjoining land or of the dominant land in relation to a restrictive covenant or easement. On the open market, such a sale might involve different terms and a possibly higher price.[47] This reliance upon the facts rather than hypotheticals is most noticeable in the area of 'costs' for works and services where the provisions for dealing with the deferred payment of tax (Stamp Duty Land Tax (Administration) Regulations 2003, SI 2003/2837, Part 4) are clearly grounded upon the basis of actual costs incurred by the taxpayer rather than the hypothetical market cost as provided for by the legislation (FA 2003, Sched. 4, para. 11).

This apparent official approach of relying upon the actual situation, whilst it may lead to a cumbersome and expensive compliance procedure with the need to file numerous returns on a provisional basis over time, avoids the even more complex and expensive arguments on valuation principles. The risk is that the taxpayer, having prepared his land transaction return on this basis, is faced with the transaction being sufficiently large for it to be referred by HMRC Stamp Taxes to HMRC's valuers who apply more traditional valuation principles. This, in theory, exposes the taxpayer to the argument that his original return was prepared negligently because he or his advisers did not apply the 'correct' valuation principles (see also *Langham* v. *Veltema* [2004]

---

47 There are difficulties in seeking to persuade HMRC valuers that such a person can be ignored even where he has declined to purchase the property, because, in their view, on a later sale he or a successor in title might take a different view so that the hypothetical purchaser might pay a higher price because of this possibility of a special purchaser on a subsequent sale.

STC 544) with the consequent risks of penalties for an incorrect return (see Chapter 14).

4.12 PARTICULAR ITEMS OF CONSIDERATION

Value Added Tax

It is provided that chargeable consideration includes any VAT which is actually payable as at the effective date, including VAT upon future instalments,[48] including variable consideration, and in effect, future rent. The fact that the purchaser or tenant or other person paying the VAT may be able to recover the input tax in whole or in part is not a relevant factor.[49]

However, where the transaction is exempt from VAT as at the effective date, the fact that the option to tax is available is ignored (FA 2003, Sched. 8, para. 2). In consequence:

- the fact that the transaction or subsequent payments could become taxable by reason of the exercise of the option to tax is ignored; and
- the actual exercise of the option to tax after the effective date is ignored even though this may affect the level of subsequent payments. The two-stage taxation of substantial performance of leases and the grant thereof (FA 2003, Sched. 17A, para. 12A; see Chapter 8) raises a particular difficulty where the option to tax is exercised between the substantial performance of the agreement for lease and the subsequent grant of the lease. The view of HMRC Stamp Taxes is that the taxable rent at the time of the grant includes the actual VAT notwithstanding that this possibly was required to be ignored at the time of the substantial performance of the agreement for lease.

Three other significant practical issues arise in relation to VAT, namely:

(1) Transfers of going concerns

It is usual to provide in the contract, in order to protect the vendor, that although the parties believe that the transaction is a transfer of a going

---

48 However, it seems that the fact that the rate of VAT may vary in the future does not make the consideration 'uncertain' for the purposes of FA 2003, s.51 because changes after the effective date are to be ignored but official confirmation from HMRC Stamp Taxes is awaited and this is its view. There are, however, possible complications where there is a lapse of time between the agreement for lease and the actual grant; see Chapter 8. Cf. *Glenrothes Corporation* v. *IRC* [1993] STC 74.

49 HMRC Stamp Taxes takes the same line of ignoring the actual or potential input tax credit when determining 'costs' such as for the purpose of FA 2003, Sched. 4, paras. 10 and 11. Since the cost is the price, i.e. the consideration payable pursuant to the contract the VAT content is, in its view, fully taxable.

concern should this not be the case the vendor will deliver a tax invoice and the purchaser will pay the VAT.[50] The problem is how such provision should be dealt with in relation to SDLT. It is currently the view of HMRC Stamp Taxes that this possible non-availability of the treatment as a transfer of a going concern means that because the VAT position is unresolved this produces 'unascertained consideration' (i.e. all of the information necessary for deciding whether the VAT is or is not payable exists on that date and the liability cannot be affected by subsequent events). In consequence, the taxpayer has to decide as at the effective date whether the tax is or might be payable (FA 2003, ss.51, 80 and 90).[51] He must then make a return of either the net or the tax inclusive amount. Should he take the view[52] that the tax may be payable he must calculate and pay the tax upon the gross amount including the VAT. It is not possible to defer the SDLT upon unascertained consideration. Should the taxpayer take the view that the VAT will not be payable the tax is calculated and payable by reference to the net price. Whichever view is taken, the SDLT position remains open until the VAT position is resolved with HMRC or cannot be challenged because the time limit for such challenges has expired. If fully paid and the taxpayer can achieve the difficult task of satisfying HMRC Stamp Taxes that VAT cannot be claimed by HMRC[53] the tax overpaid can be reclaimed;[54] but if it has not been fully paid because the taxpayer formed the view that the VAT would not be payable and the risk of payment was not included in the initial self-

---

50 There may also be issues as to whether the purchaser should indemnify the vendor against misdeclaration and other penalties and interest where the treatment is not available because of actions of the purchaser. It is considered that because the liability to pay arises by reason of breach of contract, if suitably drafted, the compensation is not part of the consideration and so does not have to be added to the chargeable consideration for the purposes of SDLT; cf. *Western United Investments Ltd* v. *IRC* [1951] Ch 392.

51 Since the parties have made provision in the contract for the possible payment of the VAT, it will be less than convincing for them to contend that they did not believe it might be payable when attacked for the numerous penalties for negligent or otherwise improper returns.

52 This view will need to be based upon appropriate advice if the taxpayer wishes to avoid the long-term uncertainty arising from the fact that he has submitted a 'negligent return', i.e. one not prepared on a proper basis. Hopefully, the basic three-year limitation period applicable for VAT will help to produce a reasonable degree of 'finality'.

53 Which is an area where HMRC Stamp Taxes has indicated, in practice, it will not be easy to persuade because of the uncertainties as to 'finality' in relation to VAT and its general position is that because this is an error or mistake by the taxpayer the overpayment cannot be recovered after three years from the effective date pursuant to FA 2003, Sched. 10, para. 34.

54 In practice HMRC Stamp Taxes is suggesting that the tax will not be repaid because the VAT position can never be closed, particularly since there may be appeals to Europe. This view is not sustainable.

assessment, the SDLT will be payable with interest with effect from 30 days after the effective date and it is probable that HMRC Stamp Taxes will seek penalties for an incorrect return.

It is generally considered that this analysis that the potential VAT is 'unascertained' rather than 'contingent' which formed the basis for the incorrect practice in stamp duty,[55] is incorrect because, for example, it is a condition for the treatment as a transfer of a going concern that the purchaser continues to carry on the same business as the transferor.[56] In consequence, not all of the conditions will be necessarily satisfied as at the effective date. Moreover, the effective date for SDLT and the tax point for VAT will rarely be the same.[57] Additionally, the contract usually requires that a payment of the VAT is conditional upon the delivery of a tax invoice. The general view is that the VAT is a contingent sum which has to be declared in the chargeable consideration, but the tax on the VAT element can usually be deferred until the position is resolved. At that time the SDLT becomes payable but without interest or penalty; but to avoid interest and penalty charges the VAT must be declared on the initial return and a deferment of payment of the related SDLT must be sought.

(2) VAT and rent

There is an issue whether actual VAT payable at the relevant effective date in respect of rent which is separately reserved as additional rent is taxable as rent or as a premium payable by instalments (pursuant to FA 2003, s.52). Current official practice[58] suggests that it is to be treated as 'rent' (see further Chapter 8), notwithstanding that it is reserved as a separate sum apparently upon the basis that 'consideration' including rent for the purposes of VAT

---

55 The revised Statement of Practice dealing with the interaction of stamp duty and VAT (SP11/91) proceeded upon the basis of unascertained consideration which justified a limited wait-and-see approach. However, the argument of the counsel for the Inland Revenue Stamp Taxes Office, which was not challenged by counsel for the taxpayer in *Prudential Assurance* v. *IRC* [1992] STC 863, was to the effect that the potential VAT was a *prima facie* sum within the contingency principle. It seems that, in practice, the Stamp Taxes Office preferred the former view notwithstanding the way in which it presented its case to the court and that the dubious view has been carried over in practice into the new tax.
56 Although there is some debate as to whether this condition is consistent with the VAT directives and may be void.
57 See the problems of VAT charges in, e.g. *Higher Education Statistics* v. *Customs and Excise* [2000] STC 332.
58 It must, however, be noted that in SP 11/91 there is a statement that VAT would not necessarily be part of the rent but would be taxed as a premium payable by instalments. This point was rarely taken in practice for stamp duty but the same risk applies to SDLT.

includes the total amount payable including the VAT (Value Added Tax Act 1994, s.19).

(3) VAT and costs

Certain consideration is taxable by reference to its market value, i.e. the price which would be paid for a sale on the open market or its open market cost (FA 2003, Sched. 4, paras. 10 and 11; Stamp Duty Land Tax (Administration) Regulations 2003, SI 2003/2837, Part 4). It appears to be the view of HMRC Stamp Taxes that the market value or market cost includes any VAT that might be payable upon the hypothetical sale, but this view ignores many issues such as the possibility of transfers of going concerns and recovery of input tax. There will be a need for preliminary negotiations as to whether the market price is the tax inclusive figure or the price net of VAT which has to be paid over to HMRC. The official view seems to be that since the VAT is part of the consideration (Value Added Tax Act 1994, s.19; see also *Glenrothes Corporation* v. *IRC* [1993] STC 74) the vendor does not account for the VAT as such, but simply includes it in his overall quarterly return, the price or cost is the tax inclusive figure. It will be necessary to press for treatment as a hypothetical transfer as a going concern or recoverable input tax if such treatments are available on the hypothetical facts. It is therefore open to challenge (see Chapter 14). The converse situation can arise, namely, where the taxpayer is assessed upon the open market cost whether 'cost' if determined upon a hypothetical basis should include VAT and, if so, whether the taxpayer's potential for recovering all or part of such VAT as a deductible input tax should be taken into account. It is considered that 'cost' is linked to cost less any recoverable input tax rather than the gross sum paid,[59] but the legislation does contain some assistance for the contrary view of HMRC Stamp Taxes because it refers to the 'price', i.e. tax inclusive consideration. There is considerable potential for a long debate over the meanings of 'price', 'cost' and 'value' in these contexts.

Postponed consideration and instalments – basic rules

The parties will frequently enter into a transaction where payment of all or part of the consideration or premium is postponed or payable by instalments,

---

59 However, the position is uncertain since the taxpayer's effective 'cost' may be lessened by other tax reliefs such as capital allowances. This could form the basis of an argument by HMRC Stamp Taxes that incidental tax reliefs or credits have to be ignored when determining the cost of a transaction. Moreover, the VAT rules as to capital goods schemes mean that the recovery may extend over a 10-year period in many cases providing a long-term continuous reporting and payment obligation (Value Added Tax (General) Regulations 1995, SI 1995/2518, Part XV).

possibly even secured by a charge on the property. This may either be because the postponed consideration is simply payable by instalments or because it is some form of overage or clawback arrangement. The distinction between these two broad categories of deferred payment is crucial because totally different rules apply (FA 2003, s.51 and Sched. 4, para. 3), and both of these differ fundamentally from the rules applicable[60] to 'periodical payments' (FA 2003, s.52; *Blendett* v. *IRC* [1984] STC 95) including certain types of premium for leases. Where the consideration is simply a delayed cash payment such as where there is a deferred or phased completion, or even a deposit on contract with the balance payable at some future date, or the vendor agrees to leave the consideration outstanding possibly secured by a charge upon the property the chargeable consideration is the full amount of the purchase price and there is no discount for the postponed payment notwithstanding there may not be any interest running in the intervening period (FA 2003, Sched. 4, para. 3). There is no right of the taxpayer to apply to postpone the payment of tax notwithstanding that the transaction takes place by instalments. Since there is no right to apply to defer the payment of SDLT for instalment payments it does not appear to make any difference whether there is simply a deferred payment arrangement or the issue of loan notes for the payment of any consideration provided at completion; both are taxable immediately upon the amount ultimately payable.[61] This is because, unlike most other forms of tax, stamp taxes fall upon the purchaser and not upon the vendor.[62] Additionally, the compliance requirements of the various categories of deferred payment will differ depending upon the characteristics of the payment in that the payment and compliance liabilities may pass to any person who acquires the relevant chargeable interest in the land (see Chapter 1 above on title investigation and due diligence).

Periodical payments and annuities other than rent[63]

Where the consideration, including any premium or payment treated as a premium, for a lease is not simply a payment delayed or by instalments, but

---

60 For example, see the issue of VAT and rent above.
61 There will be different issues where the loan notes may have a market value different from their face value because of the interest rate or absence thereof, or because the notes are convertible into shares of the company acquiring the chargeable interest.
62 The fact that the consideration is payable by instalments may be relevant in deciding whether the contract has been substantially performed, see Chapter 3. The drafting may be important in deciding whether payment has been made with a loan back or is an unpaid consideration; *Coren* v. *Keighley* [1972] 1 WLR 1556, a key issue for substantial performance.
63 FA 2003, **s.**52(6); see Chapter 8 on the possible treatment of VAT payable in relation to rent.

is an annuity or periodical payment payable either for life, in perpetuity, for an indefinite period, or for a definite term exceeding 12 years (FA 2003, s.52(1)), the chargeable consideration is limited to the aggregate of 12 years annual payments (FA 2003, s.52(2)). Although not specifically stated, it would appear that where there is an annuity or periodical payment payable for a fixed term not exceeding 12 years the chargeable consideration is the aggregate amount of the annuity or periodical payment.

'Periodical payments' or 'instalments'

This difference between the computation rules for deferred or instalment consideration and periodical payments is clearly important and there may be a significant difference in tax liability between a fixed sum payable by instalments and a series of annual payments for a similar amount, particularly if the payment period exceeded 12 years when the difference might become important. It seems that this may ultimately be a matter of drafting. For example:

- a consideration of £20,000,000 payable by 20 annual instalments if treated as a deferred consideration would be subject to SDLT upon £20,000,000; but
- a consideration consisting of £1,000,000 payable annually for 20 years would, it seems, be taxable upon a consideration of 12 years namely £12,000,000.

However, even when drafted in this way there is still the question of whether there is a periodical payment. In relation to the equivalent stamp duty provisions (Stamp Act 1891, s.56), it was held that where there was a 'distorted' payment arrangement this was not a true periodical payment because it lacked periodicity or regularity of payment (*Quietlece Ltd* v. *IRC* [1984] STC 95). Thus a payment of £1 per annum for 12 years and a payment of £1,000,000 in year 13 would not be treated as a periodical payment.

In relation to stamp duty, an arrangement for periodical payments which contained the provision for payment of the balance forthwith upon default in any instalment was held not to affect the position since the payment of 'compensation' or damages for breach was not an item that could be included in the computation of stamp duty (*Western United Investment Co* v. *IRC* [1951] Ch 392). It remains to be seen whether a similar arrangement would be equally effective for the purposes of stamp duty land tax.

Variable annuities or periodical payment

(a) INDEX-LINKED PAYMENTS

The fact that the annuity or periodical payment is adjustable in line with the Retail Price Index is ignored, although linking to any other form of index such as stock exchange indices or a modified Retail Price Index will bring the uncertain consideration rules into play. HMRC Stamp Taxes also appears to take the view that where the payment is to increase by, say, the greater of 50 per cent of the Retail Price Index increases or 5 per cent or there is a ratchet effect, in that the payment can only increase and will not be reduced if the index falls, it is not within this relief and the payment will be a variable payment (see following paragraph).

(b) OTHER VARIABLE ANNUAL PAYMENTS

Where the annual amount varies otherwise than purely by reference to 100 per cent of the change in the Retail Price Index then the consideration has to be paid upon the basis of a reasonable estimate of the amount expected to be paid over the 12-year period (FA 2003, s.51). There is, however, a particular quirk in that where the amount payable varies, or may vary, the 12 years taken into account are the 12 highest annual payments. No guidance is provided as to how to determine the estimated 12 highest payments where consideration is 'uncertain' and the payment period extends beyond 12 years; presumably the parties have to make their reasonable estimate of the 12 highest amounts expected during the lifetime of the annuity (FA 2003, s.52(4)) but the right to apply to defer payment does not apply. However, in this case although the initial return is prepared upon the basis of estimates there is no further obligation to revise the SDLT where the actual outcome differs from the original estimates.[64] This is a two-edged weapon in that there is no right for the taxpayer to recover tax should the original estimate prove to be excessive.

Debts, liabilities and mortgages

Dealings involving debts and liabilities as consideration can take many forms, for example:

- the consideration may be left outstanding as an unpaid debt. *Prima facie* the taxable amount is the face value of the indebtedness without any discount for the delay in payment (FA 2003, Sched. 4, para. 3). However, where there is the issue of a debenture or loan note it seems that the chargeable amount will be the market value of the debenture which may include a discount or premium, depending upon the interest rate;
- the vendor may be indebted to the purchaser and the chargeable interest or lease premium may be treated as being the satisfaction, whether full or

---

64 A significant discrepancy may be regarded as negligence or fraud.

UNDERSTANDING SDLT

partial, of the debt, such as may occur on foreclosure. The chargeable amount is the amount of the debt outstanding and any accrued unpaid interest or the market value of the property whichever is the lower unless the connected company charge applies;[65]
- the acquisition of the land may be part of the purchase of a business including liabilities; the chargeable amount will be the properly apportioned part of the liabilities and other consideration;
- the property may be subject to a charge or mortgage, including a mortgage to provide security for a debt, i.e. a form of contingent liability. The chargeable consideration is the actual consideration plus the mortgage liability (i.e. the amount of principal and accrued interest outstanding at the effective date) or the market value of the property if lower than the mortgage liability. This charge applies notwithstanding that mortgages are not chargeable interests.

Before the charge arises there must be an assumption of liability so that if property is transferred subject to a mortgage the transferee will not have to pay tax upon the mortgage if he does not give a personal covenant to pay, notwithstanding that he may acknowledge that the property is subject to the charge.[66] A charge arises if in connection with the transfer the rights and liabilities in relation to the mortgage are varied; this is deemed to be an assumption of liability (FA 2003, Sched. 4, para. 8 (as amended)).

A routine problem for practitioners will be when there is an assumption of liabilities such as occurs in many domestic situations. Also, it is unlikely that the parties will have sought professional advice at the inception of the transaction and the details emerge years later when there are obligations of the professional adviser to comply with the money laundering legislation and the professional adviser may face penalties for assisting in the preparation of incorrect land transaction returns (FA 2003, ss.95 and 96). For example, parents and child may jointly acquire property but on the understanding that the child will discharge the mortgage and the property will belong to him. There are difficult issues of analysis in this relationship, which will depend upon the facts of each case including whether this is an agreement to transfer the property in consideration of the child discharging the joint and several liability for the mortgage debt which at some stage becomes a chargeable

---

65 There is, however, a long-standing debate with HMRC Stamp Taxes as to whether the market value is the value of the property, subject to the mortgage, i.e. the equity of redemption. This was initially accepted by it in relation to, e.g. Finance Act 1965, s.90 but this position was later changed. The point is open for argument since the market value charge may override the charge upon the assumption of the mortgage.
66 This appears to be the basis for the HMRC Stamp Taxes's view that transfer of property to a surviving spouse designed to exploit the nil rate band of inheritance tax is not taxable if this route is adopted, although other variations upon the theme are, in its view, taxable.

transaction.[67] As constructive trusts are involved the absence of writing is irrelevant.[68]

In relation to the satisfaction of debts or assuming liabilities other than dealing with charges, the chargeable amount is the amount of the debt satisfied, released or assumed plus any accrued unpaid interest as at the effective date (FA 2003, Sched. 4, para. 3(c)). Where this is not the whole of the consideration the amount of such debt or liability satisfied or assumed is added to the other consideration (FA 2003, Sched. 4, para. 8(1)). This relates only to pre-existing liabilities of the vendor, or possibly persons connected with him, prior to the transaction; it does not apply to any debts of the purchaser as consideration for the acquisition such as unpaid or deferred consideration which is governed by the principles for deferred consideration or instalments considered above. However, if the amount of chargeable consideration would, as a result of the treatment of debts and liabilities, exceed the market value of the subject-matter of the transaction the chargeable consideration is limited to the market value (FA 2003, Sched. 4, para. 8(2)). For these purposes 'debt' means an obligation, whether certain or contingent, to pay a sum of money either immediately or at a future date. It will therefore include items such as guarantees of other persons' debts charged upon the property when the guarantee represents a contingent liability to pay the full amount of the underlying debt such as a charge upon the family home to secure borrowings of the family company (FA 2003, Sched. 4, para. 3(a)).

It is not possible to assign a liability so that the assumption of liabilities frequently takes the form of an agreement to give an indemnity in respect of outstanding debts and liabilities of the vendor, and such indemnity is, *prima facie*, taxable.[69] In this context, where a purchaser agrees to indemnify the vendor in respect of liability to a third party arising from breach of an obligation owed by the vendor in relation to the land that is the subject-matter of the transaction, neither the agreement to indemnify nor any payment made in pursuance of the indemnity counts as chargeable consideration (FA 2003, Sched. 4, para. 16). In some cases the parties seek to deal with this situation by backdating the effect of the agreement and deeming all transactions in the intervening period to have been entered into by the vendor as agent for the

---

67 Probably at the very beginning when the child moves into the house, unless the parents are in occupation when any licence to the child may not constitute possession.
68 See below on the alternative risk that this is an agreement to transfer in consideration of services taxable, at some stage, on the open market cost of such services.
69 It is considered that the assumption that a liability that is inherent in the property such as future rent reserved by a lease is not chargeable consideration for the purposes of these provisions (cf. *Swayne* v. *IRC* [1900] 1 QB 172; *Halsall* v. *Brizell* [1957] Ch 169 to the broad effect that he who takes the benefit must also take the burden); but the fact that the draftsman regarded it as necessary to introduce specific relieving provisions indicates that he clearly regarded this other provision as overriding these basic general principles.

purchaser.[70] Since the parties cannot rewrite history this is merely a mechanism for adjusting the consideration and can have adverse consequences for, *inter alia*, stamp taxes (*Metal Box Ltd* v. *IRC* [1969] 1 WLR 1620).

Special situations and reliefs

The above general rules are modified in certain cases:

1. Where property subject to a charge is transferred out of a single name into joint names or out of joint names into the name of one of the owners, only a part of the mortgage is brought into charge. This is the proportion of the property to which the incoming party becomes entitled or to which the outgoing party was entitled and, where appropriate, the lower rates of tax apply.
2. Where as part of the administration of an estate, property subject to a charge is apportioned to a legatee in full or partial satisfaction of a legacy the assumption of liability in respect of the mortgage is ignored. The same applies where the assumption of the liability is part of a variation of the estate of a deceased individual within two years of his death (FA 2003, Sched. 4, para. 8A; Sched. 3, paras. 3A and 4).
3. Where the purchaser agrees to indemnify the vendor in respect of liability to one-third arising from breach of an obligation owed by the vendor in relation to the land that is the subject of the transaction, neither the agreement nor any payment made in pursuance of it counts as chargeable consideration (FA 2003, Sched. 4, para. 16). This is potentially helpful in practice in relation to the type of indemnity required, probably unnecessarily, by vendors where there is a 's.106 development agreement' with the local authority relating to planning consents. For example, a developer may enter into a conditional agreement to acquire land if planning permission acceptable to the parties is obtained. The conditional or optional nature of this arrangement may require the participation of the current landowner as a party to the planning agreement with the local authority and he may be advised to insist upon some form of indemnity in relation to possible failures to comply with the planning agreement although he will not be the person in default. The required undertaking to indemnify the seller against such default will *prima facie* be part of the chargeable consideration for the acquisition of the chargeable interest unless this provision for the exclusion of the indemnity from the amount of the chargeable consideration applies. However, the point is far from obvious since this indemnity will not be

---

70 This is different from arrangements where the parties seek to backdate the execution of documentation or the date when the arrangement was performed which is, *prima facie*, fraud and forgery; see, e.g. *Saywell* v. *Pope* [1979] STC 824.

in respect of any breach taking place before the assignment or conveyance of the land. It represents an undertaking by the purchaser to make a payment in respect of his breach after he becomes the effective owner of the property and, in effect, the beneficiary of the planning permission. Such an arrangement may not be regarded as falling within the exemption. In consequence, it will become a highly technical debate with HMRC Stamp Taxes as to whether the utilisation of the terminology of the indemnity can convert what is essentially a payment of damages into chargeable consideration. The difficulty in the way of such an argument is that the draftsman clearly regarded an agreement to indemnify against future liabilities as chargeable consideration otherwise he would not have made undertakings to pay future rents reserved by a lease exempt from that which he regarded as a chargeable consideration (FA 2003, Sched. 17A, para. 10). If chargeable, the form of the 'indemnity' may be important, since it would appear that, upon basic principles, the payment of damages, even liquidated damages, is not part of a consideration of the transaction (*Western United Investments v. IRC* [1951] Ch 392). A payment for breach is not the same as performance of the obligation; it is expected that, although its position is technically somewhat weak, HMRC Stamp Taxes will seek to develop this argument. Prudence suggests that, for the time being pending clarification of the point in practice, striving for the strongest position to resist the claim by suitable drafting is appropriate.

4. Where there is an assignment of a lease the usual covenants by the assignee to pay the rent and to observe the covenants in the lease are not taxable (FA 2003, Sched. 17A, para. 17).

Foreign currency

Where the consideration for the transaction consists wholly or partly of non-sterling currency the tax is charged upon the sterling equivalent which is calculated by reference to the London closing exchange rate on the effective date of the transaction unless the parties have used a different rate for the purposes of the transaction (FA 2003, Sched. 4, para. 9).

Carrying out works

Where the carrying out of works, including building or construction operations, is part of the chargeable consideration and is not merely a condition of the transaction (see *Eastham v. Leigh, London and Provincial Properties Limited* [1971] 2 All ER 887) then the chargeable consideration includes the value of the works (FA 2003, Sched. 4, para. 10). The chargeable amount of the works is the amount that would have to be paid on the open market for the carrying out of the works in question (FA 2003, Sched. 4, para. 10(3)(b)).

No guidance is provided as to how to determine the 'open market cost' of the services (see *Giambrone* v. *JMC Holidays (No.2)* [2004] 2 All ER 891 on some of the problems relating to cost above). These issues are considered in Chapter 9.

Services

The provision of services, other than the carrying out of building works or works of a similar nature, is expressly brought into charge and the tax is to be calculated upon the costs or the amount that would have to be paid on the open market to obtain those services.

Amongst the difficulties of these provisions are that no guidance is provided now as to what is meant by 'the provision of services' or how to determine the open market cost of services. No doubt HMRC Stamp Taxes has in mind some sort of transaction such as where a person is granted some right in or over land in return for architectural services such as designing a building or for acting as selling agent (but note the possible effect of FA 2003, s.44A), or situations such as *Yaxley* v. *Gotts* [1999] 2 WLR 127 where a builder was to be rewarded by being granted a lease of one of the flats, which would now be a taxable transaction. There is a question as to whether the giving of a guarantee by a parent company that its subsidiary company will carry out its obligations in relation to land is a 'service' that would be part of the consideration for a land transaction.[71]

Also, a key issue for practitioners is whether domestic arrangements fall within these provisions which may raise issues of intention to create legal relations. For example, an aged person may agree, probably orally,[72] with a child or other relation that if the latter should move into the property and care for the landowner the property will pass to the latter on the death of the former. It is understood that HMRC Stamp Taxes regards this as a chargeable transaction but has failed hitherto to produce adequate guidance on how it believes the open market cost of such arrangements is to be determined in advance on a provisional basis and on the final basis when the 'services' are completed (see above).

---

71 *Curzon Offices* v. *IRC* [1944] 1 All ER 163; *Wachtel* v. *IRC* 46 TC 543. Although there may be a question as to whether the consideration is being provided directly or indirectly by the purchaser in this transaction as required by para. 1 of Sched. 4 to the FA 2003. This is, of course, unless HMRC Stamp Taxes states that the question of provision by the purchaser is limited to those situations where the consideration consists of money or money's worth within para. 1 and the restriction as to provision of the consideration directly or indirectly by the purchaser or a connected party has no relevance to any other provision for calculating the chargeable amount.
72 But legally effective as a constructive trust provided that admissible evidence can be produced of the promise, etc.

Variable consideration

Unlike stamp duty which is a once-for-all tax assessed at the time of the execution of the document with the issue of variable consideration being dealt with by the so-called contingency principle, the continued extensions of which has left many recent judicial reputations somewhat dented possibly beyond repair, SDLT seeks to deal with the problem by a form of wait-and-see with the tax being calculated initially on an estimated basis (but subject to interest and penalty risks if the estimate is incorrect) with subsequent adjustments as the uncertainties or variable elements are resolved. Regrettably for professional advisers this is merely one aspect of the fundamental provisional nature of SDLT (see Chapter 1).

It is therefore necessary initially to make an assessment and payment, including applying to defer the payment of tax where possible to avoid interest charges and penalties, and make arrangements for the obligatory revisions of this provisional assessment from time to time.

However, it is first necessary to determine into which category of variable consideration the arrangement falls since this affects not only the manner in which the initial self-assessment has to be made, but also the time of payment including the power to apply to defer payment of tax and the subsequent reporting and payment obligations.[73] Three types of variable consideration other than rent are prescribed by the legislation as outlined below.

(a) 'Contingent consideration'[74]

A contingent element is a fixed sum payable if a particular event happens or which ceases to be payable upon the happening or non-happening of a future event such as a sale of land for a fixed price with a specified additional sum if planning consent is obtained.[75] It does not apply to variable sums payable where there is not a fixed amount notwithstanding that there may be a maximum or cap.[76] Different rules apply where, for example, there is an obligation to pay 50 per cent of any resale profit with a maximum amount. A typical situation would be where the purchaser agrees to pay a basic price for

---

73 Professional advisers must bear this in mind when agreeing the terms of their retainer with the client.
74 FA 2003, ss.51, 80 and 90.
75 It is currently in dispute with HMRC Stamp Taxes whether the VAT charge, if there is not a transfer of a going concern, falls within those relatively favourable provisions.
76 FA 2003, s.80, plus the possibility of paying by instalments pursuant to FA 2003, s.91; which may affect the interest provisions for late payment: s.87(5); Stamp Duty Land Tax (Administration) Regulations 2003, SI 2003/2837, Part 4.

the land plus a further fixed sum if planning permission is obtained.[77] In such a case:

- initially, the SDLT has to be calculated and paid upon the basis that the contingent sum is payable (FA 2003, s.51); but
- although it is necessary to pay the SDLT upon any fixed or minimum amount when filing the land transaction return (SDLT 1), it is possible to apply to defer the payment of the part of the tax attributable to the contingent element in the overall sum (FA 2003, ss.80 and 91; Stamp Duty Land Tax (Administration) Regulations 2003, SI 2003/2837), subject to satisfying certain conditions such as the contingent payment may not fall due until at least six months after the effective date and obtaining the agreement of HMRC Stamp Taxes after a written submission containing the prescribed information. The importance of applying to defer is that:
  - it avoids suggestions likely to be made by HMRC Stamp Taxes that there has been fraudulent concealment of a potential tax liability if the contingent consideration is not disclosed right at the beginning of the transaction;
  - it can avoid an interest charge for late payment which normally begins to accrue shortly after the effective date rather than the date when the contingent sum falls due (FA 2003, s.91), provided that the initial estimate is not less than the amount ultimately payable; and
- this prudent treatment which is essential for the protection of the client will be initially expensive because it will require the notification to HMRC Stamp Taxes as and when the contingency cannot be satisfied so that the sum will never become payable; as well as the obligation to unwind the deferred payment situation if the contingency is satisfied and the additional sum becomes payable; but it avoids interest and penalties;[78]
- there is a refund if the contingency does not happen or the sum ceases to be payable; and any postponed tax upon the amount ceases to be payable.

---

77 A key problem area, in practice, is whether these or other related provisions apply to the potential VAT where the transaction may or may not be a 'transfer of a going concern'.

78 Fortunately, the liability to deal with the unresolved SDLT position for contingent payments does not directly pass to the purchaser except in cases of assignment of leases; but there are, for the professional advisers, practical problems of how to deal with these potential liabilities upon any assignment or sale or lease or sub-lease of land which will involve their own SDLT consequences for both the vendor and the purchaser or lessor in the current transaction, and the original landowner/lessor and purchaser/lessee in the transaction which produced the contingent liability.

COMPUTATION OF TAX

(b) 'Uncertain consideration'[79]

For these purposes the consideration, whether the purchase price or premium for the grant of a new lease,[80] is 'uncertain' if the whole or part of the amount payable depends upon future events (FA 2003, s.51(3)). A typical situation will be where there is a sale for an overage or clawback payment, where the amount payable is uncertain. These rules will apply even where there is a maximum potential amount or 'cap' on the payment. Such a sum is not 'contingent' because the amount potentially payable is variable albeit within certain fixed parameters. In these cases, the SDLT has to be paid initially upon the basis of a 'reasonable estimate' of what will ultimately be payable which will not necessarily be the maximum or cap; with an obligation to review and adjust the initial estimate in the light of later events or as any part or instalment of the variable element becomes settled and payable. This requires the taxpayer to report and pay tax (or claim a refund) as the final price or instalments become fixed and payable.[81] This will apply, for example, to the grant of a lease where the premium is a percentage of the proceeds of sale of the property in due course, or a multiple of the rent or profits in accordance with some algebraic formula, or is a sum linked to the actual square footage or net lettable area of the building to be constructed to be determined when it is finally completed.[82] Interest is payable if the initial estimate is below the final amount payable, and penalties may be imposed if the estimate is not properly prepared so that the return is 'negligent'.

(c) 'Unascertained consideration'

This is a consideration where all of the information for detemining the consideration is available but has to be processed, such as where the price is the market value on the day of completion or the premium is a multiple of the net lettable area of a building which has been completed but not measured. Tax is payable in full on the estimated total; no deferral is allowed.

---

79 FA 2003, ss.51, 80 and 90.
80 Different problems arise for assignees of leases where the variable elements of the consideration, whether premium or rent, have not been finally resolved by the original tenant at the time of the assignment.
81 FA 2003, s.80, plus the possibility of paying the tax by instalments pursuant to FA 2003, s.91; Stamp Duty Land Tax (Administration) Regulations 2003, SI 2003/2837, Part 4.
82 Such consideration may also be 'unascertained' at the time when the lease is finally granted: FA 2003, s.51.

Fortune teller tax

INITIAL CALCULATION

The initial calculation is a strange exercise even by fiscal standards since it involves a considerable element of trying to forecast the future. It is not simply a question of how much the taxpayer thinks that he may have to pay which may be nil because it is unlikely that the obligation will arise. This is because there are two components:

- how likely it is that the purchaser will have to pay further consideration; and
- upon the assumption that such a liability arises the amount which it is expected will be payable.

The taxpayer cannot take the view that it is unlikely that anything will ever be payable; he must act on the basis that if, no matter how unlikely it is, the obligation arises money will be payable and it is this sum that matters. It seems that HMRC Stamp Taxes does not regard the former as a relevant issue; it is concerned only with the latter question of the amount potentially payable. Taxpayers who rely upon the former principle and take the view that it is unlikely that there will be additional consideration run a grave compliance risk. If money does become payable they will not have declared the tax and will be liable to late payment interest as from 30 days after the effective date and possibly penalties for an incorrectly, i.e. negligently, prepared land transaction return. Their professional advisers are also exposed to a penalty of £3,000 if they have helped the taxpayer to prepare the land transaction return without explaining these issues or being aware that appropriate advice has not been obtained. If an amount is included and the tax thereon is postponed the interest runs only from 30 days after the later instalment of the consideration becomes payable (FA 2003, s.91). Parties should, therefore, include a generous estimate of the total consideration in Box 10, SDLT 1 and show the full amount of tax payable upon that sum in Box 14, but the figure in Box 15 will be only the tax upon the actual initial consideration and complete SDLT 4. An application should be made to defer the payment.

A severe practical difficulty exists in relation to preparing the initial 'reasonable' estimate of future payments,[83] particularly when the payment is linked to an event many years in the future such as a percentage of the increase on the market value if planning permission is obtained at any time in the 80 years following completion. It will also be noted that these wait-and-see rules are based upon estimates of future values and planning permission or future rents. Professional advisers are rightly refusing to make such predictions and the HMRC Stamp Taxes helpline is giving out the risky

---

83 These problems also apply to the need to predict future movements in the rent reserved by leases.

advice to use the current values or rents and ignore the variable element. Such advice cannot be relied upon and leaves the taxpayer exposed to penalties and interest for a negligent return because he has not taken proper steps to produce a reasonable estimate, i.e. notwithstanding the helpline advice, the taxpayer *prima facie* has not sought independent professional advice and thus will be penalised. As Russell LJ stated (*Crane Fruehauf* v. *IRC* [1975] STC 51) in relation to estimating the market value of shares yet to be issued, 'the parties must do the best they can'; scarcely a scientific or reasonable basis for a tax system with a harsh compliance regime. A crude but hopefully acceptable approach for HMRC Stamp Taxes is to take reasonable evidence of the impact of the planning permission for the relevant event at current values and to project this figure into the future at an inflation indexed amount plus, say, 5 per cent. This ignores the existing problems of the planning permission being unobtainable and the possibility of resale but these have to be ignored in making the self-assessment of the tax.

SUBSEQUENT NOTIFICATIONS

This initial calculation is unfortunately only the first step in a long, tedious and expensive process. As and when all or any part or instalment of the variable consideration is ascertained and falls due for payment, the purchaser must submit a new land transaction return and pay the postponed tax relevant to the amount involved (FA 2003, s.80). If the amount exceeds the estimated figures for which the tax was postponed that excess will be taxable together with interest running from 30 days after the effective date. This process and the number of returns required will depend upon the drafting and machinery contained in the contract for the payment of these amounts. Professional advisers will need to take these issues into consideration when negotiating the arrangements, particularly as this can have a significant effect upon the client's cash flow and costs. For example, in relation to a residential development involving the construction of numerous houses or blocks of flats, if the overage takes the form of a single payment when the final proceeds or profit of the development are agreed, then only one additional land transaction return will be required at the end of the project. However, if the overage takes the form of a payment equal to a specified percentage of the sale proceeds of each house in excess of a target figure, then when each house is sold or each flat let and an instalment of the additional or overage consideration can be calculated and becomes due and payable the developer will be required to make a fresh return, recalculate the tax and file and pay accordingly (FA 2003, s.80),[84] i.e. there will be a land transaction return for

---

84 There are at present no proposals for periodical block returns from developers faced with multiple reporting and payment obligations.

each house from the seller dealing with his outstanding liability for the original purchase of the land, in addition to the routine required from the purchase of the house or flat.

It will be noted that the taxation position may remain open for many years, particularly given the current tendency to seek clawback arrangements over an 80-year period, i.e. there may be an arrangement whereby if certain events occur in relation to the land in question during a period of up to 80 years from the specified date, regardless of whether the chargeable interest is within the ownership or control of the 'purchaser' in the original transaction, additional consideration equal to a specified percentage of the proceeds or 'profits' of the transaction or of the increase in the value of the land (which is hopefully defined by the agreement) will be payable by the original 'purchaser' or lessee to the original vendor. This type of arrangement which it seems the courts, without any real understanding of the practical issues especially the tax and commercial consequence involved, have held that the vendor's advisers must use reasonable endeavours to obtain (*Akasuc Enterprises* v. *Farmar* [2003] PLSCS 127), presents serious practical problems over and above the SDLT issues. There is, in consequence, for the purchaser or lessee as party to the original transaction an open tax position which may continue for up to 80 years plus any extensions available to HMRC Stamp Taxes to issue assessments, etc. for a further 21 years. This means that a liquidator of a company[85] or the personal representative of a deceased may not be able to close the liquidation or administration of the estate because the overage or other provisional tax arrangements are unresolved as matters of contract, so that since the contractual payment cannot be determined the tax position cannot be closed.

The practical consequences of this provisional assessment include:

1. Apart from the special provisions passing certain of the outstanding obligations relating to lease premiums and rent (but not variable payments relating to earlier assignments of the lease), the outstanding tax position remains with the original purchaser unless renegotiated at the time of the sale. Regrettably, attempts to deal with the situation are being met with nervousness or obtuseness by the original vendor's advisers who are afraid that the original valuations may be challenged or negligent and, more in an attempt to cover themselves rather than protect the client,[86] may insist that any such reasonable attempt to deal with the situation

---

[85] On the need for suitable warranties when purchasing shares in a company which may be affected by such a provisional SDLT situation, see Chapter 12.
[86] Professional advisers acting for the seller or landlord in such cases must also consider their position in relation to, e.g. the administration of the seller's estate. There will be an asset in the form of the chose-in-action representing the right to the deferred payment which will have to be valued for estate tax purposes and appropriated or assented in the administration of the estate with potential tax charges upon

takes the form of a novation involving the release of the original obligation and the reimposition of a similar obligation upon the third party with the start of a fresh 80-year period. This exposes the new purchaser to a charge of SDLT upon the variable or clawback amount because as part of the chargeable consideration he is assuming an uncertain liability, although it means that the original taxpayer can inform HMRC Stamp Taxes that as far as he is concerned the amount in question will not become payable and close his provisional tax position.

2. The taxpayer in many (but not all) cases will remain liable notwithstanding that he no longer owns the interest. Unless he somehow negotiates the passing of the liability to the purchaser in such a way as to cancel his own outstanding tax liability, he will require undertakings to supply information so as to be able to complete the notification and payment obligations as the deferred consideration becomes payable.

3. Where the liability for the outstanding deferred consideration and outstanding tax passes effectively to the purchaser of the interest whether pursuant to statute or otherwise such as the assignee of a lease (FA 2003, Sched. 17A, para. 11), the purchaser may need to negotiate for the delivery of the complete SDLT history of the lease so that he can deal with any possible future reporting and/or notification obligations.

4. Notwithstanding that the SDLT in respect of the vendor's outstanding tax liability relating to his acquisition does not pass with the land, there may be circumstances where subsequent purchasers need to have the SDLT history passed to them. For example, although the SDLT upon the initial grant of a lease with a variable rent will normally be resolved after the fifth year of the lease (FA 2003, Sched. 17A, paras. 7 and 8 bearing in mind the effect of a delayed 'grant'; para. 12A see Chapter 8), an assignee of the lease even after that date will need the SDLT history of the lease. In order to determine whether any subsequent increase in the rent is an abnormal increase which is measured by reference to the assumed rent and not the passing rent (FA 2003, Sched. 17A, paras. 14 and 15), the assignee will need to have details of the assumed rent, i.e. the highest 12 months' rent paid during the first five years.

Subsequent sales of the property

Where, as will often be the case,[87] the initial tax assessment is provisional only and is subject to adjustment notwithstanding that the original land

---

the beneficiary in due course. Liquidators and receivers of companies who are not advised upon how to deal with such assets will also face potential claims should they dissolve the company before assigning or otherwise dealing with such rights to payment, and the tax consequences thereof.

87 Which may also include risks of additional liability by reason of linked transaction.

transaction return has been the subject of an Enquiry and agreed by HMRC Stamp Taxes, there will be an outstanding liability for the original purchaser when he comes to deal with the land, which as a contractual or commercial matter needs to be dealt with as part of the negotiations for the sale of the property in the context of his contractual obligations to the original seller.[88] Legislative arrangements provide, *inter alia*, that where a lease is granted for a variable premium or variable rent the SDLT obligations as to payment and reporting pass to the assignee. Unfortunately, no such statutory provision exists in relation to transfers or chargeable interests subject to such variable consideration which arose otherwise than in connection with the grant of leases. For example, upon transfers of freeholds or leases purchased with such a consideration it remains essentially the liability of the initial purchaser or tenant of the land in question.[89] This means that when the initial purchaser or tenant assigns the lease or sublets the property he must consider the impact of the transaction upon the obligation itself and, if this continues notwithstanding the immediate transaction, the implications of attempts to pass on the original contractual arrangements with the original seller or landlord to the third party who will in consequence have complex SDLT of his own to resolve as 'a purchaser'. There are many ways of dealing with this issue should the sale in question not trigger the additional payment pursuant to the original contract and so terminate the original consideration provision. In such a case the original purchaser must recalculate the tax upon the basis of the actual figure and pay any additional tax falling due and claim a refund if tax has been overpaid. Usually, however, the taxpayer will have deferred the liability to pay (FA 2003, s.90; Stamp Duty Land Tax (Administration) Regulations 2003, SI 2003/2837). In such a case the postponement will cease and the appropriate amount of tax will have to be paid.

Each solution has its own set of problems requiring investigation and negotiation. Thus an indemnity from the third party will leave the taxpayer's contractual obligation unchanged and so his tax position remains unaffected. He will, however, need suitable undertakings from the third party and his successors in title to keep him informed of events over the relevant period.[90]

---

88 Attempts to attach the overage or clawback to the land as some form of restrictive covenant or other arrangement is not likely to be successful since the original vendor may not have any adjacent land of sufficient size (ransom strips are probably not adequate for these purposes) to be the dominant land benefiting from the right: FA 2003, Sched. 17A, para. 11.

89 This may cause considerable practical difficulties for personal representatives and liquidators and receivers who cannot complete their administration whilst the contractual and SDLT positions remain unresolved. Specific statutory provisions apply to the assignment of leases with such built-in liability.

90 There is no statutory power to demand such information; it is left to commercial negotiation. It is unclear at present how far HMRC Stamp Taxes expects the taxpayer to police future events.

On the other hand, a novation of the liability will bring his tax liability to an end without further payment since he will not be making any payment pursuant to the original contract.[91]

Unascertained consideration

Where the consideration is 'unascertained',[92] i.e. all of the facts relevant to the determination are available but their effect has not been agreed, the tenant must make a reasonable estimate of the amount expected to be payable. Tax must be paid upon the whole of such an estimate since there is no power to apply to postpone the payment of SDLT for such unascertained consideration (FA 2003, ss.51(4) and 90; Stamp Duty Land Tax (Administration) Regulations 2003, SI 2003/2837, Part 4). The tax position is recalculated and adjusted when the facts are 'ascertained'. For example, where a lease is granted of a completed building for a premium of £x per square foot of net lettable area[93] there must be a reasonable estimate of the expected premium, tax paid in full and adjusted when the premium is agreed. The most frequent area of difficulty, in practice, is likely to be transfers of going concerns and VAT for reasons set out above.

Reverse payments

Reverse payments, i.e. sums paid by the assignor to the assignee of a lease as an inducement for the assignee to enter into the assignment are not chargeable consideration,[94] or by a landlord as an inducement to the tenant to take the lease or by a tenant to the landlord as an incentive to accept an early surrender of the lease. These include (FA 2003, Sched. 4, para. 15) traditional types of payments moving from the assignor to the assignee in relation to the assignment of a lease such as where there are dilapidations which have to be dealt with or the current rent exceeds the market rent for equivalent premises or the terms of the lease are particularly onerous or restrictive. The need for such payments has been increased by the introduction of SDLT to deal with

---

91 Moreover, such onward movements of the property are likely to have SDLT problems even where the original contract or transfer was subject to stamp duty because, for example, it was entered into prior to 1 December 2003.
92 There is no definition but by default and elimination the explanation in the text appears to be the correct interpretation.
93 If the arrangement takes effect before the building is completed the consideration will be 'uncertain' when different rules apply.
94 This represents a bizarre view of consideration as being two items moving in the same direction where the acquirer is making a reverse payment so that the transfer and reverse payment although made by the same person can be consideration for each other. The implications of this novel theory have yet to be revealed by HMRC Stamp Taxes.

cases such as the assignment of leases where these are to be taxed as if they were the grant of a new lease (FA 2003, Sched. 17A, para. 11) so that, naturally, the assignee's advisers will require a contribution towards the additional cost of acquiring the lease as compared with adjacent premises,[95] or because there are significant long-term difficulties of SDLT associated with variable rents and the assignee requires some protection against the problems arising because of the terms of the lease when granted. These difficulties include overage and clawback provisions. Failure to deal with such issues upon the assignment and to take account of the many other taxation problems which may affect the assignee will expose the advisers to justifiable claims for breach of professional duty.

---

95 In these cases the lease may have a negative value, an important point when valuing assets or the shares in companies holding such leases.

CHAPTER 5

Exemptions and reliefs

5.1 EXEMPTIONS

It is the view of HMRC generally, not just the Stamp Taxes Office, that exemptions from tax of a general nature are a 'bad thing'.[1] Not only are they, in the official view, a springboard for wholesale mitigation of tax, merely claiming the benefit of a relief in accordance with the legislation is itself tax avoidance, and borders on fraudulent evasion. For example, during the so-called consultation process prior to the introduction of SDLT a senior representative of the Inland Revenue described the 200-year-old sub-sale relief in general and 'resting on contract' as a criminal offence moving on from the comments of the then Chancellor of the Exchequer in 1986 that a necessary relief from the cascade effect of stamp taxes was an unacceptable 'loophole' for share transactions.

In consequence, any reliefs from SDLT are of a highly focused and technical nature hedged about by numerous anti-avoidance provisions providing both short- and long-term problems and serious complications for investigations of title and due diligence. In order to avoid suggestions of fraud or failure to report 'tax avoidance schemes' in routine commercial transactions for which the relief was intended, it will be essential to ensure so far as possible that the background to the transaction is properly and contemporaneously documented because this appears to be intended to be a fundamental area for Enquiries into the land transaction return to entrap the unwary into penalties for failing to notify 'schemes'. Also, the conditions for the relief must be scrupulously considered and observed when implementing the transaction.

This approach has produced bizarre drafting in the FA 2003 which is particularly significant, raising acute problems in relation to questions of reliefs from SDLT. Not only does the one-size-fits-all plain English drafting provide relief for a wholly new set of transactions which were not exempt

---

[1] This being increasingly developed by legislation restricting reliefs where they are part of a tax avoidance arrangement; see, e.g. FA 2003, Sched. 7 (as amended).

from stamp duty, such as leases granted as variations of estates of deceased individuals or in connection with company reconstructions (see Chapter 12), but there are a variety of ways in which a transaction is relieved in whole or in part from the charge to tax. Relief may also take the form that any actual consideration is not to be treated as chargeable consideration such as actual consideration being treated as 'nil' or 'exempt' or to be ignored or not treated as chargeable consideration.[2] Because of the strange terminology adopted, the precise nature and, in particular, the compliance consequences of the relieving provision will have to be carefully noted. For example, certain exemptions provide for relief from the notification obligation and the transaction can be submitted to the Land Registry supported by a self-certificate (SDLT 60) (largely those reliefs contained in FA 2003, Sched. 3); in other cases the transaction is notifiable even though exempt (FA 2003, s.77 (as amended)). Unfortunately, the policy is not consistent in that even in respect of those exemptions where there is a relief from notification there are exclusions giving rise to notification obligations such as disadvantaged land and PFI projects (see, e.g. FA 2003, Sched. 6, para. 13; Sched. 4, para. 17(4A) (as amended)). There is no general principle other than checking the notification obligations which are scattered randomly throughout the legislation and regulations.

This dislike of exemptions and reliefs is also reflected in the complex anti-avoidance rules applicable to the individual reliefs which, in many cases, means that, consistent with the lack of finality of the tax in general, the relief is available initially only on a provisional basis. These are not merely the conditions that have to be satisfied before the relief can be taken into account in making the initial self-assessment, they include provisions cancelling the reliefs such as a clawback if certain events happen within a prescribed time period after the effective date. They also take the form of special charges upon subsequent dealings in the chargeable interest. These provisions apply on an objective basis. The mere fact of the transaction is sufficient to trigger the tax liability; there is no subjective element requiring some tax avoidance purpose or motive and there is no need for any causal link between the exempt transactions and the anti-avoidance charge which frequently falls upon unsuspecting third parties. Even routine commercial transactions are potentially vulnerable, notwithstanding that they are not connected with the relief being clawed back. Since these anti-avoidance provisions can affect third parties, the absence of any need for tax avoidance motives and, in some

---

2 There are, in these cases, issues relating to the linked transaction rules depending upon the difference between actual consideration being ignored or treated as 'exempt', i.e. the latter has to be aggregated whereas the former does not. Notification obligations where the level of consideration is involved are also affected by the outcome of the debate on these issues.

EXEMPTIONS AND RELIEFS

cases, the absence of any time limit upon the occurrence of the offending arrangement means that a taxpayer is vulnerable to traps as is a third party dealing with the taxpayer, such as a person purchasing the shares in or the business of a company.

These problems arise because reliefs take a variety of forms, have fundamental implications for notification obligations and have already been the subject of modifications to the compliance regime. It is, therefore, necessary to determine why the transaction is 'exempt'.

'Exempt'

Moreover, the precise terminology of these various types of relief and the subtle distinctions between them and their own particular meanings is likely to provide a fertile ground for traps for the unwary. For example, the word 'exempt' has given rise to problems in relation to stamp duty over many years. On a broad view, a transaction is 'exempt' if it is not liable to the tax. This is fundamentally ambiguous,[3] i.e. it could mean that it is not taxable for a variety of reasons such as it falls altogether outside the charge to tax such as the grant of a simple licence to use or occupy land which is not a chargeable interest; or it could mean a transaction that would be a chargeable transaction but for a specific relieving provision. This means that a transaction involving land that falls outside the scope of the tax such as a licence is not 'exempt' unless HMRC Stamp Taxes takes the view that licences and mortgages would be chargeable interests but for the 'exemption' in the exclusion in the definition of 'chargeable interests'. Given the subtleties, or ineptness, of the drafting and the implications turning upon such 'plain English' terminology, this is an area where taxpayers need to tread warily and, no doubt, much cost will be incurred before the pitfalls intended by HMRC Stamp Taxes have been identified and can be dealt with in practice without the related penalties and interest.

In the particular context, it has been the view of HMRC Stamp Taxes for many years that in order to be a transaction or instrument that was 'exempt' from stamp duty or was a security exempt from all stamp duties so that it was not a chargeable security for the purposes of stamp duty reserve tax (Finance Act 1986, s.99 (as amended)), it had to be an instrument that fell within the charge to tax and was specifically taken out because of a relieving provision (but see the comments in *IRC* v. *Henry Ansbacher* [1963] AC 191). The wider view of 'exempt' not being liable because the transaction did not fall into charge at all has consistently been strenuously rejected by HMRC Stamp

---

3 This is recognised to some extent by the legislation such as FA 2003, s.76 which deals with the meaning of exemption for notification purposes, dividing it into different categories.

Taxes. It is likely that, given the multitude of relieving structures in SDLT, similar issues will arise and parties completing land transaction returns will need to bear the precise legislative terminology in mind.

Procedure – 'claiming an exemption'

It is important to note that unlike stamp duty where adjudication is frequently required in order to obtain an exemption or mitigation of a charge in respect of a particular instrument, there is no equivalent procedure for SDLT and the position has been completely revised. It is no longer a case of asking HMRC Stamp Taxes to confirm that the relief is available[4] through the adjudication process, the taxpayer has to take the decision as to whether the relief applies and take the risk of the new enhanced penalty and interest regime[5] should HMRC Stamp Taxes disagree with this view in performing its downgraded role as auditor of tax returns in the course of an Enquiry. There has been a significant outsourcing of resources, cost and risk in this area from HMRC Stamp Taxes to the professions. As the tax is based upon self-assessment (FA 2003, s.76(3)(a)), the taxpayer and his advisers must take a reasoned view of the transaction[6] and decide whether the relief is available. The taxpayer will then complete the return and take this view into account by not accounting for tax in whole or in part. No doubt details of this taking

---

4 Asking for a post-transaction ruling does not produce finality, and, if a land transaction return has been filed this automatically in practice becomes a full tardy and expensive Enquiry. Even an Enquiry is not final since a discovery assessment can be issued after an Enquiry.

5 There is a possibility of depositing a sum on account of potential tax to defer interest charges and prompt disclosure which makes it difficult for HMRC Stamp Taxes to substantiate claims of fraud and negligence, but such an approach is regarded by HMRC Stamp Taxes as a sign of weakness and encourages its intransigence in the matter making it less likely that even valid claims will succeed. The parties must submit the return upon the basis that they think the relief is available and take their chances with Enquiries and penalties for incorrect returns in due course. The important principle to bear in mind is that it is essential to have well-documented records of the steps taken to decide upon the availability of the relief. Having taken such steps, it will be more difficult for HMRC Stamp Taxes to establish that the return was negligent, although incorrect, or even fraudulent.

6 And it will be important to keep records of the debates concerning the issue of the availability of the exemption. Failure to keep such records will mean that there will not be any contemporaneous evidence either that the issues were considered or for the basis for the decision being taken, which will mean that there is a significant risk that a claim for penalties in respect of the submission of a negligent return will be made. It will be necessary to establish that such a review took place and to show that the issues were fully and properly considered. The absence of contemporaneous records will make it extremely difficult to substantiate these points.

rather than claiming of the relief will require the making of appropriate entries in the land transaction return.[7]

This need for a reasoned view of the relief imposes a new area of professional risk and a potentially significant extension of professional duties, because of the need to make the decision *ab initio* and the structure of penalties for errors has changed dramatically. The penalty for error is no longer a short delay during adjudication but a risk of penalties upon an unlimited time basis (see Chapter 1 on finality) because of the decision taken. Since the time limits and risks are related to the presence or absence of 'negligence' this will be an important concept to be analysed. A mere error in the interpretation of the legislation will not necessarily be negligent but there are many areas of potential risk. A failure to carry out a suitably rigorous investigation of the facts will raise problems. Thus the editor has been involved in a consultation where leading counsel was not only, astonishingly, to give bona fide commercial reasons for the transaction[8] but actually suggested reasons why the parties had entered into the transaction. This is clearly a high risk strategy since the proper approach is to ask for the reasons behind the transaction and then to decide whether these reasons meet the criteria for commercial justification of the transaction.

There is also a potential failure to recognise the distinctions between fact, evidence and inference. Too often taxpayers seek to make an assertion to HMRC Stamp Taxes or the court that a particular fact or situation existed but are unable to provide the essential evidence to support that assertion. These are now crucial issues in relation to questions of 'negligence' in stamp taxes and it is vital to note that in seeking to carry out the professional duties owed to clients the professional advisers also assist the clients by providing them with the correct records and advice. In this area of taking exemptions from SDLT, it will be necessary to obtain protection against allegations of 'negligence' at all levels, to show that all issues were considered and properly investigated. In broad terms, a suitably ticked checklist would appear to be essential to assist the client in seeking to restrict the period of exposure to the basic Enquiry period of nine months rather than the 21 years for discovery assessments.

---

7 Various codes exist for identifying the exemption taken or claimed but as it is not easy for the prescribed forms to be amended the modification of the scope of exemptions will require increasing utilisation of the code for other exemptions which makes it extremely easy for HMRC Stamp Taxes to make a discovery because there is no disclosure of the information behind this entry (see *Langham* v. *Veltema* [2004] STC 544).

8 Which are now important for all of the reliefs for corporate transactions in FA 2003, Sched. 7 (as amended); see Chapter 12.

5.2 TYPES OF RELIEF

Small transactions

There are nil and lower rates for transactions below certain levels of chargeable consideration including rent; and there is a slightly higher nil rate threshold for land in disadvantaged areas but the nil rate does not apply for lease premiums where the rent exceeds £600 per annum. These lower rates are subject to the linked transaction rules which make the initial self-assessments provisional only and subject to subsequent review. There is also a reduced rate of 0.5 per cent for certain corporate reorganisations known as 'acquisitions relief' (FA 2003, Sched. 7, Part 2; see Chapter 12).

Exempt property

The tax applies only where there is the acquisition of a chargeable interest (FA 2003, s.43(1)). The definition of chargeable interest provides for 'exempt interests', i.e. those interests in property which are not subject to the charge. These are:

- any security interest which means an interest or right (other than a rent charge) held for the purpose of securing the payment of money or the performance of any other obligation (FA 2003, s.48(2)(a) and (3)(a));
- a licence to use or occupy land (FA 2003, s.48(2)(b)); and
- in England and Wales or Northern Ireland a tenancy at will, an advowson, franchise or manor (FA 2003, s.48(2)(c)).

Sub-sales

Highly restricted forms of sub-sale relief are available (FA 2003, ss.45 and 45A (as amended); Sched. 17A, para. 12B). Many fundamental errors are being committed in practice because it is wrongly assumed that these reliefs are modelled upon stamp duty (Stamp Act 1891, s.58(4) and (5) (as amended)). Unfortunately, these reliefs are totally different. The relief is no longer linked to the absence of a conveyance or the grant of a lease. The relief may, with care, be available notwithstanding completion; but, more importantly, the relief is not necessarily available simply because there is no conveyance or lease. It is vitally important to appreciate that the reliefs are related to the effective date which makes understanding substantial performance and keeping a watchful eye on the conduct of the clients a key issue for practitioners.

Where A agrees to sell land to B and B sub-sells the land or assigns the contract or part thereof[9] to C, no charge to SDLT arises upon B provided

---

9 There may be difficulties in assigning part of a contract; the transaction may have to be a sub-sale or a sale of an equitable interest or by means of a declaration of trust.

that he does not complete or substantially perform his contract with A prior to the completion or substantial performance of his contract with C. The simultaneous performance of his contracts with A and with C is ignored. In consequence, that payment of the outstanding balance by C directly to A does not impose a charge upon B. In many cases there will be a transfer from A directly to C; this does not constitute a chargeable transaction for B provided that there has been no prior substantial performance by B. However, the relief is available notwithstanding that there is a conveyance to B or payment of the balance of the purchase price by B provided that there is simultaneous payment of the purchase price by C to B and a conveyance from B to C. B is not taxable and so does not have to file a land transaction return. The absence of an SDLT 5 in respect of the transfer to B is explained in a covering letter to the Land Registry informing it that B is not taxable because of sub-sale relief.

C is taxable on the balance owing by B to A plus the consideration paid by C to B. It seems that, in practice, many transactions are improperly reported. In many cases this will be because of the erroneous belief that B is not liable because he has not received a conveyance. This is a fundamental error and since it involves non-reporting of the transaction it can be expected that HMRC Stamp Taxes will seek to impose maximum penalties for failure to file a return.

The other frequent error is to treat the transaction as between A and C. There are in fact two transactions, i.e. the contracts between A and B and between B and C. Two returns may be required and the return from C has to identify B as the vendor. To insert A's name in the land transaction return will be regarded as negligence, exposing the parties to discovery assessments and penalties with consequent risks of penalties for their advisers (FA 2003, ss.95 and 96). This mismatch between the transfer from A to C and the SDLT 5 identifying B as the vendor has to be dealt with in a suitably drafted covering letter to the Land Registry.

A similar relief is available for leases granted to third parties provided that the right to the lease is assigned before the original party substantially performed the agreement. This is dealt with in Chapter 8.

Relieved transactions

The charge to SDLT may be relieved or mitigated in a variety of ways with a variety of consequences. These include:

Exempt and non-notifiable

There are situations where the transaction is 'exempt' from SDLT and there is no basic obligation to report the transaction, although specific provisions require notification for certain transactions involving non-residential land in disadvantaged areas which still apply on a transitional basis and certain PFI projects. Such transactions include:

(A) TRANSACTIONS WHERE THERE IS NO CHARGEABLE CONSIDERATION[10]

This appears to be a wide exemption and it is fundamental to the utilisation of SDLT 60 since it would appear to apply where there is actual consideration which is not 'chargeable consideration'. There are situations where there is no actual consideration unless some deemed consideration rules apply to override the relief such as connected companies or the special regime for partnerships. It also applies where there is actual consideration which is ignored such as by being treated as non-chargeable in some form or is treated as nil.

The basic relief will be in respect of gifts including dividends *in specie*. It also covers assents by personal representatives and most distributions by liquidators of companies.[11] It can now apply to gifts of property subject to a mortgage but this will remain a problem for liquidators since these will usually require some form of indemnity from the shareholders (FA 2003, Sched. 4, paras. 8 and 8A; see Chapter 4). Other exempt transactions include many of those where no beneficial interest passes such as appointments and changes of trustees,[12] and transfers to or from mortgagees.

(B) DEALINGS INVOLVING REGISTERED SOCIAL LANDLORDS

Leases granted by registered social landlords are exempt if granted to one or more individuals for an indefinite term or terminable by notice of a month or less. This is pursuant to arrangements between a registered social landlord and the housing authority under which the landlord provides for individuals, nominated by the authority in pursuance of its statutory housing functions, temporary rented accommodation which the landlord has obtained on a short-term basis, i.e. the accommodation is leased to the landlord for a term of five years or less.

The housing authority is a principal council within the meaning of the Local Government Act 1972 or the Common Council of the City of London, a council constituted under s.2 of the Local Government etc. (Scotland) Act 1994 or the Department for Social Development in Northern Ireland or the Northern Ireland Housing Executive (FA 2003, Sched. 3, para. 2).

---

10 FA 2003, Sched. 3, para. 1.
11 But it must be noted that there are charges upon transactions involving connected companies: FA 2003, ss.53 and 54.
12 But special rules apply to certain transactions involving bare trustees or nominees: FA 2003, Sched. 16, para. 3; Sched. 17A, para. 11(1)(b).

EXEMPTIONS AND RELIEFS

(C) TRANSACTIONS IN CONNECTION WITH MATRIMONIAL BREAKDOWN

A transaction between one party to a marriage and the other is exempt from SDLT if it is effected:

- in pursuance of an order of a court made on granting in respect of the parties a decree of divorce, nullity of marriage or judicial separation;
- in pursuance of an order of a court made in connection with the dissolution or annulment of the marriage or the parties' judicial separation at any time after the granting of such a decree;
- in pursuance of an order made at any time under ss.22A, 23A or 24A of the Matrimonial Causes Act 1973 or ss.8(2) and 14(1) of the Family Law (Scotland) Act 1985;
- at any time in pursuance of an agreement of the parties made in contemplation or otherwise in connection with the dissolution or annulment of the marriage, their judicial separation or the making of a separation order in respect of them (FA 2003, Sched. 3, para. 3).

This relief applies to 'transactions', i.e. all forms of acquisitions and will now include new leases.

(D) VARIATION OF ESTATES OF DECEASED PERSONS

There is exemption from SDLT in respect of a transaction following a person's death that varies any disposition, whether effected by will or intestacy or otherwise, of property of which the deceased was competent to dispose provided that:

- the transaction is carried out within a period of two years after the person's death; and
- no consideration in money or money's worth other than the making of a variation of another such disposition is given for it. If there is consideration there is a partial relief in that the chargeable consideration does not include the giving up or varying of any interests in the estate. This is to deal with the situation where the person acquiring the chargeable interest has to provide an equality payment. For example, a person may be entitled to a half share in the residue valued at £400,000 and comprising a house of £250,000 and the balance in shares. The estate may be varied for the individual to take the house but in order to achieve equality has to pay £50,000 in cash to the other legatees. The tax charge is limited to the £50,000 equality, and the lower rates of tax apply since the amount of the mortgage charged upon the property is ignored.

This relief applies whether or not the administration of the estate is complete or the property has been distributed in accordance with the original dispositions (FA 2003, Sched. 3, para. 4).

It is the view of HMRC Stamp Taxes that this relief is not available in cases where the testator was seeking to mitigate the tax upon the family home by providing for the property to pass to the surviving spouse but subject to a charge equal to the nil rate of inheritance tax at the relevant time. This applies to those variations where the surviving spouse enters into some form of undertaking to pay (i.e. produce inappropriate consideration); but it currently accepts that no charge arises where the property is subjected to a charge by the will and is transferred to the surviving spouse subject to the charge and there is no assumption of personal liability.

However, it applies to leases granted as part of the variation of the estate, but the issue of rent as 'other consideration' will introduce a taxable element into the transaction.

(E) ASSENTS AND APPROPRIATION BY PERSONAL REPRESENTATIVES

The acquisition of property in or towards satisfaction of entitlement under or in relation to the will or upon the intestacy of a deceased individual, including the grant of a lease or a release of property, is exempt provided that the person acquiring the chargeable interest does not give consideration other than the assumption of a debt, including a guarantee of a debt, charged upon the property (FA 2003, Sched. 3, para. 3A). Where there is consideration other than the assumption of a mortgage liability, the chargeable consideration does not include the mortgage debt assumed (FA 2003, Sched. 4, para. 8A(1)). This indicates that the lower rates of tax are available where the other consideration does not exceed £500,000.

Exemptions requiring notification

Right-to-buy

Schedule 9 (as amended) to the FA 2003 provides for a relief for right-to-buy, rent-to-mortgage schemes and shared ownership arrangements, including arrangements involving staircasing. The conditions are similar to those that applied for stamp duty. The arrangement must relate to a dwelling and involve a qualifying body. The lease must be for a premium and a rent and a statement of the market value or a sum calculated by reference thereto must appear in the terms. The election for the special treatment of tax upon the market value must appear in the land transaction return.

Registered social landlords

An acquisition of a chargeable interest in land is exempt from charge where the person making or deemed to make the acquisition is a registered social landlord which is controlled by its tenants and:

EXEMPTIONS AND RELIEFS

- the vendor is a qualifying body; or
- the transaction is funded with the assistance of a public subsidy.

A body is controlled by its tenants if the majority of its board of members are tenants occupying properties owned or managed by it. A board member means a director of the company; if it is a body corporate whose affairs are managed by its members, a member; a trustee; or a member of the committee of management (FA 2003, s.71(2)).

A qualifying body for the purpose of being the 'vendor' means:

- a registered social landlord;
- a housing action trust under Part III of the Housing Act 1988;
- a principal council with the Local Government Act 1972;
- the Common Council of the City of London;
- the Scottish Ministers;
- a Council established under s.2 of the Local Government etc. (Scotland) Act 1994;
- Scottish homes;
- the Department for Social Development in Northern Ireland;
- the Northern Ireland Housing Executive.

A public subsidy is a grant or other financial assistance made under:

- or given by way of distribution under the National Lottery Act 1993, s.25;
- the Housing Act 1996, s.18;
- the Housing Grants, Construction and Regeneration Act 1996, s.126;
- the Housing (Scotland) Act 1988, s.2;
- the Housing (Northern Ireland) Order 1992, SI 1992/1725, art. 33 (FA 2003, s.71(4)).

Residential property

There are a number reliefs for residential property contained in Sched. 6A to the FA 2003 for part-exchanges involving new dwelling chainbreaker companies and purchases from personal representatives. These reliefs are highly technical and subject to clawback if the slightest error on implementing the transaction occurs.

Relocation relief

There is an exemption from charge where a dwelling is acquired from an employee by his employer or by a relocation company provided that the individual occupied the dwelling as his only or main residence at some time in a period of one year ending with the date of the acquisition and the acquisition is made in connection with a change of residence resulting from a relocation of employment. The consideration for the acquisition must not exceed the market value of the dwelling and the area of the land must not exceed 0.5 hectares or such larger area as is reasonable for enjoyment with the house (FA 2003, s.59). It is interesting that this relief takes the form of 'an exemption' whereas the relief for exchanges of residential property is a reduction in the chargeable consideration.

Compulsory purchase facilitating development

A compulsory purchase facilitating development is exempt from SDLT, i.e. it is an acquisition of a chargeable interest in respect of which the person acquiring the interest has made a compulsory purchase order for the purpose of facilitating development by another person (FA 2003, s.60(2)). It does not matter how the acquisition is made, so that the relief applies where the acquisition is effected by agreement or vesting order (FA 2003, s.60(3) and (4)).

Compliance with planning obligations

There is an exemption from SDLT in respect of a transaction entered into in order to comply with a planning obligation or modification of a planning obligation provided that the planning obligation or modification is enforceable against the vendor, the person making the acquisition is a public authority and the transaction takes place within a period of five years beginning with the date on which the planning obligation was entered into or modified (FA 2003, s.61).

Transfers involving public bodies

There is an exemption from SDLT in respect of a transaction entered into on or in consequence of or in connection with a reorganisation effected by or under statutory provision involving the establishment, reform or abolition of one or more public bodies or creation, alteration or abolition of functions to be discharged by them (FA 2003, s.66).

Reorganisation of parliamentary constituencies

There is a relief where an Order in Council is made and there is a transfer of chargeable interests in land from an existing local constituency association to a new association that is its successor (FA 2003, s.67).

EXEMPTIONS AND RELIEFS

Acquisitions by bodies established for national purposes

A land transaction is exempt if the person/body making the acquisition is:

- a Historic Buildings and Monuments Commission for England;
- the National Endowment for Science, Technology and the Arts;
- Trustees of the British Museum;
- Trustees of the National Heritage Memorial Fund; or
- Trustees of the National History Museum (FA 2003, s.69).

Alternative financing for purchaser

Sale and leaseback will not normally be a method of financing the initial acquisition of a house but may form part of a fundraising exercise such as an 'equity release' arrangement or a form of disguised borrowing and provided that the conditions are satisfied the leaseback will be exempt (FA 2003, s.57A (as amended)).

Special financing does, however, qualify for a limited form of relief in one narrow area designed to cope with problems of financing, where parties are restricted by rules usually of a religious nature against usury or the taking of interest and the financing must take the form of some form of participation in the profits or gains of the property and ordinary mortgages are not appropriate. However, the anti-discrimination principles mean that the relief is available to all persons not just those who subscribe to particular religious views. Two areas of relief are available:

(A) SALE AND LEASE ARRANGEMENTS

A purchase of a major interest is exempt where it is pursuant to an arrangement between an individual[13] or a financial institution which acquired its interest under this type of transaction and a financial institution being a bank (Income and Corporation Taxes Act 1988, s.840A), a building society (Building Societies Act 1986) or a wholly owned subsidiary of either whereby the institution acquires a major interest in land or an undivided interest so that the land is held for the individual and the institution as beneficial tenants in common. The institution must grant a lease or sub-lease out of that interest to the individual, the lease or sub-lease being exempt. It is necessary for the parties to enter into an arrangement under which the individual has a right to require the transfer of the major interest purchased by the institution.

The transfer of the freehold or head leasehold interest back to the individual is exempt from charge provided that the additional acquisition of the

---

13 This relief is not available to corporate employers seeking to provide accommodation for their employees.

major interest and the lease is exempt and at all times between then and the transfer of the reversionary interest the interest purchased by the institution is held by it and the lease or sub-lease granted is held by the individual.

The requirements for relief are not satisfied if the individual (FA 2003, s.72(9))[14] enters into an arrangement or holds the lease or sub-lease as trustee and any beneficiary of the trust is not an individual or the individual enters into the arrangements and holds the lease or sub-lease as a partner and any of the other partners is not an individual (FA 2003, s.72(6)).

The reliefs are also available in Scotland and specific provisions deal with the equivalent terms and practices in that country.

(B) PURCHASE AND RE-SALE

There is an exemption for the acquisition of a major interest by a financial institution[15] pursuant to an arrangement whereby the financial institution purchases the major interest in land and sells that interest to the individual. Both the acquisition by the financial institution and the on-sale to the individual are exempt from SDLT. The individual grants the institution a legal mortgage over that interest.[16]

The relief is not available if the individual enters into the arrangement as trustee and any beneficiary of that trust is not an individual or he enters into the arrangement as partner and any of the other partners is not an individual (FA 2003, s.73(4)).

Historical hangovers

A large number of ancient stamp duty reliefs for highly specialised transactions have been discovered and been carried over into SDLT by regulations (Stamp Duty Land Tax (Consequential Amendment of Enactments) Regulations 2003, SI 2003/2867). These include certain reliefs for building societies, the NHS, Welsh Development Agency and National Heritage. However, where leases are granted within the relief, special charges may apply to the subsequent assignment of the lease (FA 2003, Sched. 17A, para. 11).

---

14 Individual includes his personal representatives.
15 Which includes his personal representatives after his death: FA 2003, s.73(6).
16 For definition of legal mortgage see FA 2003, s.73(5)(b).

CHAPTER 6

Options and rights of pre-emption

6.1 OPTIONS AND EXCHANGES

It is unclear at present how far in practice the traditional stamp duty principle, that matters ancillary to the main transaction were to be ignored, applies to SDLT. The grant of an option to a tenant to acquire the reversion to the lease was not regarded as a separate taxation event if included in the lease. Unfortunately, the draftsman of the SDLT legislation has failed to deal with this point so that many difficult issues now arise.

Where land is sold by A to B who grants A an option or pre-emption right, A is acquiring a chargeable interest in land; in consequence there is technically a land exchange. Should this point be taken, as is likely to be the case, both A and B would be potentially subject to tax and notification obligations upon the market value of the chargeable interests involved. In the official view this could have a distorting effect where the strike price for the option is not the market value of the land at the time when it is exercised, i.e. such as where the option or pre-emption right has a significant value. Much may depend, however, upon the nature of the option. Where the grant of the option and the chargeable interest move in the same direction, such as where there is the grant of a lease which includes an option to renew, the option will form part of the subject-matter of the transaction and, insofar as the tenant pays a separate consideration for the option, it will form part of the chargeable consideration for the grant of the lease. However, this would be unusual and such option would rarely, if ever, have a separate market value.

Pre-emption rights

The acquisition of a right of pre-emption preventing the person granting the right from entering into or restricting the right of the grantor to enter into a land transaction, is a land transaction distinct from any land transaction resulting from the exercise of the pre-emption right (FA 2003, s.46(1)(b)).[1] This produces two stages in the tax computation:

---

1 On the nature of pre-emption rights, see *Pritchard* v. *Briggs* [1980] Ch 338.

- there is a charge in relation to the creation of the pre-emption right; and
- there is a charge in relation to the substantial performance and completion of the contract arising from the exercise of the option.

Although the grant of the pre-emption right is a land transaction in its own right, it may also be a linked transaction with the contract arising from the exercise of the right in due course (FA 2003, s.46(1)).

The effective date in the case of the acquisition of a pre-emption right is when the right is acquired as opposed to when it becomes exercisable (FA 2003, s.46(3)). Thus a right of pre-emption is acquired when granted, although it is not effective unless and until the person granting the right enters into the appropriate situations concerned with a potential sale or other disposition of the relevant property.

Options

There are three types of option: put, call and mutual, but the legislation fails to address these issues expressly. There are also certain, almost certainly incorrect, assumptions in the legislation that all forms of options are chargeable interests since the charge applies to an option binding the grantor to enter into a land transaction or to discharge his obligations under the option in some other way (FA 2003, s.46(2)).

Mutual or cross-options

Cross-options, i.e. the grant of a right to call for the sale or lease of the land in consideration of the grant of a right to require the other party to purchase or to take a lease of the land are within the definition of 'land exchange' in FA 2003, s.47. However, the charge will be limited since the 'exchange' of options is an exchange of non-major interests taxable only upon any equality money paid (FA 2003, Sched. 4, para. 5(4)).

Effective date – special rules for options and pre-emption rights

The effective date of the transaction in the case of the acquisition of an option is when the right is acquired as opposed to when it becomes exercisable (FA 2003, s.46(3)). For example, where there is an option to acquire land if planning permission is obtained, the SDLT arises upon the grant of the option, not when the planning consent is obtained.

6.2 LINKED TRANSACTIONS

The grant of the option and the substantial performance or completion of the contract arising pursuant to its exercise 'may' be linked transactions, and this is a key issue for lease renewals (see Chapter 8) and successive linked levies (FA 2003, Sched. 17A, para. 5).

Options and their exercise

The general practice is that in order to constitute a 'linked transaction' there must be 'a' scheme or arrangement or series of transactions (FA 2003, s.108). This means that there must be some form of pre-arranged and cut-and-dried understanding that an option will be exercised (see further Chapter 4). The legislation clearly recognises that there is no automatic linking of the grant of options and their exercise (FA 2003, s.46). If there are genuine commercial reasons why the option may not be exercised there will be no linkage.[2] In practice, however, it will be appropriate for both sides of the transaction to enter into contemporaneous notes of their understanding of the transaction and the reasons for adopting the option route, and, hopefully, such file notes will be mutually consistent. In the absence of contemporaneous documentation the dispute with HMRC Stamp Taxes will depend upon the evidence of the parties but the credibility of this will almost certainly be attacked by HMRC Stamp Taxes upon the basis of inference, i.e. the surrounding circumstances with the benefit of hindsight are not consistent with the explanation put forward by the taxpayer who is, in its view, in effect, seeking to mislead it and the tribunal. Since there is no control over subsequent events, contemporaneous written records will be vitally important.

Where the option and its exercise are linked because those rules operate retrospectively, it will be necessary to file a land transaction return not only in respect of the chargeable transaction arising by reason of the exercise of the option but also in respect of the revision of the grant of the option. For example, where an option is granted for a premium of £250,000 to acquire land for £2,500,000, the charge upon the option will be 1 per cent of £250,000. If the exercise is linked, the option premium will be aggregated with the strike price[3] so that retrospectively the rate applicable will become 4 per cent so that a further 3 per cent of £250,000 has to be paid and a separate return is required so that effectively at least three returns are required.

---

[2] On the question of assignees of options, see section 4.5 on linked transactions in Chapter 4 which is particularly important for assignees of leases renewing the lease.
[3] Note the drafting problems in this area referred to in *George Wimpey* v. *IRC* [1975] STC 248.

UNDERSTANDING SDLT

Option or conditional contract

There are frequently questions as to whether the parties should enter into an option or a conditional contract and a number of practical issues arise for the choice, namely:

- if a premium is paid for the option this will be taxable upon grant; a deposit paid under a conditional contract will not normally[4] be taxable until the contract is substantially performed or completed;
- entry upon the land will not involve substantial performance producing an immediate tax charge where there is an option but may do so where there is a conditional contract;
- the premium for the option may, but not necessarily, be aggregated with the price payable in respect of its exercise;[5] this depends upon whether the two stages are 'linked transactions'. However, the deposit pursuant to a conditional contract will always be part of the total chargeable consideration.

6.3 SALES OF OPTIONS

An option is a chargeable interest so that a sale of the right will be a chargeable transaction. However, the subsequent exercise of the right by the purchaser of the option will not be a linked transaction with the purchase of the option (subject to the rules of linked transactions where the parties are connected) because the grantor of the right and the seller of the right will not be the same parties, i.e. the two contracts of the purchase of the option and that arising upon exercise will be with different persons. Nor, it is thought, will the subsequent exercise of the right by the purchaser of the option be linked with the original grant because the person exercising the right is not the same person as the original grantee.

6.4 DUE DILIGENCE

Parties acquiring the benefit of options or land with the benefit of pre-emption rights or options to renew leases should obtain details of the background to the option in case HMRC Stamp Taxes establishes, contrary to the wording of the legislation, that the exercise of the right by an unconnected assignee can be linked with the initial grant to the assignor or his predecessors in title.

Since the nil rate slice has to be apportioned amongst linked leases when granted (see Chapter 8), there will be problems as to the amount of nil rate

---

4 Since it is unlikely to exceed the 90 per cent threshold for substantial performance.
5 But the drafting may matter; cf. *George Wimpey Ltd* v. *IRC* [1975] 2 All ER 45.

that can be carried forward in relation to any particular lease, and in relation to matters such as the tax arising upon subsequent rent reviews or renewals of the lease including abnormal increases in rent when the deemed new lease is automatically linked with the existing lease. Moreover, since subsequent linked transactions may affect the tax position of lease A they will also have significant implications for lease B with which lease A is linked, possibly including renewal of lease B.

6.5 COMPLIANCE ISSUE

Failure to investigate the background to the arrangement means that making the entry in Box 13 on SDLT 1 to the effect that there is not a linked transaction will be open to allegations of negligence or fraud, and the possible imposition of the statutory penalty (FA 2003, s.95) for knowingly assisting in the preparation of an incorrect land transaction return. As with so many entries on the SDLT 1 there is no opportunity to supply the detailed information behind the entry as to linked transactions so that it will be easy for HMRC Stamp Taxes to issue a discovery assessment (FA 2003, Sched. 10, para. 5), effectively extending the Enquiry period from nine months to six years (see FA 2003, Sched. 10, para. 31).

CHAPTER 7

Exchanges and partitions

7.1 GENERAL

The extension of chargeable consideration by FA 2003, Sched. 4 and other provisions has produced a complex compliance and self-assessment regime. In particular, where there is a transaction involving land and other forms of assets, the rules relating to consideration in kind rather than cash produces two sub-regimes and it is necessary as a preliminary step to determine into which category the transaction falls because the computation and reporting obligations differ significantly. The two regimes are:

- land exchanges; and
- acquisitions of chargeable interests for consideration in kind other than land.

Where there is a land exchange within the definition there are two chargeable transactions; both the persons involved are subject to a market value charge and a possible obligation to file land transaction returns. There is, therefore, a charge of potentially 8 per cent and possibly more if the VAT is included in the market value computation (see Chapter 4) as well as the cost of preparing so many land transaction returns. HMRC Stamp Taxes has, at last, achieved its long-standing ambition of a double charge upon exchanges since it is no longer possible to avoid the double charge by suitable drafting.

The special charges will, subject to a few limited and very specific reliefs, apply to all acquisitions that are exchanges such as mutual release of covenants, surrenders and regrants of leases, changes of rights to light for alterations in easements such as rights of way and sale and leaseback arrangements such as occur in equity release schemes.

It is therefore necessary to identify what are land exchanges and, importantly, who are the parties thereto for taxation and reporting purposes as well as being aware of the complex provisions for computing the tax.

This analysis turns upon what is a 'land exchange'. This is defined by FA 2003, s.47 as a land transaction entered into by the purchaser (either alone or jointly) wholly or partly in consideration of another land transaction being entered into by him (either alone or jointly) as vendor where an obligation to give consideration for a land transaction is met wholly or partly by way of entering into another transaction as vendor. This will clearly apply where A agrees to transfer or lease land to B in consideration of B transferring or leasing land (whether or not the same land) to A. Since the entering into the land transaction as vendor need be only part of the consideration to be provided there will be an exchange where there is an equality payment or other adjustment; this does not of itself take the transaction out of the land exchange charging provisions.

However, this does not solve the problem of mixed consideration such as, for example, where a life tenant in a trust fund, which includes both land and other investments, agrees to 'exchange' his life interest in part of those underlying assets in return for a transfer of the interest of the remainderman in other assets. Here there will be an exchange of mixed funds. It is considered that such arrangements, which can also arise where there are mutual transfers of businesses as going concerns such as an exchange of a hotel business with assets including goodwill[1] for a transfer of a public house business,[2] are likely to be regarded as land exchanges with extremely complex arrangements for the apportionment of the mixed consideration and the isolation of land where the market rules apply (see, e.g. Chapter 4), which may ease the apportionment exercise because 'equality payments' are to be ignored in some cases. However, as will frequently be the case in situations such as the variation of trusts, the market value principles do not apply because 'minor interests' are involved. These apportionment issues which can affect both parties for other tax purposes will often require the investment of a significant amount of time and resources.

The question of what is a land exchange has taken on a potentially enlarged meaning because of the attitude of HMRC Stamp Taxes to the word 'creation' and the conveyancing terms 'excepting and reserving'. It is the view that, in all cases other than those where the interest reserved was in existence before the conveyance in question, all rights excepted and reserved can take effect only by way of transfer and regrant.[3] Since the regrant is the creation of a new right (rather than a retention of an interest from the sale), many routine conveyances will be converted into land exchanges. Although the transferor is, in the view of HMRC Stamp Taxes, acquiring a chargeable interest, it is unlikely that he will be subject to tax since he will be acquiring a minor interest which has no or little market value and because of this low

---

1 Bearing in mind that a covenant against competition may be a transfer of goodwill, and what is frequently described in contracts as goodwill may actually be a premium payment for the land with relevant planning permission and because of its location.
2 Requiring at least two sets of fairly sophisticated form SDLT 4 (as amended) if penalties are to be avoided.
3 See, e.g. *St Edmunsbury and Ipswich* v. *Clark (No.2)* [1973] 2 All ER 902, [1975] 1 All ER 772; *Johnstone* v. *Holdway* [1963] 1 All ER 432.

market value there will be no notification obligation (Finance Act 2002, s.77 (as amended)). This approach is, however, likely to have serious implications for the purchaser of a major interest. He will be taxed upon the market value of what he is acquiring which will not be the same as the price that he is paying. For example, it is the view of HMRC Stamp Taxes that a discounted price for a quick completion or because several properties are being acquired is not a sale at market value which is the undiscounted price.[4] Thus what appears to be a straightforward sale of a new house becomes a double transaction by way of exchange because the developer/vendor reserves estate covenants.

Another issue is whether the land exchange principles are applicable to multi-party arrangements such as where A is to transfer land to B who is to transfer or lease land to C. Although it states that the consideration must be the entry by B into a land transaction as 'vendor', it does not require A to be the 'purchaser' pursuant to that contract. In consequence, an arrangement whereby B is to vest property in C could be a land exchange. A typical illustration of such an arrangement would be a development or PFI project whereby the developer is to procure the transfer or surrender of existing interests to a local authority for a cash consideration to be provided by the developer as part of the costs. Part of the arrangement may involve a lease of the site to the developer at some stage. Obviously every case will depend upon its own facts, drafting and structure which are likely to be influenced by its own particular tax and commercial considerations.[5] Nevertheless, certain of these structures may involve possible land exchanges but part of the problem, where third parties are involved, will be determining whether any consideration is provided by an appropriate person because of the basic requirement that in order to be chargeable the consideration must be provided by the purchaser or a person connected with him or a party to the transaction (FA 2003, Sched. 4, para. 1 and s.43 (as amended)).

An acquisition of land for a consideration in kind that does not include chargeable interests in land is taxable upon ordinary principles upon the value of the consideration determined where appropriate upon the provision for valuation in the legislation. However, where a land exchange is involved the position is very different and the rules depend upon whether a major or a minor interest is involved. A major interest is a freehold or a term of years absolute whether subsisting in law or equity or the equivalent in Scotland and Northern Ireland (FA 2003, s.117). All other interests are minor interests. Thus a life interest in a settlement holding a freehold or leasehold interest will

---

[4] *Lap Shun Textiles* v. *Collector of Stamps* [1976] AC 530; *Cowan de Groot* v. *Eagle Trust* [1991] BCLC 1045.
[5] Such as the possible reliefs for acquisition pursuant to compulsory powers or for certain PFI projects as in FA 2003, s.60 and Sched. 4, para. 17 (as amended).

be a minor interest because of its limited nature. Similarly, it is the nature of the interest being acquired not what the person holds at the end of the transaction that matters. Thus the acquisition of a life interest by a remainderman is the acquisition of a minor interest notwithstanding that the purchaser becomes a freeholder; the 'merger' of the interests producing something different from the two previous parts does not alter the nature of the chargeable interest acquired.

Where parties are exchanging chargeable interests, these are treated as two separate transactions each attracting the full charge to SDLT.[6] It is no longer possible to avoid the double sale charge, as in stamp duty, by appropriate drafting. The computational rules depend upon the nature of the interest being exchanged. Subject to various special rules the basic charging provisions are set out below (FA 2003, Sched. 4, para. 5).

Major interest for major interest

Where there is an exchange of major interests, i.e. a freehold is being transferred in consideration of a lease or there is a variation of a lease that amounts to a surrender and regrant, the chargeable consideration for each of the transactions is the market value of the interest being acquired, plus the net present value of any rent that may be payable where there is the acquisition of a lease. Any cash being paid or other consideration provided as equality is ignored.

Major interest for minor interest

Where there is a transfer of a major interest and the consideration consists of or includes a non-major interest such as a release of a restrictive covenant or modification of rights to light, then the chargeable consideration for each of the transactions is the market value of the interest being acquired, including any rent that may be payable where there is a lease. It would seem that any cash being paid or other consideration provided as equality is ignored. It seems that the market test applies even to the minor interests being acquired since the part of para. 5 dealing with minor interests applies only where none of the transactions involves a major interest. These current provisions must apply since these refer to 'any' (but not all) of the transactions relating to major interests. However, this may not be a significant problem since minor interests will frequently not have a market value because they cannot be sold

---

6 However, each transaction is separate for the purposes of the lower rates. Notwithstanding the attempts of HMRC Stamp Taxes, the two transactions are not linked so that mutual exchanges of property valued at £200,000 are both taxed at 1 per cent and not as a single transaction for £400,000 at 3 per cent.

separately from the dominant land on the open market. As the acquisition will be for a negligible consideration, it will not be notifiable (FA 2003, s.77 (as amended)) and any entries upon the Land Register can be supported by a self-certificate (SDLT 60). This will not always be the case since certain minor interests such as life interests in trusts may be both valuable and saleable.

Non-major interests for minor interest

Where the exchange involves chargeable interests that are all non-major interests on both sides of the transaction, such as where one party agrees to release a restrictive covenant in return for the grant of rights to light, then the chargeable consideration ignores any land interests being 'acquired' and the tax is charged only upon any consideration other than land being provided for the acquisition. In other words, the land exchange elements are ignored in determining the nature of the transaction so that there is no 'creation' of a new chargeable interest for the purpose of the charge to tax so that there is not a 'land exchange'. The charge is therefore effectively limited to the equality adjustment, if any (FA 2003, Sched. 4, para. 5(4)).

There are special rules governing situations where there are technically land exchanges in relation to:

- part-exchanges involving new dwellings (FA 2003, Sched. 6A, paras. 1 and 2);[7]
- a limited range of surrenders and regrants of leases (FA 2003, Sched. 4, para. 14).

The details of some of these reliefs are considered elsewhere (see Chapters 5 (exemption) and 8 (leases)).

7.2 PARTITION

This provision applies except in relation to partnerships (FA 2003, Sched. 15, para. 16 (as amended)) where the full land exchange charging provisions apply. In the case of a partition or division of a chargeable interest between persons who are jointly entitled (FA 2003, s.120), the mutual exchange of any undivided interest in the land is ignored and is not chargeable consideration. The charge is limited to any equality adjustment being made (FA 2003, Sched. 4, para. 6).

---

7 There are similar provisions in relation to arrangements for the relocation of employees which are, hopefully, not land exchanges. These are described in Chapter 5.

The precise scope of this provision is uncertain. It is related to the physical partition of jointly owned land.[8] In practice the equivalent provisions were reasonably applied for the purposes of stamp duty. The main areas of difficulty arise where there is what appears to be a pool of assets such as where several people own land under a variety of titles.

---

[8] It will, in consequence, not provide relief if HMRC Stamp Taxes attacks severance of beneficial joint tenancies as exchanges which may be technically open to them as land exchanges of major interests.

CHAPTER 8

Leases

8.1 GENERAL

Unlike a freehold, which continues indefinitely, a lease, to create an estate in land, must be for a term of years absolute as defined by s.205(1)(xxvii) of the Law of Property Act (LPA) 1925.[1] The conveyancing problems affecting freeholds, and in their wake the SDLT considerations, relate primarily to the change of ownership of the same estate. Each lease, however, is a separate entity with its own birth, life, inevitable death and possible continuation of the relationship of landlord and tenant (or possibly licensor and licensee) after the expiration of the fixed term of the lease by holding over or similar arrangements or possibly resurrection by means of an option to renew. Thus tax will normally be payable on the creation of a lease, and may well be payable on subsequent events such as rent reviews and assignment, or a variation of its terms, and may even be payable on its premature death by surrender or its continuation after termination of the original lease by holding over or renewal. Although as a matter of general principle the exercise of an option to renew a lease or the negotiation of a new lease whether pursuant to the Landlord and Tenant Act 1954 (as amended) or otherwise represents a completely new term, the SDLT legislation contemplates situations where the new term is 'linked' with the original lease in such a way that if two or more terms are aggregated retrospectively into a single term for the combined terms, the initial tax calculation and any revision thereof may need retrospective recalculation, returns and payment because rent reviews and fluctuations within the first five years of the term of the lease have to be recalculated by reference to the new longer deemed lease.

---

1 But note that although when defining a major interest FA 2003, s.117 refers to a term of years absolute, the definition of lease in s.76 thereof is very different and much wider. It remains to be discovered in practice just how HMRC Stamp Taxes intends to exploit and develop these two differences in definitions, one being technical the other perhaps being plain English but which may be technical intended to extend the definition of the term. This difference also raises questions as to whether 'rent' has a much wider meaning than its normal usages.

The attempts to deal with the complexities of leases have produced five sets of major amendments to the original proposals in FA 2003 which effectively have been totally replaced. New changes emerge before the ink is dry on the previous changes, and there is little transitional relief.[2] The exclusion from the changeover for agreements for leases exchanged prior to the changeover date does not apply where there is any alteration to the agreement. As HMRC Stamp Taxes takes an aggressive view on this point, anything other than a totally trivial amendment such as modification of the covenant relating to pets on the premises destroys the transitional relief regardless of the state of commercial negotiations, which may mean that it is too late to go back and renegotiate the basic principles or heads of terms because these are now too expensive to pursue. There are major problems where the agreement for lease is to grant a lease in the form of the draft Schedule with such amendments as the parties may agree. Such agreement will destroy the transitional relief. Similarly, where there are building agreements, modifications of these building specifications or asking for 'extra' when purchasing or leasing a new building could, on the current HMRC Stamp Taxes view, produce a significantly increased tax charge which has not been factored into the commercial pricing of the overall viability of the deal. Professional advisers face serious risks in assisting in the preparation of the relevant documentation if they do not give detailed advice on the risks of extra cost being undertaken by the client in such matters, even in routine purchases of newly constructed houses.

A lease, to take effect at law, must be by deed (LPA 1925, s.52) which constitutes the 'grant' of the lease,[3] a point not understood by those preparing FA 2003. This technical error gave rise to considerable problems, particularly in relation to compliance when different notification obligations applied to agreements for leases and the subsequent grant of the lease. An attempt to deal with the fundamental problems of taking possession under an agreement for lease prior to taking the grant (FA 2003, Sched. 17A, para. 12A; Sched. 4, para. 10 (as amended)), has given rise to even greater problems and increased tax liability in practice. An agreement to grant a lease must also be made in writing – a written memorandum of an oral agreement is no longer effective (Law of Property (Miscellaneous Provisions) Act 1989, s.2), and thus can be a key issue as to when the tax charge arises and numerous other problems such as the five-year period for rent reviews and the length of the term. An option for the grant of a lease may now have to be exercised in writing (*Spiro v. Glencrown* [1991] 2 WLR 931) but this is by no means clear since the terms of the lease will be the written option contract which may become a contractual document. However, where the lease is to take effect in

---

2 Note the problem in relation to leases to nominees: FA 2003, Sched. 16, para. 3.
3 An agreement for lease is not a 'grant': *City Permanent Building Society v. Miller* [1952] Ch 840.

possession for a term not exceeding three years at the best rent reasonably obtainable without a fine, it may be granted in writing, or even orally (LPA 1925, s.54). In such cases informal arrangements may amount to a yearly or other periodic tenancy, but the question of whether it is a lease or a licence, whilst important, may be difficult to determine in the absence of writing.

It must also be for a term of years absolute; the length of the term must be fixed and certain before it starts, even though it may thereafter be brought to a premature end by, for example, the operation of a break clause in the lease, or by forfeiture. A lease at a rent or premium determinable on death or marriage is not a lease for an uncertain term, as the provisions of s.149(6) of the LPA 1925 turn such a creature into a fixed term of 90 years determinable by notice after the unhappy event (see *Skipton Building Society* v. *Clayton* (1993) 66 P&CR 223); but these rules are not applied for SDLT where such leases are treated as leases for an indefinite term which begins life as a deemed lease for a year but which grows into a longer lease as the arrangement continues (FA 2003, Sched. 17A, paras. 3 and 4).[4] If, however, there is a lease which in other circumstances is to continue until the happening of an uncertain event, it is invalid,[5] and the fact that the 'agreed lease' is invalid means that entry into possession and the payment of rent may produce a tax charge totally different from that expected by the parties who will undoubtedly be exposed to penalties for filing a negligent return. This does not apply where the lease is granted for a maximum term which is expressed to be terminable on the happening of an earlier event: this is taxed as a lease for the maximum term without refund if terminated earlier by the happening of the specified event.[6] A sub-lease granted for a term of the same length as the lease out of which it is purported to be granted operates not as the grant of a new lease but the assignment of the existing lease (*Milmo* v. *Carreras* [1946] KB 306).

8.2 LEASES AND NOMINEES

Certain tax planning and commercial joint venture arrangements involve either the transfer of an interest to a nominee who grants a lease back to the transferor, or the grant of a lease to a nominee to hold absolutely for the landlord. It was held that in Scotland a lease to a nominee is invalid (*Kildrummy* v. *IRC* [1990] STC 657) but it seems that in England and Northern Ireland[7] a lease to a nominee for the lessor or a lease by a nominee

---

[4] Cf. the position of yearly and other periodic tenancies at common law.
[5] *Lace* v. *Chantler* [1944] KB 368 where a tenancy for the duration of the war was held to be invalid.
[6] But see below on break clauses and notices to quit.
[7] See *Belaney* v. *Belaney* (1867) 2 Ch App 138; *Rye* v. *Rye* [1961] 1 All ER 146; *Ingram* v. *IRC* [1999] STC 37.

to the beneficial owner is valid. Such leases are *prima facie* taxable upon their terms, but the Government has indicated that because the legal title alone has no value, the connected company charge (FA 2003, ss.53 and 54 and Sched. 16, para. 3; see Chapter 4) will not apply to deem a market value premium at least for a lease to a nominee.[8] The assignment of such a lease was between the Finance Act 2004 and the Finance (No.2) Act 2005 taxed as the grant of a new lease by the assignor to the assignee (FA 2003, Sched. 17A, para. 11 (as amended)); but is currently taxed upon grant as if the nominee rules do not apply (FA 2003, Sched. 16, para. 3 (as amended)). This new charge also applies where the freehold is transferred to a nominee which grants a lease back to the beneficial owner. When investigating title on the purchase of a lease not only is the status of the lessee and lessor a key consideration, the dates are also important.

It would seem, however, that the rules against non-merger where a leasehold interest and the immediate reversionary interest become vested in the same person remain unaffected (see LPA 1925, s.185; *Ingle* v. *Vaughan Jenkins* [1900] 2 Ch 368), and the merger of the two interests is not, at present, itself a chargeable transaction.

8.3 'LEASE'

Lease or licence

The charge is *prima facie* limited to leases or agreements for lease of land; it does not apply to licences to use or occupy land or tenancies at will which are exempt interests (FA 2003, s.48). In consequence, the distinction between a lease and a licence, so important to the question of security of tenure, has equal significance in the SDLT context of the transaction. Whether or not the parties have created a licence or a lease is a matter of construction in each case.[9] It should be remembered that the courts look at the substance of the transaction, not necessarily at the name that the parties have chosen to give it (*Addiscombe Garden Estates* v. *Crabbe* [1957] 3 All ER 563), but a statement in the document to the effect that the parties do not intend to create the relationship of landlord and tenant may tip the balance in borderline cases (*Ogwr Borough Council* v. *Dykes* [1989] 2 All ER 880). This is in accordance with general principles of construction that parties cannot enter into an

---

8 This view may be incorrect since, subject to any contrary legislation a transaction involving a nominee is a non-event for SDLT: FA 2003, Sched. 16, para. 3 (as amended).
9 But subject, according to Lord Templeman, to certain presumptions in relation to residential arrangements (*Street* v. *Mountford* [1985] 1 AC 809), or domestic arrangements where the parties may and intend to create legal relationships of landlord and tenant as in *Facchini* v. *Bryson* [1952] 1 TLR 1386.

agreement containing such a statement and then contend for the contrary position unless the contract is clearly inconsistent with the provisions (*Massey* v. *Crown Life* [1978] 2 All ER 576; *Readymix Concrete* v. *Minister for Pensions* [1968] 1 All ER 433) or there is a clear legislative policy contrary to such an arrangement.

HMRC Stamp Taxes starts from the proposition that if the arrangement confers exclusive possession upon the occupier and otherwise contains terms appropriate to a lease, it may be held to have created a tenancy, even though called a licence (*Street* v. *Mountford* [1985] 2 WLR 877). There may, however, be differences between arrangements relating to business property and those affecting domestic arrangements, since in relation to the former category the judiciary have generally rejected Lord Templeman's rigid formulation and have been prepared to pay some attention to commercial needs and the wishes of the parties where security of tenure for individual tenants is not involved.

However, difficult issues of classification can arise under building arrangements where a developer who is entitled to the benefit of an agreement for lease is allowed into occupation of the premises in order to carry out the building works. In practice he may have the equivalent of exclusive occupation and if he is paying a fee or fees HMRC Stamp Taxes may claim that the licence to enter and to build is some form of tenancy.[10] Moreover, such an arrangement may involve the prospective tenant taking possession and so substantially performing the agreement for lease triggering an effective date with a tax charge and an obligation to notify the transaction; although an early effective date will operate to exclude from charge many building contracts and fitting out arrangements, provided that the taxpayer ensures that any licence he has to enter upon the land amounts to taking possession of the whole or substantially the whole of the land (see Chapter 3).

Definition

As part of this exercise 'lease' is defined (FA 2003, Sched. 17A, para. 1), at least for England and Wales and Northern Ireland, as:

- an interest or right in or over land for a term of years (whether fixed or periodic); or

---

10 Such argument arose from time to time when licences were subject to stamp duty pursuant to the 'Bond Covenant' head of charge. The removal of the charge in 1971 has meant that the argument has lain dormant because of the lack of opportunity to attack such arrangements; but the point arose from time to time. It is likely to resurface significantly and FA 2003, ss.44A and 45A represent an intention to attack such arrangements.

- a tenancy at will[11] or other interest or right in or over land determinable by notice at any time.

It is unclear whether the draftsman intended this as some form of plain English explanation of what is a lease or whether it is intended to apply to any arrangement whereby a chargeable interest in land such as an easement is acquired for a limited period, such as a right to pass over adjoining land during the development phase, and is to be treated as a 'lease'.[12] This would be an interest in land for a term of years and in relation to the notification obligations it may have to be treated as a lease (FA 2003, s.77(2)). It is considered that HMRC Stamp Taxes will take this point. It is, however, questionable whether any payments made for the limited right will be 'rent' which term is not defined. It may not be helpful to describe such payments as 'rent' in the documents. If not regarded by HMRC Stamp Taxes as rent for the purposes of computation they are likely to be treated as consideration other than rent, i.e. a premium governed by the rules relating to periodical payments other than rent (FA 2003, s.52).

Deemed leases

Certain transactions are treated as giving rise to the grant of a new lease. These include:

(a) Assignments

Assignments of leases are treated as involving the grant of a new lease by the assignor (FA 2003, Sched. 17A, para. 11) where the original lease was exempt because:

- it was part of a sale and leaseback arrangement (FA 2003, s.57A);
- group relief or reconstruction or acquisition relief applied (FA 2003, Part 1 or 2 of Sched. 7);
- it was a transfer involving public bodies (FA 2003, s.66);
- charities relief applied (FA 2003, Sched. 8);
- it was a lease granted to nominees between the Finance Act 2004 and Finance (No.2) Act 2005; or
- it fell within any such regulations as are mentioned in s.123(3) of FA 2003 (regulations reproducing in relation to SDLT the effect of enactments providing for exemption from stamp duty) (Stamp Duty Land Tax (Consequential Amendment of Enactments) Regulations 2003, SI 2003/2867).

---

11 However, tenancies at will are not chargeable interests: FA 2003, s.48(2)(c)(i).
12 Fortunately when defining 'major interest' in FA 2003, s.117 the phrase 'term of years absolute' is utilised which suggests that other interests for a limited time such as a right of way for five years although possibly a 'lease' is not a major interest.

The grant is treated as being:

- for a term equal to the unexpired term of the original lease; and
- on the same terms as those on which assignee holds that lease after the assignment.

In consequence, the assignee will be taxed upon any consideration paid for the assignment that is properly allocated to the land and fixtures, plus the net present value of the rent for the balance of the term. There will be the obligation to adopt the complex multiple reporting requirements for dealing with variable rent. It seems that the five-year period and abnormal rent increase provisions apply with full force to the deemed new lease with the relevant date commencing on the effective date for the actual assignment.

This charge does not apply where the relief in question is group relief, reconstruction or acquisition relief or charities relief and is withdrawn as a result of a clawback event occurring before the effective date of the assignment.

(b) Increase of rent

Two areas of rent increase (but not rent reduction which is treated differently) (FA 2003, Sched. 17A, para. 15A and s.43(3)(d)) produce deemed new leases, namely:

- an increase in the rent otherwise than in accordance with the terms of the lease such as where a landlord pays a sum to the tenant to agree to an increase in rent (FA 2003, Sched. 17A, para. 13);
- where after the expiration of the fifth year of the term of the lease there is an abnormal increase in the rent (FA 2003, Sched. 17A, paras. 14 and 15).

These issues of rent variations are considered later in this chapter, but it should be noted that these deemed new leases remain separate from the original lease for the purposes of calculating the rent duty and for general compliance purposes (but see FA 2003, Sched. 17A, para. 14(6)).

8.4 LEASES AND COMPLIANCE

A number of practical problems exist:

- it appears that as a result of the changes made in the Finance Act 2004 (inserting FA 2003, Sched. 17A, para. 12A) unlike all other forms of chargeable transactions with only one effective date the same lease arrangement may have at its commencement two effective dates producing two separate chargeable transactions, i.e. substantial performance of the agreement and the grant of the lease;

- in virtually every case the tax will be required to be calculated initially on an estimated basis under the sanction of interest and penalties if the estimate is unsatisfactory;
- assignees of leases may have to take over the original tenant's outstanding tax liability (FA 2003, Sched. 17A, para. 12);
- special linked transaction rules apply which can affect assignees of the lease and even other leases and deemed new leases (FA 2003, Sched. 17A, paras. 14 and 15) which are linked because of the need to apportion the nil rate slice for rents between linked leases and because of the possibility of linked successive leases.

8.5 'DOUBLE CHARGE'

Effective date for leases

The effective date for leases is now split. The starting point is that virtually every agreement for lease will contain a provision that it is to be completed by a 'conveyance', i.e. the grant of the lease so that substantial performance of the agreement becomes an issue (FA 2003, ss.119 and 44). There is an effective date at substantial performance with another at grant if these two events have the misfortune to be separated. There is now a potentially significant downside in resting upon the agreement for lease and postponing the actual grant.

Substantial performance – deemed grant

The basic rules of substantial performance apply to agreements for lease (see also Chapter 3), namely substantial performance occurs, when there has been no prior or simultaneous actual grant of the lease, such as where the lessee enters upon the land before the deed is executed, at the earliest of:

- payment of the whole or substantially the whole of any premium (i.e. 90 per cent of the premium where this is a cash payment);
- first payment of rent. This applies when rent is actually paid rather than the quarter or other date when it becomes due.

Substantial performance of agreement for lease and later grant

The failure of the draftsman of FA 2003 to understand conveyancing practice, and the meaning of key technical terms such as 'grant' has produced amending legislation which is defective in concept but the defects are being exploited by HMRC Stamp Taxes to enlarge the tax base and compliance obligations significantly, namely:

- substantial performance of an agreement for lease (where the actual lease has not been previously granted or is not granted simultaneously with such substantial performance) is to be treated as the grant of a lease; and
- when the lease is formally granted there is a deemed surrender of the deemed lease arising upon substantial performance of the agreement for lease, but the tax in respect of the rent has the benefit of a credit for the rent, but only the rent, taxed at the time of substantial performance (FA 2003, Sched. 17A, para. 12A).

Whilst this was apparently intended to remove the compliance problems arising from the original different reporting obligations for leases and for agreements for lease, it is currently being exploited as creating two chargeable events in relation to the same lease. For example, HMRC Stamp Taxes has already stated that where the substantial performance of an agreement for lease is exempt because it is an intra-group transaction within Part 1 of Sched. 7 to FA 2003 this exemption no longer automatically carries over to the actual grant of the lease. The exemption has to be reassessed by reference to the facts, intentions and circumstances existing as at the date of the grant of the lease. It is questionable whether the interpretation is correct given the apparent purpose of the amendment but there is limited support for the aggressive approach in the legislation.[13] If the interpretation is correct, a wide range of consequences follows from the official position including:

- a new effective date creating a new five-year review period for variable rents (FA 2003, Sched. 17A, paras. 7 and 8). This is a key issue for assignees of leases to investigate;
- the possibility that there is a new assumed rent for years after the fifth year of the new term arising from the grant affecting linked transactions and subsequent abnormal rent increases;
- any exercise of an option to renew which is a linked transaction will be linked with the actual lease rather than the agreement for lease, since linked successive leases relate back to the effective date for the renewed lease;
- a different discount rate may apply for the net present value of the rent;
- the tax upon the rent has to be recalculated from the date of the grant by reference to the then passing rent subject to the limited credit mechanism;
- where the option to tax the rent for VAT has been exercised after substantial performance but before the grant the tax computation will have to include the VAT upon the rent although it was ignored at the time of substantial performance;

---

13 Such as the rent credit mechanism which would not be necessary if the grant of the lease related back to substantial performance of the agreement for lease in para. 12A itself; and the specific backdating of the relief for works such as building and fitting out works to the substantial performance of the agreement for lease by FA 2003, Sched. 4, para. 10 (as amended).

- the rates, exemptions and charging provisions may differ from those applied to the substantial performance of the agreement for lease, subject to any transitional provisions where the law is changed;
- the term of the lease will differ from the term taken into account for the agreement for lease (i.e. it will be shorter, from a later date) which will be a complicating arithmetical factor when calculating the new tax on the rent;
- although rent payable under the agreement for lease would be 'rent' and taxed initially as such, it may be regarded as rent paid in respect of the lease but prior to its effective date and so taxed as a premium. However, it seems that HMRC Stamp Taxes's argument is vulnerable because of its view that the grant is a new lease so that the rent is paid in respect of a different lease;
- the relief for rent reviews in the last quarter of the fifth year of the term (FA 2003, Sched. 17A, para. 7A(c)) although available for the agreement for lease will almost inevitably not be available in respect of the later grant of the lease which will be much closer to the first review date than the prior substantial performance and be well after the three months from the term commencement date.

There may be arguments against certain of these potential applications of the charge by HMRC Stamp Taxes but it will be clear that given the relatively relaxed approach, in practice, to the actual grant of the lease, particularly for shorter terms, the taxation consequences can be arbitrary and capricious but severe. Professional advisers who do not discuss with their client the desirability of ensuring that substantial performance and grant coincide may, justifiably, find themselves in difficulty.

Two reliefs against the double charge are provided but unhelpfully these also provide support for the argument that the same transaction now has two effective dates. These reliefs are:

- the chargeable rent reserved by the new lease is reduced by reference to the rent payable under the agreement for lease (FA 2003, Sched. 17A, para. 12A); and
- the exemption for works including fitting out executed after the effective date applies to all works carried out after the effective date for the agreement for lease, notwithstanding that they are carried out before the effective date for the grant of the lease (FA 2003, Sched. 4, para. 10 (as amended)).

It is considered that because the deemed surrender is not expressed to be in consideration of the grant of the lease and vice versa, there is not a deemed surrender and regrant so that no charges arise by reference to the value of the interests involved which could be quite substantial because of the works carried out in the interim period. HMRC Stamp Taxes's view is not known, but the transaction is a land exchange outside the exempting provisions and is regarded as unsustainable on the legislation.

8.6 GRANT OF LEASES TO THIRD PARTIES

A frequent practical situation is where a person such as a developer enters into an agreement for lease and subsequently enters into arrangements with a third party pursuant to which he directs the grant of the lease to the third party (cf. *Att-Gen* v. *Brown* (1849) 3 Exch 662). Alternatively a person may agree to take leases of several flats,[14] hoping to dispose of the lease without paying stamp taxes. For such persons the stamp tax planning strategy has fundamentally altered, but the one-size-fits-all drafting means that leases are now eligible for a form of sub-sale relief (FA 2003, s.45 (as amended)) and a special albeit limited relief is now available (FA 2003, Sched. 17A, para. 12B).

Unfortunately, although because of the potential double charge upon the deposit by the original tenant the specific relief may be less favourable in many cases, it is provided that the original relief pursuant to s.45 cannot be claimed where the specific para. 12B is available, but where the new para. 12B relief does not apply the basic relief of s.45 of FA 2003 (as amended) may be available (see Chapter 5).

Specific relief

The specific relief for leases to third parties applies where a person enters into an agreement for lease and before he substantially performs that agreement he assigns his interest as lessee to a third party. In such a case the original agreement takes effect as if it were with the assignee who is treated as providing as part of the consideration under that agreement for lease including any consideration given for the assignment.[15] Where the original contract has been substantially performed prior to the assignment, the assignment is a separate chargeable transaction. In consequence, the original

---

14 Which will be linked transactions even if embodied in separate legally independent contracts.

15 This provision will be somewhat random in its effect. It will apply where a person agrees to acquire several flats intending to on-sell them at a profit. Normally he will not substantially perform his contract and he will escape the charge to tax. However, a developer will frequently have substantially performed his contract by taking possession in order to commence construction, if only to protect his building costs from tax. The assignee runs the risk of an element of double taxation. He will usually reimburse the original tenant for any sums such as deposits paid to the lessor. Unless HMRC Stamp Taxes is prepared to treat the new contract as being modified to exclude sums paid by the assignee prior to the assignment such sums will be effectively brought into the computation twice.

tenant pays tax when he substantially performs and the assignee pays tax upon the sum paid to the original tenant for the lease. The third party in this case will need to investigate the original party's position since this fundamentally affects his tax liability; suitable indemnities may be required.

It is a condition that the person 'assigns' his interest as lessee under an agreement for lease. These rules do not apply where there is a sub-lease granted by the original party to the agreement for lease but, that apart, the scope of the provision is unclear. 'Assign' would, in context, seem to require a formal transfer of the right, i.e. sufficient documentation to vest the right to call for the lease to be granted in the third party.[16] This will be a potentially limited situation since these tripartite arrangements are usually part of a development arrangement whether of building new houses or flats or constructing commercial premises; an outright assignment would be difficult until the end of the construction phase because there will be outstanding building arrangements and obligations which the third party will not wish to take over. Moreover, at this stage the right to call for the lease is likely to be conditional upon the satisfactory completion of the buildings so that an outright assignment is not really possible. The normal arrangement would seem to be for the original lessee to agree to procure the grant of a lease to the third party as and when the right to call for the lease becomes unconditional.[17]

There is also the difficulty in that the draftsman has failed to deal with the routine situation of a residential or industrial site developer dealing with several third parties who may each require separate leases of their house or business premises. There is no provision dealing with the assignment of the right to call for a part lease. It would seem prudent to include express provision in the original agreement for lease to call for or assign the leases separately or in parts.

Although the legislation does not deal with the situation clearly, it is tentatively suggested that 'assign' includes 'agrees to assign' which will include 'agrees to procure the grant of the lease' and also applies to dealings in part of the land. Unless the legislation is stretched in this way the provisions of para. 12A of Sched. 17A are effectively redundant and s.45 of FA 2003 will continue to apply to most cases.

8.7 THE CHARGE TO TAX ON LEASES

There are two basic elements to tax upon leases. There is a charge upon the rent and a separate charge upon consideration other than rent. For convenience the latter will be described as 'premium'. The tax upon the rent is

---

16 It is interesting to compare the drafting of FA 2003, s.45 (as amended) which refers to a person becoming entitled to call for a conveyance.
17 But note the potential application of FA 2003, ss.44A and 45A; see Chapter 9.

payable in addition to any tax upon the premium (FA 2003, Sched. 5, para. 9(4)) which includes not only cash payments but also deemed premiums such as where market value rules apply and consideration in kind such as land or other property including shares in companies and building works[18] and other services. It must also be noted that where a sum described as 'rent' is paid in respect of periods before the grant of the lease (which appears to include substantial performance of the agreement for lease) this is taxed as a premium (FA 2003, Sched. 5, para. 1A). This may occur where, for example, the rent is expressed to be payable from the immediately preceding quarter day prior to the grant of the lease.

8.8 RENTS

SDLT is chargeable upon the net present value of the rent (FA 2003, Sched. 5, para. 2; Sched. 6, paras. 5 and 9). However, where there are linked transactions the net present value is not taken into account when determining the chargeable consideration for those transactions (FA 2003, Sched. 5, para. 9(5)), but the nil rate band for lease premiums is not available if the average annual rent exceeds £600.

The charge upon rents is not imposed solely upon the grant; there are numerous charges and reporting obligations arising in relation to:

- substantial performance of the agreement for lease;
- the grant of the lease with a rent credit for rent payable pursuant to the previously substantially performed agreement for lease;
- variations of rent during or at the end of the first five years of the term including routine rent reviews;
- 'abnormal' increases in the rent after the end of the first five years of the term;
- increases of rent other than pursuant to the terms of the lease;
- reductions in the rent (FA 2003, Sched. 17A, para. 15A);
- assignments of leases that were within certain exemptions when granted or were granted to nominees. These are taxed as the grant of a new lease taxable, *inter alia*, upon the then passing rent (FA 2003, Sched. 17A, para. 11).

It must also be noted that certain variations of lease operate as surrenders and grants of new leases which will be taxable in respect of the rent but with certain credits for previous tax charges upon the rent (FA 2003, s.43(3)(d) and Sched. 17A, para. 15A (as amended) and para. 9).

---

18 See further on building works in Chapter 9.

Provisional tax[19]

Moreover, many of the assessments and returns have to be prepared on an estimated or potentially temporary basis particularly where rent is concerned and, broadly, almost every land transaction will be subject to subsequent charges throughout and beyond its life. Matters that trigger retrospective adjustments to the previous rent calculations include:

- variable rents during or at the end of the first five years of the term;
- later linked leases possibly including renewals of existing leases whether of the same or other premises;
- exercise of options to renew leases where these are linked transactions;
- holding over producing an extended lease;
- continuation of periodic and similar tenancies.

This virtually continuous process of taxation of leases can pass over to third parties who need to obtain full disclosure of the SDLT history of the lease (FA 2003, Sched. 17A, para. 12).

Taxable amount – net present value of the rent

Rent is no longer taxed upon one year's rent calculated by averaging the rent over the term of the lease; the new charge is upon the aggregate of the rent over the whole term of the lease, suitably discounted. There are, however, many oddities in the calculation of this amount where certain special or deeming provisions override the actual situation, but these artificial assumptions have produced many situations where the initial calculation is subject to either retrospective adjustment or wide-ranging anti-avoidance provisions that apply to all transactions and do not require any tax avoidance purpose before they are applied. This objective element in the tax avoidance provisions will cause long-term commercial difficulties for dealings in the leases.

The formula for determining the amount of the rent upon which the SDLT is to be charged is

$$v = \sum_{i=1}^{n} \frac{r_i}{(1+T)^i}$$

In this formula:

v   is the net present value of the rent for the purposes of SDLT, i.e. the taxable sum;
Σ   is the mathematical symbol generally utilised to denote the sum or aggregate of the various elements in a series of numbers; in this case it

---

19 See Chapter 1.

means the aggregate of the rent (or deemed rent) for each year of the term of the lease after it has been discounted, at the specified rate, i.e. (I + T);

ri is the rent or estimated or assumed rent where there is a 'variable rent' payable in year 'i';

i is first, second, third, etc. years of the term producing r_1, r_2, r_3 etc. being the rent for years 1, 2 and 3 respectively;

n is the term of the lease; and

T is the temporal discount rate,[20] i.e. the rate at which each year's rent is discounted over time. The current rate is 3.5 per cent giving a figure for (I + T) of 1.035.

Although not specifically stated, it appears from the general computational provisions in relation to the 'effective date' which appear to apply to only one date that the temporal discount rate of the effective date applies to all subsequent computations which 'relate back' to the initial computation of the SDLT as at the effective date. In consequence, the original rate will apply to any recalculation of the SDLT upon the grant of the lease or where an uncertain rent becomes less uncertain and further notification and calculation are required (see, e.g. FA 2003, s.80(2)(c)), notwithstanding that the temporal discount rate may have been changed by regulations in the intervening period.[21]

It will still remain necessary for the taxpayer to input the correct data which will involve both identifying the 'rent' for the premises and making the necessary estimates and calculations of the 'assumed rent' for periods after the fifth year as well as acceptable assumptions as to the rent during the first five years. It is essential that these estimates are carried out on a proper basis in order to avoid penalties for incorrect returns. HMRC Stamp Taxes has provided an online facility to enable solicitors and other professional advisers to calculate the tax. The so-called helpline is supplying incorrect and inappropriate advice on rents such as suggesting that the taxpayer utilises simply the initial rent and should ignore the impact of rent reviews. This advice,

---

20 Assuming a lease for five years at a fixed rent of £100 the net present value of the rent would be the aggregate of:

$$\frac{£100}{(1.035)} + \frac{£100}{(1.035)^2} + \frac{£100}{(1.035)^3} + \frac{£100}{(1.035)^4} + \frac{£100}{(1.035)^5}.$$

The position for variable rents is somewhat more complicated and is described below.

21 Persons seeking to utilise the promised online facility for calculating the SDLT may need to investigate whether the rate has been changed and that they are accessing the correct facility. Unless HMRC Stamp Taxes preserves the existing facility, notwithstanding the introduction of new rates, the facility will rapidly become useless. Nevertheless, as the point may be overlooked in the updating process the appropriate due diligence will be required.

which cannot be relied upon even to mitigate penalties, is incorrect and means the return is not properly prepared. In addition, substantial interest costs for tax underpaid will be incurred, and there are likely to be difficulties raised by a well-advised potential purchaser of the lease.

There are certain key elements in the application of the formula to determine the net present value of the rent which require detailed explanation; these are as follows.

'Rent'

Basic position

'Rent' is not defined and so it would appear that the normal meaning of the term is applicable, i.e. a payment made by a tenant to a landlord for the exclusive possession of the land (see, e.g. *T & E Homes* v. *Robinson* [1976] STC 462; *Gable Construction Co* v. *IRC* [1968] 1 WLR 1426), and is officially regarded as including mineral royalties. If the payment is not reserved out of the land, it is not rent (*Hill* v. *Booth* [1930] 1 KB 381). This lack of statutory definition is important since 'lease' is defined (FA 2003, Sched. 17A, para. 1) in such a way as possibly to include rights such as easements granted for a limited time. The SDLT charge will depend upon whether any annual 'fees' or royalties paid for such a right are 'rent' in the strict sense or some form of annual or other periodic payment,[22] which may constitute some form of periodic consideration for the grant of the right taxed upon a chargeable consideration derived by 'capitalising' the annual payment pursuant to s.56 of FA 2003.

On this there are various points to note:

Drafting issues – service and other charges

For the purposes of calculating the SDLT upon 'rent', a single sum expressed to be payable either:

- in respect of rent; or
- in respect of rent and other matters but not apportioned,[23]

is to be treated entirely as 'rent' (FA 2003, Sched. 17A, para. 6(1)). This suggests that the reservation of various items as 'rent' (but not it is thought, reservations as 'additional rent'), in order to provide the landlord with

---

[22] Taxable pursuant to FA 2003, s.52. It is considered that on general principles they are not 'rent' but the description of them as 'rent' may mean that they are 'rent'. In many cases it may be that the SDLT charge as 'rent' is lower than an annual payment taxed at 4 per cent.

[23] Where the sum is apportioned between various items such apportionments must be made on a 'just and reasonable' basis: FA 2003, Sched. 4, para. 4.

possible additional powers in relation to the enforcement of the covenant to pay the rent may have adverse effects upon the tenant, possibly sufficient in some cases to make the proposed lease commercially unattractive.

Where the service charges are not 'rent' they are not taxable (FA 2003, Sched. 17A, para. 10). There is, therefore, the basic drafting issue as well as a commercial negotiation between the landlord and the tenant as to whether certain items are to be payable 'as rent' or are separate payments.

VAT and rent

Only VAT contractually payable at the effective date is taxable (FA 2003, Sched. 4, para. 2). Where the lease rent is exempt at that date, both the possible and actual exercise of the option to tax are ignored when calculating the net present value of the rent because such VAT arising after the effective date is to be ignored (FA 2003, Sched. 4, para. 2). However, since HMRC Stamp Taxes has introduced two effective dates for leases (FA 2003, Sched. 17A, para. 12A), there will be a charge upon the VAT where the option to tax is exercised after substantial performance of the agreement for lease but before the grant thereof.

Rent or premium

The effect of FA 2003, Sched. 17A, para. 6(1) may be that where the VAT and the rent are not expressed as a single sum but are reserved as two separate items, the VAT is not 'rent'. In this case it would seem that the VAT not being reserved as 'rent' may constitute a periodical premium (FA 2003, s.52(6)). HMRC Stamp Taxes has publicly stated that where VAT was reserved separately from rent in relation to stamp duty it was a periodical premium within the provisions equivalent to s.52 (Stamp Act 1891, s.56; SP11/91, para. 9). Since the basic structure has not changed the risk of an attack on this basis remains. Where VAT is treated as rent which generally produces a reasonably favourable result for taxpayers, HMRC Stamp Taxes does not appear to challenge this treatment in practice.

Service and other charges and payments

This exclusion applies to other routine payments and includes both the covenant and underletting and any payments made whether by way of performance of the covenants, such as a payment towards landlord's insurance premiums, or in respect of a breach of covenant such as damages for dilapidations. The excluded matters are considered later in this chapter in relation to 'premiums'.

'Back dated rent'

Some leases reserve sums as rent payable from some date prior to the grant of the lease. Such sums are taxable not as rents but as 'premium' (FA 2003, Sched. 5, para. 1A).

Deemed rent

Employment

Where a lease is granted in consideration of a person's employment or the employment of a person connected with him which generates a benefit in kind within Chapter 5 of Part 3 of the Income Tax (Earnings and Pensions) Act 2003, there is a charge to SDLT upon an amount equal to the cash equivalent of the benefits chargeable under that Act as if it were a sum of rent (FA 2003, Sched. 4, para. 12). This sum is added to any actual rent reserved. As this charge is based upon a notional rent equal to the cash equivalent charged to income tax and that cash equivalent is variable (see Income Tax (Earnings and Pensions) Act 2003) this notional rent would appear to be 'uncertain' within s.51 of FA 2003 so that the initial payment of SDLT will be based upon a reasonable estimate of the amount of the chargeable consideration, i.e. the estimated notional rent with obligations to notify, recalculate the tax and pay the additional tax[24] at the end of the fifth year taking into account the income tax calculation charges.[25]

Fortunately this provision is unlikely to have a significant impact in practice since, in general, the interest of the employee is likely to be an exempt interest as a licence (FA 2003, s.48(1)(b)) or as a tenancy at will (FA 2003, s.48(1)(c)(i)). Even where the interest created is a lease, it is likely that the level of the actual and/or notional rent will not exceed the nil rate threshold so as to give rise to a positive charge to tax and as the contractual term is likely to be for less than seven years the grant of the lease will not be notifiable (FA 2003, s.77(2)(b)(ii)) as the nil rate applies. The problem will be how the term of such a lease is to be computed. Such tenancies are unlikely to be for a fixed term, but will be linked to the duration of the employment[26] or be of a periodic nature. The tenancy will be, in most cases, treated as being a tenancy for one year when the taxable sum will be the deemed rent with a discount which applies even for the first year's rent. Should the tenancy continue it will become a two-, three- or four-year lease with the net present value of the rent correspondingly increasing. There is, therefore, a risk that notwithstanding

---

24 Or possibly a claim for repayment of overpaid tax.
25 It may be necessary to investigate and keep copies of Form PIID or its equivalent.
26 If such arrangement is not void for uncertainty as may well be the case: *Lace* v. *Chantler* [1944] KB 368.

the increasing impact of the discount the net present value of the rent may exceed the nil rate slice and tax become payable. At this stage and every year thereafter there will have to be a retrospective recalculation of the tax or any additional tax due and a need to file a complete land transaction return.[27]

Deemed new leases

In certain cases of rent increases (FA 2003, Sched. 17A, paras. 13 and 14) these are treated as being the grant of a new lease. The rent for the new term is, broadly, the additional rent, although this varies between the different situations (cf. FA 2003, Sched. 17A, paras. 13(1) and 14(3)), and the tax is charged upon the net present value of the deemed rent in accordance with the above formula. These deemed new leases are described at appropriate places in this chapter.

Rent credit

In certain cases (FA 2003, Sched. 17A, para. 9) involving surrenders and regrants of leases of substantially the same premises or the grant of a new lease pursuant to Part 2 of the Landlord and Tenant Act 1954 (as amended), which relates back to the end of the contractual term of the original lease but SDLT has been paid in respect of the holding over (FA 2003, Sched. 17A, para. 3), the rent reserved by the new lease is, broadly, reduced by either the rent payable in respect of the balance of the term surrendered or during the holding-over period but the latter provision is not particularly well drafted.

However, it seems that this credit is available only where the original lease being surrendered or held over was within the charge to SDLT and does not apply to leases granted within the stamp duty regime even when granted on or after 1 December 2003.

Variable rents

Rents are likely to change during the course of a lease in a variety of ways whether by reason of rent review or because they are linked to some form of turnover or participation figure in relation to sub-lease rents received from occupational tenants. The new tax becomes immensely complicated in relation to compliance if not calculation and recalculation in relation to such leases in that there are two sets of problems; namely:

---

[27] Fortunately, as a result of amendments it will no longer be necessary to notify the existence of the lease after the end of the fifth year when the tenancy becomes a lease for a term of seven years or longer. Notification is required only when tax is payable.

- how such rents are to be taxed on the effective date; and
- whether any variation in the rent subsequently gives rise to either a liability to pay further tax or a refund of overpaid SDLT and/or an obligation to notify HMRC Stamp Taxes of the variation.

To some extent the computation procedure depends upon the nature of the variation of the rent since the following are not variable rents:

- indexation to the Retail Price Index is ignored (FA 2003, Sched. 4, para. 4(3)). There is a doubt from the drafting as to whether an upwards only indexation increase is within this provision, since this exclusion applies only where the rent adjustment is 'in line with' the Retail Price Index. Adjustments related to a modified version of the index may not be accepted as excluded by HMRC Stamp Taxes. Rent reviews linked to some factor other than the Retail Price Index such as a review to indexation, or 5 per cent, whichever is the greater are not covered by these provisions. This will be a significant compliance problem for finance leases, *inter alia*, where the rent is linked to movements in interest rates which is likely to be the case where there are sale and leaseback and similar arrangements intended as a fundraising exercise, although there is an exemption for leases in certain sale and leaseback arrangements on the initial grant (FA 2003, s.57A (as much amended));
- the increase of rent by reason of VAT does not appear to give rise to a chargeable transaction when the option to tax is exercised after the effective date or the rate changes (FA 2003, Sched. 4, para. 2); and
- rents where the first review or variation occurs after the expiration of the fifth year of the term (FA 2003, Sched. 17A, para. 7A), although this is complicated by the double charge on leases described above.

However, virtually every other type of rent will be taxed as a variable rent if it is capable of alteration during the first five years of the term. The fact that it may be changed after that date is ignored unless any variations after that date involve an abnormal increase in the rent (FA 2003, Sched. 17A, paras. 14 and 15; see later in this chapter). Thus a ground rent which doubles every 25 years will be a variable rent but the initial calculation will be based upon the rent for the first 25 years being treated as the rent for the whole term. The subsequent adjustments are ignored unless they are 'abnormal'.

Uncertain rents

Variable rents, like variable consideration, can take many forms and the basic types of variation namely contingent, unascertained and uncertain are the same as for variable consideration in s.51 of FA 2003 considered in Chapter 3. However, unlike variable consideration including variable premiums, the tax due in respect of rent even though estimated has to be paid in full within 30 days after the effective date, with a right to a refund if the initial guestimate of future rents is too high. There is no power to postpone the payment of tax upon rents. The procedure is:

- where there is a contingent rent, i.e. a basic rent which is to increase by a fixed amount should a specified event happen, the tax is calculated initially upon the basis that the contingent rent is payable with adjustment should the contingency not occur;
- where the rent is 'unascertained', such as rent based upon the square footage of a building which has been completed but not measured, the rent is taxed upon the basis of a reasonable estimate with an adjustment when the rent is finally agreed;
- where the rent is 'uncertain', such as a turnover rent including rent reviews the tax on the rent has to be calculated initially upon a reasonable estimate of the rent during the first five years and the position reviewed during or at the end of the fifth year of the term.

The situation may change over time since the initial self-assessment calculation of the SDLT upon the rent has to be carried out as at the effective date when the rent, although not variable, may be uncertain such as where the rent is expressed to be a fixed sum per square foot of 'lettable area' when the building is completed or as a percentage related to the final development costs. It may be that the effective date is before the completion of the building so that the rent cannot be ascertained, or before the parties have reached agreement on the final figure. In such a case, s.51(2) of FA 2003 applies and the SDLT is self-assessed on the basis of a reasonable estimate of the amount of rent expected to be paid. This will involve a certain degree of speculation and the position has to be revisited with the tax recalculated and the transaction notified again when the uncertainty is resolved such as the square footage being agreed (FA 2003, s.80).

Rent reviews to market rent and similar arrangements

The most frequently encountered variable rents will be those within the 'uncertain' category, i.e. the precise amount payable cannot be pre-determined. In general, rents linked to turnover, occupational rents, overage arrangements and so on are likely to fall into the definition of 'uncertain' consideration since the amount of rent payable depends on uncertain future events, i.e. the level of future profitability, turnover or rents received and payments made by tenants; or a period of uncertainty when there are no sublettings in place and the future market rent may be substituted for the rent received in the rental formula. There may also be adjustments required in calculating the amount of the payment for the deduction of relevant expenditure by the tenant such as insurance or cost of providing services. Such rent is totally dependent upon future events. These have to be dealt initially upon the basis of reasonable estimates of future rent, so far as there is no fixed rent for the particular year, and subject to review of a retrospective nature at some time during or at the end of the fifth year of the term of the lease.

For these purposes, however, it has to be noted that there are potentially two such five-year periods producing different calculations, but with a credit. There is the initial five-year period from substantial performance of the agreement for lease and a replacement five-year period starting from the date of the actual grant which terminates and supplants the initial five-year period. When making the second calculation, credit is available by reference to the rent taxed at substantial performance of the agreement to lease.

This need for review (and the double five-year period) produces a complex multiple reporting obligation, namely:

(i) Initial calculation – at both effective dates[28]

As at the effective date for the agreement for lease or date of grant,[29] it is necessary to put into the formula set out above the actual or estimated rent for the first five years of the term and an assumed rent for all years after the expiration of the fifth year.[30] Where there is an initial fixed rent or a rent holiday for a few years followed by a review to, say, market rent, it is necessary to insert the initial rent (or nil or the reduced figure for a rent holiday). If the first review date falls after the expiration of the fifth year of the term or within the final three months of the five-year period (FA 2003, Sched. 17A, para. 7A) there will be a fixed rent and this is also the assumed rent for the remainder of the term; but there is a high risk of taxable abnormal increases thereafter.

For each year in the period after the first review date it is necessary to make a reasonable estimate expected to be payable including the expected effect of any review until the end of the five-year period. For periods after the expiration of the fifth year of the term, the rent to be taken into account ('assumed rent') is the highest amount of rent expected to be paid in any 12

---

28 Should there be a temporal separation between entry into possession, i.e. substantial performance and 'completion' in the technical sense. The initial return will effectively lapse and have to be replaced by a totally new return with the limited rent credit relief. There will, therefore, be a new and provisional return for the same lease with the time frame of five years moved.

29 For convenience the double chargeable transaction will be referred to as the effective date but it must be remembered that there is a second effective date as of the grant of the lease pursuant to FA 2003, Sched. 17A, para. 12A.

30 There may or may not be a minimum rent payable. However, the existence of a minimum rent would appear to be no longer the sole relevant factor in determining the net present value of the rent. The existence of the minimum rent is merely one of the elements to be taken into account in making the necessary estimates of future rent. In consequence, the general provisions concerned with variable consideration would appear to be applicable.

consecutive months during the first five years. It has to be noted that this is any 12 months and is not necessarily linked to rent periods which may lead to inconvenience in practice, particularly for leases at a monthly rent reserved by reference to turnover if HMRC Stamp Taxes takes a strict view of this requirement. The SDLT is, therefore, calculated by reference to the initial actual rent until review and subsequent estimated rents for the first five years (FA 2003, s.51), and for the balance of the term it is the 'assumed rent'.

(ii) First five years

Where the rent varies during the first five years of the term so that the rent for the balance of the five years becomes fixed during the first five years, the tax is recalculated as from the effective date on the basis of the actual rents paid in the past and fixed for the future, i.e. upon the basis of the reviewed rent. The actual rent paid to the review date and the reviewed rent for the period between review dates are inserted into the formula for the first five years and, in general, the reviewed rent will form the basis of the assumed rent for the balance of the term.

(iii) Fifth year cut-off

Where the rent does not become certain during the first five years of the term, as will be the case in turnover or similar rents, a retrospective reassessment of the position is required after the end of the fifth year of the term of the lease. This is carried out upon the basis of the rent actually paid during that period, and as regards the rent for each year of the term of the lease after the fifth year this is assumed to be an amount equal to the highest amount of rent payable in respect of any consecutive 12-month period during the initial five years. This 'assumed rent' is a key factor in relation to the taxation of the lease and is involved in many subsequent charges and calculations such as holding over and abnormal rent increases; assignees will require its details.

Rent reductions

It is possible for rent to reduce in accordance with the terms of the lease such as where there is a decline in turnover during the first five years. This will be taken into account on the revision calculation at the end of the fifth year. Although upwards and downwards rent reviews are currently rare, where they do exist the downward movement may mean that tax has been overpaid. In these situations a repayment claim is possible, together with interest from the date of payment (FA 2003, s.80(4)). Different principles apply where there is a rent reduction not pursuant to the terms of the lease (FA 2003, Sched. 17A, para. 13).

Perpetual review – abnormal increase risk

Although the basic provisional SDLT position is intended to be terminated at the end of the fifth year of the term of the lease and subsequent reviews or variations are to be ignored,[31] there is an anti-avoidance provision (FA 2003, Sched. 17A, paras. 14 and 15) whereby an abnormal increase of rent is deemed to be the grant of a new lease[32] for the increased rent and the balance of the unexpired term of the original lease.[33] However, the base rent is not the previous passing rent but the assumed rent for all years after the fifth in the initial calculation or the previous abnormally increased rent. A rent increase is abnormal if it is greater than 5 per cent of the existing rent plus the increase in the Retail Price Index over the relevant period but this has to be calculated in accordance with a complex formula. It is, apparently, the view of HMRC Stamp Taxes that this applies not merely to rent reviews, but also to fluctuating rents such as profit-sharing or turnover rents. It can apply even in commercial situations such as where there is a lease on favourable terms in a new development which proves to be successful so that rents soar upon review. The lease may provide a power for one party to alter the rent basis such as a right to convert from a profit-sharing rent to market rent where there is an assignment of the lease to take account of the different activities of the assignee. The exercise of this power may produce an abnormal increase for these purposes. This means that reviews and other variations in rent such as exceptional fluctuations in turnover, or rents received from sub-leases, need to be regularly monitored, possibly annually, in order to be able to comply with this obligation to calculate the tax and notify HMRC Stamp Taxes should it produce an abnormal increase.

This trap exists in many routine situations; for example:

- although rent holidays or rent-free periods appear to offer a reasonably low SDLT charge it is virtually inevitable that the first review of the rent after the rent-free period will produce an abnormal increase in the rent giving rise to a deemed new lease at the new rent (FA 2003, Sched. 17A, paras. 14 and 15);
- rents are frequently linked to rents received from sub-tenants, turnover or business profits arising from a development and similar factors. Such rents do not have an element of stability and change frequently by reference to future circumstances which will require frequent notification of transactions and recalculation of the SDLT payable or reclaimable;

---

31 Provided that these are pursuant to the terms of the lease.
32 But this is linked with the original lease: FA 2003, Sched. 17A, para. 14(5).
33 There would appear to be no carry forward of the discounting under the existing lease.

- the lease may contain provisions whereby one party has the power to change the rent basis such as an election to switch from a profit-sharing to a market rent.

Reasonable estimates

The 'rent' for the purposes of calculating the tax and completing the return form is a reasonable estimate of the amount or value of the rent (FA 2003, s.51). To avoid allegations of fraud and negligence the parties will, therefore, be required to make a reasonable estimate of the rents they expect to receive over the first five years of the term of the lease in order to apply the formula for determining net present value. This will involve additional complexity when applying the formula since there will need to be a separate reasonable estimate of the future rent for each of those five years. Simply inserting the current rent, as frequently suggested by the so-called helpline, as an estimate of future rent for the calculation will clearly not be acceptable. In preparing the land transaction tax return the reasonable estimate of the future rent levels must be prepared on a reasonable basis, i.e. supported by such professional advice, economic and other analysis as is regarded appropriate by HMRC Stamp Taxes. Notwithstanding the difficulty of obtaining professional advice because advisers are not fortune tellers, failure to carry out a 'proper' exercise will undoubtedly be regarded as producing a 'negligent' return with all the appropriate penalties imposed including the possibility that HMRC may raise an assessment against the taxpayer and his professional advisers for a period of up to 21 years (FA 2003, Sched. 10, para. 31(2)). As an underestimate will involve interest charges since an increase of 5 per cent plus Retail Price Index is regarded as 'abnormal' and rents may be regarded as a function of interest rates, a 'guestimate' based upon indexation plus a few per cent could perhaps be defended as not being negligent.

Other variations of rent including deeds of variation of rent

(i) Increase of rent

A lease can be varied by deed such as where a landlord makes a payment to a tenant to purchase the benefit of the tenant's improvements and increase the rent accordingly, or simply pays cash to increase the rent in order to enhance the value of the freehold reversion. The variation is treated as if it were the grant of a new lease in consideration of the additional rent made payable by it (FA 2003, Sched. 17A, para. 13). If the rent is increased only to the next rent review date there will be a fairly short lease. On the other hand, if the rent operates to increase the minimum rent for the whole of the term unexpired, the new lease will be treated as being for that unexpired term. As this is deemed to be a new lease the tenant will be the purchaser liable for the tax.

(ii) Reduction and commutation of rent

A reduction of rent if made for consideration provided by the tenant will be a chargeable transaction. It is a variation of the lease within the basic definition of 'acquisition' (FA 2003, s.43(3)(d) and Sched. 17A, para. 15A (as amended)).

Practical problem

Unfortunately, the draftsman has not seen fit to provide any test for determining whether there has been an increase or reduction in the rent which is not always obvious and there are fundamental differences in the manner in which the provisions operate. An increase in rent is taxable whether or not there is chargeable consideration and the tenant is always taxable even where the landlord pays the consideration; reductions are taxable only if there is consideration. There may also be calculation complications since it is not always the passing rent that is involved in the comparisons; it may be the artificial 'assumed rent' for years after the fifth year. Some cases will be fairly obvious but others will be a source of uncertainty. For example, it is not clear whether there is an increase or reduction where there is a change in the review date. In some cases the parties may negotiate a change in the rent basis from a turnover rent to a profit-sharing rent or switch to a market rent. Since many of these rent bases will be uncertain in their own right, it will be difficult if not impossible to carry out a realistic comparison of the situation before and after the change, or to assess whether any variation involves an abnormal increase. It seems, although there is no guidance in the legislation, out of the possibilities available the comparison should be carried out upon the basis of the net present value of either the preceding rent or the assumed rent and the net present value of the new rent. These calculations will involve estimates but since the two rents themselves will or may be commercially uncertain, this provides as reasonable a basis as any other in the absence of an official policy.

Holding over and rent[34]

There can be two forms of holding over regime:

(i) Where a lease for a fixed term has expired and the tenant is holding over 'by operation of law' (which probably means pursuant to a statute such as Part 2 of the Landlord and Tenant Act 1954 (as amended) or its agricultural equivalent and may not apply to contracted-out tenancies; but

---

[34] As the provisions refer back to the effective date of the acquisition of the original lease, it is considered that these provisions do not apply to holding over of leases granted before the introduction of SDLT. Holding over a stamp duty lease at present does not give rise to SDLT issues in the view of HMRC Stamp Taxes.

HMRC Stamp Taxes does not draw this distinction in practice at present) at the start of the first year of holding over, the original lease is deemed to have been extended by one year. If the holding over continues beyond one year the original lease is deemed to have been for a term equal to the original term plus two years, or three or four years and so on.

The SDLT paid upon the original lease has to be recalculated on the basis of a lease for the longer deemed term at the end of each extended term, i.e. every year of the holding over. Tax may become payable for the first time or the transaction become notifiable on a different basis if the term exceeds seven years but there is no obligation to notify simply because the effect of the holding over is to produce a lease for seven years or longer. The rents payable under the holding over arrangements may initially be a continuation of the rents payable during the final years of the contractual term, but may be subject to variation such as an order for interim rents. However, where the initial rent is variable the rent taken into account during the holding over period is the assumed rent for all years after the fifth year not the passing rent. It remains to be seen whether, as is likely, HMRC Stamp Taxes intends to charge orders for interim rents as a deemed new lease for the notional increase over the assumed rent.

Where the new lease is granted pursuant to the Landlord and Tenant Act 1954 and is to be treated as relating back to the contractual termination of the original lease (FA 2003, Sched. 17A, para. 9), the taxable rent for the new lease is reduced by the amount of the rent taken into account for SDLT in the interim period between the termination of the old lease and the actual grant of the new lease (FA 2003, Sched. 17A, para. 9).

(ii) Where a tenant holds over at the expiration of the contractual term otherwise than 'by operation of law' which it seems will include holding over at common law and contracted-out tenancies although this is in general law treated as a new lease of a periodic nature giving rise to a potential charge to SDLT, HMRC Stamp Taxes has indicated that it does not intend to take the point and will treat this as a holding over by operation of law as described above. It is considered that this view may be incorrect but it will usually be beneficial to the taxpayer. The practice may change.

Taxpayers need to exercise care during a holding over including statutory tenancies such as agricultural holdings. During any negotiation the parties may modify the terms of the arrangement which may be a form of surrender and regrant, and thereby create a new tenancy for the purposes of SDLT.[35]

---

35 And, for the time being, taxpayers crucially lose the benefit of no taxation when holding over a stamp duty lease.

8.9 LINKED TRANSACTIONS AND RENEWALS OF LEASES

The basic linked transaction rules (FA 2003, s.108; see Chapter 4) apply to leases as regards premiums and rents, but there are special problems for leases:

- in certain situations such as an abnormal increase in rent and the assignment of leases exempt when granted (FA 2003, Sched. 17A, paras. 14, 15 and 12 respectively) the transaction is taxed as the grant of a new lease which, by statute, is linked with the actual lease;
- where there are linked leases the nil rate slice for the rent has to be apportioned between them. This apportionment is made on the basis of the proportion that the net present value of the rent for the particular lease bears to the total net present value of the rents for all linked leases (FA 2003, Sched. 5, para. 2(5) and (6) (as amended)). Since the linked transaction rules apply on a retrospective basis the allocation to any particular lease may be reduced subsequently. This is likely indirectly to affect assignees of leases who are bound to notify (FA 2003, s.81A and Sched. 17A, para. 12) and who will require an undertaking from the vendor to supply relevant information to enable him to recalculate his tax in respect of the lease or which may affect his abnormal increase calculation and, in consequence, he may require an indemnity against any additional tax arising.

Successive linked leases

The basic planning strategy for leases is to operate upon the basis of short-term leases possibly with options to renew exploiting the multiple use of the nil rate slice upon rents. Such options are ignored initially in determining the term of the lease (FA 2003, Sched. 5, para. 6(5)) and the short term will mean in many cases that the amount by reference to which the SDLT is to be charged will fall within the nil rate band. However, where successive linked leases are granted of the same or substantially the same premises, the leases are treated as a single lease granted at the time of the grant of the first lease for a term of the aggregate of the terms of all the leases in the series for the time being in consideration of the aggregate net present value of the rent payable under all such leases (FA 2003, Sched. 17A, para. 5).

The practical problem will be most frequently encountered in relation to options to renew leases. The general position would appear to be governed by ss.46(1) and 108 of FA 2003. As the linked transaction rules apply only as between the same parties or connected persons, it seems that the new lease arising upon the exercise of an option in an existing lease cannot be linked where the original lease has been assigned to some persons unconnected with the original tenant, because the exercise of the option to renew is not between the same parties. The view of HMRC Stamp Taxes is not known but any suggestion that assignees could be directly affected is generally considered to be incorrect, but as discussed elsewhere the exercise of an option to renew may indirectly affect the tax position of an assignee of another linked lease and require him to report and pay additional tax. He should insist upon suitable indemnities. Where the option is exercised by the original tenant, it appears to be necessary to investigate the grant of the original lease and whether there was an arrangement or understanding between the landlord and the tenant that the option would be exercised. If there is established on the evidence that there was a postponed genuine commercial decision as to whether the option would or would not be exercised the original lease and the new lease are not linked (see further Chapter 4).

8.10 THE TERM OF THE LEASE

The term of the lease is important for various reasons including:

- the calculation of the net present value of the rent (FA 2003, Sched. 5 (as amended));
- whether the lease is for less than seven years or seven years or longer when different reporting obligations apply (FA 2003, s.77 (as amended)).

There are at least four important dates in relation to the length of a lease:

- the date from which the term is to be computed which may frequently be earlier than any agreement for lease, substantial performance or the actual grant (*Alan Estates Ltd* v. *W.G. Stores Ltd* [1981] 3 All ER 481);
- the date of the agreement for lease; such agreements are not taxable (FA 2003, s.44(2), but the date of the agreement for lease may be information required for the purposes of completing the land transaction return;
- the date of the substantial performance of the agreement for lease;
- the date of the grant of the lease itself.

Three of these may be important in relation to the charging and reporting obligations for SDLT:

- the 'start date' or term commencement date, i.e. the date from which the term of the lease is calculated. This date has no bearing on the length of the lease. Its main practical significance is in determining whether a rent review takes effect during the final three months of the first five years of the term (FA 2003, Sched. 17A, para. 7A);
- the date of substantial performance of the agreement for lease, i.e. the effective date which starts certain of the notification and payment provisions and is the relevant date for fixing the term in calculating the SDLT (FA 2003, Sched. 5, para. 6(2), but amendment unclear);

- the date of the actual grant of the lease being the date from which the 30-day notification and payment provisions run (FA 2003, ss.44(8) and 77) even where there has been prior substantial performance of an agreement for lease (FA 2003, s.44(8)).

Term of the lease for rent duty calculation

Where an agreement for lease has been entered into[36] and the agreement is substantially performed otherwise than by 'completion' so that an effective date has been triggered and subsequently the actual lease is granted pursuant to an agreement, the term of the lease is:

- initially the period from substantial performance until the end of the contractual term specified in the lease; or
- where there is a subsequent grant from the date of the grant until the end of the contractual term.

Fixed terms

It is provided (FA 2003, s.120) that references to a lease for a definite term are to leases for a fixed term (FA 2003, s.120(2)(a)).

Special cases

(i) Renewals of leases

The existence of an option to renew or extend the lease is to be ignored when initially determining the contractual term of the lease for calculating the stamp duty upon the rent (FA 2003, Sched. 5, para. 6(5)).[37] Where a lease is renewed such as by the exercise of an option it may be a linked transaction and the original and new terms have to be aggregated (FA 2003, Sched. 17A, para. 9), so that the initial tax has to be reviewed on the basis of a lease for the combined term of the two leases as described later in this chapter.

(ii) Holding over

The holding over or continuation of periodic tenancies is treated as a retrospective extension of the term. Although such a possibility of holding over or continuation is ignored in making the initial calculation, that initial

---

36 Where the parties do not adopt the unusual course of proceeding directly from negotiation to the actual grant.
37 This raises the question of the effect of an option to extend the lease which appears to be different from an option to renew; see *Baker* v. *Merckel* [1960] 1 QB 657.

assessment has to be revisited and revised when holding over commences and the tax recalculated on the basis of the term increased by one year, with a subsequent revision every year thereafter whilst the lease is held over or the periodic leasing continues. This will affect assignees of the lease.

Where a new lease is granted by order of the court under the Landlord and Tenant Act 1954 or other legislation, the new lease may be treated as if it began on the expiration of the previous lease (FA 2003, Sched. 17A, para. 5), for the purposes of obtaining a credit in respect of the charge upon the rent.

(iii) Break clauses and notices to quit

For the purposes of the calculation, no account is taken of any right of either party to determine the lease such as by notice to quit, forfeiture or otherwise. A potential area of difficulty would be break clauses since it is provided that a lease terminable by notice is a lease for an indefinite term (FA 2003, Sched. 17A, para. 4(5)(c)), but it is provided that, *inter alia*, break clauses are to be ignored, to counteract any suggestion that a lease terminable by notice is a lease for an indefinite term, although the drafting is less than helpful (FA 2003, Sched. 17A, para. 2(b)).[38] The tax is calculated on the basis of the maximum term and there is no refund if the break clause should be exercised.

(iv) 'Indefinite' terms[39]

For the purposes of computing the SDLT upon the rent, a lease for an indefinite term is treated as if it were a lease for one year. Where there is a lease for a fixed term and thereafter until terminated by notice, it is for an initial term equal to the fixed term plus one year. This originally expressly applied to, *inter alia*:

- a perpetual lease which is treated by the Law of Property Act 1925 as a lease for 2,000 years;
- a lease for life which is treated by the Law of Property Act 1925 as being a lease for 90 years;[40] or
- a lease determinable on the marriage of the lessee.[41]

Although these provisions do not appear expressly in the amended Sched. 17A, it seems clear that such leases are to be treated as being for an indefinite

---

38 See *Baker* v. *Merckel* [1960] 1 QB 657.
39 It must not be overlooked that a lease for an unascertainable term is void for uncertainty; see, for example, *Lace* v. *Chantler* [1944] KB 368.
40 Subject to determination upon the relevant death: Law of Property Act 1925, s.149(6).
41 These three types of lease appear to fall within FA 2003, Sched. 17A, para. 4(2).

term because of the provision excluding the effect of other legislation upon the term of the lease which is applied to:

- a periodic tenancy or other interest or right[42] determinable by a period of notice;
- a tenancy at will in England and Wales or Northern Ireland. Although a tenancy at will is not a chargeable interest (FA 2003, s.48(2)(c)(1)), this is presumably necessary to identify those interests that may be exempt; and
- any other interest or right determinable by notice at any time (FA 2003, s.120(2)(b)).

A lease for an indefinite term is treated (pursuant to FA 2003, Sched. 17A, para. 4(1)) as being initially a lease for a fixed term of one year. If it continues into a second, third or subsequent year it is treated 'retrospectively' as a lease for two, three, four years and so on, and the tax calculation will have to be revised on the basis of a longer term. In such cases at the start of each new year of the lease, i.e. at the end of the current deemed fixed-term lease, it is necessary to reassess 'retrospectively' as from the original effective date taking it into account as an initial grant of a lease for the current deemed fixed term.

8.11 THE PREMIUM

Subject to certain exclusions mentioned later, where there is chargeable consideration other than rent in respect of a lease then not only the rent but also the other consideration is subject to SDLT (FA 2003, Sched. 5, para. 9(1)).[43] A premium will therefore include everything that falls within the general definition of 'chargeable consideration' contained in Sched. 4 to FA 2003.

It is a fundamental question as to what is consideration for the lease including building works and services and land exchanges including surrenders of other leases. As *Eastham* v. *Leigh, London and Provincial Properties Limited* [1971] 2 All ER 887 clearly shows, what is described as a 'condition' may in fact be the consideration for the grant of the lease. Subject to special rules, the basic computational rules will apply with the right to apply to defer payment of the tax in cases of variable premiums. In theory, when calculating the premium, any lessor's costs paid by the lessee should be included, but as a matter of practice, HMRC Stamp Taxes ignored them for

---

42 On the meaning of the words 'interest or right' in this context see Chapter 2 above.
43 Where the lease for a rent or a variation is a linked transaction with another transaction for the purposes of s.55 of the FA 2003, no account is taken of the rent in determining the relevant consideration: FA 2003, Sched. 5, para. 9(5).

beneficial stamp duty ((1959) *Law Society Gazette* 95). It is not yet clear whether the practice is to continue into SDLT.

However, there is a major practical difference between sales and leases in that the liability to deal with the open or provisional estimated initial assessment will pass to the assignee in the case of a lease premium (FA 2003, Sched. 17A, para. 11). In consequence, he is vulnerable to the problems arising in connection with the resolution of this open tax position even though he may not contractually assume the liability for the payment of the deferred consideration to the landlord.

A grant of a lease or substantial performance of an agreement for a lease of an inadequate consideration, such as where the premium is below market value or the rent is low[44] is, in general, taxable only upon the actual premium and/or rent unless the connected company charge or other provisions such as the partnership regime expressly impose tax upon a deemed market value premium plus the net present value of the actual rent (FA 2003, s.53). It is important to note that the market value charge applies only to the premium. HMRC Stamp Taxes seems to have abandoned its previous attempt to find a 'market rent' for leases which is an immensely complicated exercise and virtually impossible to apply in practice for tax purposes even with the wait-and-see rules for rents.

Particular situations – with special lease modifications

The following situations apply the normal rules for computation but with significant modification.

(i) Variable premiums

Where a lease is granted for a variable premium the normal rules for contingent, unascertained or uncertain consideration apply including the right to apply to defer payment (FA 2003, s.90; Stamp Duty Land Tax (Administration) Regulations 2003, SI 2003/2837).[45] In consequence, the tax will be paid initially on an estimated basis with an obligation to notify and reassess the tax as contingencies occur or the consideration becomes ascer-

---

44 HMRC Stamp Taxes has great difficulty in dealing with what appear to be low rents which it, and other divisions of HMRC, seem to think is more or less automatically not a market value situation. However, low rents can be commercially agreed such as rent holidays where the tenant is incurring the fitting out or similar expenses and prefers a low rent to a reverse premium to reimburse him for carrying out the works. These commercial issues will need to be carefully documented in case HMRC Stamp Taxes contends that the low rent produces a market value charge for SDLT purposes in those situations where market value is involved such as connected companies, partnerships or land exchanges.

45 There is no right to defer tax in relation to variable rent.

tained (FA 2003, ss.51, 80 and 90 on instalments; see Chapter 4); but the obligation to deal with the subsequent adjustment in the tax passes to the assignee of the lease (FA 2003, Sched. 17A, para. 13), notwithstanding that he may not be personally affected by or assume all or any part of the liability to pay the outstanding or deferred consideration to the landlord. Assignees of leases will need to investigate these issues.

(ii) Instalments and periodical payments[46]

Where the premium consists wholly or partly of sums other than rent payable by instalments or periodically (FA 2003, s.52(6)), the SDLT is payable upon the total payment of the instalments or aggregate of the periodical payments; but where the periodical payments are payable for life, in perpetuity,[47] an indefinite period or a definite period exceeding 12 years, the amount is limited to the amount payable over 12 years (FA 2003, s.52(1) and (2) ignoring linking to the Retail Price Index (FA 2003, s.52(3)).

One particularly important 'periodical payment' will be VAT where this is not reserved as part of the rent or additional rent. In relation to the equivalent provisions for stamp duty HMRC Stamp Taxes indicated that it regarded such VAT as consideration not rent which is payable periodically, i.e. a 'premium'. The question whether it is to be taxed as a periodical premium or as 'rent' could substantially affect the SDLT liability (see Chapter 4). The main issue in practice will depend upon the drafting and whether, where the VAT is not reserved as rent or an additional rent, it is taxable as a periodical premium pursuant to s.52 of FA 2003 as outlined above. However, as described elsewhere, at present in practice HMRC Stamp Taxes does not appear to be pursuing this point and does not appear to be challenging or enquiring into land transaction returns which treat such VAT as 'rent'.[48]

(iii) Works[49]

Chargeable consideration includes 'works' which are not restricted to building works but include improvements, repairs (but note the exclusion for repairs in FA 2003, Sched. 17A, para. 11) and other items (see Chapter 9) chargeable upon open market cost with relief for works to be carried out on the land being demised.

---

46 FA 2003, s.52; see Chapter 4.
47 Although this is unlikely in relation to leases which should have a definite or ascertainable date for termination.
48 Obviously failure to deal in some way with such actual VAT will mean a possible attack for a negligent or fraudulent return and leave the taxpayer open to a discovery assessment.
49 FA 2003, Sched. 4, para. 10 (as amended); see Chapter 9.

However, these charging provisions will give rise to a particularly acute problem in relation to leases because of the problem of the exemption for works constructed upon the land to be demised at the cost of the tenant but not making use of the landlord or anyone connected with the landlord as a builder (FA 2003, Sched. 4, para. 10(2)). The exclusion from charge for the tenant's own works is available only where these take place after 'the effective date', i.e. only those works constructed after the effective date of the grant of the lease if appropriate will qualify for the exemption. Works carried out on the land to be demised before the effective date will be taxable where the carrying out of the works is part of the chargeable consideration (as in *Eastham v. Leigh, London and Provincial Properties Limited* [1971] 2 All ER 887).

This means that the issue of 'substantial performance' of the agreement for lease will be crucial and, in particular, whether the entry on to the land by the builder for the purpose of carrying out the works before the right to call for the lease becomes 'unconditional' will be treated as taking 'possession' will have important consequences, possibly avoiding the need to insert artificial steps such as the payment of £1 'rent' to generate substantial performance.[50] The problem of para. 12A of Sched. 17A to FA 2003 creating two effective dates where substantial performance of the agreement for lease precedes the grant of the lease is specially provided for (FA 2003, Sched. 4, para. 10(2A)) and works executed before the grant of the lease but after substantial performance of the agreement for lease are within the exemption. Clearly, organisation of these arrangements in the future will require considerable delicacy and prudence.

(iv) Land exchanges involving leases

Land exchanges will involve a charge upon a consideration (FA 2003, s.47) equal to the market value of any of the leases being acquired plus any rent reserved by that lease so tax is charged upon the market value of the property received, not the property transferred (FA 2003, Sched. 4, para. 5).[51] In conse-

---

50 However, it must be noted that in the Inland Revenue Tax Bulletin August 1995 dealing with contingent rents Stamp Taxes indicated that if it took the view that a sum was artificially inserted as 'rent' solely for the purpose of mitigating stamp duty it would not regard that sum as a true rent and be ignored. The correctness of this approach is open to fundamental objection and so far as is known it was never actually raised in practice. It remains to be seen whether this type of argument will be raised for the purposes of SDLT which, being a transaction tax, is more vulnerable to arguments based upon the approach of cases such as *Ramsay v. IRC* [1982] AC 300 and *Furniss v. Dawson* [1984] STC 153.

51 It should be noted that in such transfer and leaseback class of transactions it has for a decade been the view of HMRC Stamp Taxes that the value of the land transferred is determined upon a vacant possession basis ignoring the obligation to grant the lease back.

quence, where a lease is granted in consideration of the transfer of other land the lessee is liable to tax upon a notional premium equal to the market value of the lease, if any. If the lease is at a full rent it is unlikely to have a market value and the tax charge will be limited to the net present value of the rent.

This charge upon the premium arising from the land exchange rules is subject to exceptions where the premium is not taxable such as:

- relief for leases back entered into as part of an exempt sale and leaseback arrangement but these are subject to tax on assignment (FA 2003, s.57A); and
- two categories of surrender and grant of new leases which are taken out of the land exchange charge; namely:
  - surrenders and grants of new leases of different premises (FA 2003, Sched. 17A, para. 16); and
  - surrenders and regrants of the same premises;[52]
- certain reliefs exist for land transactions entered into in connection with a limited range of PFI projects (FA 2003, Sched. 4, para. 17 (as amended)).

Deemed premium – connected companies and partnerships

Where a lease is granted to a connected company or to or by a partnership in a transaction between connected parties (FA 2003, Sched. 15, Part 3), it will be subject to tax upon the net present value of the rent reserved by the lease. If that rent is below the market rent there will also be a deemed premium equal to the market value, if any, for a lease on those terms, because an arrangement involving a lease to a connected company or to or by a partnership is deemed to take place at market value (FA 2003, s.53 and Sched. 15, Part 7). Reliefs have been made available for leases to connected companies where:

- the lease or agreement is with a corporate trustee[53] and immediately after the transaction the corporate trustee holds the property as trustee in the course of a business that it carries on that includes or consists of the management of trusts; or
- immediately after the transaction the corporate trustee holds the property as trustee and the lessee is connected with the corporate trustee only by reason of the lessor being the settlor.

There is an exemption for certain transactions in a liquidation of a company but it is most unlikely that these transactions will involve the grant of leases by a liquidator.

---

52 FA 2003, Sched. 17A, para. 16 with a limited additional relief for rent in the overlap period: FA 2003, Sched. 17A, para. 9.
53 The position is obscure where there are both corporate and individual trustees. It is thought that the charge is not intended to apply in such cases.

8.12 EXCLUSIONS FROM THE CHARGE ON PREMIUMS

A number of items of consideration are excluded from the scope of chargeable consideration other than rent.

(a) Reverse premiums

Inducements paid by a landlord to a tenant to take the lease are not taxable (FA 2003, Sched. 17A, para. 18). However, it must not be overlooked that a reverse premium, i.e. an inducement to the tenant to take the lease will usually mean a higher rent because the landlord may recover the payment through the rent. Such rent will be subject to the heavy charge to SDLT upon rents (FA 2003, Sched. 5). In these situations it is likely to be more SDLT efficient for the tenant to choose a rent holiday rather than a reverse premium (which would be subject to tax as income); the lower rent would attract a lower charge to SDLT although there is a greater risk of abnormal rent increases in the unlikely event that the rent holiday exceeds five years (FA 2003, Sched. 7, para. 5).

(b) Indemnities given by tenants

Where a tenant agrees to indemnify the landlord in respect of liabilities to a third party arising from breach of an obligation owed by the landlord in relation to the land that is the subject-matter of the transaction, neither the agreement nor any payment made in pursuance of it counts as chargeable consideration (FA 2003, Sched. 4, para. 16).

(c) Covenants and miscellaneous obligations under the lease

It is provided (FA 2003, Sched. 4, para. 13) that the following do not count as chargeable consideration.

1. Any undertaking by the tenant to repair, maintain or insure the demised premises or, in Scotland, the leased premises.
2. An undertaking by the tenant to pay any amount in respect of services, repairs, maintenance or insurance or the landlord's costs of management.[54] It is provided that if a single sum is expressed to be payable by way of rent then it should be treated as entirely rent even though it may relate to other matters such as services. The benefit of this exclusion of a charge to services from tax as a premium may be lost if the payment

---

54 This will need to be considered in connection with the provisions of para. 4(1) of Sched. 5 to FA 2003.

of rent wraps up the service charges as part of a single unapportioned sum (see further the discussion of 'rent' earlier in this chapter).

3. Any other obligation undertaken by the tenant that is not such as to affect the rent that a tenant would be prepared to pay on the open market. This is an extremely cryptic provision since virtually every restrictive covenant or restriction in a lease may have some effect on the rent that a tenant on the open market might be prepared to pay. A user covenant of commercial premises affects value, otherwise tenants would not be prepared to pay substantial sums for their release or relaxation. Moreover, the structure of this provision suggests that the giving of a covenant is part of the consideration for the lease. Since a covenant is a chargeable interest this points to a normal lease transaction which is technically a land exchange taxable upon market value.

4. Any guarantee of the payment of rent or performance of any other obligation of the tenant under the lease.[55] Again this is an odd provision because there is no obvious acquisition of a chargeable interest, unless a right of reimbursement by means of subrogation is a chargeable interest which seems difficult to justify as the right to recover rent is an integral part of the lease and not a separate right.[56] It seems bizarre that the draftsman of the legislation thought that a payment by a third party, i.e. a non-tenant, could be consideration for the 'acquisition' of a chargeable interest. The consequence of this view is that third parties can provide chargeable consideration, but only if they are connected with the purchaser (FA 2003, Sched. 4, para. 1) so that a bank guarantee would not be within these provisions. Additionally, the mere giving of a guarantee is the provision of consideration which is, if chargeable, substantially performed when the contract of guarantee is given because at that stage the contract is simultaneously completed. Therefore, whilst this provision relieves many routine transactions where third parties give, and make payments pursuant to, guarantees, the fact that it was believed to be necessary to provide this relief means that there are many situations where it is believed by HMRC Stamp Taxes that a chargeable transaction occurs.

5. Any penal rent, or increased rent in the nature of penal rent payable in respect of any breach of an obligation of the tenant under the lease.

---

[55] Without this provision the charge upon services pursuant to FA 2003, Sched. 4, para. 11 would include a charge to SDLT upon the market cost of obtaining a third party guarantee on the tenant's obligations.

[56] But special relief applies to leases granted to the guarantor: FA 2003, Sched. 17A, para. 9(1)(d).

UNDERSTANDING SDLT

The exclusion from charge applies not merely to assuming the obligation but also to any payment made in discharge of the obligation (FA 2003, Sched. 4, para. 13(2)). The assumption or release of any such obligation in relation to the assignment of the lease is not chargeable consideration (FA 2003, Sched. 17A, para. 17). However, two points should be noted:

1. If the sum is drafted as part of the 'rent' then it may be chargeable as rent notwithstanding this exemption (FA 2003, Sched. 17A, para. 6).
2. Payments made in respect of a breach of any of these obligations are, *prima facie*, not chargeable. However, as *Banning* v. *Wright* 48 TC 421 indicates, a payment in respect of a breach of covenant may also be in whole or in part a payment for a variation of the covenant which is a chargeable transaction (FA 2003, s.43(3)(c) and (d); Sched. 17A, para. 15A); this has become a significant issue following the reinstatement of a charge upon all variations of leases for a consideration. There is also a question of whether HMRC Stamp Taxes intends to attack settlements of disputes involving breaches of leasehold and other covenants as a release of all or part of a chargeable interest. This exclusion would apply to the extent that the payment was not merely compensation for the breach but was for a modification of the covenant. The problem also remains whether HMRC Stamp Taxes will wish to contend that payment for the release of a restrictive or other covenant which might affect the amount of the rent is a taxable variation of a lease as a release of a chargeable interest for a chargeable consideration. This may be a difficult argument to maintain because it would mean that covenants in leases (at least in those cases where they might affect the rent) are separate chargeable interests granted to the landlord by the tenant so that every lease would be a land exchange taking place at market value; in consequence in the absence of aggressive or provocative planning it is unlikely that HMRC Stamp Taxes would pursue the point.

8.13 VARIATIONS OF LEASES

It is provided that 'acquisition' of an interest includes the 'variation' of a chargeable interest (see Chapter 2) but this has been modified in relation to leases (FA 2003, s.43(3)(d) and Sched. 17A, para. 15A (as amended)).[57] In consequence, a variation of a lease is taxable where:

- it involves a surrender and regrant;
- it reduces the rent;
- it increases the rent otherwise than pursuant to the terms of the lease;

---

57 Different rules apply for periods prior to March 2005.

- it reduces the term of the lease (FA 2003, Sched. 17A, para. 15A (as amended)); or
- it is any other variation made for a consideration.

These charging provisions which are the product of several piecemeal amendments and changes of policy are fraught with difficulties of interpretation. For example, the draftsman has not made clear whether a release of a covenant in a lease such as a change of user restriction is chargeable as a variation of a lease or a release (see also *Banning* v. *Wright* 48 TC 421).

There is an express charge upon a variation that reduces the term of a lease; but such a variation will be a surrender and regrant which is chargeable as a land exchange with a certain amount of relief (FA 2003, s.47; Sched. 17A, paras. 9 and 16). It is difficult to find any routine situations where this might apply since a termination of a lease by means of a notice to quit or break clause is difficult to regard as a variation which suggests that the lease continues albeit in a modified form rather than ceases to exist altogether. Similarly, inserting a break clause although potentially shortening the lease does not actually vary the term.[58]

Surrenders and regrants

A lease may be surrendered for a lease of other premises where there is an exclusion from the land exchange rules. Where the new lease is between the same parties and for the same premises there is a reduction in the taxable rent (FA 2003, Sched. 17A, paras. 9 and 16). A surrender and regrant may be effected expressly.

Where a tenant enters into a deed of variation increasing or reducing either the term or the demised premises, it is a surrender and regrant. A typical situation will be where a tenant of a flat enlarges the term of the lease.[59] Occasionally a landlord and tenant agree to what purports to be a variation in the terms of the lease, but which, in the probably unwitting eyes of the parties, has the effect of a surrender of the old lease, followed by a regrant. The best example is where the parties agree to a variation in the length of the lease as in *Baker* v. *Merckel* [1960] 1 QB 657. A variation of the rent by deed of variation will only result in an implied surrender and regrant if that is the intention of the parties (*Gable Construction* v. *IRC* [1968] 1 WLR 1426).

---

[58] Inserting a break clause after Finance (No.2) Act 2005 is chargeable if for a consideration provided by the tenant.

[59] However, if the tenant takes an overriding lease and merges the existing lease the merger does not give rise to a chargeable transaction. The overriding lease will be taxable upon any premium paid and rent reserved. This may not be as efficient as on a surrender and regrant since the latter may qualify for a rent credit pursuant to FA 2003, Sched. 17A, para. 9.

There will be an exchange in the form of a surrender in consideration of the grant of the new lease and vice versa. This produces a, *prima facie*, multiple charge pursuant to the land exchange rules as major interests are involved (FA 2003, s.51 and Sched. 4, para. 5). However, two provisions modify the application of these basic charging provisions, namely:

1. It is provided that in the case of a surrender of a lease and the grant of a new lease, whether of the same or different premises, the exchanges of the property interests are ignored. The general effect for most cases appears to be:

    - the landlord will not be providing any chargeable consideration so that his 'acquisition' will be exempt;[60] and
    - the tenant will not be regarded as 'exchanging' land so that:
        - his acquisition will not be at market value but for the actual consideration, if any, supplied to the landlord for the variation of the lease; and
        - the tenant will be taxable upon the rent reserved by the new lease but he will be entitled to a form of credit where he has paid SDLT upon the original lease being surrendered provided that the new lease relates to substantially the same premises as the original lease. The 'credit' takes the form of reducing the amount of rent reserved by the new lease to be included in the rent formula by an amount equal to the rent for each particular year of the unexpired balance of the term of the original lease.

2. Where the premises are the same, the chargeable rent is reduced by reference to the rent payable for the balance of the surrendered term.

8.14 ASSIGNMENT OF LEASES

The assignment of an existing lease is an acquisition by the assignee of a chargeable major interest generally notifiable (FA 2003, s.77 (as amended)). Tax will be chargeable upon any consideration provided by the assignee, but the undertaking by the assignee to pay all future rent is not chargeable consideration and any covenant by the assignee to perform the covenants in the lease and, presumably, indemnify the assignor against any liabilities in respect of a breach of covenant is ignored in computing the tax (FA 2003, Sched. 17A, para. 17; see also Sched. 4, para. 16).

---

60 FA 2003, Sched. 3, para. 1 which will have important implications for his reporting obligations, see FA 2003, s.77.

Where the assignee pays a lump sum to the assignor which is part of the consideration attributable to the land as opposed to, for example, chattels,[61] this is taxed as a consideration. In this area there is a major issue of principle of whether a payment for goodwill is in law an additional sum payable for the land rather than true goodwill (*Whiteman Smith Motor Co* v. *Chaplin* [1934] 2 KB 35; *Mullins* v. *Wessex Motors* [1947] 2 All ER 727).

Where the assignor makes a payment to the assignee as an inducement to take the assignment, a 'reverse premium', such payment is not chargeable consideration (FA 2003, Sched. 4, para. 15(1) and (2)(b)).

Problem areas

The assignment of leases is, however, not entirely straightforward. For example, it is specifically provided (FA 2003, Sched. 17A, para. 12) that where there has been an assignment of a lease and subsequently there is an event or transaction which:

- requires an adjustment in respect of a variable premium such as a premium that is linked to the profits or proceeds of the development by the tenant; or
- requires an adjustment of uncertain rent pursuant to s.80 of FA 2003 during the first five years of the lease (FA 2003, Sched. 17A, paras. 7 and 8); or
- requires a return because there is a later linked transaction so that an earlier transaction becomes notifiable and tax payable[62] which seems to include the exercise of options to renew; or
- requires a return because of the provisions relating to holding over (FA 2003, Sched. 17A, para 4); or
- involves an adjustment of the rent during or at the expiration of the fifth year of the lease (FA 2003, Sched. 17A, para. 8),

the responsibility for dealing with these situations is passed to the assignee of the lease. In consequence, it will be necessary for the assignee to obtain undertakings from the assignor to disclose the relevant information. Assignors will also require undertakings to disclose relevant information where the liability to deal with their outstanding tax liability is not passed to the assignee or they have agreed to indemnify the lessee, when they may wish to have the conduct of the matter with HMRC Stamp Taxes. For example, should a rent review during the first five years of the term produce a higher

---

61 On fixtures and chattels see Chapter 2.
62 FA 2003, s.81A; but as the lease has been assigned there is a fundamental question as to whether the later transaction can be linked because it will not necessarily be between the same parties or persons connected with them. See Chapter 4.

rent than that used in estimating the rents upon the initial assessment this would affect the overall tax liability and require the reallocation of the relevant proportion of the nil rate slice to all linked leases, whether past, present or future. The original tenant will, therefore, need to know what the assignee is doing in relation to the assigned lease. Provision may also be required to deal with issues of additional tax being payable or tax being refundable because of the assignor overestimating or underestimating the relevant rent levels, such as on the five-year adjustment. Assignees will not wish to bear tax[63] and late payment interest because the assignor underestimated or relied upon the advice of the helpline to prepare the return upon the basis of the actual rent and ignore the possible effect of the rent review. Conversely the assignor may be reluctant to allow the assignee to recover overpaid tax as a windfall if he overestimated the possible increase in the rent.

The risk of and the responsibility for dealing with the possibility of an abnormal rent increase lies with the assignee (FA 2003, Sched. 17A, paras. 14 and 15).

Exempt leases

Where the original grant of the lease or substantial performance of the agreement for lease was exempt from SDLT because it was granted:

- in connection with a sale and leaseback transaction (FA 2003, s.57A);
- in connection with an intra-group transaction (FA 2003, Sched. 7, Part 1);
- in connection with a scheme of reconstruction or reorganisation of a company (FA 2003, Sched. 7, Part 2);[64]
- to an exempt public body (FA 2003, s.66);
- to a charity (FA 2003, Sched. 8 (as amended));
- within regulations bringing old stamp duty reliefs into the new tax (Stamp Duty Land Tax (Consequential Amendment of Enactment) Regulations 2003, SI 2003/2867);
- to a nominee prior to Finance (No.2) Act 2005,[65]

the first assignment of that lease that is not also exempt from SDLT by reason of those exemptions is deemed to be the grant of a new lease to the assignee as tenant for the unexpired term of the original lease at the rent

---

63 The position on penalties is uncertain in this case. It is thought that they remain a problem for the original tenant but this is unclear.
64 The provision operates particularly harshly where the lease is granted in connection with a scheme of reorganisation which is not exempt but qualifies only for the reduced rate of 0.5 per cent, which, it seems, is available in relation to both premiums and rent. There is no credit for the reduced rate of SDLT paid pursuant to this provision so that there is an approximate charge of 1.5 per cent upon the rent in such a case.
65 FA 2003, Sched. 3, para. 1 and Sched. 16, para. 3; but such leases are now fully taxable pursuant to Finance (No.2) Act 2005.

reserved (FA 2003, Sched. 17A, paras. 7 and 8). Being treated as the grant of the new lease there will be no benefit of discounting for the expired term of the lease and the assignee faces all of the difficulties of the commencement of a new five-year period for variable rents (FA 2003, Sched. 17A, paras. 7 and 8). The relevant rent is that passing at the effective date for the agreement to assign. This charge may precede the assignment where the assignee substantially performs the purchase contract such as by being allowed into possession before completion to fit out or make alterations to the premises; this risk applies even where the agreement is still conditional upon landlord's consent. This is a harsh provision because it applies even though there was no tax avoidance motive relating to the original grant; nor is there any time limit so that an assignment of the lease which takes place say 15 years after the initial grant and is totally unconnected therewith is taxable under this provision. Assignees need to investigate the tax history of the lease, even where this lease is acquired as simply one of the assets in a bona fide purchase of a business.[66]

8.15 TERMINATION OF LEASES

Lapse of time

Prima facie the termination of a lease by lapse of time is not subject to SDLT. This does not involve a release or surrender and, in general, there will be no consideration when the lease expires. This does not mean that no payments will be made. For example, the tenant may be making payments to the landlord in respect of dilapidations or the landlord may be making payments to the tenant by way of compensation pursuant to the Landlord and Tenant Act 1954 (as amended). Many such payments such as the payment of compensation will not be chargeable consideration since they are not the price being paid for the termination of the lease but are being paid pursuant to statute or as compensation for breach of an obligation. In addition, para. 13 of Sched. 4 to FA 2003 provides that both entering into covenants to repair premises and payments made in pursuant of such a covenant and possibly as damages for breach do not count as chargeable consideration.

Notice to quit and break clauses

The term of the lease for the purpose of SDLT is determined without regard to the existence of a break clause, i.e. the term of the lease for the purposes of the formula for determining the net present value is the maximum length

---

[66] This charge does not apply if the exemption or relief in respect of the original grant of the lease has been withdrawn as a result of a clawback within the relevant three-year period.

of the term; but there is no right to a repayment of tax if the lease is terminated early by the exercise of such powers.

Termination by notice to quit or the operation of a break clause would not seem to be within the charge to SDLT even though the landlord giving the notice to quit may be required to pay some form of compensation either under the terms of the lease or otherwise. A surrender and a notice to quit are different forms of legal operation (*Barrett* v. *Morgan* [2000] 1 All ER 481) and so termination by notice to quit cannot be included under a 'surrender' or 'release' since these require the participation of the tenant whereas a notice to quit is a unilateral action of the landlord; but HMRC Stamp Taxes is apparently considering its position.

Surrenders

HMRC Stamp Taxes spares the dying lease on its deathbed from natural causes or, where the lease is forfeited for breach of covenant, any further exactions. Not so, however, where there is a surrender to the landlord of a fixed term before its expiry by effluxion of time. A surrender of a lease whether by operation of law (FA 2003, s.43(2)) or by deed (LPA 1925, s.52) by a tenant in consideration of a payment or other property or services by the landlord will give rise to a charge to SDLT in respect of which the landlord will be the 'purchaser'. Tax is escaped where there is a 'reverse premium' and the tenant pays the landlord to relieve the tenant of the lease (*Re Duke of Westminster's Settled Estates (No.2)* [1921] 1 Ch 585). Where the other property is a chargeable interest in land there will be a land exchange with each party being subject to tax upon the market value of what he receives (FA 2003, Sched. 4, para. 5). In some cases where the lease of one set of premises is being surrendered in return for the grant of a new lease of other premises this is a land exchange but there is a relief which excludes the land exchange charge in such cases (FA 2003, Sched. 17A, para. 16), so that the tenant is taxable only upon the rent reserved by the new lease and any premium he is paying for the new lease. If the landlord is making a payment to the tenant, it may be important whether this payment is regarded as consideration for the surrender such as payment by the landlord to induce the tenant to surrender; or the grant of a new lease of different premises when it appears to be taxable; or a reverse premium or inducement to take the new lease when it is not taxable (FA 2003, Sched. 4, para. 15); or it is a payment as a contribution to removal expenses, disturbance of business or to fitting out when it appears to be outside the scope of SDLT.

Merger

The extinction of a lease by a merger into the reversionary interest is not, of itself, a chargeable transaction, although the tenant may be facing a tax charge in respect of the transaction(s) by means of which he became entitled to the two interests involved.

Reversionary interest

The removal of stamp duty has removed many of the problems affecting landlords and persons acquiring reversionary interests. There is no longer a charge to tax upon the landlord's counterpart so that, for example, a landlord may sue the tenant for arrears of rent or breach of covenant notwithstanding that the tenant has not paid SDLT.

In relation to the purchase of a reversionary interest, there is no longer any need for any form of denoting upon the transfer of the reversion that any lease to which it is subject has been duly stamped or SDLT has been paid. Where the lease is registered, it can be assumed that some form of SDLT return has been filed. Fortunately, if the tax has not been paid or insufficient tax has been paid and a successful challenge has been mounted by HMRC Stamp Taxes, this has no effect on the title of the person acquiring the reversion or a landlord seeking to sue in respect of the lease.

8.16 EXEMPTIONS FROM LEASE DUTY

There are certain leases and agreements for lease which are exempt from SDLT. These are predominantly the same as the general range of exemptions because the one-size-fits-all drafting of the reliefs applies to both conveyances and leases in the absence of contrary provisions, although certain of the anti-avoidance rules apply only in the case of leases. The basic details of the general exemptions are considered in detail in Chapter 5. There are, however, certain points that require special comment.

Nil rate for premiums

Where the premium for a lease does not exceed £120,000 and the rent reserved does not exceed £600 per annum, the SDLT upon this premium is nil, and if the term of the lease is for less than seven years it is not necessary to notify HMRC Stamp Taxes and as such a lease is not registrable it is not necessary to prepare an SDLT 60 which is only required for registration by the Land Registry (FA 2003, s.77 (as amended)).

Subject whereto the lower rates of SDLT and the linked transaction rules apply to agreements for lease and leases.

Relief for premiums

There are reliefs for certain surrenders and regrants which are taken out of the land exchange rules considered earlier in this chapter.

Rent credits

There are certain situations largely concerned with the reduction of the chargeable rents where preceding rent has been taxed and there is an 'overlap' between the old tax and the new lease. These include:

- surrenders and regrants of leases applying to the same premises (FA 2003, Sched. 17A, para. 9);
- grants of new leases pursuant to the Landlord and Tenant Act 1954 (as amended) (FA 2003, Sched. 17A, para. 9);
- the grant of a lease where there has been a deemed grant upon the substantial performance of the agreement for lease (FA 2003, Sched. 17A, para. 12A).

General exemptions for leases

Charities

The two forms of relief from SDLT upon an agreement for lease or lease granted to a charity pursuant to FA 2003, Sched. 8 are available for leases provided that the numerous conditions are satisfied.

Where a lease has been granted to a charity in addition to the two clawback regimes, within the exemption where the exempt lease is assigned in a non-exempt transaction the assignee is taxed upon the basis that he is being granted a new lease of the unexpired term at the current rent.

Gifts

A grant of a lease for no chargeable consideration is exempt (FA 2003, Sched. 3, para. 1). HMRC Stamp Taxes considers that a lease for a peppercorn rent is for no chargeable consideration and is within the exemption; but a token rent of £1 is chargeable consideration unless the lease is to a connected company when the market value is taxed as a premium (FA 2003, s.53) or the lease is between a partnership and connected persons (FA 2003, Sched. 15, Part 3).

Matrimonial breakdown

A lease granted in relation to a divorce or judicial separation may be exempt (FA 2003, Sched. 3, para. 3).

LEASES

Variations of estates of deceased persons

There would seem to be no reason why the 'exemption' for certain variations of the estates of deceased persons should not extend to a lease granted as part of those arrangements provided that the other conditions are satisfied (FA 2003, Sched. 3, para. 4; see Chapter 5).

Intra-group transactions

The relief for intra-group transactions applies to leases (FA 2003, Sched. 7, Part 1; see Chapter 12); but such relief is subject to clawback and there is a charge upon assignments as the deemed grant of a new lease (FA 2003, Sched. 17A, para. 11).

Reconstructions[67]

The relief for reconstruction and reorganisation of companies may have been inadvertently enlarged to exempt leases as land transactions entered into for the purposes of or in connection with (see *Clarke-Chapman John Thompson v. IRC* [1975] STC 567) the transfer of the undertaking. Subject to the issue of whether there is an undertaking where a lease is granted, it may no longer be necessary to transfer the entire land interests of the company whose business is being transferred in order to qualify for the relief. Granting a lease of the premises utilised or occupied for the purpose of carrying on the activities may now be eligible for relief. This may be helpful where the purpose of the reorganisation is to separate the trading activities of the company from its land but grants of leases do not necessarily qualify as transfers of going concerns for VAT and payment of such tax will cancel the reliefs.

Lease and underlease back

It is provided that the relief for sale and leaseback (FA 2003, s.57A) applies to lease and leaseback transactions such as where one party wishes to keep certain capital allowances. In consequence, where:

- A transfers or grants,
- a major interest in land to B, and
- wholly or partly as consideration B out of that interest grants a lease or sub-lease to A,
- of the same premises as those transferred to B,
- the transaction is not part of a sub-sale arrangement,

---

67 FA 2003, Sched. 7, Part 2; see Chapter 12.

- the consideration for A's transfer to B does not consist of or include anything other than the payment of money[68] or the satisfaction, assumption or release of a debt, which means an obligation whether certain or contingent to pay a sum of money either immediately or in the future, and
- the parties are not members of the same SDLT group,

then the lease or sub-lease is not subject to SDLT.[69] However, B is taxable upon the transfer.

Where this relief is not available, the transaction whether by way of sale and leaseback or lease and underlease back will be subject to two charges to SDLT as a land exchange and HMRC Stamp Taxes is continuing to contend that the transfer of a head lease has to be valued upon a vacant possession basis and without regard to the impact upon the valuation of the terms of the leaseback. This view is considered to be incorrect; it was originally part of the legislation but has disappeared from the current much amended version and this weakens HMRC Stamp Taxes's argument.

'Assignments' of agreements for lease

A form of sub-sale relief is introduced (FA 2003, Sched. 17A, para. 12B) for leases to deal with the situation where A enters into an agreement for lease with B who directs A to grant the lease to C. In certain situations B is not subject to tax but many problems pass to C (see also FA 2003, s.45). The details of this relief are described earlier in this chapter.

Registered social landlords

Limited reliefs are available for short leases granted by registered social landlords as part of an arrangement to provide short-term accommodation with a housing authority (FA 2003, Sched. 3, para. 2).

Right-to-buy and shared ownership

Reliefs are available (FA 2003, Sched. 9 (as amended)) for leases granted in relation to right-to-buy transactions and shared ownership leases, including staircasing transactions.

Rent-to-mortgage[70]

Rent-to-mortgage transactions qualify for relief.

---

68 Whether sterling or a foreign currency.
69 Although 'exempt' the leaseback is fully notifiable: FA 2003, s.77.
70 FA 2003, Sched. 9, para. 6.

PFI projects

Reliefs (FA 2003, Sched. 4, para. 17) are provided for certain leases granted in relation to a limited range of PFI projects.

8.17 RELIEFS NOT AVAILABLE FOR LEASES

Certain reliefs are not available for leases, namely:

- part-exchange of new houses (FA 2003, Sched. 6A);
- relocation relief (FA 2003, Sched. 6A);
- certain exemptions involving compulsory purchase (FA 2003, s.60); reorganisations of public bodies (FA 2003, s.66) and parliamentary constituencies (FA 2003, s.67) appear to require outright transfers so that the grant of a lease would seem to be an unlikely event and may not be exempt. The exemption for land transactions in compliance with planning obligations (FA 2003, s.61) may include the grant of leases;
- alternative finance relief is not available except where the relevant transactions involve an outright sale of the interest in land (FA 2003, ss.72 and 73); the relief does not apply for example to a lease and underlease back arrangement.

CHAPTER 9

Construction, fitting out and other 'works'

9.1 BACKGROUND

HMRC Stamp Taxes has consistently attacked sales and leases of land and related building agreements. This was intended to be changed by para. 10 of Sched. 4 to FA 2003. HMRC Stamp Taxes thought that the legislation reversed the stamp duty position completely but has been advised that its arguments were totally unsustainable upon the legislation. It has, however, produced massive tax charges for developers of new residential and commercial property and tenants fitting out. The whole focus of the tax charge has moved in a manner increasing the costs, particularly for first time buyers and for local authorities and others desirous of providing social or affordable housing. This is because, unless care is taken, purchasers and tenants may have to pay tax upon their own construction costs or fitting out expenditure.

A further attack was introduced by the Finance Act 2004 (now Finance Act 2003, ss.44A and 45A). Where a person enters into a contract which gives him a power to direct a conveyance either to himself or to another person, the substantial performance of that contract gives rise to a charge to SDLT. This is intended to apply where, in order to avoid a charge to the developer, the developer would not agree to purchase the land but would enter into a building agreement with the landowner for a consideration related to the disposal proceeds of the development, thereby escaping the double taxation of transactions because there was no acquisition of land for the purposes of SDLT. It is now provided that if the contract is substantially performed, which has a limited meaning in the context (FA 2003, s.44A(6)), a charge to SDLT arises (see further Chapter 2). This legislation is defective and somewhat haphazard in its application (see also FA 2003, s.45A for its application to 'sub-sales' or assignments of the right to direct the conveyance; Chapter 2), so that it is a potential trap for all persons entering into building contracts and its terms should be checked as a matter of prudence in all such cases.

Land transactions frequently occur in the context of arrangements for the development of land which may be the land being acquired or other land. Broadly, three areas of difficulty arise for the purposes of SDLT, namely:

CONSTRUCTION, FITTING OUT AND OTHER 'WORKS'

- the sale or lease of land where the parties enter into a more or less simultaneous agreement whereby the vendor or landlord is to carry out works on the land in question at the cost of the purchaser or tenant;
- the sale or lease of land where the purchaser or lessee is to carry out works on land other than that to be acquired such as land owned by the vendor or lessor;
- the sale or lease of land with arrangements pursuant to which the purchaser or tenant is to carry out building or fitting out works on that land being acquired.

In each of these cases there is the question of whether the works to be carried out form part of the chargeable transaction so as to form part of the purchase price or taxable premium for the grant of the lease.

Sale or lease of land and related building contracts – vendor/lessor as builder

A person may agree to sell or lease land and, at the same time, enter into a contract to construct a building upon the land at the cost of the purchaser/tenant. The question is whether there is a single contract for the sale/lease of a completed building when the SDLT is chargeable upon the aggregate consideration for the land and the building works or there are two separate contracts with SDLT chargeable only upon the land contract. The former stamp duty position[1] has not been altered by para. 10 of Sched. 4 to FA 2003. The position for SDLT is that, provided that the land and the works contracts are legally independent and not 'contractually interdependent', only the land price is taxable. The linked transaction rules do not apply to aggregate the two contracts but the consideration must be apportioned between the land and the works upon a just and reasonable basis (FA 2003, Sched. 4, para. 4). Attempts to reduce the SDLT by loading the consideration on to the works may be fraud (*Saunders* v. *Edwards* [1987] 2 All ER 651).

Works to be carried out by the purchaser/tenant

Works to be carried out by the purchaser or tenant at his own expense may now be chargeable consideration. Consequently, it must not be overlooked that

---

1 *Prudential Assurance Co Ltd* v. *IRC* [1992] STC 863; this has been confirmed by HMRC Stamp Taxes; *Kimbers & Co* v. *IRC* [1936] 1 KB 132. The decision in *Macleod* v. *IRC* (1885) 22 SLR 674 was generally regarded as perverse in law and on its facts; see the comments of the same Judges in *Paul* v. *IRC* [1936] SC 443, and the comments in *Kimbers & Co* v. *IRC* [1936] 1 KB 132. See also SP8/93 and its predecessors which still contain much helpful guidance.

what appears to be a conditional arrangement may be in law the provision of the consideration (*Eastham* v. *Leigh, London and Provincial Properties* [1971] 2 All ER 887). The effect is that an agreement for lease that is expressed to be 'conditional' upon the tenant completing the construction of a building is potentially taxable upon a 'premium' equal to the cost of the works.

Chargeable consideration

This is not limited to the infrastructure costs but may also include the costs of implementing planning agreements with the local authority such as the provision of social housing or swimming pools and schools.[2] There is also a special restricted relief for acquisitions by charities such as registered social housing landlords where such bodies acquire land for development for social housing as part of a joint project (see FA 2003, Sched. 8 (as amended)). There are also difficult issues arising from the financing of such arrangements which may add to the SDLT costs of the transaction, as well as of compliance costs of multiple notifications (see FA 2003, ss.51 and 80).

The issues differ depending upon whether the works are to be carried out upon land to be acquired, for which a limited relief is provided, or upon land owned by the vendor as landlord or a third party (see below). Where a purchaser or tenant is to carry out works the open market cost of those works may be subject to tax as part of the charge upon the land transaction.

(a) Works on land not being acquired

It will be relatively easy for HMRC Stamp Taxes to establish chargeable consideration where the purchaser or lessee is to construct works on land retained by the vendor such as a lease from a local authority on terms, *inter alia*, that the lessee will construct a new school on other land.[3]

It must be noted there is no exemption for such building costs.

---

[2] There is a fundamental issue of technical legal analysis of whether any stipulations as to the construction of works contained in a 's.106 agreement' are merely, non-taxable, conditions related solely to the implementation of the planning consent or are consideration for the acquisition of chargeable interests in land from the local authority. It is considered that any indemnity given to the seller/lessor of land relating to failure to observe the stipulation in the s.106 agreement is not taxable (FA 2003, Sched. 4, para. 16 – the argument is reinforced by the terms of FA 2003, Sched. 17A, para. 17). If the local authority is not contributing land the stipulations in the s.106 agreement as to social housing or swimming pools are not part of the taxable consideration; but the position is less clear where the local authority is transferring land to the developer since there is an argument that construction obligations are consideration. That position can be helped where the s.106 agreement and the land contract are separate documents and do not cross-refer.

[3] But note the possibility of relief for PFI transactions pursuant to FA 2003, Sched. 4, para. 17.

(b) Works on land being acquired

It may seem rather a strange concept that an arrangement under which a person acquires land in circumstances where he is to carry out works on the land to be acquired is regarded as providing consideration for the acquisition of the land such as where there is an agreement to grant a lease subject to the construction of a satisfactory building. This derives some support from the decision in *Eastham* v. *Leigh, London and Provincial Properties Limited* [1971] 2 All ER 887. This line between a condition and the provision of part of the consideration is one that is likely to prove to be of considerable importance in practice and much will depend upon how the attitude of HMRC Stamp Taxes develops once it begins to understand the tax raising potential of its position. Much will depend upon the drafting and structuring arrangements. A tenant may simply be given permission to enter upon the land to fit out if he wishes. *Prima facie*, because there is no obligation to fit out, the costs of the works are not taxable and it is immaterial whether the limited access given to the tenant amounts to taking possession. However, since landlords usually require the fitting out to be done expeditiously and to a good standard so that the tenant can commence trading as soon as possible, they may impose obligations upon the tenant to carry out the works. In such a case, it is probable that the works will constitute some form of chargeable consideration other than rent for the lease. If the agreement merely provides that the tenant may, if he wishes but is not obliged to, enter upon the land the fitting out works will probably not be chargeable consideration. On the other hand, if the tenant is required by the contract to fit out or the lease is 'conditional' on fitting out within a specified time, this is likely to be regarded as chargeable consideration. The charge is avoided where the works are carried out after the effective date for the transaction as described below.

Other arrangements may create tax problems; although taking possession ahead of the grant of the lease may accelerate the tax charge, it may be prudent to consider early possession to protect the costs of the works from tax (see Chapters 3 and 4).

For example, the developer agrees to the vendor having access to infrastructure works being constructed by the developer on the land to be acquired. Such rights are likely to be some form of easement or similar chargeable interest in or over land and the tax position may depend upon the form in which the rights are brought into existence. If the land is transferred to the developer who grants[4] new rights to the vendor then such rights are, *prima facie*, consideration in kind for the transfer of the land or part of a

---

4 There are also issues where such rights are excepted and reserved. See, e.g. *Johnstone* v. *Holdway* [1963] 1 All ER 432; *St Edmundsbury and Ipswich* v. *Clark (No.2)* [1973] 3 All ER 902, [1975] 1 All ER 772; *Shannon, The* v. *Venner Ltd* [1965] 1 All ER 590; see Chapter 2.

premium for the lease. This produces a land exchange and SDLT will be chargeable upon the market value of such rights.[5] Strictly, the land exchange ignores the actual or other chargeable consideration and is taxed upon the market value of the interest received. This suggests that costs of works or variable consideration are to be ignored. Where land is transferred to a developer for a cash sum plus a leaseback of one of the flats to be constructed, this is a land exchange and the building costs are ignored along with the cash sum. It may be that by suitable timing the developer's tax can be mitigated because the land has a low market value because it is undeveloped and the leaseback to the seller may be of small value if granted before the works are started. This may in some cases be more tax efficient than a transfer of land for a cash sum plus an obligation to build a house upon the land retained by the vendor when the building costs would become an issue for the developer, particularly if the lower rates are available to the seller on an exchange or leaseback arrangement.

9.2 WORKS

'Works' as chargeable consideration include the carrying out of works of:

- construction of a building;
- improvement of a building;
- repair of a building; or
- other works to enhance the value of land; but this is apparently not limited to the land being acquired or land retained by the vendor or landlord. Works carried out upon adjoining land may enhance the value of the land such as by providing access to a road or mains services.

It is, in consequence, a word of wide application in this context.

Exclusion from charge

Such works to be carried out on the land being acquired are not subject to SDLT where (FA 2003, Sched. 4, para. 2):

- the works are carried out after the effective date of the transaction;
- the works are carried out on land acquired or to be acquired under the transaction or on other land held by the purchaser or a person connected with him; and

---

5 This will be a difficult issue to determine since the rights themselves are not capable of realistic sale separate from the land, although they may substantially enhance or support the value of the land retained by the vendor.

CONSTRUCTION, FITTING OUT AND OTHER 'WORKS'

- it is not a condition of the transaction that the works are carried out by the vendor or lessor or a person connected with him, i.e. it must not be a term of the lease or sale contract that the builder is to be the seller.

Should the fitting out be a premium for the grant of the lease, it will be necessary to ensure that the initial entry by the tenant constitutes substantial performance of the agreement for lease because there is an exclusion from the charge to SDLT for the cost of building works carried out on the land to be acquired after the effective date.[6] This key issue will depend upon the terms upon which the tenant is permitted to enter. It must be noted when structuring and drafting these arrangements that the tenant must take possession of at least substantially the whole of the land. There will, in consequence, be difficulties where only partial access is granted such as access to only part of the land to be demised or access limited as to time, especially in cases where the landlord remains in occupation of the land because the main building works have not been completed.

The same issues can apply to developers who are entering into arrangements whereby their construction operations are consideration. To avoid the charge the developer must take possession of substantially the whole of the land before commencing operations. This can be a problem where he is acquiring the land in phases. Such arrangements should be structured as separate contracts rather than as a single contract with phased completion, because in the latter case there may be major problems in establishing substantial performance.

9.3 SITE ASSEMBLY

A key element in the costs of any development is the taxation of the assembly of the site to be developed from the existing owners, whether or not with the assistance of a local authority or other body having compulsory acquisition powers.[7] Traditionally, this additional cost in the prices of new houses and

---

[6] The problem of the double effective date for agreements for lease and leases arising pursuant to FA 2003, Sched. 17A, para. 12B is specifically covered by a provision that in relation to the grant of the lease the cost of the works carried out prior to the grant of the lease but after the effective date for the agreement for lease are taxable.

[7] For which there may be relief from SDLT pursuant to FA 2003, s.60; but this relief is subject to many restrictive conditions and HMRC Stamp Taxes has already taken points in practice which clearly indicate that this relief will be attacked and restricted whenever and as far as possible. For example, difficulties have arisen in relation to both the meaning of the word 'development' and the nature of the development arrangements which have to be in place as at the effective date of the acquisition in question. There are also difficulties of analysis and the effect of arrangements where the local authority will be acquiring the land under compulsory powers and will be granting leases out of the land so acquired to the developer. These issues include

commercial developments was mitigated by sub-sale relief (Stamp Act 1891, s.58(4) and (5) (as amended)); but one of the major policy objectives of the introduction of SDLT was the removal of this key relief[8] regarded as vital to the reasonable operation of the tax over two centuries ago. The effect is that although the relief remains available, with careful planning for the short-term speculator, the person who is the developer of the land such as the constructor of houses for first time buyers, is now to be hit by the new tax in situations where previously no tax would normally arise. Moreover, this hit occurs at an early stage in the transaction so that in addition to the new tax charge there is an additional carrying cost in the form of an interest charge incurred to pay the tax[9] enhancing the cascade effect of stamp taxes in this area which is also increased because of:

- the charge to SDLT upon VAT even where recoverable input tax;
- the acceleration of the time of the tax charge from documents to transactions and to substantial performance rather than 'completion' cancelling the cost benefit of resting on contract;
- the extension of the scope of taxable transactions, in particular in this context the potential charge to SDLT upon works to be carried out by the person acquiring the interest in the land (FA 2003, Sched. 4, para. 10 (as amended)); and
- there may be overage or other arrangements which increase the tax charge and the compliance costs (see Chapter 4) because of the need to prepare and file several land transaction returns.

Restricted sub-sale relief

Previously, it was possible to control the stamp duty costs by not taking a transfer; but the previous stamp duty device of resting on contract and dealing with the matter by way of sub-sale transfer is no longer a realistic option in most cases (see Chapter 5). Although there is a highly limited form of relief for sub-sales and assignments (FA 2003, s.45) or the grant of leases to third parties (FA 2003, Sched. 17A, para. 12B; see Chapter 8) these reliefs are not available where the first purchaser or tenant has substantially

---

whether payments made by the developer to the existing landowners are chargeable consideration for the acquisition by the local authority as required by FA 2003, Sched. 4, para. 1, and whether any arrangement for the grant of leases by the local authority out of the land acquired to the developer involves land exchanges chargeable in accordance with the provisions of FA 2003, s.47 and Sched. 4, para. 5.

8 And this attack upon sub-sale relief has been extended by the anti-avoidance provisions upon similar arrangements in FA 2003, ss.44A and 45A.

9 There is also a commercial issue since the status of the contract to acquire the land may be conditional upon completion of the construction works and so there may be difficulties in providing acceptable security to the lender.

performed the contract. In effect, the relief is available only for the speculator (see Chapter 5). The developer who enters upon land to commence the works will almost certainly not escape a new and early charge to tax because he will have substantially performed the contract by either providing about 90 per cent of the consideration, or going into possession such as by commencing building or fitting out works operations; or where the interest being acquired by the developer is a lease the taxpayer has made the first payment of rent, even if this is only a token £1 rent during the development phase (FA 2003, s.44).

Even though the developer or prospective tenant is only a licensee,[10] during the development phase it will be difficult to create a situation where the terms of the licence avoid entering into 'possession' so as to trigger a charge to SDLT and the consequent payment and compliance obligations.[11] On the other hand, a speculator who has no interest in developing or refurbishing the land and obtains a discount from the developer[12] can avoid SDLT altogether. He may take an option to purchase or call for a lease or a contract conditional upon obtaining planning permission. Alternatively, he may enter into an agreement to acquire leases of several flats intending that the leases will be granted to individual purchasers. Provided that he avoids substantial performance of his contract, which should be relatively easy because he merely intends to profit by turning his contract in these situations, he will not be subject to tax. The true developer cannot normally escape the charge to tax because of the effect of entering upon the land to carry out the development or refurbishment.

Developer trap – phased development

It is provided that, in general (FA 2003, Sched. 4A, para. 10; see above), works effected on the land acquired or to be acquired for the improvement of

---

10 It should also be noted that HMRC Stamp Taxes takes the view that where there is any licence to enter upon land to carry out building works and under the terms of the licence the landlord granting the licence has a right to enter upon the land in question in order to ensure that the building works are progressing satisfactorily, it is an indication that the licence confers exclusive possession upon the developer and may amount to some form of tenancy although this is merely an indication of tenancy. It may be possible to minimise this risk by making the licence non-exclusive, see the comments in *Street* v. *Mountford* [1985] 1 AC 809; *Addiscombe Garden Estates Ltd* v. *Crabbe* [1957] 3 All ER 563; but note the decision in *Ogwr* v. *Dykes* [1989] 2 All ER 880 where there is the suggestion that the inclusion of a provision in the agreement that the arrangement is not intended to create the relationship of landlord and tenant may be effective to prevent the creation of a tenancy.
11 Attempts to escape from this restriction are possibly vulnerable to FA 2003, s.44A mentioned above.
12 But such a discount will almost inevitably produce linked transactions, cancelling the lower rates that should be chargeable with the tax.

the land are excluded from the charge to SDLT but only where these are carried out after the effective date for the agreement, i.e. after the date of substantial performance or taking possession.

Substantial performance requires taking possession of the whole or substantially the whole of the land in question. Entry into possession of part of the land will not necessarily operate as substantial performance. This should be noted, particularly where there is to be a staged development and the land is to be drawn down in tranches by the developer from time to time. Whilst this may operate to delay the effective date for the transaction and so postpone the payment of tax, it represents a trap where the works in question are part of the chargeable consideration since in many cases what may appear superficially to be a condition may prove to be part of the consideration (*Eastham* v. *Leigh, London and Provincial* [1971] 2 All ER 887). The relief for building works by the developer upon what is effectively his own land is not available in these circumstances since having only limited access to the land the purchaser or tenant is not taking possession of substantially the whole of the land. As a result of the changes, taxpayers may find themselves subject to tax upon their own building works.

9.4 CALCULATION AND PAYMENT

The tax is charged upon the open market cost of the works or services, i.e. the amount that would have to be paid for the works on the open market (FA 2003, Sched. 4, para. 10(3)). No statutory guidance is given as to how this novel fiscal test is to be applied but it seems that, strictly, actual costs are to be ignored and the tax calculated upon the prices that would be charged by contractors or sub-contractors operating for a profit and on an arm's length basis. It seems probable that the tax will be charged upon the price that would have been charged for the supply of the building works upon a stand-alone basis and not as part of the overall land acquisition arrangement. There will, therefore, have to be a profit element included in the 'cost' which may include VAT. As discussed elsewhere (see Chapter 4), there is some doubt as to the meaning of 'cost' but HMRC Stamp Taxes's position is that 'cost' is the price on the open market including VAT even where recoverable as input tax and ignoring the issue of the capital goods scheme. However, it seems that, in practice, HMRC Stamp Taxes may prefer to work on the basis of actual cost at least in those cases where sub-contractors are engaged. The treatment of situations where an in-house labour force is employed remains problematic but this is likely to be an area where the open market cost will be relied upon by HMRC Stamp Taxes, i.e. the price that would be charged simply for the building works unrelated to the overall transaction.

It may be that in some cases even on this hypothetical basis the 'costs' may not be finally determined on the effective date because an open market contract would include an adjustment for costs to the hypothetical sub-contractor plus a mark-up thereon. Detailed rules are provided for the payment and deferment of tax in this situation (Stamp Duty Land Tax (Administration) Regulations 2003, SI 2003/2837, Part 4).

CHAPTER 10

Trusts, wills and intestate estates

10.1 CREATION OF TRUSTS

The whole concept of a trust is based on equity's insistence that a man follows the dictates of his conscience (as interpreted by equity). Looking, as ever, at the substance of the transaction rather than the form, equity (as opposed to statute) does not require any formalities to be observed on the creation of a trust (*Paul* v. *Constance* [1977] 1 WLR 527). All that is necessary for a trust to arise is the presence of the three certainties of intention, subject-matter and objects. If the property and interest therein to be the subject-matter of the trust are ascertainable, the beneficiaries identified or identifiable by reference to a sufficiently certain formula, and, above all, it is clear from the words or deeds of the person making the disposition that a trust is intended, a trust will come into being. These issues of oral arrangements and the need for writing may be of crucial importance in relation to many domestic transactions which almost certainly will not be adequately documented; such as where a child agrees to care for an elderly parent on the 'understanding' that the house will pass at some stage to the child. Such arrangements may not have the necessary evidence as to the parties' intention to create legal relationships (see, e.g. *Facchini* v. *Bryson* [1952] 1 TLR 1386 on the presumptions for domestic agreements) and there may be issues as to whether there is some form of trust created with a life interest to the parent and remainder to the child. The fact that the transaction is oral will not necessarily render the arrangement legally ineffective. Thus an oral declaration by the settlor that he intends thenceforth to hold stated property upon trust for stated beneficiaries will create an immediate and valid trust, as in *Paul* v. *Constance* [1977] 1 WLR 527 where there was an oral declaration of trust concerning money in a bank account by the use of the words, uttered by the settlor to the beneficiary, 'The money is as much yours as mine' (see also *Choithram (T) International* v. *Pagarani* [2001] 2 All ER 492).

Equity's permissive view has, however, long been modified by statutory provisions requiring the observance of written formalities in many cases, and in practice an oral declaration of trust is only unaffected by statute when limited to personalty. Section 53(1)(b) of the Law of Property Act (LPA) 1925 states: 'a declaration of trust respecting any land or any interest therein must be manifested and proved by some writing signed by some person who is able to declare such trust or by his will'. Like s.40 of the same Act before its repeal by s.2(8) of the Law of Property (Miscellaneous Provisions) Act (LP(MP)A) 1989, the above provision is evidential only, and does not require that the trust should necessarily be declared by writing. There must, however, at some stage, be written evidence of the declaration signed by the competent party or, probably, some act of reliance upon the oral arrangement which can be utilised to establish a constructive or similar trust which does not require writing.[1]

However, the absence of writing does mean that there may not be a trust and the potentially taxable passing of property. LPA 1925, s.136 requires transfer of legal title to choses-in-action to be in writing. If the settlor does not do all in his power, according to the nature of the property given, to vest the property in the trustees (as in *Re Rose* [1949] Ch 78), equity will not interfere to perfect the trust because, in the absence of consideration given by a beneficiary, there is an imperfect gift and (in the absence of an estoppel or the creation of a constructive trust which does not require writing), as was said in *Milroy* v. *Lord* (1862) 4 De GF & J 264, 'there is no equity in this Court to perfect an imperfect gift', and in certain situations trustees may be ordered by the court not to enforce a deed of covenant unless there is separate consideration as partner within the marriage consideration (see, e.g. *Re Kay's Settlement* [1939] Ch 329; *Re Cook's Settlement Trusts* [1965] Ch 902).

The position may differ where the proposed trustees are the personal representatives of the deceased settlor who thereby become vested with the legal estate (see, e.g. *Strong* v. *Bird* (1874) LR Eq 315) or the legal title otherwise 'accidentally' vests in them (see, e.g. *Re Ralli* [1964] Ch 288). It remains to be seen how far the judges who were trained upon the now repealed doctrine of part performance bring back a similar set of principles re-labelled 'constructive trust' as in *Yaxley* v. *Gotts* [1999] 2 WLR 1217 which can operate to pass an equitable interest in land without writing. It is immaterial when the written memorandum is produced, but until there is a written declaration, the trust remains unenforceable by court action, but not invalid and ineffective. HMRC Stamp Taxes may seek to contend that even in the absence of a written memorandum such arrangements are valid, albeit unenforceable by the court (see *Forster* v. *Hale* (1798) 3 Ves 696; *Rochefoucauld* v. *Boustead* [1897] 1 Ch 196) and the position differs from that of a transaction which is void unless effected in writing.[2] However, although there may be a tax charge

---

1 LPA 1925, s.53(2); LP(MP)A 1989, s.2(6); *Yaxley* v. *Gotts* [1999] 2 WLR 1217; *Binions* v. *Evans* [1972] 2 All ER 70, where, in effect, the trust arose in favour of a person who was not a party to the transaction.
2 This also means that the legislative requirement may be invalid pursuant to the human rights legislation as an obstacle to the protection of validly created property rights. This is a fundamental issue as to how far the rules of evidence and procedure can continue to regulate property ownership and its protection.

in the meantime, the beneficiaries will not, in the case of land, be able to enforce the trust by court action.

10.2 RESULTING AND OTHER SIMILAR TRUSTS

The formalities for the creation of a trust of land do not affect the creation or operation of resulting, implied or constructive trusts (Law of Property Act 1925, s.53(2)). By their very nature such trusts arise without the formality of documentation recording their existence, but as they invariably attach themselves silently, the transaction itself will bear any tax payable. The difficulty of such trusts arising by operation of law rather than by specification of the parties, although it may be the actions of the parties that enable the law to create such trusts, is identifying the effective date i.e. the date at which the tax charge and the notification obligations arise. As there is likely to be an oral arrangement it may be difficult for HMRC Stamp Taxes to establish that there is an effective binding contract between the parties that provides for completion by a conveyance so that the effective date will be 'completion' whatever that may mean in the current context since FA 2003, s.117 is silent on the subject.

Moreover, there will be some fundamental technical issues of principle depending upon the nature of the implied trust and the circumstances giving rise to the trust. For example, certain 'resulting trusts' arise because the person concerned has failed to make an effective disposition of the entire equitable interest in the property (*Vandevell* v. *IRC* [1967] 1 All ER 1). This raises certain issues as to whether the entire equitable interest leaves upon the effective date and the balance reverts to the transferor or only the relevant part of the equitable interest passes and the balance remains. In the latter case there is only one possible chargeable transaction. In the former case there are two chargeable transactions, namely there are reciprocal movements of the equitable interest; this being so, the question arises whether they are 'consideration' for each other so that a land exchange arises pursuant to FA 2003, s.47. It will become an important issue of principle about whether the attempt to transfer a partial interest in property is a transfer of a limited interest with a reservation (i.e. a single transaction) or an outright transfer of the whole with a re-transfer of a limited interest back (i.e. a land exchange with two chargeable transactions). Much may turn upon the structuring of the arrangement and whether in law it is possible to reserve or except the interest in question or a regrant is required. To some extent it may be possible to overcome these difficulties by utilising nominees whose existence is generally ignored for the purposes of SDLT; but increasing anti-avoidance legislation is restricting the scope for such simple mitigation of a possibly unnecessary charge which only arises by reason of the lack of flexibility in general property law. It is considered that, in general, such a resulting trust does not give rise to a chargeable transaction. However, in some situations there will be a potentially chargeable transaction such as where equitable interests are acquired because of contributions to the acquisition and maintenance of the property or acting upon the oral promises of the other party when there may be an actual increment from the promiser or other person who becomes a trustee as in *Yaxley* v. *Gotts* [1999] 2 WLR 1217.

Many such implied trusts are really remedies imposed by equity to counteract improper conduct such as breaches of trust and fiduciary duties. Such remedial arrangements are usually intended to prevent the equitable interest from passing from the original owner so that any transferee acquires only the legal title in a fiduciary capacity. Consequently, such arrangements are unlikely to involve chargeable acquisitions.

10.3 TRUSTS: GENERAL

The draftsman's view of equitable interests behind trusts and similar arrangements as chargeable interests and the extension of chargeable consideration mean that there has been a significant increase in transactions where trusts and estates are involved which are subject to the full impact of SDLT as compared with the former stamp duty regime.

Terminology

Two types of trust situation exist in the SDLT provisions, namely:

- a bare trust; and
- a settlement.

These are usually created expressly; but implied, resulting and constructive trusts are nevertheless indirectly important both for their direct and indirect effect because they may result in the acquisition of a chargeable interest and they may affect the identity of the vendor and/or the purchaser. Such trusts which can arise notwithstanding the absence of writing[3] may mean that a totally oral transaction can be effective even though the conditions of s.2 of LP(MP)A 1989 are not satisfied (*Yaxley* v. *Gotts* [1999] 2 WLR 1217). They are also important for compliance reasons in identifying the purchaser or the vendor for the purposes of paying the tax and completing the land transaction return (SDLT 1 and 2) since the legal title and Land Register are no longer relevant for these purposes. The existence of fiduciary obligations such as in the case of agents who are affected by the implied trust rule may affect

---

3 LPA 1925, s.53(2); see *Neville* v. *Wilson* [1997] Ch 144 criticising *Oughtred* v. *IRC* [1960] AC 204 and effectively reversing it on the relationship between LPA 1925, s.53(1)(c) and (2).

who can sign the return. The relevance of the legal title and registration is much diminished and the significance of beneficial ownership is much increased. Accurate analysis of the legal relationship between the various interested parties and the land is now fundamental to the compliance regime if taxpayers and their advisers are to avoid penalties for incorrect returns and assisting in the preparation thereof. Whilst professional advisers may be liable only for 'knowing' assistance, pleas of ignorance of the underlying law may be less convincing and certainly embarrassing (FA 2003, ss.95 and 96).

The vast majority of trusts and settlements are created voluntarily (i.e. without consideration), so that on the basis that there is a general exemption (subject to certain exclusions) for transactions where there is not chargeable consideration (FA 2003, Sched. 3, para. 1), it might be thought that there were no significant SDLT issues in respect of trusts. However, this is not an entirely accurate appraisal of the situation: there are problems in relation to SDLT. Not all dealings in trust assets or interests are voluntary in the sense that there is no consideration. Where there is consideration such as the mutual exchange of equitable interests upon the variation of a trust or an estate, such deeds of family arrangement were not liable for stamp duty in general sales (*Henneker* v. *Henneker* (1852) 1 E&B 54); this analysis is no longer relevant because of the much broader basis of SDLT which is not limited to 'sales' in the general meaning of the term. In consequence, a much wider range of transactions involving trusts and estates are potentially within the charge to tax in the new regime.

Moreover, there is an increased risk that the variation or partition of a trust or an estate may be a sale possibly attracting two charges to tax where land is involved on both sides of the transaction. There are also anti-avoidance provisions such as the connected company charge pursuant to FA 2003, ss.53 and 54 which include transfers of land into and out of the settlement, with very limited exemptions applying to dealings with or by trustees. These charges may apply upon the transfer or leasing of property into a trust, dealings in equitable interests and transfers of property out of the settlement.[4]

Settlement or bare trust

The distinction between a bare trust or nominee and settlement is important since in the case of a bare trust the existence of the trust is ignored and all

---

[4] Moreover where, as is probable, the estate of the deceased or the trust fund includes or may receive interests in shares and loan stock of companies, questions of the much wider liability to the directly enforceable stamp duty reserve tax can arise (see Finance Act 1986, s.87 and following), it having been from time to time the view of HMRC Stamp Taxes that the definition of 'chargeable securities' contained in Finance Act 1986, s.99 (as amended) is probably sufficiently wide to encompass interests in shares and other securities held as part of a trust fund; however it appears that at present this view which would in many cases be incorrect is not taken.

transactions in relation to the land are treated as having been performed by the beneficial owner (FA 2003, Sched. 16, para. 3(1)). In consequence, transactions involving nominees such as a change of nominee[5] will not normally incur any liability to SDLT but, contrary to this general principle, an increasing number of such situations are attracting tax consequences. Where there is the grant of a lease to a nominee this is now fully taxable (FA 2003, Sched. 16, para. 3(3)); however, such transactions are not without consequences. A lease granted between July 2004 and March 2005 to a nominee may not attract a charge to SDLT, but any subsequent assignment of the lease is treated as the grant of a new lease by the assignor (FA 2003, Sched. 17A, para. 11 (as amended)) which will include the beneficial owner of the lease.

On the other hand, the 'purchaser' is the beneficial owner who, subject to limited exceptions, is the only person who can sign the declaration on the land transaction return or self-certificate. There can no longer be any secrecy such as a person acting as agent for an undisclosed principal. The signing of the return by the agent will be invalid and a return will not have been filed on time. This will, of course, produce frequent situations where there is a divergence between the persons identified as vendors and purchasers and signing the land transaction return and included in the SDLT 5 certificate and the Land Registry documentation. For example, where parents combine with a child to purchase property jointly and beneficially but which is to be registered solely in the name of the child, the SDLT 1 and SDLT 5, to be correct, should refer to the three parties, but the Land Registry transfer will be in the child's name. The Land Registry now recognises these and other problems and has indicated that it is prepared to act on the basis of an explanatory letter. Similar problems will apply to partners and others and may affect even vendors where the property is held by a nominee or pursuant to an uncompleted sale contract, such as a sub-sale arrangement. These principles mean that it is no longer permissible to rely solely upon the Land Register or the parties to the contract who may be acting in an undisclosed fiduciary capacity.

These look through rules which affect liability to pay and the compliance obligations mean that it is, therefore, necessary to be able to recognise which situation is relevant.

---

5 The position of nominees and the connected company charge (FA 2003, s.53) has not been expressly dealt with but as there is no transaction it seems that the connected company charge does not apply. The Government indicated that as only the legal title passed there was no significant market value for the purposes of the tax so that no charge arises. Unfortunately, the official view means that an SDLT 1 is required because there is chargeable consideration. The correct view means that an SDLT 60 would be sufficient.

Bare trust

A bare trust is a trust under which property is held by a person as trustee,[6] either:

- for a person who is absolutely entitled as against the trustee. A person is treated as absolutely entitled to property as against the trustees if he has the exclusive right, subject only to satisfying any outstanding charge, lien or other right of the trustee to resort to the property for payment of duty, taxes, costs or other outgoings or to direct how the property is to be dealt with (FA 2003, Sched. 16, para. 1(3)) or who would be so entitled but for being a minor or other person under a disability. The distinction turns upon whether the beneficial interest is held absolutely without successive interests and, in particular, whether the holder of the legal title has any powers or discretions of his own or is totally controlled by the beneficial owner (see, e.g. *Cowan de Groot Properties Ltd* v. *Eagle Trust plc* [1991] BCLC 1045). General law would indicate that a nominee is a person who merely holds the legal title for some person absolutely and has no power or discretion but must act under the direction of the absolute beneficial owner. Successive, as opposed to joint, interests such as to A for life and then to B absolutely will be a 'settlement' and not a bare trust notwithstanding that both A and B are of full age and capacity and between them absolutely entitled to the property (*Saunders* v. *Vautier* (1841) 4 Beav 115). The ability of the owner of the legal title to take decisions on his own initiative would point towards a 'trust';
- for two or more persons who are or would be jointly (FA 2003, s.121) so entitled (FA 2003, Sched. 16, para. 1(2)). This will apply to many domestic or family transactions such as purchase by husband and wife or partners where statutory trusts may apply (Trusts of Land and Appointment of Trustees Act 1996).

10.4 TRUSTS AND SDLT

SDLT (and where shares and other securities are involved stamp duty reserve tax) arises in relation to trusts upon:

- the establishment of the trust and the initial vesting of property;
- the appointment and retirement of trustees;

---

[6] It is important for trustees and personal representatives to note that their status may change where interests change such as where a person becomes absolutely entitled on the death of the life tenant or a power of appointment or advancement is exercised but the legal title is not immediately transferred. Appropriation by executors may have similar consequences.

- vesting assets in the trustees;
- changes of investments by trustees;
- dealings in equitable interests in the trust; and
- distribution by trustees to beneficiaries including exercises of powers of appointment and revocation.

10.5 PROPERTY INTO TRUST

Property may become part of the trust assets in various ways:

- the trustees may purchase the property; or
- the settlor may transfer the property into the trust, usually but not invariably by way of gift; or
- there may be an appointment by the trustees of one settlement into a new trust or a subtrust.

However, the exemption for gifts is subject to the connected company charge (FA 2003, s.53) and certain dealings involving partnerships (FA 2003, Sched. 15, para. 25 (as amended)). Trustees are connected with the settlor and, it seems, with other trustees so that the appointment and changes of trustees as well as vesting property in a corporate trustee upon the initial creation of the settlement may be within the charge. The Government has accepted that a transfer to a bare trustee does not attract a significant charge to SDLT pursuant to s.53 of FA 2003 because the legal title itself is of negligible value. It remains to be seen whether it will accept that the connected company charge has no application upon the wider basic principle that there is no change of beneficial ownership such as occurs on the change of trustees; it is expected that this view will be adopted in practice.

10.6 PURCHASE OF LAND

Where trustees of a settlement purchase land they are deemed to be purchasers of the whole of the interest acquired, including the beneficial interest and are taxable upon general principles save that the return or self-certificate may, it seems, be given by one or more of the trustees (FA 2003, Sched. 16, paras. 5 and 6; SDLT 6).

10.7 INITIAL VESTING OF TRUST ASSETS

Different considerations arise where it is intended that the nominated trustees shall take over the control and management of the property to give effect to the trust. In these circumstances, notwithstanding the presence of the three certainties, the trust will be imperfectly constituted until such time as the property is properly vested in the trustees by the manner appropriate to the nature of the property. Until this happens and the property is in their hands, the trustees are trustees of nothing (*Richards* v. *Delbridge* (1874) LR 18 Eq 11). Cash and goods can be transferred by delivery, but land must be conveyed or assigned by deed, shares by a stock transfer form or directives through CREST where the default liability to the principal charge to stamp duty reserve tax will apply (Finance Act 1986, s.87) unless appropriate steps are taken to enable the utilisation of those transaction indicators or 'flags' which indicate that the transaction is for one of the relevant reasons not liable to stamp duty reserve tax and for the obtaining of a stamp duty relief at fixed rate of £5 which cancels the charge to stamp duty reserve tax. Solicitors should note that stamp duty reserve tax is directly enforceable and it is required under penalty that appropriate records are maintained so that upon audit by HMRC the parties can substantiate their utilisation of the particular flag and reporting the tax.

A written assent by personal representatives in favour of themselves as trustees of the will is required in order to prove that they have ceased to act as personal representatives and are acting as trustees for sale.[7] Consideration, however, is not unknown in the shape of a financial inducement to persuade the tenant in tail in remainder to bar the entail, and resettle on further trusts.

If, on the other hand, the settlor first conveys the property to trustees on trusts yet to be declared, no beneficial interest passes as there is an immediate resulting trust back to the settlor (see *Vandervell* v. *IRC* [1967] 1 All ER 1). The conveyance or transfer will not give rise to a tax charge because there is no change of beneficial ownership and the legal title is held on a bare trust (FA 2003, Sched. 16, para. 3), unless it involves a lease to a nominee (see FA 2003, Sched. 16, para. 3(3) (as amended)). In such a situation subsequent attempts to create an effective trust are likely to be required to be in writing in order to comply with LPA 1925, s.53(1)(c). The trust instrument, when executed, will have the effect of shifting the beneficial interest away from the settlor and into the hands of the beneficiaries, and thus bear the full charge to SDLT but only if for a chargeable consideration.

---

7 Administration of Estates Act 1925, s.36(4) and (7); *Re King's Will Trusts* [1964] Ch 542; *Re Hodge* [1940] Ch 260; but not it seems if they purport to sell as personal representatives (*Re Ponder* [1921] 2 Ch 59).

10.8 APPOINTMENT AND RETIREMENT OF TRUSTEES

There is no specific provision dealing with appointments and retirement of trustees, but normally such transactions will not be for a consideration and so not subject to tax pursuant to FA 2003, Sched. 3, para. 1. It may be that land held by the trustee is subject to a charge and so the change of trustee would appear to be vulnerable to a claim pursuant to FA 2003, Sched. 4, para. 8, but since this charge requires the assumption of a liability and there is no fundamental change of the ownership of the property it seems that HMRC Stamp Taxes will not normally seek tax.[8] However, it seems that it intends to impose a charge when the change of trustee is in connection with the transfer of the property between specific trusts or where there is no change of trustee but some form of appropriation and apportionment to themselves as trustee of a separate settlement, and the liability to repay the mortgage changes.

Should the connected company charge be applied by HMRC Stamp Taxes to changes of trustees the exclusions contained in s.54 will apply. Transfers to corporate trustees carrying on the business of managing trusts or which are otherwise unconnected with the settlor apart from the settlor/trustee relationship will be exempt. For the time being, however, appointments or changes of trustees involving family companies will be vulnerable to attack and should be avoided until some guidance of the official view has been provided. This will be a particular problem where there is an advancement or appointment into a new trust with corporate trustees, notwithstanding the exemption since HMRC Stamp Taxes will almost certainly seek to apply the connected company charge even though it is essentially merely a change of trust interests.

It would seem from the definition of 'conveyance' for certain purposes in relation to the effective date (FA 2003, s.119) that it is intended that any written instrument which creates the trust (or which is treated as creating it) could be treated as a 'conveyance', possibly triggering the payment and notification obligations, if any, but these are likely to be rare circumstances because of the exclusions for gifts or other transactions where there is no chargeable consideration[9] and such transactions are usually relieved from the need to notify being dealt with by self-certification (SDLT 60).[10]

---

8 But note the potential charge if the rights or liabilities of the parties to the mortgage are charged in connection with the transfer: FA 2003, Sched. 4, para. 8 (as amended).
9 But note transfer subject to mortgage (FA 2003, Sched. 4, para. 8) and connected companies (FA 2003, ss.53 and 54).
10 But note disadvantaged land requirements (FA 2003, Sched. 6, para. 13).

10.9 DISPOSITIONS OF TRUST PROPERTY – DEALINGS IN EQUITABLE INTERESTS

The area of dealings in equitable interests and lack of formality may be important since LPA 1925, s.53(1)(c) requires most dealings to be in writing and, *prima facie*, in the absence of writing there is no transaction. For example, if instead of transferring the beneficial interest direct to the intended donee, the donor orally instructs his trustees to hold the donor's beneficial interest for the donee in lieu of the donor, this is in substance also a disposition of the equitable interest, since it is an equitable assignment (see *Re Tyler* [1967] 3 All ER 367; *Letts* v. *IRC* [1957] 1 WLR 201) and the direction to the trustees must be in writing if it is to be effective (*Grey* v. *IRC* [1960] AC 1). If as a result of the interaction of such legislation there is no effective transaction there is no charge to tax.

It is well established that where equity would order specific performance of the contract once payment in full is made (see *Michaels* v. *Harley House (Marylebone) Ltd* [1999] 3 WLR 244 for part payment and vendor's liens), the equitable and beneficial interests pass to the purchaser, i.e. a constructive or implied trust arises in his favour (*Walsh* v. *Lonsdale* (1882) 21 Ch D 9). This raises the question of the interaction of the charging provisions and LPA 1925, s.53(1)(c) which requires writing for the effective disposition of the equitable interest. However, there are substantial limits upon the application of s.53(1)(c). This refers only to the actual dispositions of the equitable interests; it does not itself require any contract to dispose of the interest. That is a possible matter for other legislation and the question whether LP(MP)A 1989 affects arrangements dealing with trust interests particularly where land is not the sole asset in the fund. Additionally, *Neville* v. *Wilson* [1997] Ch 144 effectively disposes of the fundamental errors of the House of Lords in *Oughtred* v. *IRC* [1960] AC 206 so that s.53(2) which dispenses with the need for writing prevails over s.53(1)(c) so that many such transactions will be effective even without writing. The problems of constructive and resulting trusts will, therefore, be particularly important in practice if family arrangements are entered into informally and are effective to pass interests in land and give rise to tax payments or reporting obligations because a constructive or similar trust arises since LPA 1925, s.53(2) and LP(MP)A 1989, s.2(6) provide that writing is not required for the effective creation of implied, resulting or constructive trusts (see on the current law *Yaxley* v. *Gotts* [1999] 2 WLR 1217).

10.10 INTERESTS OF BENEFICIARIES

A trust arises, however, whenever one person holds property subject to an obligation, enforceable by equity, to use the property in whole or in part for another. The classic example is where the legal estate or interest in, say, land or shares is vested in the trustee or trustees with a direction to hold upon stated trusts for the beneficiaries. It has long since been recognised that the rights of the beneficiaries, though originally *in personam* only against the trustees, have acquired the status of interests in property enforceable historically against the whole world, save for the time-honoured bona fide purchaser for value of the legal estate without notice, actual or constructive, of a prior equitable interest in the property, or those deriving title through such a person. This rule has been substantially displaced by the doctrine of overreaching as enshrined in s.2 of LPA 1925, whereby a purchaser of a legal estate in land can ignore equitable interests regardless of notice provided he takes the appropriate safeguards, e.g. by paying his money to the appropriate number of trustees in the case of a trust for sale or strict settlement. Nevertheless, pending overreaching, the equitable rights arising out of the trust remain firmly interests in property, as illustrated with a vengeance by the House of Lords in its decision in *Williams & Glyn's Bank Ltd* v. *Boland* [1981] AC 487. This aspect of the decision is reinforced by ss.1(6) and 2(6) of LP(MP)A 1989, both of which define an interest in land for the purposes of the sections as 'any . . . interests . . . in or over land or in or over the proceeds of sale of land'.

Moreover, this view has been adopted and extended by the draftsman of the SDLT legislation. It is clearly his view that beneficiaries interested in trusts governed by English law have interests in land, i.e. their interests are chargeable interests.

Equitable interests in trusts where the trust fund includes land in the UK are regarded as chargeable interests. This emerges impliedly from the rules dealing with certain types of trust. It is provided that although foreign trusts may differ from English trusts in the sense that the beneficiaries may not have some form of equitable interest in the underlying property, i.e. a proprietary interest that may entitle them to trace the property to a certain extent but have merely a personal right against the trustees to compel proper administration of the trust and to sue for breach but without any rights of a proprietary nature in relation to the underlying property (see *Garland* v. *Archer-Shee* 15 TC 693; *Archer-Shee* v. *Baker* 15 TC 1), the fact that the foreign law merely gives an *in personam* right is overridden by legislation (FA 2003, Sched. 16, para. 2). Therefore, interests in foreign trusts are treated as though the trust was governed by English law, i.e. if the English law would give the beneficiary some form of proprietary interest in the underlying property then notwithstanding the trust is governed by foreign law and administered by trustees outside the UK, the interest of the beneficiary, who may be non-resident, is a

UNDERSTANDING SDLT

chargeable interest and dealings in that interest for consideration will be subject to SDLT.[11]

As a consequence of this, variations of trusts involving disposals of a beneficial interest where the trust assets include land will involve potentially chargeable transactions if done for a consideration notwithstanding that the trust assets are held by non-resident trustees under a trust created by a non-residential settlor and the beneficiaries are resident offshore holding under a trust governed by foreign law. In such situations it would seem prudent for the trustees to hold any chargeable interests in UK land through an offshore company, if this does not lead to adverse tax consequences in other areas.

Since 'acquisition' includes not merely assignments but also the creation of interests as well as releases and surrenders, but not disclaimers, many dealings in interests in trusts will be subject to SDLT if done for a consideration.[12] For example, an assignment by a life tenant of all or part of his interest will require the purchaser of that interest to pay SDLT and make a return. Similarly, the release of a life interest if done for consideration will be chargeable as will be a surrender of an interest if done for consideration.

Frequently there will be consideration since the adjustment in the rights of beneficiaries will be part of a variation of the trust under which interests are exchanged such as where a life tenant and remainderman agree to combine their interests in order to partition the fund. This arrangement will not qualify for the special treatment for partitions since the interest will not be jointly owned, i.e. the parties are not joint tenants or tenants in common but hold interests in succession (FA 2003, s.121). In such a situation the life tenant and remainderman will be 'exchanging' interests in land so that charges to SDLT will arise (FA 2003, s.47).

10.11 SEVERING JOINT TENANCIES

There is a highly technical but ultimately less than convincing argument that certain arrangements converting a beneficial joint tenancy into a tenancy in

---

11 The assumption of the draftsman that the tracing remedy of beneficiaries under English trusts is an interest in land in the general sense is questionable, but with the legislation having been prepared on the basis that it is a chargeable interest it will be difficult to persuade the current judiciary that the legislation was prepared on a false premise. The argument will be that by necessary implication for the purpose of SDLT the interest of the beneficiary is a chargeable interest. However, the question then arises as to whether the interest of the beneficiary is a 'major interest' since it is neither a leasehold nor a freehold interest in equity but is a limited interest. This will be important in relation to the rules for calculating SDLT upon exchanges of interests and reporting obligations.

12 Assuming that such exercises are not tainted as frauds on the power.

common are land exchanges.[13] As these interests will usually exist in relation to freeholds and leaseholds the beneficial interests 'exchanged' will be 'major interests' with two market value charges (FA 2003, Sched. 4, para. 5). The issue is whether the arrangement is 'contractual'. Insofar as the situation is dealt with by one party serving the appropriate notice (LPA 1925, s.36(2)), it is arguable that there is no contract; but a mutual agreement to bring about this result could be vulnerable to attack. At present, fortunately, HMRC Stamp Taxes has not shown any intention to take this point.

A somewhat more frequent occurrence will be an arrangement whereby one party releases or assigns his interest in favour of the other party for a consideration probably consisting of other property held within the trust. This will be a straightforward transfer of an interest in land in consideration of the interest in the other property being received. It will be taxable upon the open market value of the property as interest therein received.

Unfortunately, most trust funds are not simply land but consist of a wide mixture of investments.[14] This means that the interests involved in the variation will involve interests in land and other property. There will, in consequence, be a completely mixed arrangement involving mutual transfers or acquisitions of a mixed fund only part of which is land. Unless the transaction is carefully structured, there will not be a straightforward exchange of minor interests in land with tax only upon the equality; there is a significant risk that HMRC Stamp Taxes will take the view that each interest in land is being transferred for consideration in kind, with the relevant proportion of the consideration provided being allocated between the land and other assets pro rata. It will be difficult to persuade HMRC Stamp Taxes to isolate the two land interests into two separate transactions for mixed considerations not a 'land exchange' treatment; each equal interest is transferred for mixed consideration of the other interest not a simple land for land exchange with an adjustment for equality. The beneficiaries may both be faced with arguments for tax because there is not a simple land exchange with equality. It may be necessary to fragment the transaction so that one equitable interest consists solely of land 'exchange' for the other land interest and a balancing interest of other assets. This means a double charge upon the apportioned consideration and not a single charge upon the equality adjustment, if any.

---

13 This turns upon the technical interpretation of FA 2003, s.47. This will not be a 'partition' since the land is not physically divided.
14 Which is, of course, an argument that the equitable interest is a separate chose-in-action and not a bundle of interests in the individual trust assets which is the view of the draftsman.

10.12 COMPUTATIONAL ISSUES

Two areas of computation problems arise.

(a) Apportionment

Insofar as the trust fund consists of a mixture of investments including both shares and land, and only one interest includes land such as where the life tenant surrenders his life interest in the land and possible other assets in return for the remainderman surrendering him interests in other assets, presumably, it will be necessary to apportion any cash consideration paid upon an assignment of the interest between the interest in the land and the interest in the other assets on a just and reasonable basis (see FA 2003, Sched. 4, para. 4). Only the consideration apportioned to the former would appear to be within the charge to SDLT.

(b) 'Exchanges'

More frequently, however, the arrangement will involve mutual transfers of beneficial interests which may include land on one side or the other or both. The computation rules will differ depending upon whether there is an exchange of interests in land or there is only one interest in land and the property being received does not include any land interest such as where a life tenant agrees to transfer the interest including the interest in any land held in the trust by the remainderman in consideration of becoming absolutely entitled to shares held by the trustees.

In the case where only one side of the bargain involves the acquisition of an interest in land, the SDLT will be charged upon the consideration, i.e. the apportioned value of the shares relevant to the proportion of the land interest being 'acquired' received from the trustees at the direction of the remainderman. However, where the interests being exchanged both involve interests in land the land exchange rules (FA 2003, s.47) may apply if HMRC Stamp Taxes, contrary to its expected position set out above, treats the arrangement as two disposals for mixed consideration because both sides of the transaction include non-land assets and the parties have not sought to break out the separate assets and consideration in their documentation. This gives rise to a conceptual difficulty as to the nature of the interest of the particular beneficiary. A major interest is defined (FA 2003, s.117) as being a freehold or leasehold interest whether subsisting at law or in equity. The interest of the beneficiary in a trust is only a limited interest in such land and, *prima facie*, would appear not to be a 'major interest'. In consequence, where the exchange does not involve the acquisition of a major interest on either side then the chargeable consideration is the amount or value of any consideration provided other than the disposals that are given (FA 2003, Sched. 4, para. 5(4)(a) and (b)). This would appear to limit the charge to any consideration that represents equality or other adjustments. The value of the interests in land being mutually exchanged is ignored.

10.13 DISCRETIONARY TRUSTS

Beneficiaries of discretionary and similar trusts do not have interests in the underlying property.[15] There are merely personal rights against the trustees for proper administration. In consequence, in general, dealings in such interests are not dealings in chargeable interests even if done for consideration. However, it is specifically provided (FA 2003, Sched. 16, para. 7) that where a chargeable interest is acquired pursuant to the exercise of a discretion or power of appointment vested in the trustees of a settlement, the acquisition is treated as being made for a sum equal to any consideration that was given by the person in whose favour the appointment or discretion was exercised before becoming an object of the power or discretion. Therefore, if a person pays a sum of money whether to the trustees or to the settlor or to any other party in order to be included within the class of discretionary beneficiaries or appointees, that money will rank as chargeable consideration in respect of any land transferred out of the trust.[16] This charge is, however, not limited to discretionary trusts but appears to be intended to apply to situations where rather than purchasing an equitable interest in a fixed interest trust, which is potentially taxable, the money is paid to be included within the class of persons to whom an appointment can be made which, apart from this provision, would not appear to be taxable.

An interest in a trust fund is a chose-in-action, enforceable only by court action against the trustees at the instance of a beneficiary. A purchaser or an assignee of a chose-in-action must remember to protect his interest by giving notice to the person obliged to distribute the property. There may, of course, be questions whether such notices are in substance equitable assignments (see, e.g. *Brandt's (Wm)* v. *Dunlop Rubber Co* [1905] AC 454). It is thought that in order to be an equitable assignment the notice would require to be signed by at least the transferor or seller. In the case of a legal chose-in-action, express written notice must be given to the debtor, trustee or other person from whom the assignor would have been entitled to claim the debt or chose-in-action. An equitable interest in a trust fund should be protected in exactly the same way under the rule in *Dearle* v. *Hall* (1828) 3 Russ 1. Since 1925 the notice to the trustees must be in writing (LPA 1925, s.137) and to

---

15 *Gartside* v. *IRC* [1968] AC 553; *Holmden* v. *IRC* [1968] AC 685; but query where there is only one discretionary beneficiary and no power to accumulate the income.
16 Assuming that the exercise is not tainted as a fraud on a power or similar breach of trust.

give maximum protection should be served on all the trustees (*Re Wasdale* [1899] 1 Ch 163). Failure to serve notice may cause the donee to lose priority in the event of a subsequent dealing with the same interest. However, SDLT is not affected by issues of priority or the potential loss of the interest purchased. Tax will be payable by reference to substantial performance or completion in the sense of the delivery of the assignment notwithstanding that full title does not pass because the requisite notice has not been given. There will be no right to reclaim the tax if the transaction proves to be valueless through loss of priority because this is not the annulment or rescission of the contract within FA 2003, s.44(9).

10.14 CREATION OF DERIVATIVE TRUSTS

As an alternative to disposing of his equitable interest outright, the assignor may care to create a derivative or subtrust, leaving himself as a buffer between the head trustees and the ultimate beneficiary. Thus if a beneficiary has, say, a life interest in property which he wishes to sell to another, instead of assigning the interest outright he can convey it to a new set of trustees to hold on the stated trusts, or continue to hold it himself as trustee, having moved the beneficial interest down one step by a declaration of trust. In either case the original trustees will remain owners of the legal estate and interest, and liable to account for the income to the new trustees of the life interest or the original life tenant, as the case may be. They or he in turn must pass the income down the line to the beneficiary. If trustees of the life interest are to be appointed, exactly the same principles as above apply in properly constituting the trust, but as the subject-matter of the conveyance to the trustees is a subsisting equitable interest, the conveyance must be in writing to satisfy s.53(1)(c) of LPA 1925 or pass the equitable interest by constructive trust where this is permitted without writing (see *Neville* v. *Wilson* [1997] Ch 144). This applies even though the property in the hands of the head trustees consists of property capable of transfer by delivery. Similar principles to those discussed above also apply in determining whether the contract, if any and if in writing, to dispose of the equitable interest is within Finance Act 1999, Sched. 13, para. 7 or the assignment to the trustees or the declaration of trust bears the *ad valorem* stamp.

Where, however, the former beneficial life tenant chooses himself to remain trustee, he can make the declaration of trust orally, at least if the property out of which the trust has been created is personalty. If the trust is of land, unless a bare trust or a strict settlement governed by the Settled Land Act 1925 is involved, the legal estate will be held on trust for sale by the original trustees. As such the property is treated by equity as personalty by the application of the doctrine of conversion. Nevertheless, the safer view appears to be that the beneficial interests are still in land until sale actually takes place. Certainly the interest of a tenant in common in equity under a trust for sale was held in *Cooper* v. *Critchley* [1955] Ch 431 to be an interest in land for the purpose of s.40(1) of the LPA 1925 before its repeal by s.2 of LP(MP)A 1989. Section 53(1)(b) of LPA 1925 governing the formation of trusts in land (which has not been repealed) is very similar in wording and purpose to the old s.40.

10.15 INTERNAL REARRANGEMENT OF BENEFICIAL INTERESTS

It should be remembered that a release of a beneficial interest under a trust will amount to a disposition if in writing and if its effect is to move or create a beneficial interest in favour of another and will constitute an 'acquisition' by the person benefiting from the transaction. Thus, if instead of a life tenant selling his interest to the remainderman, he purports for consideration to surrender or release it, the effect is the same: the reversion is accelerated and falls into possession immediately (*Platts Trustees* v. *IRC* (1953) 34 ATC 292). In the case of a gift, the desired result could be achieved by the trustees exercising their powers of advancement under s.32 of the Trustee Act 1925 with the requisite consent of the life tenant. The consent of the life tenant to the arrangement is not a release of an interest (*Re Pauling's Settlement* [1962] 1 WLR 56). The powers are limited by the statute to the advancement of one half only of the actual or presumptive entitlement of the reversioner, but in a properly drawn trust deed these powers can and should be enlarged. The exercise of a power of advancement may be a dutiable transaction when the power is exercised in favour of a connected company which can include a corporate trustee of a derivative settlement because of the connected company charge (FA 2003, ss.53 and 54) or where the person benefiting has provided consideration in order to become an object of the power (FA 2003, Sched. 16, para. 7). Where the alteration of the equitable interest is effected with the assistance of the court pursuant to the Variation of Trusts Act 1958 the court order is potentially subject to SDLT if there is consideration provided for the variation. Acquisitions include transactions effected by a court order so that these variations can be chargeable transactions if the conditions are satisfied. Such arrangements are not normally transactions for consideration (*Henniker* v. *Henniker* (1852) 1 E&B 54) and so will not normally attract SDLT but this is not a universal principle and tax may arise in the particular circumstances where there is chargeable consideration (see, e.g. *Oughtred* v. *IRC* [1960] AC 206).

Instead of one party wishing to rearrange the beneficial interests so that an advantage is conferred on another, there may be a rearrangement of the interests under which neither party gains. But if there is chargeable consideration moving between the parties the transaction may be caught as chargeable (*Oughtred* v. *IRC* [1960] AC 206). The same problems arise where interests in land are involved in the exchange or variation. In such case the structure of the variation of the equitable interest is important because the transaction may be either land exchange or transfer of a chargeable interest for consideration in money's worth where the computational rules differ significantly. An illustration likely to be quite common in practice would be where land is held for A for life remainder to B and the beneficiaries agree to divide the land between themselves. Such an arrangement is not a partition because the interest is not held 'jointly' (FA 2003, s.121), i.e. concurrently, but consecutively. In consequence, there are exchanges of interests in land. However, since these, like most interests in trusts are merely limited interests in freehold land and leaseholds, this will be an exchange of minor interests. In consequence, although the parties become entitled to a freehold interest in their respective part of the land, the tax is chargeable only upon any consideration provided by way of equality,[17] but, as considered above, in other situations the issues as to whether HMRC will argue for two 'sales' are more complex and structuring issues may arise.

10.16 POWERS OF APPOINTMENT AND ADVANCEMENT

Chargeable interests include powers over land (FA 2003, s.48) and there is no reason why this should not include powers of appointment exercisable by trustees. Given the general exemption for gifts (FA 2003, Sched. 3, para. 1), except where connected companies or partnerships are involved,[18] the normal exercise of powers by trustees is unlikely to give rise to a charge to SDLT because there will be no chargeable consideration. However, where a chargeable interest is acquired by virtue of the exercise of a power of appointment and the person in whose favour the appointment is made gives consideration to become an object of the power, the chargeable interest is taxed as if that consideration was consideration for the appointment (FA 2003, Sched. 16, para. 7). Where consideration is provided, assuming that this does not constitute some form of fraud on a power, then insofar as the property appointed or advanced out of the settlement includes land there will be a chargeable transaction as far as the appointee is concerned. Where the property appointed is subject to a mortgage (FA 2003, Sched. 4, para. 8) there is a potential charge to tax if the transferee assumes personal liability for the mortgage (FA 2003, Sched. 4, para. 8). However, if the transferee whilst taking the property subject to the charge does not assume personal liability,

---

17 FA 2003, Sched. 4, para. 6; but note the special rules where partnerships are involved: FA 2003, Sched. 15, para. 16 (as amended).
18 FA 2003, ss.53 and 54 where the previous stamp duty exemption for distribution out of trusts contained in Finance Act 2000, s.120 has not been continued in relation to SDLT, and Sched. 15, paras. 13 and 24 (as amended).

i.e. there is no personal covenant to repay the mortgage or a recharging of the property as banks are unfortunately prone to requiring which does not include such a covenant, there is no charge because there is no assumption within the charging provisions; but if as part of the arrangements there is a variation of the rights and liabilities of the parties there is a deemed assumption of the liability and this is deemed to be chargeable consideration producing a chargeable transaction.

'Subgifts'

As indicated above, the 'gift' to the trustees may be subject to SDLT as it may complete more than one transaction. A classic illustration would be where the settlor has agreed to purchase the property and directs the seller to transfer the property directly to the trustees. Such a purchase and 'sub' gift may escape SDLT as a 'sub-sale' since the second limb (i.e. the gift to the trustees) is not a sale for the market value of the property.[19] The effect of s.45 of FA 2003 is that if the two transactions are substantially performed or completed at the same time, the original purchaser escapes liability notwithstanding that he pays the contract price in full, and possibly receives a transfer. This is upon the basis that the contract between A and B and the arrangements between B and the trustees are completed at the same time. It would appear possible to vest the property in the trustees free of tax provided that the trustees are not within the connected company charge.

10.17 RESERVATION OF BENEFIT

A difficult area arises where the settlor wishes to vest the property in the trustees whilst reserving some benefit for himself whether by way of contract or otherwise, or wishes to dispose of only a partial interest in the property. Here the conveyancing mechanics imposed by the general law or the machinery adopted by the parties can affect the SDLT costs significantly since 'land exchanges', which are widely defined (FA 2003, s.47), are potentially subject to a double charge. It is not always possible to transfer land reserving an interest or simply gifting a partial interest; the transaction may have to take the form of a transfer and a regrant of the retained interest. This type of problem will frequently arise where the settlor wishes to transfer the freehold of his home to the trustees but retaining the right to continue to

---

[19] There is, however, a technical argument on the badly drafted legislation that in order to obtain sub-sale relief, the 'sub-sale' arrangement must be for consideration. The view of HMRC Stamp Taxes on this point is not known, but, although a weak argument, there is a significant risk that it may make it. Payment of a few pounds may be prudent protection in this situation.

reside there, or is entering into some form of equity release or home annuity arrangement where there may have to be an outright transfer of the main interest and the grant of some form of right of occupation that has the appropriate value. Such arrangements are likely to create leases for life rather than licences (*Skipton Building Society* v. *Clayton* (1993) 66 P&CR 223) and there may be an intention to grant or reserve a lease for a fixed term for the settlor. HMRC Stamp Taxes takes an aggressive position on this area and has contended that where there is a transfer of the title to trustees who agree to delay delivery of vacant possession indefinitely this is a lease for life[20] and is not a licence to occupy since it confers exclusive possession upon the transferor/donor. HMRC Stamp Taxes may take the view that there is a sale and leaseback rather than just the gift of a reversionary interest.[21]

Pursuant to FA 2003, s.47, the SDLT upon the transfer will be charged upon its market value and the leaseback will be taxable upon a deemed premium equal to its market value and upon a rent reserved. The exemption for sale and leaseback arrangements will not necessarily apply because there may not be a cash sum payable for the 'sale' plus any rent reserved.[22] HMRC Stamp Taxes, after long resistance, is beginning to accept that the land transferred is to be valued subject to the obligation to grant the leaseback.

It was formerly possible to mitigate these multiple charges by arranging for the first stage to be the grant of the lease to a nominee followed by a sale of the reversionary interest to the third party subject to and with the benefit of the lease. However, it is now provided that where a lease is granted to a nominee[23] or by a nominee to the beneficial owner it is taxable.

10.18 ESTATES OF DECEASED PERSONS

There is no specific general exemption for property passing on death but such arrangements will normally, but not invariably, be for no chargeable consideration and they will not be chargeable transactions.

---

[20] Treated initially as a lease for one year but increasing each year for the purposes of the charge upon any rent reserved during which the lease continues; becoming a two-, three- or four-year lease, etc.

[21] There are issues as to whether there is a contractual relationship between the settlor and the trustees. See *Nichols* v. *IRC* [1973] STC 497; [1975] STC 278; *Park* v. *IRC* [1970] 1 WLR 626; *(No.2)* [1972] Ch 385.

[22] See FA 2003, s.57A (as amended), but note that the conditions for this relief are not identical with the reliefs for inheritance tax.

[23] It is currently possible in England to create valid leases in this situation but there may be difficulties in Scotland. See, on dealings between nominees and beneficial owners, *Lady Ingram* v. *IRC* [1999] STC 37; *Rye* v. *Rye* [1961] 2 All ER 146. See also *Kildrummy* v. *IRC* [1990] STC 657.

However, arrangements taking effect on death may be chargeable transactions for a variety of reasons. Whilst a *donatio mortis causa* will normally be a 'gift' it will be exempt notwithstanding that it takes effect outside any will or intestacy. Other extra-testamentary dispositions becoming effective on death may, however, be taxable. For example, constructive trusts such as those arising because the satisfaction of the conditions is the performance of consideration creating a contractual type of relationship.

Provisions within the will also raise issues. For example, it may be provided that, in broad terms, the matrimonial home is to pass to the surviving spouse subject to some arrangement such as the payment of an amount equal to the nil rate band of inheritance tax possibly charged upon the property and the surviving spouse may provide a loan note on the assumption of liability. There are many such arrangements but the general view of HMRC Stamp Taxes is that such arrangements are taxable as 'sales' for the amount of the 'debt' (see Guidance Note 12 Nov. 2004). It is far from obvious that its analysis is correct in all cases; but, since it accepts that it is possible to transfer property subject to a mortgage without incurring a charge provided that no personal liability for the debt is assumed, this seems, for the time being, to offer a relatively unprovocative method of dealing with the situation free of tax for the time being.

Deceased's liabilities

When the deceased has entered into a chargeable transaction, the responsibility for payment and clearly the SDLT will pass to the personal representatives who become personally liable for the tax but with a right to deduct the tax paid out of the assets and effects of the deceased (FA 2003, s.106(3)). It might be thought that this is unlikely to be a significant difference but the assumption is incorrect. In addition to incomplete transactions of purchase there are many structures where there are outstanding taxation liabilities and until these have been resolved it will not be possible to complete the administration of the estate. Typical structures will include:

- leases with reviewable rents where there may be an obligation to make a further notification upon review and at the end of the fifth year of the term of the lease or any subsequent review producing an abnormal increase;
- acquisition of land where the consideration is variable within FA 2003, s.51 where instalments of the overage or other payment are outstanding (FA 2003, s.80). Where the variable payment is a premium in connection with the grant of the lease (FA 2003, Sched. 17A, para. 12), the liability passes to an assignee of the lease, but in all other cases the obligation to resolve the taxation issue remains with the original purchaser of the land; and

- where there are arrangements for SDLT upon a prior transaction these are payable by instalments (FA 2003, s.90; Stamp Duty Land Tax (Administration) Regulations 2003, SI 2003/2837).

These outstanding liabilities can delay the administration of the estate for many years and will require careful planning when disposing of or assenting the land in question. It seems that if in the course of the administration of the estate the personal representatives discover that the deceased made an error in a land transaction return they are under a duty to correct that error within a reasonable time or suffer a tax-related penalty (FA 2003, Sched. 10, para. 8).

10.19 WILLS AND INTESTACIES

The SDLT areas relating to wills where tax may arise are:

- transfers of assets to specific legatees and devisees;
- appropriation of assets in satisfaction of legacies;
- dealings in interests in the estate after a variation;
- variations of the estate of the deceased.

It would seem that interests in the estates of deceased parties may amount to interests in land in the UK. A specific devisee would have such an interest, assuming that the estate was not insolvent when he might not receive anything at all.

Residuary estates may be more difficult since until the residue has been administered and all creditors and liabilities have been provided for, the residuary beneficiaries do not have any interest in the underlying assets (*Commissioner of Stamps* v. *Livingston* [1964] 3 All ER 692 (PC)). However, it would seem that when the administration is complete an interest in the property vests and a chargeable interest arises. There would seem to be no reason why the estates of persons dying non-domiciled or not resident in the UK may not produce chargeable interests where the estate holds land in the UK. The overseas factor does not appear to affect the situation so that the tax applies. It will, however, be necessary to analyse the rights of the various devisees and residuary beneficiaries under the law governing the administration in order to determine the nature of their rights. It seems that the provisions applying to trusts will not, as such, apply to the estates of deceased persons during the administration. However, there seems to be no reason why the provisions affecting foreign trusts should not apply to trusts arising under wills or intestacies of persons non-domiciled or not resident in the UK.

TRUSTS, WILLS AND INTESTATE ESTATES

10.20 TESTAMENTARY TRUSTS

Testators frequently leave all or part of their estates subject to trusts and statutory trusts may arise upon intestacy. It seems that trusts created by the wills of deceased persons are governed by the basic trust regime, although there may be some questions as to when the land ceases to form part of the estate of the deceased person or becomes trust property or the person's representatives become nominees (FA 2003, Sched. 16, para. 1) with all of the compliance issues related to the change of status, and whether an assent or other appropriate vesting arrangement has been entered into by the executors, particularly where these are the same persons as the trustees of the testamentary settlement. Such trusts arising upon death will usually be for no consideration and therefore exempt from SDLT. The vesting of the land in the trustee or the personal representative becoming a trustee will not be a notifiable transaction. Any change in the Land Register that the parties believe to be necessary can be dealt with on the basis of a self-certificate (SDLT 60).

One issue of compliance arises. At this stage there is a change of status, the personal representative became trustee and different principles apply. Normally executors will be the vendors so that their identification on the land transaction return may not be a significant issue in practice. However, it remains to be seen whether, although there is no tax loss HMRC Stamp Taxes will, as seems likely, seek to impose a penalty for an incorrect return upon the 'purchaser'.

10.21 ASSENTS AND APPROPRIATIONS

However, persons other than specific devisees of land may be affected by SDLT. For example, a pecuniary legatee may enter into an arrangement with the personal representatives that a particular parcel of land be appropriated to him in satisfaction of his right to the pecuniary legacy (*Jopling* v. *IRC* [1940] 2 KB 282). However, frequently wills provide that the personal representatives may appropriate property in satisfaction of other types of legacy without the need for the consent of the beneficiary. Specific exemptions have been subsequently introduced as FA 2003, Sched. 3, para. 3A, whereby the acquisition of property by a person in or towards the satisfaction of his entitlement under or in relation to the will or intestacy of a deceased person is exempt such as where the matrimonial home is appropriated towards the interests of the surviving spouse (FA 2003, Sched. 3, para. 3A). The exemption applies where the property is assented subject to a mortgage; but the acquirer must not give any other consideration. However, where there is any other consideration such as where the legatee may have to make a payment because the value of the property exceeds the amount of his legacy, the charge is limited to the amount of the actual consideration (FA 2003,

Sched. 4, para. 8A). As the relief is included in Sched. 3, there is no notification obligation regardless of the value of the property where there is a transfer of a major interest, i.e. a freehold or a lease unless it relates to land in a disadvantaged area (FA 2003, Sched. 6, para. 13) and would be exempt by reason of those provisions.

10.22 VARIATION OF ESTATES OF DECEASED PERSONS

It has long been possible for beneficiaries under a will or on intestacy to rearrange by agreement between themselves their respective testamentary or statutory entitlements (Inheritance Tax Act 1984, s.142; Taxation of Chargeable Gains Act 1992, s.62). Insofar as the interest of any of the parties to such a transaction is a chargeable interest then such an arrangement will, *prima facie*, give rise to a charge to SDLT if done for consideration. Much may depend upon the circumstances of the arrangement. For example, a disclaimer of a legacy which would usually be without consideration should not give rise to a charge to SDLT even though the interest vests in some other person. Moreover, even if there is consideration, it is considered that no charge to tax arises since a disclaimer is not within the definition of an acquisition. However, there may be some other form of disposition within the definition of 'acquisition' whether a release, surrender or otherwise in return for some reciprocal arrangement or the payment of consideration directly. Insofar as the consideration for the disposal of the chargeable interest in land consists of consideration other than entering into another land transaction in the land exchange provisions (FA 2003, s.47), the SDLT upon the person acquiring the interest will be by reference to the amount or value of the consideration provided. However, where there is some form of reciprocal arrangement whereby interests in one property are released or surrendered in consideration of other interests being released or surrendered so that the parties are in effect exchanging interests in land then the land exchange provisions will apply (FA 2003, Sched. 4, para. 5). In this situation the question as to whether the particular devisee has a major or non-major interest will be important. For example, where there is a specific devise of a freehold interest to A it would seem that, *prima facie*, A has a major interest albeit his interest subsists in equity (FA 2003, s.117). However, where the interest is part of some form of testamentary trust or a limited interest is granted such as a right to occupy for life the interest may not be a major interest. This affects the computation and notification obligations.

Insofar as there is an exchange involving one or more major interests such as where one beneficiary is exchanging the freehold land left to him for freehold land devised to some other beneficiary then there will be two charges to SDLT based upon the market value of the interest being acquired. Any equality adjustment would appear to be ignored (FA 2003, Sched. 4, para.

5(3)). However, where the transaction involves 'exchanges' of interests all of which are not major interests the mutual exchange of interests is ignored in determining the extent of the chargeable consideration which is limited to any other consideration provided such as any equality payment or other consideration providing such an adjustment (FA 2003, Sched. 4, para. 5(4)).

However, SDLT may be payable on any element of consideration in kind deemed to be dutiable, as, for example, a mutual transfer of an interest in land for an interest in shares. For example, where the family home is demised to the children jointly, one child may wish to take the house absolutely and the other children are agreeable to this provided that they are appropriately compensated such as by receiving the assets in the estate. *Prima facie* there is a chargeable transaction (which may be a linked transaction because all of the parties are 'connected') involving an acquisition of land for a consideration in kind consisting of the compensation adjustment. The liability to *ad valorem* stamp duty on such rearrangements with other arrangements is relieved by FA 2003, Sched. 3, para. 3. There is a limited exemption from SDLT in respect of certain variations of the estates of deceased persons. It is provided (FA 2003, Sched. 3, para. 4) that no charge to SDLT arises in respect of the variation of an estate of a deceased person provided that:

- the deceased was competent to dispose of the chargeable interest in question. This means that the deceased was not acting as trustee or had a special power of appointment over the property. It would seem that where the deceased had a special power of appointment over the property whether exercisable by deed or will, he is to be regarded as competent to dispose for these purposes;[24]
- the transaction is carried out within the period of two years after the death;
- no consideration in money or money's worth other than the making of a variation of another such disposition is given for the variation; and
- it is immaterial whether or not the administration of the estate is complete or the property has been distributed in accordance with the original dispositions,

provided that the consideration if any consists solely of other interests in the estate. If the variation is made for any consideration in money or money's worth other than consideration consisting of the variation in respect of another of the dispositions, such as the child receiving the house has to resort to borrowing from a bank to provide all or even part of the compensation, the relief remains available but on a restricted basis. The tax is charged upon

---

24 He may be competent to dispose where he had a general power of appointment, see, e.g. *Re Penrose* [1933] Ch 793.

the external consideration but the benefit of the lower rates is available by reference only to such external consideration.

10.23 PURCHASERS OF LAND FROM PERSONAL REPRESENTATIVES

In order to facilitate the administration of estates, a relief is provided for a property trader whose business includes purchasing dwellings from personal representatives where the deceased individual occupied the property as his only or main residence at some time in the two years preceding his death. The property trader must acquire by transfer a major interest; the grant of a new lease is not exempt. The land must not exceed 0.5 hectare and such larger area as is reasonable for the property. The property trader must not spend more than a limited amount on refurbishment (i.e. £10,000 or 5 per cent of the consideration paid up to a maximum of £20,000). The property trader must be a company, a limited liability partnership, or a partnership comprised solely of companies, and must not permit its employees to occupy the premises nor grant a lease or licence. If the conditions are subsequently breached the tax is clawed back (FA 2003, Sched. 6A, paras. 3, 8, and 11(3)).

CHAPTER 11
Partnerships

11.1 GENERAL

Partnerships are governed by a complex stamp tax regime. Their ordinary acquisitions of assets are governed by the normal principles of stamp duty, stamp duty reserve tax and SDLT, although there are certain modifications for compliance in the last case.

However, where there are acquisitions or disposals of land between a partnership and partner or persons connected with them, a special regime applies.

Where there are transactions which constitute transfers of interests in a partnership there is a relief to the extent that the assets of the firm are free of stamp taxes such as book debts, a charge of 0.5 per cent where there are shares or marketable securities and a charge to SDLT where the partnership property includes land by reference to the market value of such land.

Certain issues arise as to the terminology since the same terms such as 'transfer' can bear different meanings in different parts of Sched. 15 to FA 2003, and possibly from other parts of the SDLT regime.

'Partnership'

For these purposes 'partnerships' are widely defined but they are excluded from the definition of 'company'. The definition includes all forms of partnership formed or established in the UK including general partnerships under the Partnership Act 1890, limited partnerships under the 1907 Act and limited liability partnerships. The legislation indicates that the charge for the tax overrides any such limited liability. It also includes a firm or entity formed or established abroad having a similar character to any of those formed under English law; but no guidance is provided as to the possibly relevant criteria. Moreover, the legal personality of a partnership is disregarded to the extent that the chargeable interest held by or on behalf of the partnership is treated as held by or on behalf of the partners and the land transaction is treated as having been entered into by or on behalf of the partners as such (FA 2003, Sched. 15, para. 2) but the partnership is deemed to continue notwithstanding changes in the membership.

'Partner'

No explanation is given of who is to be treated as a partner for these purposes. Persons who are 'salaried partners' as opposed to equity partners may not be partners in law (*Stekel* v. *Ellice* [1973] 1 All ER 465), but they may be liable as partners by reason of estoppel or holding out (see, e.g. Partnership Act 1890, s.14), or because they have not given notice of their retirement or seen to the removal of their names from the notepaper (*Tower Cabinets* v. *Ingram* [1949] 2 KB 397). It seems probable that HMRC Stamp Taxes will seek to rely upon these principles in order to collect the tax.[1]

11.2 STAMP DUTY

Basic rules of stamp duty continue to apply to acquisitions by partnerships,[2] but there are difficulties since the language is not consistent even within Sched. 15 to FA 2003.

- There is a charge to stamp duty at the rate of 0.5 per cent on acquisitions by a partnership of shares or marketable securities and if such stamp duty is not paid then there will be a liability to the principal charge to stamp duty reserve tax at the same rates.
- There is a charge to SDLT on land acquisitions outside the special regime.
- There is an exemption from both the above charges for the acquisition of property including land on the initial incorporation of a limited liability partnership.
- Where there is an instrument operating or a written agreement (Finance Act 1999, Sched. 13, para. 7) to 'transfer' an interest in a partnership there is now an obligation to apportion the consideration between non-chargeable assets, shares and marketable securities, and land.
- The consideration attributable to non-chargeable assets such as goodwill,[3] book debts and intellectual property of the firm is not subject to stamp taxes in any form.
- To the extent that the consideration relates to stock or marketable securities owned by the partnership the consideration allocated will be subject to stamp duty at the rate of 0.5 per cent (Finance (No.2) Act 2005, Sched. 10, para. 21; FA 2003, Sched. 15, para. 33 (as amended)). It seems that

---

[1] They may, however, be less willing to press the argument simply for the purpose of imposing penalties such as for submitting an incorrect land transaction return by not including such persons as 'purchasers'.
[2] HMRC Stamp Taxes does not seek to apply stamp duty reserve tax to dealings in partnership interests even in relation to limited liability partnerships.
[3] But note the problem of whether it is goodwill or land value.

HMRC Stamp Taxes does not regard this aspect of the transaction as being within the charges to stamp duty reserve tax.
- The SDLT charge upon the consideration attributable to land that is 'partnership property' is 4 per cent and is considered in more detail below.

The situation is not simplified by the fact that different principles apply for each of the taxes involved and different rules for computing and reporting the tax are applicable. Valuation exercises will frequently be required, which are likely to involve costs disproportionate to the tax involved, particularly at the rate of 0.5 per cent. Regrettably, the desire to avoid such extra costs is likely to expose the taxpayer's advisers to allegations of negligence and extended discovery assessment periods which will involve even higher costs and interest and penalties.

11.3 STAMP DUTY LAND TAX

Ordinary transactions

Basically the ordinary rules of SDLT which apply to all persons apply to 'partnerships'. Given the provisional nature of much of SDLT and the continuing nature of the partnership notwithstanding the changes in the membership, there will be difficult questions for incoming and outgoing partners as to the liability to the tax and interest and penalties which may need to be resolved because there are certain modifications to the general compliance regime.

Liability

An ordinary acquisition by a partnership is treated as being made by the partners. In consequence, the liability falls upon the 'responsible partners' who are the partners as at the effective date and any person who becomes a partner after that date.[4] Retirement does not appear to relieve a partner from liability. Anything done or to be done is a matter for the responsible partners; liability for the tax, penalties and interest can be enforced against the partners individually on a joint and several basis (FA 2003, Sched. 15, paras. 6 and 7) notwithstanding that this liability may exceed the limited capital contribution of the partner to the firm. However, tax and interest may not be recovered from responsible partners who were not partners as at the effective date. Penalties may be recovered against new partners where these accrue on a daily basis after their admission or the act or default occurred after their

---

4 Such partners are also liable to penalties but with limitations in respect of periods prior to their admission: FA 2003, Sched. 15, para. 7.

UNDERSTANDING SDLT

admission even where the effective date predates such admission (FA 2003, Sched. 15, para. 7 (as amended)).

Compliance

Acquisitions by a partnership must be dealt with by means of a land transaction return (SDLT 1) which must be signed by the appropriate persons. Strictly, this is all of the partners. This will not merely be the persons to whom the legal title passes such as the first four named who will be acting effectively as nominees for all of the partners as beneficial owners (FA 2003, Sched. 16, paras. 1 and 3 (as amended)). However, it is provided that the administration of compliance with the tax (and the initial liability to pay) can be dealt with by representative partners (FA 2003, Sched. 15, para. 8). These are persons who are nominated by the majority of the partners whose nomination has been approved in advance by HMRC Stamp Taxes, who must also sanction any changes in the list of representative partners (FA 2003, Sched. 15, para. 8). In practice, however, HMRC Stamp Taxes treats a partnership as a single purchaser so that when inserting the name of the vendor or purchaser in the land transaction return (SDLT 1) or the self-certificate (SDLT 60) only the partnership name is required (Notes for Guidance (SDLT 6)).

Special transactions

There is a group of transactions entered into after 22 July 2004 subject to special charges, where the counterparty to the transaction is a partner or a person who is connected with the partner[5] whether as 'vendor' or 'purchaser' and the chargeable interest becomes or ceases to be utilised as partnership property, i.e. 'used' for the purposes of the partnership business in whole or in part such as a lease by the partnership to a partner and 'transfers' of 'partnership interests' where the partnership property includes chargeable interests. Special charges also apply to persons about to become a partner and it seems retired as well as retiring partners.

Special transactions in relation to partnerships can be divided into three broad areas:

- 'transfers' of property to partnerships from partners or connected persons, whether for cash or in consideration of the issue of shares or the increase of shares in partnerships;

---

[5] A person may be connected with a partner without necessarily being a connected company.

- 'transfer' of partnership interests[6] which can include in the view of HMRC Stamp Taxes, a wide range of transactions;
- the transfer of partnership property from a partnership to partners or persons connected with them such as the withdrawal or repayment of capital *in specie* on retirement or where the partnership leases or sells land to one of its members or a connected person.

General

The legislation relating to dealings between partners and connected persons within the special regime, i.e. transfers of chargeable interests into and out of partnerships, is complex but the broad policy appears to be that insofar as the land remains owned by the same connected persons (other than persons who are connected simply by reason of being partners) there should be no charge to tax, unless there is 'actual consideration' moving between the parties. This favourable treatment, however, does not extend to transfers of partnership interests but since the charge to tax requires actual consideration (FA 2003, Sched. 15, para. 14) transfers of partnership interests by way of gift should not be taxable; but if in either case there is any actual or deemed consideration, no matter how small, the chargeable consideration is, broadly, upon a proportion of the market value. Unfortunately the discrepancy between the treatment of partnership capital and partnership income profits provides a trap for the unwary unless the allocations made for the purposes of the charging formula described below are carefully considered and appropriately applied. To some extent fiction prevails over reality in coping with transactions that are not intended to be taxed but consistent application of this policy has proved to be beyond the skills of those structuring and drafting the legislation.

Terminology

The plain English drafting has produced many specialised if unusual meanings of routine terminology that have to be noted. These include:

Partnership shares and interests

The SDLT legislation refers at various times to 'partnership shares' and 'partnership interests'. There is no definition of a 'partnership interest' but

---

6 There are many issues relating to what is a partnership 'share' and these issues vary from tax to tax because the jurisdictional rules differ and questions of corporate personality are differently treated. The provisions of FA 2003, Sched. 15 apply only for the purposes of SDLT; see para. 1 ('for the purposes of this Part'). There are many unanswered questions as to partnership 'shares' and 'interests' and how these relate to capital and loans and the nature of rights of partners in a limited liability partnership.

only a 'partnership share'. This is the share in the income profits of the partnership to which the person is entitled at the relevant time which, as mentioned below, is itself a problem. It has no relevance to his capital.[7]

This raises a whole range of problems and the current indications are that these many ambiguities are intended to be exploited by HMRC Stamp Taxes. For example:

PARTNERSHIP SHARE

This is the person's share in the 'income profits' of the firm. The current indications are that a hard line is to be taken in relation to partnership participation in 'profits' for these purposes. Not only is a change in profit sharing ratios regarded officially as a 'transfer',[8] but 'profits' will be widely interpreted.

PARTNERSHIP PROFITS

There is no definition of 'income profits' of the firm notwithstanding its importance. HMRC Stamp Taxes is taking a wide view. Included in a partner's share are not only the profits ultimately allocated but also there are added back prior allocations of profits such as special remuneration and possibly interest on partnership loan capital. The final profit shares in the agreement may not be the correct figures to apply. These rules are unworkable in the context of a transaction-based tax since profits and profit shares are fixed on an annual basis. Whilst a prior charge of X per cent of profits to one partner can be determined and added back to modify the agreed division of the ultimate profits, this cannot work where a partner is entitled to a fixed amount payable whether or not there are profits or there are special arrangements for dealing with rent if any property of the firm is sublet again regardless of profits for the year. No guidance as to how to deal with such issues has been provided by HMRC Stamp Taxes, which appears to be unaware of the defects in this legislation.

PARTNERSHIP INTEREST

In other cases, the legislation refers to partnership interest. The above problematic approach to partnership 'shares' raises the question as to whether a partnership 'interest' is to be treated as the capital or economic participation in the firm. The current approach of HMRC Stamp Taxes is that partnership 'interest' is the interest in the net assets of the firm, but without indicating

---

[7] But note the flexibility when determining the sum of the lower proportions mentioned above.

[8] But taxable only if there is some form of consideration pursuant to the statutory provisions (FA 2003, Sched. 15, paras. 14 and 36).

whether the 'net' position is arrived at by deducting partners' loans to the firm (including undrawn profits). Since these are not 'liabilities' of the firm they are likely to be treated as assets attributable to the percentage involvement of the partner of that 'repayment' of 'loan accounts' and can involve a change in profit sharing ratios which, in the official view, produces a transfer of a partnership 'share' potentially subject to tax. There is also the question, given the amendments contained in para. 17A of Sched. 15 relating to repayment of loan accounts, as to whether a partner's interest will be not merely his participation in capital but his entire economic involvement with the firm such as any partner loan account including monies advanced to the firm or possibly including undrawn shares of profits, although the amendments in para. 17A suggest that these latter items would not be included since this could incorporate an element of double counting, particularly where partnership shares are concerned.

'Transfer' of chargeable interests and partnership interests

The special charges are based upon 'transfers' which are defined in terms similar to 'acquisition' (FA 2003, s.43, Sched. 15, para. 9); but there are extensions to the definition such as 'transfer' includes property becoming or ceasing[9] to be partnership property which includes, in the official view, chargeable interests being utilised by licence in relation to 'partnership property'; and there are transactions deemed to be transfers of partnership interests. Unfortunately the draftsman has not made it clear whether the definition of 'transfer' in the latter case is in addition to the general definition of transfers or is in substitution for it.

'TRANSFER'

There are several definitions of transfer for the purposes of the special regime, namely:

- a general definition equivalent to 'acquisition' of a chargeable interest. This does not apply to transfers of partnership interests (FA 2003, Sched. 15, para. 9(2));
- a definition of transfers to or by a partnership in terms of a chargeable interest becoming partnership property, considered above (FA 2003, Sched. 15, paras. 35 and 37); and

---

9 It remains to be seen how HMRC Stamp Taxes intends to treat termination of leases by lapse of time. Fortunately these will rarely be for actual consideration, and so not taxable, but they may have to be notified by SDLT 1 (FA 2003, s.77 (as amended)).

UNDERSTANDING SDLT

- a special definition of 'transfer' of a partnership interest (FA 2003, Sched. 15, para. 36).

The particular meaning has to be noted in each separate context.

PARTNERSHIP PROPERTY

Although the provisions refer to transfers and chargeable interests, there is a definition of 'partnership property' (FA 2003, Sched. 15, para. 34(1)) as an interest (note, not a 'chargeable interest') held by or on behalf of a partnership, or one or more of the members of a partnership or for the purposes of the partnership business, and there is a transfer of a chargeable interest to a partnership whenever a chargeable interest becomes partnership property and a transfer by a partnership, *inter alia*, where a chargeable interest ceases to be partnership property (FA 2003, Sched. 15, paras. 34, 35 and 37).

These definitions are widely interpreted by HMRC Stamp Taxes. For example, it is its view that where a partner who owns land grants a licence to the partnership his whole freehold interest becomes partnership property, but if he grants a tenancy at a rent which rent acts as 'actual consideration' the partnership property is the tenancy interest. This transaction would not on general principles be taxable because there is no 'transfer' of a chargeable interest, but on HMRC Stamp Taxes's argument the freehold becomes partnership property. This difference between what is acquired and what becomes partnership property has to be noted because, in addition to the general definition of 'transfer' in terms of 'acquisition', there is also for the purposes of the special regime a transfer to or by a partnership when a chargeable interest becomes or ceases to be partnership property (FA 2003, Sched. 15, paras. 35 and 37(a)), or an interest is created out of partnership property (FA 2003, Sched. 15, para. 37(b)). It is, therefore, a major question whether this provision brings the whole freehold value into charge upon the grant, variation or termination of a licence to use or occupy the land. It seems that these provisions are intended to maximise the scope of the charge by maximising the extent of the property acquired in order to enhance the chargeable consideration where there is a transfer of a partnership share (FA 2003, Sched. 15, para. 14). Since the charge upon 'transfers' of partnership interests is related to the market value of the partnership property, the question of the extent of the partnership property is crucial in many cases. Where a partner has granted a short lease at a rent to the firm,[10] the chargeable amount is related to the actual lease but if he merely grants a rent-free licence, albeit of

---

10 Which is unlikely to be excluded from the computation by FA 2003, Sched. 15, para. 15.

a limited nature, the entire freehold interest or the entirety of the chargeable interest is owned by the licensor.

11.4 ACQUISITIONS OF CHARGEABLE INTERESTS FROM CONNECTED PERSONS

There is a chargeable transaction where there is what is effectively an acquisition of land by a partnership, i.e.:

- a transfer of a chargeable interest by an existing partner into the partnership; or
- a transfer by a person who becomes a partner such as on the initial contribution of capital; or
- a transfer by a person connected with an existing partner; or
- a transfer by a person connected with a person who becomes a partner.

'Transfer' is defined in the same manner as 'acquisition'.

These provisions will apply to situations where an owner of property who is either a partner or connected with partners sells or leases land to the partnership on an arm's length basis. They will also apply where a person contributes land to the partnership as his initial contribution of capital on being admitted to partnership or as an *in specie* increase of his partnership share when he is already a partner.

The problem of what is 'transferred' in such cases is considered above. The chargeable consideration is a mixture of the market value and any actual consideration and is determined in accordance with the formula

$$(MV \times (100 - SLP)\%) + (AC \times SLP\%)$$

MV   is market value
AC   is actual consideration
SLP is the sum of the lower proportions.

If there is a lease solely for a rent there is a deemed premium of market value (taking into account the rent). If there is an actual premium as well as rent, the market value charge still applies to guard against the lease being at an undervalue notwithstanding premium and rent. The charge includes both the actual premium and the amount needed to bring the premium up to open market value.[11] Tax is charged upon the premium and the proportion of the net present value of the rent pursuant to the formula

---

11 On the determination of market value note the provision in FA 2003, Sched. 15, para. 38.

(MV (i.e. deemed premium) × (100 − SLP)%) + (AC (if actual premium) × SLP%) + ((NPV rent) × (100 − SLP)%).[12]

It should be noted that although the same formulae apply to disposals of land by partnerships, the SLP is determined in a different way, as described below.

11.5 ACTUAL CONSIDERATION

There are various problems in relation to the drafting of these provisions such as in relation to mortgages. An early version of the draft notes for inclusion in the *Stamp Duty Land Tax Manual* gives an illustration that indicates that where the property transferred is subject to a mortgage this is not included within the scope of the 'actual consideration' but this does not appear in later versions.[13]

There will obviously be costs in determining market value and the net present value of the rent, but the key issue is determining SLP, i.e. the sum of the lower proportions. To do this it is necessary to apportion the interest of the transferor amongst partners connected with him (including himself). The lower proportion is the proportion so allocated or the proportion of the property measured by that partner's income share. The greater the sum of the lower proportion (i.e. the share of the property retained by the transferor and connected partners) the smaller the market value falling into charge; but the chargeable actual consideration will increase. It seems to be the official

---

12 It is important to note some confusion in the drafting of 'AC': in relation to premiums it is the 'actual chargeable consideration' whereas it normally means the actual consideration. It seems that for some reason the draftsman of the legislation intended the charge upon these premiums to be on a narrower basis, i.e. the charge is not upon the entire 'actual consideration' but only upon that part of the 'actual consideration' that falls within the definition of chargeable consideration; deemed consideration albeit chargeable is not included in the calculation.

13 No explanation is given for this treatment unless 'actual consideration' means consideration in law as opposed to consideration within the extended definition of this term in the charging provisions. Some support for this can be found in other parts of the special provisions relating to partnership acquisitions which refer to both 'actual consideration' and 'actual chargeable consideration'. This suggests that 'actual chargeable consideration' means actual consideration that is chargeable consideration, i.e. there is a double test; and 'actual consideration' means only that consideration that falls within the general law. There is old authority in stamp duty that taking over property subject to a mortgage does not involve the mortgage as part of the chargeable consideration. It was for these reasons that it was necessary for the predecessor of the Stamp Act 1891 to be enacted, i.e. taking over liability in respect of a mortgage is not 'consideration' in general law.

view that where the parties are dealing with unconnected persons, the whole value of the property will be subject to charge by reason of the market value charge and the actual consideration is ignored but it is difficult to support this by reference to the legislation.

It is, in consequence, important to understand the complex process to determine the SLP but, as indicated above, if all of the parties are 'connected' no market value charge should arise and tax is payable only if there is 'actual consideration'. It is the current practice of HMRC Stamp Taxes to apply a broad rule of thumb and to indicate that there is no charge where such a connection exists. In such a situation, where the SLP is 100 there will be no chargeable consideration but because the exemption pursuant to FA 2003, Sched. 3, para. 1 does not apply, the transaction will be notifiable upon a land transaction return (SDLT 1).

For example:

H, W and S being parents and child are in partnership in equal shares. H transfers a freehold into the partnership as additional capital. There is no actual consideration. The value is apportioned one-third each; the partnership shares are one-third each. The sum of the lower proportion is $3 \times \frac{1}{3}$, i.e. 100. The chargeable amount is MV $\times (100 - 100) = 0$.

11.6 SUM OF THE LOWER PROPORTIONS

In order to determine sum of the lower proportions (SLP) it is necessary to identify the owner of the chargeable interest and the persons who are connected with him and who are partners (known as 'corresponding partners'). The owner's interest in the chargeable interest is apportioned between the corresponding partners and the owner if he is involved in the partnership. This apportionment can, in the view of HMRC Stamp Taxes, be made in whatever proportions produce the lowest tax for the parties. The apportionment does not have to be made by reference to shares in the partnership income; it can be made by reference to capital interests to deal with situations where there is a difference between income entitlement and level of capital. However, since the maximum reduction is limited to the partner's income share, allocations on this basis will normally produce the best result; but, given that profits are not always on a simple fixed basis, this is not an easy test to apply as at the effective date. For each partner the 'lower proportion' is the lesser of the proportion of the chargeable interest apportioned to him and the proportion equivalent to his 'partnership share' (i.e. his share in the profits – not capital – of the firm) (FA 2003, Sched. 15, para. 34(2)) immediately after the transaction. The sum of the lower proportions is the aggregated lower proportion for each connected partner.

For example:

H and W own land equally and are entering into partnership with S and D. All parties are connected. The capital shares are H and W 50:50; the profit share are H:W:S:D – 10:10:60:20.

Allocating on the basis of capital shares produces H:W:S:D – 50:50:0:0 but the lower proportions, i.e. income shares, are 10:10:0:0 i.e. 80 per cent of the market value is chargeable (because the allocated shares of S and D are below their income shares and those allocated to H and W exceed their income shares). Allocating on the basis of income shares produces 10:10:60:20, i.e. 100 per cent so that there is no charge to tax.

In a case where A and B are unconnected parties entering into a partnership whereby A contributes land and B contributes cash there can be no actual consideration. Assuming that the profit and capital shares are 50:50, SLP will be 50 so that there is a charge upon 50 per cent of the market value. This applies even where A receives cash from the partnership intended to balance the capital share, since HMRC Stamp Taxes does not regard this as actual consideration or as a withdrawal of capital not subject to tax. It seems, from the draft materials for inclusion in the Manual, that these arrangements are not affected by para. 17A of Sched. 15 to FA 2003 which may not apply to the 'debt' arising upon the initial contributions of capital; but for the time being pending clarification of the policy behind these provisions it seems prudent to pay cash at once.[14]

As will be clear, there are major difficulties to be addressed upon the acquisition of land by a partnership where profit and capital shares differ, especially where there is to be some form of cash adjustment between the parties who are connected.

Where the partnership consists solely of bodies corporate if the sum of the lower proportion is 75 or more, the charge is imposed fully upon the market value and any actual consideration is ignored.[15]

11.7 REMOVAL OF LAND FROM PARTNERSHIP

There are many ways in which property can be taken out of a partnership, i.e. situations where the property ceases to be within the definition of partnership property such as, if HMRC Stamp Taxes is correct, the termination of a licence to use land held by one of the partners or whilst the chargeable

---

[14] However, the draft materials indicate that there may be problems, particularly in relation to 'transfers' of partnership shares where cash is received from the partnership and 'lent' back.

[15] Should there be an SDLT group, the transaction is forced into intra-group relief because there are more and longer term anti-avoidance charges applicable.

interest remains partnership property an interest is carved out of it, such as the grant of a lease or a sub-lease or an easement or profit is created. As no specific provisions are made for winding up of partnerships these rules apply to distributions of land to the members in such circumstances. Property ceases to be partnership property and there is a transfer of an interest out of the partnership if it ceases to be partnership property or a sub-interest such as a lease or sub-lease is created out of the partnership property and this sub-interest does not itself become partnership property. As indicated above, where the partnership utilises land for its business which is owned by one of the partners otherwise than pursuant to a lease at a rent such as a licence, the whole interest of the licensor/parties becomes partnership property. The termination of the 'licence' will, in the official view, result in the 'transfer' of the entire chargeable interest already owned by the transferee. Partners may wish to reduce their capital or retire and take the repayment of their capital *in specie*. The partnership may be dissolved and the land distributed to the partners either pro rata or in accordance with some form of liquidation agreement whereby certain assets are allocated to particular partners and others are distributed elsewhere.[16] There may also be 'removals' of assets from the partnerships by reasons of partnership mergers and demergers.[17] Unfortunately, many of these transactions are governed by different principles and it is necessary to identify into which category the transaction falls.

The rules are somewhat similar in concept to those concerned with land going into a partnership and the same formulae apply. The policy appears to be that to the extent that the property remains vested in persons who are partners or persons connected with partners or possibly former partners, the

---

16 Although there are special rules for dealing with partitions of chargeable interests held by partnerships in FA 2003, Sched. 15, para. 16, there is a fundamental question, where the land held by the partnership is divided amongst the partners, whether this is in fact a 'partition' within the general rules or is some form of complicated land exchange provision. This affects the application of the charging provisions which differ between partitions and land exchanges in FA 2003, Sched. 4, paras. 5 and 6. Although there is some doubt upon the point, it seems that in practice HMRC Stamp Taxes is inclined to the view that a division of a pool of assets rather than the physical division of a single asset held under a single title can constitute a partition.

17 It seems that FA 2003, Sched. 15, para. 16 may have some relevance in such cases because it refers to the acquisitions (although not referred to as a transfer there is presumably intended to bring in the full definition of 'acquisition' which is the same for most purposes as 'transfer') and a chargeable interest in a partnership in consideration of entering into a land transaction. However, since a partnership interest as such is not a chargeable interest notwithstanding the look through provisions, it seems that entering into partnership would not be a land exchange; but an assignment of a partnership interest in return for land would be a land exchange for these purposes. This narrow interpretation gives a correspondingly narrow application for the modification of the rules relating to exchanges and partitions.

market value charge is reduced and tax will be computed on a proportion of the actual consideration,[18] if any. To the extent that the property vests in persons who are partners but not connected with the transferor partners in any other manner than being partners, the market value charge will arise and the amount of chargeable consideration will be correspondingly reduced. Appropriate proportions of the net present value of the rent passing under a lease that is transferred out of the partnership are included in the chargeable amount.

The key issue is again SLP. It is necessary to apportion the proportion of the chargeable interest held by the connected transferee after the transaction amongst the partners who are the transferees and partners connected with them.[19] This allocation can be made on the most favourable basis. SLP is the aggregate of the lower of either the proportion so allocated or the partner's income share. In consequence, in practice, it will usually be beneficial to reduce the market value charge to allocate on the basis of income share since this represents the maximum extent of the relief.

The formulae described above apply but only with the modification that when determining SLP (FA 2003, Sched. 15, para. 20) it is necessary to identify the interest of each partner or a person connected with the partner in the chargeable interest in question prior to the transaction. The interest held by the 'transferee' of the chargeable interest after the transfer is then allocated to him and partners connected with him. The SLP is the lower of the interest as so allocated to him and each connected partner or each partner's share in the income profits of the firm.

Where there is a transfer of chargeable interest out of a partnership which consists wholly of bodies corporate and the SLP is 75 or greater, the charge is essentially upon the market value of the interest transferred (FA 2003, Sched. 15, para. 13).

Where there is a transfer to another partnership such as a merger or demerger or incorporating a limited liability partnership (where the relief is not available), the tax is calculated upon the basis of an acquisition by a

---

18 The special rules also apply where the person 'has been' a partner or is connected with a 'has-been' partner. There is no obvious time limit on the separation of the former partner from the firm. For example, there is no suggestion that the transaction has to be in connection with ceasing to be a partner. It seems odd that there should be a special charge when the person acquiring the chargeable interest ceased to be a partner for bona fide commercial reasons unconnected with the current transaction several years previously; but the legislation could be utilised to support such a charge.
19 There are certain harsh transitional rules which treat the share as nil where the land was vested in the partnership prior to July 2004 unless *ad valorem* stamp duty was paid (the fixed £5 is not sufficient) or an SDLT charge has been incurred and tax paid if any tax was due.

partnership or a disposal by a partnership whichever produces the higher risk.

11.8 TRANSFERS OF PARTNERSHIP INTERESTS

General

The transfer of 'an interest' in a partnership is a complex and usually expensive stamp tax calculation because certain of the consideration will be apportioned to partnership assets that are not subject to tax such as 'goodwill' and book debts which are tax free, or shares held by the partnership where a charge of 0.5 per cent may arise on the apportioned consideration and chargeable interests in land where there is a potential charge of up to 4 per cent upon the market value rather than the actual consideration.

It will be obvious that this will involve a valuation of each individual asset in the partnership and an apportionment of the consideration to them, which may be a difficult matching exercise because the consideration may well take account of the liabilities of the firm.[20] There may also be problems because of the way in which professional and other firms treat 'goodwill' which, as mentioned elsewhere, may not be business goodwill but a key element in the valuation of the partnership's land. It remains to be seen how willing HMRC Stamp Taxes is to act upon the basis of the partners' valuations if supported by independent advice or arm's length negotiations. However, the actual consideration may be influenced by the provisions in the partnership deed as to how matters are to be dealt with or that provide arbitrary procedures for calculating 'values' or attributing assets, such as relating to 'goodwill' to previous years' average profits or to future profits.

SDLT

A key point to note is that this charge applies to partnership 'interests' rather than 'shares' which latter is limited to profit shares. Issues of capital shares and loan capital are potentially involved. There is a chargeable transaction where there is a transfer of an interest in a partnership for consideration and the partnership property includes a chargeable interest in land (FA 2003, Sched. 15, para. 14). It is important to note that notwithstanding the existence of a form of look through, the effect of these provisions is not such as to convert a partnership interest itself, in whole or in part, into a chargeable interest.

---

[20] Note the provision dealing with liabilities in FA 2003, Sched. 15, para. 32.

UNDERSTANDING SDLT

This charging provision does contain a number of problems:

- There has to be a 'transfer'. This is defined[21] as being either:
  - a direct transfer (i.e. an assignment) of all or part of a partnership interest from one person to another whether an existing or a new partner. HMRC Stamp Taxes takes the view that a change in profit sharing ratios is a transfer within this part of the definition. This, in the official view, includes changes in partnership participation in either income or capital. A change in profit sharing ratios will on this view be a transfer; whilst this is debatable as a general proposition it is unlikely to prove a significant problem in practice since the chargeable consideration on the proportion of land value is likely to fall within the nil rate band and there is no obligation to notify in such cases (FA 2003, Sched. 15, para. 30); or
  - where a person becomes a partner and an existing partner reduces his interest or ceases to be a partner. This situation deals with a new partner coming into the firm and contributing capital where there is a simultaneous or a related withdrawal of capital pursuant to 'arrangements' whether in whole or in part by one or more existing partners (FA 2003, Sched. 15, para. 36(2)).[22]

It seems likely that HMRC Stamp Taxes will try to argue for it as being an extension of the definition.[23] This means that there may be a potential charge where there is:

- an outright assignment from A to B of his partnership share;
- the retirement of A linked with a withdrawal of his capital from the partnership related to a transaction whereby B is admitted into partnership

---

21 FA 2003, Sched. 15, para. 36; but it has to be noted, as has been commented upon above, that there is also another definition of 'transfer' for the purposes of the special charging provisions which 'includes' variation, release and creation. It is an open question as to whether a 'transfer' of a partnership interest 'includes' variation, etc. The context of the legislation suggests otherwise since there is a specific definition which, upon old-fashioned principles of statutory construction, should override a general provision, but the current judiciary take a more 'flexible' attitude to legislation and it is not at present clear whether HMRC Stamp Taxes intends to develop the wider general interpretation in this context.

22 It is possible that a concession may be made by HMRC Stamp Taxes to exclude situations where such related admissions and retirements are pursuant to provisions contained in the partnership deed. Details of this proposed concession have not been made widely available to practitioners.

23 It is believed that HMRC Stamp Taxes may be considering operating a concession, probably not to be published, to the effect that where the admission and retirement and related dealings in partnership 'capital' are pursuant to a pre-existing partnership deed, this will not be regarded as an 'arrangement' in this context. As a hitherto unpublished concession the position is vulnerable to attack, and concessions cannot be relied upon if there is 'tax avoidance' involved.

and contributes capital. It is the view of HMRC Stamp Taxes that a withdrawal of capital by one partner as part of a commercially related transaction whereby another partner contributes capital may be an assignment of a partnership interest and for certain purposes this has been given statutory effect (FA 2003, Sched. 15, para. 36) and extended (FA 2003, Sched. 15, paras. 17 and 17A);[24]

- a withdrawal of part of his capital by A related to a transaction whereby B contributes new capital or increases his capital. This is regarded as a transfer of part of a partnership interest;
- adjustments in profit or income sharing ratios such as where there are adjustments in contributions to capital. It seems that HMRC Stamp Taxes intends to treat this as a 'transfer' of a partnership interest; but as a variation or transfer as such is not taxable since there has to be a transfer for 'consideration' there may be difficulties for it unless there are either direct payments between the partners or related withdrawals and contributions of capital. It must be noted that although the transaction must be for 'consideration' before a charge arises, the chargeable consideration ignores that amount of actual consideration and is related to a proportion of the market value of land that is 'partnership property';
- the admission of a new partner who contributes capital without there being any related retirement or withdrawal of capital by the existing partners. Although this may affect profit sharing ratios, there may not be a 'transfer'; and
- the retirement of a partner and withdrawal of capital without any related admission of new partner or increase of capital by the existing partners. As with the preceding point, notwithstanding the change in profit sharing ratios this may not be a 'transfer';
- consideration for the 'transfer'. For these purposes:
  – in the case of a direct transfer of a partnership share there is consideration if money or money's worth is given by the assignee of the interest;
  – a contribution and withdrawal of capital consideration is regarded as being provided if there is a withdrawal of money or money's worth from the partnership by the person ceasing to be a partner or reducing his interest (FA 2003, Sched. 15, para. 14(4)).

The effect of these provisions has to be noted because they can apply to commercial partnerships where there are the usual annual retirements and admissions to partnership. Technically these could be treated as transfers of partnership interests to the extent that the partnership has a chargeable

---

24 HMRC Stamp Taxes is also of the view that giving guarantees of borrowings by the partnership and leaving profits undrawn can constitute relevant consideration in the context of transfers of partnership interests.

interest in land,[25] but it is believed that there may be an informal concession to be operated where the 'arrangements' are routine provisions in the partnership deed. Transfers of partnership shares are not notifiable if the consideration (or deemed consideration) for the transaction does not exceed the nil rate threshold. This will protect most commercial partnerships unless the chargeable consideration exceeds the nil rate threshold. This also ignores the amount of any 'actual consideration' or deemed consideration for the transfer. The level of the contribution or withdrawal of capital is not, of itself, relevant for these purposes. The nil rate band is usually £150,000 (upon the basis that this is the relevant nil rate because the land held by the partnership is usually non-residential). Insofar as certain of these provisions depend upon the existence of 'arrangements', it is believed that HMRC Stamp Taxes is contemplating operating an unofficial concession that normal retirements and admissions pursuant to the terms of the partnership deed will not be arrangements and so outside the scope of the tax – details are awaited.

Exemptions

The market value charges override the exemption for gifts producing a reporting obligation even in relation to gifts of land or partnership interests, but all other reliefs apply in respect of contributions of land into or out of the partnership or transfers of partnership shares. Charity relief applies to transfers of partnership shares to charities and intra-group relief is available for transfers of land into and out of partnerships and the reliefs for company reconstruction apply. These reliefs are subject to the usual clawbacks relevant to the particular relief (FA 2003, Sched. 15, para. 27).

Anti-avoidance for special transactions

Anti-potential avoidance legislation means that other situations are brought into the charge to tax. These include:

- situations where there is a transfer of land to a partnership and there is a subsequent transfer of a partnership interest which is not otherwise a chargeable transaction; for the purposes of Sched. 15, para. 17, this is a chargeable transaction effected for a chargeable consideration equal to a proportion of the market value of the chargeable interest transferred previously into the partnership (FA 2003, Sched. 15, para. 17); or

---

25 This applies to all chargeable interests in land including leases other than certain leases granted solely for a full reviewable market rent where the rent has to be reviewed at least once every five years (FA 2003, Sched. 15, para. 15).

- where within the three years after the transfer of a chargeable interest to a partnership there is a withdrawal of money from the partnership which is not a distribution of income such as a person contributing land, withdrawing capital or reducing his interest or ceasing to be a partner, or there is a repayment of a loan made by the person contributing the land (FA 2003, Sched. 15, para. 17A). It is an open question whether HMRC Stamp Taxes intends to apply this provision to delayed payment of any money owing in respect of the initial establishment of the firm such as where one of the partners contributes land as capital and a balancing adjustment is made to reflect the intended capital and/or income interests.

The two anti-avoidance provisions are designed to bring into the charge to tax transactions whereby a person contributes land to the partnership, subsequently another person becomes a partner and eventually the original contributor retires so that the 'new partner' effectively became the owner of the land. There are, of course, many variations upon this theme intended to be entrapped by this legislation so that, in general, retirements and admissions will henceforth require careful scrutiny taking into account these provisions. The acquisition of the land and the deemed transfer are linked transactions.

CHAPTER 12

Corporate transactions

12.1 BACKGROUND

Although the primary focus of this book is on acquisitions of land, there are problem areas for property transactions where bodies corporate are involved as sellers or purchasers of land[1] as well as where their shares are the subject-matter of the contract. This chapter is essentially not only a survey of the problems for property lawyers when one of the parties is a company but also a summary of the broad issues involved since the detailed principles involved are beyond the scope of this book.

The problems involved include:

- acquisitions of land where the connected companies' charge applies;
- acquisitions of land from companies where, in addition to the problems which generally affect persons acquiring land who are forced by statute to take over the provisional tax liabilities of the vendor, there are special rules, particularly important in practice, where the vendor is a body corporate and reliefs for companies may have been obtained on a previous transaction;
- new areas for warranties and indemnities for share purchases and a new set of related problems for valuing the securities in a body corporate; and
- the anti-avoidance provisions upon reliefs for companies which have long-term risks for both purchasers from the company and the company, its shareholders and the directors.

12.2 'COMPANY'

It is first necessary to identify those entities which are affected by these provisions since there are complex definitions of 'company' and the meanings vary within the charging and compliance regimes. Detailed scrutiny of the relevant

---

1 Such as the need to file SDLT 4 (as amended) in virtually every case no matter how straightforward.

definitions is essential, and there are long-term subtle practices of HMRC Stamp Taxes which frequently lie dormant but, from time to time, re-surface to trap the unwary and it must not be assumed that 'company' and 'body corporate' mean the same thing, although the EU rules against discrimination are having an impact in this area (note *Ministre de Finances* v. *Weidert* [2005] STC 1241).

The basic definition for SDLT is that a 'company' means any body corporate or unincorporated association but not a partnership (FA 2003, s.100), but this applies mainly for compliance purposes and is frequently modified for charging and exempting provisions such as unit trusts and open-ended investment companies. It will include clubs and similar organisations even where these are not bodies corporate by their controlling legislation. Partnerships that are bodies corporate such as limited liability partnerships are not treated as companies (FA 2003, Sched. 15, Part 1).

12.3 ACQUISITIONS BY COMPANIES

In general the acquisition of a chargeable interest by a company is subject to SDLT only by reference to the actual consideration but special charges apply to acquisitions by a 'connected body corporate'.

Connected companies

Two areas of special charge apply (FA 2003, s.53), where either:

- an estate or interest in land is acquired by a company which is connected with the person transferring or vesting the estate or interest; or
- an estate or interest in land is transferred to or vested in a company and some or all of the consideration for the transfer or vesting consists of the issue or transfer of shares or securities issued by a company with which the 'vendor' is connected.[2]

The acquisition is deemed to be for a consideration not less than the market value of the chargeable interest immediately before the effective date. Where the transaction involves the grant of a lease, or possibly a deemed grant of a new lease (such as pursuant to FA 2003, Sched. 17A, para. 12A), there is a charge upon a deemed premium equal to the market value of a lease at that rent plus the net present value of the actual rent. It is specifically provided that this charge overrides the exemption for gifts and other transactions for non-chargeable consideration so that the transaction is fully

---

2 It seems that for these purposes the company must be connected with the other party (the vendor) prior to the transaction. The charge does not apply where the vendor becomes connected only as a consequence of the transaction.

notifiable. The intention is to prevent landowners converting land into shares to provide a more stamp tax efficient package for persons wishing to acquire land; but since there is no tax avoidance notice required before the charge can operate, it applies to routine commercial transactions such as the incorporation of a business or a grant of a lease to the family farming or manufacturing company intended to provide it with the premises from which it can carry on business. It will also be potentially applicable in relation to corporate incorporations in restructuring operations although the reliefs in FA 2003, Sched. 7, Parts 1 and 2, described below, may apply. However, these reliefs carry the anti-avoidance charge of the first non-exempt assignment of such a lease being taxed as a deemed new lease (FA 2003, Sched. 17A, para. 11) unless there has been a prior 'de-grouping' or other clawback of the initial relief, and now require a bona fide commercial intention and the absence of a tax avoidance motive.

Exemptions from connected company charge

FA 2003, s.54 provides that the connected company charge does not apply to acquisitions by connected companies where the consideration, if any, does not consist of or include shares or securities in the following cases.

Trusts

Settlors (and certain members of their family) are connected with the trustees of the settlement. This means that, *prima facie*, a market value charge arises upon transactions whereby property is vested in corporate trustees except where the connected company which is to hold the estate or interest as trustee:

(a) is a person carrying on a business which consists of or includes the management of trusts; and
(b) is to hold the estate or interest as trustee acting in the course of that business; and
(c) apart from s.839(3) of the Taxes Act 1988 (trustees as connected persons), it would not be connected with the 'vendor' (FA 2003, s.54).

It should be noted that these exemptions do not protect companies controlled by trustees. For example, where trustees, whether corporate or individual, decide to transfer UK land into a company of which they are the sole shareholders there will be a market value charge notwithstanding that the company is incorporated outside the UK.

Nominee or bare trustee companies

These provisions are essentially aimed at settlements and there is no specific exemption for transfers to nominee companies. However, the Government stated in the debate on the Finance Bill 2003 that because no beneficial interest vests in the nominee company the value of the interest which it acquires, i.e. the bare legal title, is valueless so that no charge arises in practice. Since all acquisitions by a nominee are treated as acquisitions by the beneficial owner and there cannot be an acquisition from oneself, a transfer between a nominee and the beneficial owner is not an acquisition or chargeable transaction[3] in any event. This has, however, been modified subsequently. Finance Act 2004 imposed charges upon the first assignment of leases granted by nominees (Sched. 17A, para. 11), but this was replaced by provisions in Finance Act 2005 treating the grant of the lease as a fully chargeable transaction. These latter provisions also apply a full charge to a lease by the nominee company to the beneficial owner. Conveyancers will need to investigate whether the tenant selling the lease is a nominee or beneficial owner or trustee of a settlement and the dates on which the lease was granted or the agreement for lease was substantially performed.[4]

Distribution by companies

Dividends *in specie*, distributions by liquidators and purchases and redemptions of share capital *in specie*, are *prima facie* exempt because there is no chargeable consideration.[5] However, where the distribution is to a connected company the market value charge would *prima facie* apply[6] but there is an exemption (FA 2003, s.54) for such acquisitions unless the chargeable interest being distributed was acquired by an exempt intra-group transaction within the preceding three years.

Routine transactions

Liquidation

The liquidation of the company does not involve a disposal or acquisition of assets but it may operate to cause a clawback of some previously obtained exemption for intra-group transactions or company reorganisations.

---

3 However, there is a charge upon any dealing with the lease (FA 2003, Sched. 17A, para. 11).

4 The key dates are 22 July 2004 and 19 May 2005. This may also raise the conveyancing issue of whether a receipt from two trustees is required pursuant to LPA 1925, s.27 since there will be actual knowledge of the trust and this may affect the overreaching principles.

5 A charge to tax may arise where the property distributed is subject to a charge and the persons acquiring the land assume or are deemed to assume the liability in respect of the mortgage (FA 2003, Sched. 4, para. 8).

6 The charge may be relieved if the conditions for exemption for intra-group transactions can be satisfied.

Receiverships

The appointment of receivers and similar arrangements does not cause the same de-grouping as liquidations and so does not pose the same risk of clawback. However, a sale of a subsidiary company by the receiver may trigger a clawback of previously obtained relief.

12.4 PURCHASES FROM COMPANIES

Particular issues arise as regards to the investigation and due diligence in connection with acquisitions from bodies corporate. Not all of these are unique to companies and may apply to acquisitions from other persons, but are more likely to arise with companies because of the tendency to utilise companies as nominees or bare trustees or other convenient vehicles for joint ventures.

The problem areas for investigation are:

- acquisitions of leases from nominees granted between July 2004 and May 2005; these may be taxable as the grant of new leases (FA 2003, Sched. 17A, para. 11 (as amended));
- assignments of leases which were exempt when granted pursuant to:
    - sale and leaseback arrangements (FA 2003, s.57A (as amended));
    - group or reconstruction relief (FA 2003, Sched. 7, Parts 1 and 2). This differs from clawback relief and applies even where the chargeable interest is acquired as part of the assets in an undertaking or business as a going concern. It will, in consequence, not always be obvious that this provision might apply so that it must become routine for questions to be asked;
    - relief for charities (FA 2003, Sched. 8), including corporate charities.

    There is no time limit on this charge upon assignment.

12.5 'TIME BOMBS'

Share acquisitions and valuations may be adversely affected by the company's position since, as described elsewhere, much of the tax is provisional and it is difficult to achieve finality. Purchasers of shares need to be aware of these long-term issues ticking away within the company. Not all of these have a time limit when the tax risk expires.

Reliefs are available for reconstructions but these are subject to numerous conditions and long-term problems such as clawback or special charges upon later unrelated transactions. The long-term issues affecting provisional tax positions such as a variable consideration or rent and possible abnormal increases of rent upon later rent reviews, clawback of relief or the charge upon the assignment of certain leases may have a significant impact upon the company's assets. Clawbacks operating over 80 years can leave the company with an open tax position for many years with a serious risk that the original provisional return was underestimated. It seems that such deferred or potential tax charges are not being adequately reflected in companies' accounts by the auditors who are apparently signing off accounts without recognising these issues in the notes to the accounts.

In consequence, it is not sufficient to merely ask for warranties and indemnities to the effect that the company is up to date with its SDLT. The possibility of Enquiries which may challenge a relief that has been claimed or disposals at market value or market rent included in the self-assessment and any related penalties and interest will have to be taken into account. Deferred tax issues in relation to postponed payment of tax or the enforced assumption of tax liability in relation to the assignment of leases will require investigation.

12.6 CORPORATE REORGANISATIONS

Notwithstanding that there is no 'look through' in relation to companies so that shares and marketable securities are not, as such, subject to SDLT, many transactions involving companies are affected, directly or indirectly, by the tax. A corporate reorganisation may:

- involve clawback implications for previous transactions and possible warranty or indemnity claims in share sale contracts;
- have problems of its own as regards reliefs;
- set up new clawback charges;
- create the risk of any assignment of a lease being taxed as the grant of a new lease;
- create 'time bomb' situations within the company that may have a bearing upon share sales in the future;
- involve payment of tax deferred from previous acquisitions.

Due diligence

The obtaining of these reliefs or their equivalent for stamp duty[7] may be relevant in deciding whether there is to be an immediate clawback of any

---

[7] The clawback and exclusion events will be related to share transactions and so within the realms of stamp duty and its reliefs such as s.42 of the Finance Act 1930 and ss.75 and 77 of the Finance Act 1982. As the clawback is related to a company leaving the group or a change of control, the relieving events for the clawback will be linked to the share transfers. Both sets of relieving provisions must, therefore, be noted.

intra-group relief obtained within the preceding three years (FA 2003, Sched. 7, para. 4). In consequence, when planning a reconstruction of a company or a group and the possible utilisation of these reliefs it is now necessary to consider whether the proposed transaction will either:

- trigger a clawback of previously obtained reliefs;[8] or
- set up a new three-year period in relation to land in the UK involved in the reconstruction; or
- involve a roll-over of previously obtained relief so that the clawback risk passes into the new group for the balance of the three-year period (see, e.g. FA 2003, Sched. 7, para. 4(6) and (7)).

Warranties

As there is power to recover the clawback amount from other companies in the same group as the acquiring company or lessee body corporate, the potential impact upon the proposed arrangements has to be investigated possibly where there are plans for the liquidation of any company liable directly or indirectly for the clawback amount. This will involve a need for careful planning of any arrangements to fund any SDLT[9] actually clawed back since this may involve a payment in cash as part of the reconstruction which is not permitted by the terms of the section granting the relief intended to be relied upon, thereby destroying the exemption being sought. The possible roll-over of the clawback into the new group will also need to be investigated where the particular stage is merely one step in a much larger reconstruction involving onward movement of shares which may be inconsistent with the roll-over treatment of the clawback.

12.7 PROCEDURE

As with all reliefs from SDLT, there is no formal procedure for applying to HMRC Stamp Taxes 'claiming' the relief as with equivalent stamp duty reliefs. The parties simply take the relief by making appropriate entries in the land transaction tax return and not self-assessing any tax or paying the lower amount of SDLT and hoping that any subsequent HMRC Stamp Taxes Enquiry agrees with their views. The usual range of penalties and interest will apply if the interpretation adopted by the parties proves to be incorrect, but provided that they have considered all relevant matters properly and can

---

8 Including a relief from stamp duty obtained within the preceding two or three years (depending upon the date of the instrument for which the relief was obtained) since such relief remains subject to clawback (see FA 2003, Sched. 19, para. 6).
9 Or stamp duty from the previous regime.

prove this by having made and retained contemporaneous written records they may not be subject to the additional penalties for 'negligence' or 'fraud' in making the return.

Two areas of relief are available in relation to corporate reorganisations involving the 'acquisition' of chargeable interests in land, namely:

- total exemption for a limited range of corporate reconstructions (FA 2003, Sched. 7, para. 7); and
- a reduced rate of 0.5 per cent for certain types of corporate reorganisations (FA 2003, Sched. 7, para. 8). There is also a relief for intra-group transactions (FA 2003, Sched. 7, para. 1).

Reconstructions

Paragraph 7 of Sched. 7 to FA 2003 provides for exemption from SDLT for chargeable transactions in land entered into pursuant to or in connection with[10] a scheme for reconstruction of a body corporate, which includes foreign incorporations but not partnerships (FA 2003, s.110), whereby another body corporate, including foreign companies, acquires the whole or part of the undertaking of the other body corporate. The consideration for the acquisition (*Crane Fruehauf* v. *IRC* [1975] 1 All ER 429; *Central and District Properties* v. *IRC* [1966] 1 WLR 1015) must consist either:

(a) wholly of the issue[11] of non-redeemable shares in the company acquiring the undertaking to either the company whose undertaking is being acquired or all or any of that company's shareholders; or

(b) partly of the issue of non-redeemable shares and the balance being the assumption or discharge of the liabilities of the company whose undertaking is being acquired; this limitation on the type of consideration permitted means that it is important to ensure that the transfer of the undertaking escapes the charge to VAT as a transfer of a going concern. Should there be a payment of cash such as VAT, this takes the transaction outside the scope of the exemption from stamp duty.

Where the parties believe that the transaction involves a transfer of a going concern but make the usual provision that should the transaction not qualify as a transfer of a going concern the purchaser will pay the VAT upon delivery of an appropriate tax invoice, such payment in cash must inevitably exceed the permitted 10 per cent limit. There is little evidence of the approach of HMRC Stamp Taxes in practice. Insofar as extra consideration is required, it should consist of an obligation to issue further shares but this still leaves liquidity problems. The most

---

10 *Clarke Chapman John Thompson Ltd* v. *IRC* [1975] STC 567, holding that these are wide words including matters not directly part of the scheme.
11 This requires registration (*Oswald Tillotson* v. *IRC* [1933] 1 KB 134).

prudent course is to provide that the consideration consisting of the issue of shares is inclusive of VAT, if any is payable. This avoids the possibility that HMRC Stamp Taxes might refuse the relief upon the ground that the obligation to issue shares in satisfaction of the VAT was not an issue of shares within the relieving provisions. Hopefully, since the relief requires a transfer of an undertaking the transaction may qualify for exclusion from VAT as a transfer of a going concern.

Additionally, immediately after the acquisition:

1. Each shareholder appears in the register of members of both companies holding shares in the same proportion or as near thereto as is possible. Underlying beneficial ownership of the shares is irrelevant. The share register controls the exemption. For example, if A and B each own one share in the target company and B holds that one share as nominee for A who is the sole beneficial owner, the relief is available only if, after the transaction, the shares in the acquiring company are registered equally in the name of the two members; the relief is refused if only one share is issued to the nominee notwithstanding that this reflects the underlying beneficial ownership. Subscriber shares can easily upset the proportions of the registration of the consideration shares. It is possible to reduce the number of shares to be issued to any of the subscribers so that after the transaction the correct proportions are maintained.
2. The acquisition must be effected for bona fide commercial reasons and must not form part of a scheme of arrangement of which the main purpose or one of the main purposes is the avoidance of liability to stamp duty, income tax, corporation tax, capital gains tax or SDLT. This is usually established by producing a copy of any clearance letter from HMRC in relation to capital gains tax,[12] but the preparation of the clearance application may require careful drafting since such correspondence has been utilised by HMRC Stamp Taxes to refuse the relief (see, e.g. *Swithland Investment* v. *IRC* [1990] STC 448).

Various aspects of these conditions raise highly technical issues; and as in relation to the equivalent reliefs from stamp duty where strict observance of the conditions was insisted upon so that a divergence in shareholding percentages that emerged only at the seventh place of decimals could lead to a rejection of the relief, it can be expected that an approval will be similarly difficult for SDLT.

---

12 In the event of a different response from HMRC, the capital gains tax clearance usually prevails over the refusal of a clearance for the purpose of Income and Corporation Taxes Act 1988, s.703.

Reconstruction defined

A scheme of reconstruction requires that an existing company transfers its undertaking to another company which carries on substantially the same activities and that both companies are owned by substantially the same shareholders. Although total shareholder identity is an express condition for this relief (FA 2003, Sched. 7, para. 7(4)) and the test for reconstruction requires only 'substantial identity', merely satisfying the former condition is not necessarily sufficient to satisfy this test. There may be situations where, notwithstanding the mirror share capital condition is satisfied, there may not be a scheme of reconstruction and the relief lost. For example, where there is a pre-sale reorganisation and there are plans for the onward movement of the shares in the acquiring company to a third party which have become so integrated into the contracts that they are part of 'the scheme', the onward sale can affect what is the consideration and/or whether there is shareholder identity (*Central and District Properties* v. *IRC* [1966] 2 All ER 433). Where there are plans for the injection of fresh outside capital into the acquiring company the documentation relating to and the timing of such contributions can affect whether there is a scheme of reconstruction (see the discussion in *Crane Fruehauf* v. *IRC* [1975] 1 All ER 429). The word therefore raises a larger time frame in testing for the entitlement to the exemption.

Acquisition of undertaking

There must be the acquisition of the whole or part of an undertaking (see also *R.* v. *Industrial Dispute Tribunal, ex p. Courage and Co. Ltd* [1956] 1 WLR 1062), i.e. the assets transferred must constitute a 'business' or 'part of a business' of the transferring or target company. Not every asset of the company will be an undertaking (see also *E. Gomme Ltd* v. *IRC* [1964] 1 WLR 1348).

There is accordingly a question of fact in each case, whether the assets concerned formed part of a business or were mere investments not constituting a business as such (*Baytrust Holdings Ltd* v. *IRC* [1971] 1 WLR 1333). The holding of investments such as holding land and receiving the rent can itself constitute a business (scc, e.g. *IRC* v. *Tyre Investment Ltd* [1924] 12 TC 646) and be an undertaking.

12.8 PARTITIONS AND REORGANISATIONS OF COMPANIES – REDUCED RATE

A reduced rate of SDLT of 0.5 per cent (but without any adjustment to the chargeable consideration) is available where:

- a body corporate which now includes foreign companies acquires the whole or part of the undertaking of another body corporate which can include foreign companies for a consideration which consists either:
  - wholly of the issue of non-redeemable shares in the acquiring company; or
  - partly of the issue of non-redeemable shares in the acquiring company and partly of either the assumption or the discharge of liabilities of the disposing company and/or cash not exceeding 10 per cent of the nominal value of the non-redeemable shares issued as part of the consideration. This can include VAT if the transaction does not constitute a transfer of a going concern which clearly cancels the relief;
- such consideration shares being issued either:
  - to the company whose undertaking is being acquired; or
  - to all or any of the shareholders in the company whose undertaking is being acquired;
- the acquiring company is not associated with another company that is a party to arrangements with the company whose undertaking is being acquired which relate to shares issued by the company in connection with the transfer of the undertaking or part.

It will be seen that these conditions are virtually the same as those in relation to the reliefs for reconstructions outlined above and the terms bear the same meaning.

Disqualifying conditions

The relief is not available unless the acquiring company is not associated with another company that is a party to arrangements with the target company relating to shares of the acquiring company issued in connection with the transfer of the undertaking or part (Finance Act (FA) 1986, s.76(3A)). For these purposes companies are 'associated' if one has control of the other (as defined by Income and Corporation Taxes Act 1988, s.416) or both are controlled by the same person or persons (FA 1986, s.76(6A)(a)), and 'arrangements' includes any scheme, agreement or understanding whether or not legally enforceable (FA 1986, s.76(6A)(b)).

This condition will preclude the relief where there is a plan for the consideration shares to be sold to a third party (although this might also give rise to a clawback problem). It would also appear to strike down the relief in cases where the transaction for which the relief is being sought is a preliminary step to injecting the business into a joint venture. The terms of the articles of association of the joint venture company and any shareholder agreements may make the claim for relief vulnerable to these provisions. It remains to be seen how aggressive HMRC Stamp Taxes intends to be where bona fide commercial arrangements of this nature are involved.

This condition does not apply where the relevant arrangements are not with a body corporate but with individuals or possibly partnerships even where these include corporate partners. It must, however, be noted that limited liability partnerships are bodies corporate and arrangements with these may fall within this restriction upon the relief.

Clawback of both of these reliefs

Clawback of both of these reliefs can occur where:

- relief has been obtained under either of the above provisions; and
- control of the acquiring company changes;
- before the end of the period of three years beginning with the effective date of the transaction or more than three years after that date where the change of control is in pursuance of or in connection with 'arrangements', which include any scheme, arrangement or understanding whether or not legally enforceable (FA 2003, Sched. 7, para. 9(5)(a)) made before the end of the three-year period;
- at that time the acquiring company still holds the interest that was acquired by the exempt transaction or an interest derived therefrom and that interest has not subsequently been acquired at market value under a chargeable transaction in relation to which relief pursuant to either para. 7 or para. 8 of Sched. 7 to FA 2003 was available but was not claimed then.

The relief in relation to the exempt transaction or an appropriate proportion of it is withdrawn and SDLT becomes chargeable (FA 2003, Sched. 7, para. 9).

Taxable amount

The amount of tax payable is the tax that would have been chargeable in respect of the exempt transaction but for the relief if the chargeable consideration for that transaction had been an amount equal to the market value of the chargeable interest and any related property.[13] The appropriate proportion means an appropriate proportion having regard to the subject-matter of the relevant exempt transaction and what is held at the time of the change of

---

13 This is an odd provision since, in most cases on such a reconstruction, it is likely that the companies will be 'connected companies' when the transaction will be deemed to be at market value in any event (see FA 2003, s.53).

control by the acquiring company or by that company and any relevant associated companies (FA 2003, Sched. 7, para. 9(3)).

Exclusions from clawback

The exemption for land acquired in connection with a scheme of reconstruction is not withdrawn where the change of control arises:

- as a result of a transaction in shares that is between one party to a marriage and the other party which is effected in connection with a transaction that qualifies for the matrimonial breakdown relief (FA 2003, Sched. 3, para. 3);
- as a result of a transaction varying a disposition following a person's death that is within the relief for variations within two years after the death (FA 2003, Sched. 3, para. 4);
- where the control of the company acquiring the land changes as a result of an intra-group transfer of shares which qualifies for exemption pursuant to s.42 of the Finance Act 1930 or s.11 of the Finance Act (Northern Ireland) Act 1954;
- as a result of a transaction in shares which qualifies for exemption pursuant to s.42 of the Finance Act 1930 (or Finance Act (Northern Ireland) 1954, s.11); the clawback is not terminated but merely held over for the balance of the three-year period. In consequence, the clawback applies where there is a 'de-grouping' of the relevant companies during the unexpired portion of the three-year period which is not itself excluded from the clawback under the provisions mentioned in this and the surrounding paragraphs;
- where the control of the company acquiring the land changes as a result of transfer of shares to another company in relation to which relief pursuant to s.77 of the Finance Act 1986 applies.

12.9 RELIEF FOR INTRA-GROUP TRANSACTIONS

An exemption from SDLT is available for chargeable transactions if both parties are bodies corporate within the same SDLT group as at the effective date of the transaction which includes unlimited companies, foreign incorporations, certain local authorities, charter corporations and other bodies provided that they have the necessary share capital structure and are the parent company of the group.

Group

This requires that:

- one body corporate is the 75 per cent subsidiary of the other; or
- both are 75 per cent subsidiaries of a third company.

75 per cent subsidiary

The 75 per cent shareholding test requires that:

- the parent company is the beneficial owner of not less than 75 per cent of the ordinary shares of the ordinary share capital of the subsidiary, i.e. all the issued share capital, by whatever name known, of the company other than capital, the holders of which have a right to a dividend at a fixed rate but have no other right to share in the profits of the company; and
- the parent company has a 75 per cent economic interest in the subsidiary company, i.e. 75 per cent of the assets in a winding up and 75 per cent of the dividend.

These tests can be satisfied by both direct and indirect shareholdings, through other companies, but certain types of loan capital are treated as shares for the purpose of the economic interest test. In consequence, the rights of creditors of the subsidiary company must be investigated to determine whether they affect the group structure.

The parent company must also have control of the relevant subsidiaries and there must be no arrangement in place whereby another person could acquire control of the acquiring company but not of the vendor company.

Anti-avoidance provisions

The relief is not available where there are arrangements whereby:

- the consideration, or any part of the consideration for the conveyance or transfer is to be provided or received, directly or indirectly by an outsider, i.e. a person other than an appropriately associated body corporate; or
- the disposing company and acquiring company are to cease to be associated by reason of the acquiring company ceasing to be a 75 per cent subsidiary.

The relief is also not available where the intra-group transaction is a sub-sale or an assignment of a contract with a vendor who is not a member of the SDLT group (FA 2003, s.45(5)(a); cf. *Escoigne Properties Ltd* v. *IRC* [1958] AC 549).

12.10 ARRANGEMENTS

'Arrangements' include any scheme, agreement or understanding whether or not legally enforceable. It is necessary for there to be some involvement with a third party such as a purchaser of the shares. It is difficult to have a unilateral arrangement no matter how strong the intention to sell or to bring about the desired result may be, but it seems that the practice may continue to be based upon the views set out in relation to stamp duty in Statement of Practice SP3/98. As regards the provision and receipt of the consideration and ceasing to be associated, the practice set out in that Statement of Practice will be applied in relation to SDLT. One area of uncertainty is the provision excluding the relief where there is an arrangement whereby the consideration or part thereof is to be received by a non-associated person, such as where an intra-group lease is granted prior to the sale of the reversionary interest whereby rent becomes payable to a non-group landlord. Hitherto this has not proved an obstacle to obtaining the relief.[14]

12.11 CLAWBACK OF INTRA-GROUP RELIEF[15]

The intra-group exemption is withdrawn and the SDLT becomes payable where, within three years after the effective date,[16] the acquiring body corporate whilst still holding the land ceases to be a member of the same group as the vendor/lessor. Also, at the time, it or another relevant associated company[17] ceases to be a member of the same group whilst it holds the agreed chargeable interest or an interest derived from a chargeable interest that was acquired by such exempt transaction and that has not subsequently been acquired at market value under a chargeable transaction for which the exemption from SDLT for intra-group transactions was available but was not claimed. The amount of tax chargeable is the tax that would have been chargeable in respect of the transaction for which the exemption was obtained for the intra-group lease. This is on the basis that the chargeable consideration for that transaction had been an amount equal to the market

---

14 However, such an arrangement faces other problems such as clawback and assignment, pursuant to FA 2003, Part I and Sched. 17A, para. 11.
15 See also Chapter 13 on enforcement of clawback and Appendix C on warranties and indemnities.
16 Or longer if arrangements are in place for de-grouping during the three-year period.
17 A 'relevant associated company' means a company that is controlled by the company that acquired the land pursuant to the exempt transaction immediately before the control of that company changes and of which control changes in consequence of the change of control of that company (FA 2003, Sched. 7, para. 9(4)).

value of the chargeable interest acquired by that transaction together with any interest or right appurtenant or pertaining to the chargeable interest that is acquired with it.

Exclusions from clawback

The exemption for intra-group transactions is not withdrawn where the purchaser/lessee ceases to be a member of the same group as the vendor/lessor as a result of:

- a transaction in shares of the vendor company (FA 2003, Sched. 7, para. 4(2));
- anything done for the purposes of or in the course of winding up the vendor/lessor or another company that is above the vendor/lessor in the group structure (FA 2003, Sched. 7, para. 4(4)). A company is 'above' the vendor/lessor in the group structure if the vendor/lessor or another company 'above' the vendor/lessor is a 75 per cent subsidiary of the company (FA 2003, Sched. 7, para. 4(5));
- an acquisition of shares by another company, in relation to which the share transfer is exempt from stamp duty pursuant to FA 1986, s.75, immediately after which the purchaser/lessee is a member of the same group as the company acquiring those shares (FA 2003, Sched. 7, para. 4(6)). However, in this case the exclusion of the clawback is not on a permanent basis: the position is merely held over. SDLT is clawed back if the purchaser/lessee ceases to be a member of the same group as the company acquiring the relevant shares within three years of the effective date of the transaction for which the intra-group exemption was obtained; or after the three-year period when in pursuance of or in connection with arrangements made before the end of this period; and if at the time it ceases to be a member of the same group, the purchaser/lessee (or any company that ceases to be a member of the same group as the company acquiring the shares in consequence of the purchaser/lessee ceasing to be a member) holds a chargeable interest acquired under the transaction for which the intra-group exemption was obtained, or derived from an interest so acquired, but not subsequently at market value, under a chargeable transaction for which intra-group exemption was obtained (pursuant to FA 2003, Sched. 7, para. 1) but not claimed.

12.12 SHARE SALES, WARRANTIES, INDEMNITIES AND DUE DILIGENCE

The change to SDLT from stamp duty and, in particular, that it is a self-assessment tax that is directly enforceable with severe penalties for non – or inadequate – compliance and the fact that there is no finality until the end of the Enquiry period, which, in certain circumstances, may run for 21 years from the effective date of the transaction, has introduced a whole new area of due diligence in relation to share sales. These include the time bombs mentioned above. Unlike adjudication for stamp duty, obtaining the SDLT 5 is merely the start of the process; it is not a guarantee that the correct amount of SDLT has been paid. HMRC can challenge an SDLT 1 on the basis that the figure inserted as market value was not correct, that the estimated future payments were not property prepared, that the exemption claimed was not available or that the transaction was linked or was affected by later linked transactions.

It remains to be seen whether assignees taking an exempt lease as part of the purchase of the business will insist upon some adjustment in the price or some reverse payment in respect of the additional stamp duty cost of the transaction. This may mean that certain leases could have a 'negative value' in that it may cost money to dispose of them.

The problems of proper compliance, leases of negative value, subsequent adjustments for variable payments, etc., remain within the company and are not, as such, affected by the change of ownership of its shares. Purchasers of shares will therefore need to investigate the SDLT position of the company in depth in order to discover what current and long-term problems may be locked within the company and adjust the price and/or take suitable warranties and indemnities.

12.13 COMPLIANCE SITUATION

A purchaser of a company will require appropriate warranties that the company is up to date with its SDLT compliance. This will require undertakings that all forms that should have been filed have been filed and that the correct forms have been lodged and the information contained within them was correct and they are not open to challenge. There must also be some form of contractual provision that there are no current Enquiries in progress and that there are no reasons to believe that if there is an Enquiry launched in relation to any particular transaction undertaken by the company this will lead to the imposition of extra tax, interest and penalties. As with all taxes based upon self-assessment, these warranties will need to be wide ranging since self-assessment will require the parties to form a view as to matters such as market value or present and future market rents and, in relation to SDLT, the fundamental problem of 'cost' for the supplies of services and works all of which can be challenged by HMRC.

The company may have bought land on some overage or earn-out basis where the tax was originally paid on an estimated basis. This will require review as and when instalments are payable.

There may also be a risk of penalties and interest should a land transaction return be challenged.

12.14 DEFERRED OR PROVISIONAL TAX

In certain situations, particularly those related to variable payments, whether by way of premium or rent, the original tax calculation is provisional only. The first SDLT 1 will have been filed on the basis of estimated payments. In many cases the taxpayer company may have been able to defer the payment of the tax on the variable amount. Details of these matters will be required to be disclosed and taken into account in fixing the price, as well as undertakings that the amount in respect of which the tax has been deferred is the correct amount. Also, that no additional tax over and above that estimated and postponed will fall due and that the company has made adequate provision in its accounts for the payment of the deferred tax.[18] No doubt the shareholders may take the view that the company may have overestimated and over-provided for this postponed tax. They may want some provision for the adjustment of the consideration in the event of the company receiving a refund or paying less tax than that predicted.

Additionally, this possibility related to deferred taxation may apply to land that is no longer owned by the company. As described elsewhere, transfers of land subject to overage and clawback arrangements do not pass the liability to deal with the tax in respect of the initial transaction unless it is some form of variable premium or variable rent in the lease where the liability passes to the assignee. However, in such cases there may be contractual arrangements between the company and the purchaser or assignee of the property concerning the tax situation. For example, the company, when assigning a lease, may have given a warranty to the assignee that the amount of tax paid to HMRC is the correct amount and, if it is insufficient, the company may have to indemnify the assignee. All such indemnities and similar arrangements including any undertakings to provide or receive information affecting outstanding tax liabilities will need to be disclosed.

---

18 As an incidental point since this tax is purely estimated and the figures may prove to be higher as circumstances develop, particularly over a long period of time, the question of the level of the provision may have to be reviewed from time to time and this may have important consequences as to the level of the company's distributable profits and reserves for dividend policy. Discussions with the company's auditors would seem to be appropriate.

In the case of leases with variable rents, as described elsewhere, this tax position has to be reviewed at some stage during the first five years of the term of the lease. This may result in increased taxation being payable or a refund of tax already paid. Purchasers of shares in a company will require protection against the company having seriously underestimated the tax charge with the problems of related interest and penalties. This will apply even where the lease has been assigned and appropriate contractual arrangements have been entered into with the assignee.

Variable rents raise problems beyond the expiration of the fifth year of the term of the lease. All leases with variable rents are potentially vulnerable to the special charge that arises on the basis of a deemed new lease where any subsequent increase represents an abnormal increase in the rent. Whilst it may prove commercially difficult to safeguard the purchase of shares against a subsequent increase giving rise to such a charge, the purchaser of shares may find it prudent to obtain the full SDLT history of all leases granted on or after 1 December 2003 within the SDLT regime and discover their SDLT position including the base rent for abnormal increases, namely the highest rent paid during any 12 months during the first five years of the term. Other forms of relief are subject to clawback if there is a change in the share ownership or control within a three-year period. The details of these clawback provisions are considered elsewhere but share purchasers will need appropriate warranties that neither the immediate transaction nor any previous transaction will or has given rise to a clawback. This may go beyond the immediate company since in some situations, although there may have been a change of ownership or control, the relief is not immediately clawed back but the liability continues to follow the company under its new ownership for the balance of the three-year term.

It is no longer possible because of the provisional nature of the tax structure to deal with the situation by means of a simple warranty that all of the company's documents are duly stamped; the fundamental changes made in relation to both the charge to SDLT and its administration mean that there is no finality in most cases because using an SDLT 5 is not the equivalent of adjudication and HMRC Stamp Taxes has up to 21 years to investigate the transaction. In consequence, there are problems of the comfort needed that there are no risks of an Enquiry or discovery assessment but since these can produce additional tax, interest and penalty charges provision for them has to be made, particularly since a successful Enquiry does not necessarily preclude a subsequent discovery.

CHAPTER 13

Liability for the tax

13.1 GENERAL

The payment and compliance regime for SDLT is based upon self-assessment, subject to a somewhat long-term open ended regime for HMRC Stamp Taxes to challenge the return.[1] This regime requires the person identified by the legislation as 'the purchaser' to provide prescribed information by means of completion of one or more of the land transaction returns (SDLT 1–4 (as amended)), to calculate and pay the tax and to arrange for the keeping of records. Moreover, since much of SDLT other than in relation to very basic house purchases is of a provisional nature, there are continuing obligations upon the purchaser to file and pay for many years after the effective date, possibly to the consternation of personal representatives and liquidators as well as the purchasers of shares. Each component in this process has its own detailed provisions and it is not surprising that the so-called simplification of stamp taxes has produced a compliance regime that contains an amount of legislative materials about 10 times larger than the actual charging and relieving provisions. Whilst it may be possible to discover what to do if a charge arises by working through the legislative maze, the imbalance in the legislation means that it is not so easy to determine whether a charge arises and how to self-assess the tax. Nor is there clear guidance on what procedures need to be adopted in order to produce a land transaction return that is not vulnerable to discovery assessments and is not 'negligent' so that a 21-year opportunity exists for HMRC Stamp Taxes discovery attacks.

13.2 THE TAXABLE PERSON – 'THE PURCHASER'

The first step is to identify the party to the transaction within the definition of 'purchaser'. This goes not merely to the question of who is liable to pay the tax, but may affect whether there is chargeable consideration provided by

---

1 On the absence of 'finality' in SDLT, see Chapter 1.

UNDERSTANDING SDLT

the right person[2] and the nature of the transaction. Other issues turn upon the identity of the purchaser such as linked transactions and various reliefs and who may sign the return.

13.3 THE ISSUES – A MOVING TARGET

The legislation refers throughout to the 'purchaser' although this is generally the 'taxpayer' but it has to be noted that there is no total identity of 'purchaser' with 'taxpayer' because the legislation provides that persons who are not parties to the transaction and are, in consequence, not 'purchasers' may nevertheless become 'taxpayers' in the full sense of the term including both compliance and payment and persons may become 'taxpayers' as a consequence of transactions where they have no involvement whatsoever because the liability for any tax adjustments passes by legislation to them. Three key points of practical importance have to be noted:

1. SDLT, unlike the traditional stamp duty which it replaces and which attached to documents, attaches to persons rather than documents and this may change over time. It also does not attach to the land[3] as such but may follow the land to some extent so that other persons such as assignees of leases become responsible for another person's tax (see, e.g. FA 2003, Sched. 17A, para. 11) but does not represent a title issue in quite the same way as stamp duty (see Chapter 1), but there is a need for title investigation and due diligence, including the provision for completion and contractual terms for dealing with the situation where the vendor does not have registered title and the release of funds by mortgagees (see Chapter 1).
2. The provisional nature of much SDLT, particularly in relation to variable payments and rents and linked transactions when the initial tax return is usually prepared upon an estimated basis and has to be revised from time to time, means that the original taxpayer has an open or unfinalised tax position which may continue for many years.
3. In some cases involving the assignment of leases, the open tax position and related notification obligations (FA 2003, s.81A; Sched. 17A, para. 12) pass to the assignee so that, notwithstanding the above comments, the tax liability passes to the assignee (FA 2003, Sched. 17A, para. 12).

---

2 FA 2003, Sched. 4, para. 1 requires chargeable consideration to be provided by the purchaser or a person connected with the purchaser. The absence of chargeable consideration for this reason means that the transaction is exempt pursuant to FA 2003, Sched. 3, para. 1 and is, in general, not notifiable so that the approach to the Land Registry is to be made relying upon a self-certificate (SDLT 60).
3 At present there is no 'HMRC charge' upon the land for unpaid or underpaid tax, interest and penalties.

In other cases, such as sales of freehold land with a clawback arrangement, the open tax position remains with the original taxpayer indefinitely unless resolved at the time of the sale. This will clearly affect persons such as personal representatives, liquidators and receivers of companies as well as the warranties and indemnities for both land and share sales and the valuation of shares in corporate taxpayers.

In consequence, these mobile liability and compliance obligations require professional advisers to undertake a major re-think of conveyancing practices and due diligence in order to protect the interests of their clients (see further Chapter 1). Even where the outstanding tax liability may not pass with the land on the particular transaction, the full SDLT history of the property will be relevant to the third party whose future tax position may be affected. One of these issues is determining where the liability to pay (or reclaim) tax and compliance obligations lie at any particular time. Another is whether future events will need to be notified, particularly by or to the unfortunate third party compelled to take over the taxation liability.

Significance of purchaser

The purchaser is a key figure upon whom the liability to pay (FA 2003, s.85) and the compliance obligations (FA 2003, s.76) are imposed. In particular, at present, the purchaser is important for many reasons other than payment of the tax; the most important in practice are:

- only the purchaser is permitted to sign the land transaction return but special rules apply (FA 2003, s.81B). Even where other persons are entitled to sign the land transaction return the identity of the purchaser has to be disclosed on SDLT 1 (and SDLT 2 where there are more than two purchasers);
- consideration is not chargeable, i.e. the transaction is exempt, unless the consideration is provided by the purchaser or a person connected with him (FA 2003, Sched. 4, para. 1(1)) and this may also affect the taxation of sub-sales and assignments (FA 2003, ss.45(3) and 45A (as amended)). This is likely to give rise to difficulties in identifying the relevant party where there is a multi-party transaction such as where third parties provide inducements or where A agrees to transfer property to B in return for which B agrees to transfer or lease property to C or to release a restrictive covenant over C's land;[4] where, because this is a 'land exchange' (FA 2003, s.47; see Chapter 7), special computational rules apply if a charge arises which may override the question of whether C has provided consideration. The attitude of HMRC Stamp Taxes is currently unknown

---

4 Such arrangements appear to fall within the land exchange provisions of FA 2003, s.47.

UNDERSTANDING SDLT

but although the drafting is possibly technically defective, it is likely to take an aggressive position (see further Chapter 3 on third parties and chargeable consideration);
- linked transactions are restricted to transactions between the vendor and the purchaser or persons connected with either of these (see Chapter 3);
- it is necessary to identify the purchaser because many provisions depend upon other parties involved in the transaction being connected with the purchaser such as the connected company charge, the special partnership regime and certain reliefs for residential property;
- it may affect the taxation of building work and fitting out (FA 2003, Sched. 4, para. 10(2));
- possession can be taken by the purchaser or a connected person with him so as to constitute substantial performance of the contract to purchase (FA 2003, s.45);
- the purchaser is liable to any penalties imposed (FA 2003, Sched. 10, para. 8);
- the purchaser is subject to special obligations to keep records (FA 2003, Sched. 10, para. 9);
- the identity of the vendor and the purchaser is important for certain reliefs such as intra-group transfers and leases, company reconstructions and reorganisation, formation of unit trust schemes;[5]
- much of the special regime for partnership transactions depends upon who is the true vendor or purchaser and persons connected with them (FA 2003, Sched. 15, Part 3).

'Purchaser' defined

However, since chargeable transactions include transactions other than sales, it is clear that 'purchaser' must include persons other than a buyer of property in its normal meaning, and 'vendor' must mean something other than the seller of the property.

A 'purchaser' is defined as the person acquiring the subject-matter of the transaction (FA 2003, s.43(4)), i.e. the person who becomes entitled to the interest being created or the person whose interest is benefited or enlarged by reason of the surrender or release of a chargeable interest or the person benefiting from a variation of a chargeable interest which in the case of a lease may be either the landlord or the tenant.[6] A person so acquiring is a purchaser even if there is no consideration which may seem strange, espe-

---

5 FA 2003, s.64A; but this relief contains an ambiguity as to whether the unit holder after the transaction is the registered owner of the land or the beneficial owner. It is considered that the units should be issued to the beneficial owner.
6 Certain variations of leases are deemed to create a new lease in which case the purchaser will be the tenant.

cially since if there is no actual or deemed consideration there is no chargeable transaction (FA 2003, Sched. 3, para. 1). It is, however, necessary to have a 'purchaser' so that there is a person who may sign the return or self-certificate (SDLT 60) and be the target for all of the compliance obligations. However, a person is not to be treated as a purchaser unless he has given consideration for or is a party to the transaction (FA 2003, s.43(5)).

13.4 'VENDOR'

The 'vendor' is defined as the person disposing of the subject-matter of the transaction.

There is no requirement that consideration is received for a person to be a vendor as it may be provided by the purchaser to a third party. Thus a donor will be a vendor for the purposes of completing returns.

As with the purchaser, the nominee rules apply to vendors so that the registered title is not conclusive and it is theoretically necessary to investigate the underlying ownership where the vendor is or may be holding in a fiduciary capacity such as a nominee, trustee or personal representative. The investigation of the status of the apparent vendor by the purchaser's advisers is becoming more important in practice because certain transactions involving nominees are taxed in special ways. For example, transfers of leases originally granted between July 2004 and March 2005 (FA 2003, Sched. 17A, para. 11 (as amended)) to a nominee may be taxable as if the assignment were the grant of a new lease which may produce a tax surprise for the assignee, who may also be affected by later linked transactions entered into by persons of whose existence he might be unaware if the appropriate due diligence has not been exercised.

The identity of the vendor is not always vital to enforcement of the tax but the vendor's identity may be important for the purposes of computing the charge where certain provisions apply, such as the connected company provisions, linked transactions, some partnership arrangements and various reliefs such as intra-group transactions. It remains to be seen whether HMRC Stamp Taxes will take a strict line in relation to penalties where the vendor is not correctly identified or some only of the vendors are disclosed upon the land transaction return, where, as will usually be the case, there is no loss of tax, but there may be issues as to whether appropriate records have been prepared and retained by the true vendor.

13.5 LAND REGISTRY ISSUES

It will be noted that there will frequently be a discrepancy between the SDLT certificate SDLT 5 or 60 and the Land Registry transfer particularly where nominees or bare trustees including statutory trustees (LPA 1925, s.27) are involved (FA 2003, Sched. 16, para. 3 (as amended)).[7] It will not necessarily be correct to rely upon the contract and the persons described as the parties thereto since these may be nominees or agents, whether disclosed or undisclosed. Lack of proper investigation of these issues will open up allegations of a negligent land transaction return. SDLT 1 or 60 requires identification of beneficial owners, so that SDLT 5 or 60 may not be the same as the Land Registry application. It seems that the Land Registry is prepared to give effect to registration applications in such cases provided that there is a covering letter explaining the discrepancy.

This point also arises in relation to sub-sale and similar transfers of legal title. The Land Registry transfer may have to be accompanied by two land transaction return certificates (SDLT 5 and SDLT 60) providing a chain of title with a covering letter of explanation. However, where the initial purchaser is claiming sub-sale relief in respect of the whole of the land there is no chargeable transaction (FA 2003, s.45 (as amended); see further on sub-sales in Chapter 5); notwithstanding that the original purchaser is receiving a Land Registry transfer, he will not be required to file a land transaction return and so will not have a certificate. A covering letter from the ultimate transferee to the Land Registry explaining that the first purchaser is not subject to tax because of sub-sale relief will be sufficient to enable the transferee to obtain registration of the instrument. It seems that the Land Registry does not have the power to challenge such a letter.

13.6 CONNECTED PARTIES

In general, connected parties are not liable for another person's tax, but a key issue around the identity of 'vendor' and 'purchaser' is that of 'connected persons'; such persons are important in order to identify:

- whether any consideration is chargeable; this depends upon whether it is provided by the purchaser and a person connected with him;
- whether there is a connected company charge;
- whether the transactions are linked because the linkage applies only where the parties are connected with the vendor or the purchaser;
- whether the special regime for partnerships applies.

---

[7] It is no longer possible to hide behind a nominee, and the use of a nominee may incur a substantial tax charge.

Special cases

Special rules apply to particular categories of purchaser. These rules need to be noted since they affect the issue of who is liable for the tax and/or who may sign the land transaction return and/or who is otherwise subject to the compliance obligations; namely:

Joint purchasers

Where two or more people acquire land jointly, i.e. as joint tenants or tenants in common, or their equivalents in Scotland and Northern Ireland (FA 2003, s.121), unless special rules apply such as in respect of partners and trustees, all must sign the return and any liability for payment of the tax or penalties is a joint and several liability of the purchasers (FA 2003, s.103(2)(c)) but may be discharged by any of them (FA 2003, s.103(2)(a) and (4)) such as in the case of purchases of matrimonial homes and other similar jointly occupied premises. The test is, however, based upon beneficial or equitable ownership, not the legal title as such. All beneficial owners must sign even though only one is taking the legal title (see also LPA 1925, s.27).

Agents

The basic principle is that individuals must sign personally and there are only limited situations where an agent can sign the return on their behalf, namely:

- a person authorised to act on behalf of an individual by a written power of attorney (in Scotland a factory and commission) signed by the individual can sign the declaration. As the power of attorney must authorise the person to act in relation to the matters to which the return (SDLT 1) or certificate (SDLT 60) relates, it seems to be the view of HMRC Stamp Taxes that the power of attorney must refer to the particular transaction. General powers of attorney, other than enduring powers for persons under a disability to which special rules apply (FA 2003, s.106(1)), may not be adequate; and
- in order to avoid the need for the client to attend completion meetings an individual purchaser, or each of them, may authorise an agent to complete the form provided that they or each of them make a declaration that with the exception of the effective date, the information in the land transaction return is to the best of his knowledge correct and complete. The return must be in the special prescribed form which contains the special declaration by the agent that the effective date is to the best of his knowledge correct (FA 2003, Sched. 10, para. 1A), which may require him to ensure that the client informs him of all dealings in relation to the property such as fitting out, investigating minerals or carrying out repairs before formal completion (see Chapter 3). Lack of knowledge through

lack of attention is likely to expose the adviser to problems with HMRC Stamp Taxes.

However, these rules merely relate to the signing of the form. The purchaser, not the agent, remains liable for the tax and all other compliance obligations such as notifying later linked transactions or relevant rent reviews and paying any extra tax.

Nominees and bare trustees

Where the person involved in the transaction is a nominee or bare trustee (FA 2003, Sched. 16, para. 1), the transaction is treated as being carried out by the beneficial owner and not by the bare trustee (FA 2003, Sched. 16, para. 3). This will include situations where the transfer or lease is taken in the names of the four individuals who are the maximum permitted by LPA 1925, s.27 who hold upon trust for themselves and the other beneficial owners. It will also apply to other forms of joint purchases such as where parents and child combine to purchase a house which is to be taken into the name of the child who may, depending upon the facts, be a bare trustee for himself and the parents. All three are 'purchasers' and must be identified in and sign the land transaction return. In such a situation, therefore, the person liable to the tax is the beneficial owner and, importantly, the only person who can sign the declaration included in the land transaction return is the beneficial owner or his duly authorised agent as considered above. Signature by the nominee would not in theory be a valid declaration and penalties could be imposed for an incorrect return (FA 2003, Sched. 10, paras. 3–5 and 8), but HMRC Stamp Taxes has stated that since any action of the nominee is deemed to be the action of the principal, signing of the declaration by the nominee will be treated as signing by the beneficial owner and will be accepted as valid.

There is an increasing number of situations where transactions entered into by nominees may be subject to a special tax regime as far as the purchaser is concerned such as the assignment of leases (FA 2003, Sched. 17A, para. 11 (as amended)).

Companies

For these purposes companies can act only through human agency and this requires special rules as to both liability and compliance, particularly since the tax applies to companies incorporated and/or resident, i.e. centrally managed and controlled outside the UK, and unit trust schemes and open-ended investment companies[8] but not partnerships.

---

[8] For the position of special companies such as unit trusts and open-ended investment companies, see FA 2003, s.101.

LIABILITY

The liability to pay the tax falls initially upon the 'proper officer' of the company (i.e. the secretary or the person acting as secretary) or any person having actual or apparent authority to act for the company[9] or a liquidator or administrator, but he may retain out of money he receives on behalf of the company sufficient to pay the tax and if this is insufficient he is entitled to be indemnified by the company. This may be of little comfort if the company is insolvent and there is a large penalty and interest charge which also appear to be his liability. In relation to foreign companies the tax can be recovered from the proper officer.

COMPLIANCE

The compliance obligations are the primary responsibility of the proper officer.

Unincorporated associations, clubs and societies

Unincorporated associations, other than partnerships, are treated as companies. It should be noted that many 'associations' such as industrial and provident societies are made bodies corporate by their governing legislation and so they fall within the preceding paragraph. These provisions will, in consequence, apply to clubs and similar organisations. Moreover, since the tax applies to such unincorporated collective enterprises established abroad, it will be necessary to investigate the legal status under the foreign law of the association or syndicate in question. This will be a particularly important investigation for foreign associations that at first sight appear to be similar to partnerships formed or established under English law.[10]

The treatment of non-partnership associations as bodies corporate may affect the identity of the owner of the property, i.e. who or what is the vendor or purchaser but this will mean that the taxpayer is the statutory quasi-entity not the committee. Unfortunately, for such associations that may not be deemed to be bodies corporate there is, at present, no clear or simple answer and the issue of beneficial ownership and the question of whether the

---

9 Specific board resolutions may be helpful on this point.
10 Once again, lawyers in Scotland are badly served by the draftsman who pays little regard to Scots law where, *inter alia*, partnerships are treated differently. He regards all foreign lawyers as being sufficiently familiar with English law so as to realise that special rules apply to their client, and that English and Scottish lawyers understand foreign law sufficiently to spot these problems when dealing with an overseas investor in land in the UK.

members are 'absolutely entitled' as against the trustees or the committee (see, e.g. *Neville Estates* v. *Madden* [1962] Ch 832) and the powers of the members to intervene will be areas of considerable difficulty that may have to be investigated. Although in general liability and compliance are normally imposed upon the same person, in the context of special situations this unity of the obligations is not always clearly observed and there is an open question of whether the fiction of corporate personality applies to shield the individual members or the committee from personal liability for penalties and interest for late payment.

Where the taxpayer is an unincorporated association which is treated as a body corporate such as a club taking a lease of premises, the person primarily liable for the tax and compliance is the person who is the secretary or is acting as the secretary; or the person acting as treasurer; or any person who for the time being has the express, implied or apparent authority of the association to act on its behalf for the purpose of SDLT; or a liquidator if one has been appointed. In practice, a resolution of the committee nominating the appropriate person is likely to avoid any uncertainty. The proper officer, i.e. the treasurer or the secretary or other person held out by the committee as having authority is personally liable for any tax due but he is given a right of indemnity (FA 2003, s.100(4)).

Liquidators and administrators

If a liquidator or administrator has been appointed for the company or an association or body of persons that is treated as a company then the liquidator or the administrator is the proper officer (FA 2003, s.100(7)(a)). If two or more administrators are appointed to act jointly or concurrently then the proper officer is such one of them as is notified to HMRC Stamp Taxes by those persons or, if HMRC Stamp Taxes is not so notified, such one or more of those persons who HMRC Stamp Taxes itself may designate as the proper officer (FA 2003, s.100(7)(b)).

Partnerships

Separate rules apply to partnerships which are specifically stated as not being within the definition of 'company' and this is reinforced by a provision which specifically lifts the corporate veil of partnerships that, like limited liability partnerships, are under the legislation, whether English or otherwise, governing their formation or establishment treated for general legal purposes as 'bodies corporate'. There are numerous areas of special provisions applicable to partnerships arising pursuant to Sched. 15 to FA 2003 (as amended) (see Chapter 11). The immediate difficulty is the problem of determining whether non-English business associations are to be treated as partnerships

LIABILITY FOR THE TAX

or as bodies corporate. No statutory criteria are provided and it is unclear what relative weight has to be attached to the various possibly relevant factors such as limited liability, corporate personality, participation in management or existence of a general unlimited partner.

Two regimes apply to partnerships:

(A) ORDINARY TRANSACTIONS

Where a partnership is subject to SDLT upon an acquisition of land in the ordinary course of business, i.e. outside the special regimes, from persons other than partners or persons about to become partners or persons connected with either of these, the purchaser for the purposes of SDLT is all of the responsible partners who are defined as the persons who are partners as at the effective date of the transaction. Any person who becomes a member of the partnership after the effective date of the transaction is not liable for unpaid tax, penalties and interest on penalties (FA 2003, Sched. 15, para. 6(2) (as amended)). As regards the payment of tax or interest on unpaid tax or any penalty or interest on a penalty the liability of the responsible partners is a joint and several liability of those partners (FA 2003, Sched. 15, para. 7(1) and (1A)).

However, the land transaction return may be signed by only some of the partners (known as 'representative partners'). These are partners who are nominated by the firm and approved in advance by HMRC Stamp Taxes. HMRC Stamp Taxes in the Notes for Guidance (SDLT 6), by concession, will accept the firm's name as purchaser or vendor and does not require details of all of the partners on numerous SDLT 2s.

(B) SPECIAL TRANSACTIONS

There are broadly three areas of land transactions involving partnerships where special rules apply, namely:

- acquisitions of chargeable interests from persons connected with partners. In such cases the responsible partners, i.e. the persons who are partners as at the effective date of the transaction and persons who become partners after the effective date who include any partner who is the vendor as regards the transaction are liable for the payment and compliance obligations including interest and penalties on a joint and several basis. The partners may nominate one or more partners to deal with the compliance obligations in advance of the transaction provided that such person(s) has been approved by HMRC Stamp Taxes (FA 2003, Sched. 15, para. 8), but this does not affect liability;

- transfers and deemed transfers of partnership 'interests'.[11] In these cases the purchaser is the person who acquires an increased partnership share,[12] or becomes a partner. This person will be fully liable for the tax and compliance obligations;
- acquisitions of land from partnerships by persons connected with the partnership, including another partnership. In these situations it seems that the normal definition of 'purchaser' as the person benefiting from the transaction applies for both payment and compliance obligations.

Receivers

A receiver appointed by a court in the UK[13] having the direction and control of any property is responsible for discharging any obligations in relation to SDLT in relation to a transaction affecting that property as if the property were not under the direction and control of the court (FA 2003, s.106(4)). Since specific provision is made for receivers and others acting for persons suffering from some incapacity these provisions would seem to be intended to apply to commercial or insolvency arrangements providing a different regime from administrators. This would appear to impose a personal liability upon such a receiver to pay the tax, interest and penalties due from the company including, it seems, tax and penalties owing in respect of transactions entered into prior to the appointment. There is no statutory reference to any indemnity for payments made on account of the purchaser's liability.

Trustees

The payment of tax, penalties or interest may be recovered from one or more of the responsible trustees who are the persons who are trustees at the effective date of the transaction or any person who subsequently becomes a trustee (FA 2003, Sched. 16, para. 5(3)). However, no amount may be recovered in respect of a penalty or interest on a penalty from a person who did not become a responsible trustee until after the time at which the penalty accrued. In relation to any daily penalty or interest the liability in respect of such penalty or interest does not apply to trustees appointed after the effec-

---

11 Not defined but the view of HMRC Stamp Taxes appears to be that it is not limited to the share in the capital of the firm but applies also to 'loans' by partners to the firm including, *inter alia*, undrawn profits, which, in the unlikely event of its being held to be the correct approach, will involve consideration problems where there is simply a repayment of such 'indebtedness' of the firm.
12 Which is defined as the share in the income profits of the firm.
13 No specific provisions are made to deal with the situation of receivers appointed pursuant to the terms of any contract or security.

tive date except to the extent that the penalty or interest accrues after the date of their appointment (FA 2003, Sched. 16, para. 5(2) and (4)).

Persons acting in a representative capacity other than trustee or agent and nominee

INCAPACITY

The person having the direction, management or control of the property of an incapacitated person is responsible for the obligations of the purchaser in relation to SDLT, i.e. he is required to file any returns, pay the tax personally and is presumably subject to penalties. He may be indemnified in respect of any payments made on behalf of such a person (FA 2003, s.106(1)). This will usually be the person holding the enduring power of attorney, and different rules apply to receivers appointed by the court (FA 2003, s.106); and to situations where the Official Solicitor is involved (FA 2003, s.81B (as amended); Sched. 10, para. 1B).

MINORS

The parent or guardian of a minor is responsible for discharging any obligation where the minor is a 'purchaser' (FA 2003, s.106(2)), i.e. is responsible for the payment of the tax, filing returns, keeping records and is in consequence liable to the appropriate penalties.

DECEASED PERSONS

Personal representatives of deceased individuals are affected by SDLT in many situations. For example, it must not be overlooked that personal representatives may also be affected by SDLT issues in relation to the administration of the estate such as in connection with assents or appropriations of property to beneficiaries and variations of the dispositions pursuant to the will or intestacy (FA 2003, Sched. 3, paras. 3 and 3A (as amended)), and they may be required to investigate whether they are at the relevant time personal representatives or bare or other trustees of the chargeable interest involved (see Chapter 10). Even where there is no immediate outstanding liability of the deceased there may be contractual arrangements arising from previous disposals of chargeable interests, or potential liabilities in respect of reviews of rent such as where the deceased was carrying on a business.

As regards transactions entered into by the deceased, the personal representatives of a person who was the purchaser under a land transaction are responsible for discharging the obligations of the 'purchaser' such as payment and filing of the returns in relation to the transaction. The personal representatives of a person who was a purchaser under a land transaction are liable for the tax but have a right of indemnity from the estate. They may reimburse themselves for the tax out of the assets of the estate of the deceased person (FA 2003, s.106(3)). It seems that they are also liable for any interest or penalties arising on a personal basis but it is not clear whether they are entitled to be indemnified in respect of such liabilities.

This apparently simple situation hides a mass of complex issues largely arising from the lack of finality of the tax, although certain HMRC powers are limited to three years after the individual's death (FA 2003, Sched. 10, para. 31(4)). However, it must not be overlooked that the obligations to pay tax may be deferred over a long time such as where the deceased purchased land with a clawback or overage consideration, or his business includes a lease with a reviewable rent. There are potential tax liabilities in such situations that have to be dealt with as part of the administration of the estate (see Chapter 10).

Assignees of leases[14]

Assignees of leases will be 'purchasers' under normal circumstances and will be liable for tax upon their purchase of the lease pursuant to the normal principles and under normal circumstances. The purchaser of an existing lease would justifiably expect his liability to the tax to be limited to a charge upon the price that he is paying for the lease (after deducting therefrom any amount that is justly and reasonably allocated to the purchase of chattels including equipment attached to the land that for whatever reason has not lost its character as a chattel (see Chapter 2)). To support this it is specifically provided that undertakings to pay future rent, certain indemnities for breaches of covenant and reverse premiums such as sums paid by the assignor/original tenant to the assignee to compensate for excessive rents or outstanding obligations relating to dilapidations are not subject to tax (FA 2003, Sched. 17A, paras. 10 and 17).

However, in certain situations, assignees of leases do become responsible for reporting and paying any tax arising in relation to the original chargeable transaction. The legislation is drafted on the basis of various obligations passing to the assignee and there is no reason to believe that HMRC Stamp Taxes intends this to be limited to reporting obligations. The provisional nature of the original tenant's tax return means that the assignee is required to deal with the final resolution of the original tenant's open tax position,[15]

---

14 See further, Chapter 8.
15 But also, it seems, become entitled to reclaim any tax initially overpaid by the assignor.

i.e. is substituted for the original purchaser, in the following situations (FA 2003, Sched. 17A, para. 12B):[16]

- where any contingent or uncertain premium becomes payable or ascertained (FA 2003, s.80 and Sched. 17A, para. 12(1)(c)), the obligations to deal with subsequent payments of the variable sum have to be satisfied by the current tenant;
- where there is a later linked transaction (FA 2003, s.108) including a successive linked lease (FA 2003, Sched. 17A, para. 5) pursuant to the exercise of an option to renew (FA 2003, Sched. 17A, para. 12(1)(b)), the original calculation of the tax on the rent, including where necessary the allocation of the nil rate slice between linked leases, has to be revised to take account of the linked transaction. This has to be carried out by the current tenant of each of the leases. This does not appear to be limited to transactions involving the assignee whose tax position may be affected by transactions between other persons (see Chapter 4). He will, in consequence, require undertakings for information potentially relevant to his tax position to be provided;
- where a periodic tenancy continues or there is a holding over there is a deemed extension of the original term. The original tenant should have dealt with the tax as of the effective date but this has to be revised retrospectively as the tenancy continues because the length of the term in the equation has increased. The obligation to deal with this revision of the original tenant's tax position passes to the assignee of the lease (FA 2003, Sched. 17A, paras. 3, 4 and 12(1)(c));
- where during or at the end of the first five years of the term of the lease the variable rent becomes 'certain' (FA 2003, Sched. 17A, paras. 8 and 12(1)(d)), the original assessment has to be revised. This revision must be carried out by the tenant at the time who may be an assignee of the lease.

13.7 ACCOUNTABILITY FOR THE TAX

At present there are no general provisions for any person other than certain assignees of leases to be liable to account for the tax owed by some other person. Particular rules apply to certain persons in fiduciary positions such as personal representatives (FA 2003, s.106) but for the moment solicitors and other professional advisers are not personally accountable for the client's tax. This is, however, expected to change as e-conveyancing is introduced, as

---

16 Also, there are possible issues of taking over the SDLT upon the original agreement for lease where this is assigned prior to substantial performance of that agreement by the original tenant.

UNDERSTANDING SDLT

HMRC Stamp Taxes is given power to reduce the return period from 30 days to nil so that some form of banking arrangements or accounts will be required holding money to be transmitted instantly the land transaction return is filed whether physically or electronically.

13.8 REGISTRATION OF TITLE

Although SDLT is a transaction tax and the tax status of the transaction does not appear upon the document either in the form of an impressed *ad valorem* stamp, or some form of certificate indicating that the transaction is exempt or attracted only a fixed duty, it is necessary to produce the equivalent of these stamp tax flags to the Land Registry in the form of certificates. This is a far more complex process, now that dealing with the matters routinely over the counter at the local Stamp Office has been replaced by self-assessment and postal delays and increased opportunities for HMRC Stamp Taxes to lose documents including cheques.[17]

Broadly, but at some slight risk to accuracy, the former *ad valorem* charge is represented by the need to produce an SDLT 5 certificate; the former fixed duties and reliefs which relied upon the certificates contained in Land Registry transfers and on the reverse of stock transfer forms are replaced by the self-certificate (SDLT 60). However, this simple carryover has not been achieved because of the extension of the full charge to tax and the complexity of the structure for exemptions and reliefs and their different compliance requirements (see Chapter 5).

In order to make certain changes in the Land Register in any relevant jurisdiction it is necessary to produce one of two types of certificates (FA 2003, s.79(1) and (3)). These certificates are:

- a certificate issued by HMRC Stamp Taxes that a land transaction return has been delivered in respect of the transaction (an SDLT 5) (FA 2003, s.79(3)(a)); or
- a certificate issued by the taxpayer, a self-certificate, that no transaction return is required (an SDLT 60) (FA 2003, s.79(3)(b); Sched. 11).

The form of the certificate depends upon whether or not it is necessary to deliver a land transaction return in respect of the transaction (FA 2003, s.79(3)).

It should be noted that these requirements for the production of an SDLT 5 or an SDLT 60 for the purposes of registration are not identical with the situations where it is necessary to notify HMRC Stamp Taxes by filing a land

---

[17] It is vitally important that any cheques sent as payment bear the bar code number on the SDLT 1 as they may become separated whilst being processed, and there will be difficulty in proving payment.

transaction return SDLT 1 (together with such of SDLT 2, 3 or 4 (as amended) as may be appropriate). There are many transactions that are notifiable on a land transaction return which will automatically produce an SDLT 5 but this latter form will be irrelevant as regards title since there is nothing to register. For example, it is necessary to file a land transaction return upon the five-year review of variable rents or the deemed new lease upon an abnormal rent increase and upon an increase of rent otherwise than pursuant to the terms of the lease, or the clawback of various reliefs and the payment of instalments of overage consideration. In such cases there will usually be no need to amend the Land Register and, therefore, no practical need for the SDLT 5 other than as a rather elaborate receipt and proof of payment of the SDLT shown in the original SDLT 1, which is, of course, no comfort on the point that the correct amount of SDLT has been paid.

This requirement applies to every land transaction (FA 2003, s.79 (as amended)) except:

- where the entry is required to be made without any application or so far as the entry relates to an interest or right other than the chargeable interest acquired by the purchaser under the land transaction that gave rise to the application (FA 2003, s.79(1)); or
- a contract for a land transaction such as an agreement to sell a freehold or to grant a lease under which the transaction is to be completed by a conveyance (FA 2003, s.79(2)(a)). This will apply to virtually all contracts for sale and agreements for lease since standard form provisions usually include an obligation upon the vendor or lessor to execute an appropriate written instrument such as a Land Registry transfer or a formal lease under seal where appropriate. As the test must, to be workable in practice, be applied on the objective basis of the written terms of the contract the actual intention of the parties that they will rely upon the contract rather than 'complete' in the formal sense of executing a document will be irrelevant. In practice, therefore, all contracts will be registrable without either form of certificate. Such transactions can be entered on the register without any form of certificate since simply entering into a contract does not, of itself, give rise to a charge to SDLT (FA 2003, s.44(2)) and there is possibly no obligation to notify HMRC Stamp Taxes so that no land transaction return certificate could be obtained;
- an arrangement involving a sub-sale, assignment of benefit of a land contract or other similar arrangement (FA 2003, s.79(2)(b)). The effect of s.45 of FA 2003 is that where A has contracted to sell land to B and B either contracts to sell the land to C (a sub-sale) or B contracts to assign the original contract to C (an assignment) the arrangement between B and C is not a chargeable transaction (FA 2003, s.45(2)). In consequence, an entry in relation to the contract between B and C can be put upon the register without production of the certificate;

UNDERSTANDING SDLT

- where the transaction arises pursuant to substantial performance of a contract (FA 2003, ss.44(4) and 45; Sched. 17A, para. 12B);
- substantial performance of a contract with power to direct a conveyance or an assignment thereof (FA 2003, ss.44A(3) and 45);
- substantial performance of an agreement for lease (FA 2003, Sched. 17A, paras. 12A(2) and 19(3));
- an increase or reduction of rent or of the term (FA 2003, Sched. 17A, paras. 13 and 15A);
- where the entry relates to a notice pursuant to the Land Registration Act 2003, s.34 (or the Land Registration Act (Northern Ireland) 1970, s.38) and the land transaction is a variation of a lease.

It would seem that, since contracts as such are not taxable, purchasers can protect their contracts by appropriate entries in the register without the need for a certificate and there is no need to produce a certificate where that contract is substantially performed before being completed. Certificates may be needed to register options and pre-emption rights since these are taxable at the contract stage (FA 2003, s.46).

In order to obtain an SDLT 5 certificate it is necessary to file a land transaction return with the declaration duly signed and make payment of the tax shown upon the face of the return. The certificate is simply a statement that these requirements have been satisfied. It is not a statement that the return is correct and the tax paid is correct or that the taxpayer is entitled to the exemption claimed. This is the function of the Enquiry or discovery assessments. However, if the certificate is produced to the relevant Land Registry and acted upon with changes in the register the entry cannot be challenged because it subsequently emerges that the tax was not correctly assessed or the exemption was not available.

13.9 NOTIFIABLE TRANSACTIONS

It is therefore necessary to know when an SDLT 1 is required. Notifiable transactions are those where a land transaction return (SDLT 1 together with the supplementary forms SDLT 2 to 4 (as amended)) is required, namely:

- grant and substantial performance of a lease for seven years or more for a chargeable consideration;[18]
- grant and substantial performance of a lease for less than seven years where either the premium or the rent exceeds the nil rate band. In this case a rent of £600 per annum cancels the nil rate band for the premium making the lease notifiable if there is a premium, which includes backdated

---

18 A peppercorn rent is not chargeable consideration, but £1 is.

rent. Notification is required even where the lease is exempt such as a lease to a charity;
- the assignment of a lease if either a notional grant of the lease at the time of the assignment would be notifiable or the assignment is for a consideration which is taxable at 1 per cent or higher or would be so taxable but for exemption;
- substantial performance of contracts for and completion of the acquisition of freeholds unless exempt pursuant to Sched. 3 to FA 2003 (as amended) which exemption is described below in relation to self-certificates; or the land is residential property and the chargeable consideration is less than £1,000;
- acquisition of minor interests (i.e. all interests in land other than freeholds and leases) where the consideration falls within the nil rate band;
- substantial performance of an agreement with a power to direct a conveyance pursuant to s.44A of FA 2003 (as amended);
- rent reviews during the first five years of the lease;
- abnormal increases in rent after the fifth year of the term;
- when unascertained consideration or premium becomes certain;
- as and when contingent or uncertain consideration becomes certain or instalments are paid;
- where there is a later linked transaction;
- if treatment as a transfer of a going concern is not granted by HMRC;
- where any relief is granted subject to clawback, such as transactions involving charities, residential property within Sched. 6A to FA 2003, intra-group transactions and company reconstructions, and such reliefs are forfeited during the relevant period;
- where any chargeable interest is varied for a sufficiently large consideration such as the extension of an option exercise period;
- where a lease is varied.

This list is steadily increasing as new reporting events and chargeable transactions are added.

13.10 THE TWO CERTIFICATES

(a) Land transaction return certificate (SDLT 5)

These certificates are obtained by lodging a land transaction return and paying the tax where required.

UNDERSTANDING SDLT

(b) Self-certificate (SDLT 60)

These are statements by the taxpayer that the transaction being submitted to the relevant Land Registry is not one requiring notification to HMRC Stamp Taxes. For compliance purposes they are treated as equivalent to land transaction returns and can be the subject-matter of an Enquiry. Such certificates can be utilised where a transaction is not notifiable but an entry is required upon the Land Register namely:

- the grant of a lease for a term of seven years or longer where there is no chargeable consideration. A peppercorn rent is regarded as not chargeable consideration, but a nominal £1 is chargeable consideration;
- the grant of a lease for a contractual term of less than seven years where no SDLT is payable, i.e. either:
  - the premium is below £125,000 or £150,000 and the rent is below £600 a year; or
  - there is no premium and the net present value of the rent is below £125,000 or £150,000;
- acquisition of freeholds and leases which are exempt pursuant to FA 2003, Sched. 3, namely:
  - there is no chargeable consideration. This applies where there is no actual or deemed consideration such as gifts, dividends *in specie*, appointments and distributions by trustees[19] and liquidators, changes of trustee. It also applies where there is actual consideration but the legislation provides that the consideration is not chargeable and is to be treated as nil. However, this latter circumstance is subject to two important exclusions in practice: transactions relating to disadvantaged land or within the exemption for PFI transactions are fully notifiable;
  - certain leases involving registered social landlords;
  - transactions in connection with matrimonial breakdown;
  - transactions exempt as variations of the estate of a deceased person within two years after the death;
  - appropriations by personal representatives to legatees that are exempt.

Technically the grant of certain leases by registered social landlords are not notifiable but the current version of SDLT 60 contains no provision for such transactions. HMRC Stamp Taxes has indicated that the taxpayer may draw his own box and make an appropriate entry upon the SDLT 60. However, in

---

19 But note the changes pursuant to FA 2003, Sched. 6, para. 8 (mortgaged property) and Sched. 16, para. 7.

practice, such leases are likely to be for low rents and for less than seven years and within SDLT 60 on this latter basis.

13.11 SELF-ASSESSMENT

When completing the land transaction return (SDLT 1) the taxpayer has to give details of the amount and nature of the chargeable consideration (see also SDLT 4). On the basis of this information, he must calculate the tax due and arrange for payment of that amount to HMRC Stamp Taxes.

Where the taxpayer considers that an exemption or relief is available, the tax is self-assessed upon the basis that the relief is available. HMRC Stamp Taxes will not generally question the SDLT 1 at this stage since it has only limited powers to 'correct' the return for obvious errors and omissions and will issue the SDLT 5 on the basis that the exemption or relief has been correctly taken so that the Land Register can be altered. Similarly, where the exemption is within the category of those where the party can utilise self-certificate SDLT 60, this cannot be questioned by the Land Registry who must act upon it on the basis that it is correct. The availability of the exemption or relief will be tested subsequently upon an Enquiry. If the relief is not available, the appropriate amount of SDLT together with penalties and interest will become payable. However, the entries on the Land Register are not affected by this so that, for example, mortgagees do not need to retain funds to cover the possibility that the relief will not be available, once the title has been registered.

CHAPTER 14

HMRC powers and enforcement

14.1 GENERAL

Traditional stamp duties were frequently described as a voluntary tax for a variety of reasons, one being that HMRC Stamp Taxes could not enforce the payment of tax. That has been fundamentally changed by SDLT. The counterpart to the self-assessment regime shifting the obligation, under severe penalties, to the taxpayer to calculate accurately the tax liability is the conversion of the Inland Revenue generally from tax inspectors to a form of auditors with extensive powers to collect the tax directly and to reopen transactions for up to 21 years in the many cases which will arise, inevitably, because of the defects in the self-assessment regime and the limitations of the presented forms. This will make it unbelievably easy for HMRC Stamp Taxes to issue a 'discovery assessment' (*Veltema* v. *Langham* [2004] STC 544). Moreover, to make good the deficiencies in the powers of HMRC Stamp Taxes to investigate transactions there is an obligation unlimited in time under tax-related penalties, imposed upon taxpayers to report any errors in their return, even where the return was not made negligently or fraudulently, when they become aware of them (FA 2003, Sched. 10, para. 8).

14.2 ENQUIRIES

The key weapon in enforcing the tax in practice will be the Enquiry which is the main means for HMRC Stamp Taxes to investigate the transaction. It differs in theory from the traditional adjudication of stamp duty, although currently these Enquiries seem to be conducted in the same way as adjudications, i.e. by correspondence asking the same questions as for the equivalent stamp duty and a refusal to explain the questions or justify the conclusions, and then claiming the tax, supported only by copying out the legislation without any real attempt to apply that legislation to the evidence and facts. It is, in consequence, proving to be an expensive process for taxpayers, although there is a power for taxpayers to apply to the General or Special Commissioners for an order requiring the Enquiry to be completed within a

HMRC POWERS AND ENFORCEMENT

set time because HMRC Stamp Taxes is being dilatory or inefficient or, possibly, asking irrelevant questions and not justifying its claims for tax on a proper basis (FA 2003, Sched. 10, para. 24).

Importantly, it differs from adjudication in that it is not final and conclusive for at least two reasons. There can be an Enquiry into a land transaction return that is effectively provisional such as the initial return for variable rent and a further return is required after the rent review date. A further Enquiry can be launched into the second and subsequent returns. Secondly, HMRC Stamp Taxes can issue a discovery assessment notwithstanding that there has been a previous Enquiry (FA 2003, Sched. 10, para. 30(3)(b)), and there are restrictions upon what it is deemed to know at the end of the Enquiry (FA 2003, Sched. 10, para. 30). Therefore, although HMRC Stamp Taxes may have accepted the land transaction return and possibly corrected it and have issued the appropriate certificate (SDLT 5), it can Enquire into it or issue a discovery assessment for potentially up to 21 years after the effective date.[1]

Enforcing payment

Although the primary obligation is on the taxpayer to enclose payment with the land transaction return, HMRC Stamp Taxes is given wide powers to sue for any part of the tax unpaid, interest and penalties. This applies even where the tax arises as a result of its own assessment such as determining on an Enquiry that tax has been unpaid, or where it discovers that insufficient tax has been paid. It may also assess and sue for tax where no land transaction return or self-certificate has been produced.

HMRC Stamp Taxes may also sue to enforce interest and penalties.

14.3 ASSESSMENTS BY HMRC

Determinations

HMRC Stamp Taxes may make a determination of the tax at any time within the six years following the effective date of the chargeable transaction where no return has been delivered calculating the tax to the best of its information and belief (FA 2003, Sched. 10, para. 25). This tax, so assessed, forms the basis for interest and penalties. However, after the service of such a determination the taxpayer may deliver a land transaction return with a

---

[1] The problem will be how, in practice, HMRC Stamp Taxes will be in a position to obtain information sufficient for it to make a discovery, but see the situation in *Veltema v. Langham* [2004] STC 544.

self-assessment and this takes over the process from the determination (FA 2003, Sched. 10, para. 27).

Discovery assessments

HMRC Stamp Taxes may, upon 'discovery' that tax that ought to have been assessed has not been assessed, or an assessment is or has become insufficient or that a relief or exemption claimed is or has become excessive, make an assessment for what, in its opinion, is the correct amount of the tax still outstanding (FA 2003, Sched. 10, para. 28). This includes a power to reclaim any tax that has, in its view, been incorrectly repaid.

Such discovery assessment may only be made if there was fraud or negligence causing the underpayment of the tax or at the end of the Enquiry period HMRC could not on the basis of the information made known to it have been aware of the underpayment of the tax. There are certain statutory assumptions as to the information available to HMRC Stamp Taxes (FA 2003, Sched. 10, para. 30). This is limited to information produced to it 'for the purposes of an Enquiry' which suggests that it is entitled to ignore information supplied to it voluntarily in a covering or explanatory letter sent with the land transaction return. It should be noted from these conditions that a discovery assessment can be issued notwithstanding that there has been an Enquiry and the information in question was not available because HMRC Stamp Taxes failed to ask the right questions, i.e. did not through its own ineptness discover the relevant information.

Moreover, in practice, this gives HMRC Stamp Taxes virtually unlimited power to issue discovery assessments because there is no real method of disclosing the full facts with the original return. For example, the boxes relating to the consideration require the taxpayer to insert market value or reasonable estimated future rent but there is no way to disclose the methodology adopted to determine that value or 'guestimate'. Similarly, many boxes although listing code numbers for various transactions usually contain a code '0' for other transactions so that the relief taken cannot be fully disclosed. Attempts to pre-empt the situation by submitting a detailed covering letter setting out all information will be unavailing since the general policy of HMRC Stamp Taxes is not to refer to such letters so that it is not restricted by them. Additionally, it intends to take the view that the persons receiving such letters are authorised only to receive the land transaction returns and to give them the basic scrutiny required by the legislation and have no authority to take cognisance of such correspondence so that even if they read it or place it on the file, if any, maintained by HMRC Stamp Taxes at this stage, it will not fetter them in any way whatsoever.[2] Also, such a letter is not within

---

2 See the successful argument for the Inland Revenue to this effect in *Matrix Securities v. IRC* [1994] STC 272.

the prescribed list of information treated as being available to HMRC Stamp Taxes (FA 2003, Sched. 10, para. 30(4)).

A discovery assessment may be made at any time up to six years after the effective date, unless there is fraud or negligence involved when the time limit is extended to 21 years. As negligence includes not merely errors as to the analysis of the basic legislation but also incorrect preparation of the land transaction return such as not taking proper or officially approved steps to make an estimate of future value of the rent or property, there will be ample opportunity for this longer period to be applied in practice. Moreover, it must not be overlooked that much of SDLT is of a provisional nature with subsequent returns being required, each of which start a new time period for these and other compliance purposes.

A potentially powerful tool for HMRC Stamp Taxes to extend time limits beyond the basic Enquiry period and to enlarge their powers to issue discovery assessments into the nature of the chain of title. Whilst conducting an Enquiry into a particular chargeable transaction HMRC Stamp Taxes may claim that it is necessary to inspect or investigate documents relating to other transactions because these somehow impact upon the title or transaction in question which will provide it with ample opportunities to make discoveries relating to those other transactions, since the immediate transaction may depend for its effectiveness on the analysis of its precise legal effect upon the title of one or other of the parties to that transaction. Even a vendor may be vulnerable because he and his advisers can be required to produce both documents and oral information which may provide sufficient information for HMRC Stamp Taxes to attack his acquisition of the chargeable interest in question.[3] Since in its view the non-payment of tax is at least proof of negligence, if not fraud, there is a serious risk of a minimum 21-year period of risk for taxpayers. Moreover, these problems for taxpayers are likely to increase as the amount of information that has to be disclosed to the Land Registry also increases. All such information will be instantly available to HMRC Stamp Taxes in the same way that every transaction in shares effected through CREST is passed on to it providing it with ample opportunity to make a discovery in relation to transactions other than the one for which the entry in the Land Register is being sought. HMRC Stamp Taxes is empowered to conduct an Enquiry into the return and the transaction which it reports. It is also entitled to conduct an Enquiry into self-certificates.

---

3 It also seems highly probable that in any such Enquiry or request for information HMRC Stamp Taxes will take any stamp duty objection available to it (Stamp Act 1891, s.14; *Parinv* v. *IRC* [1998] STC 305) in order to require the payment of additional tax, interest and penalties.

14.4 ENQUIRIES INTO LAND TRANSACTION RETURNS (SDLT 1)

An Enquiry into a land transaction return can be launched:

- in relation to a land transaction return, during the period of nine months after the filing date if the return was delivered on or before the date;
- nine months after the date on which the return was delivered if the return was delivered late;
- where the return was amended, nine months after the date of the amendment.

14.5 ENQUIRIES INTO SELF-CERTIFICATE (SDLT 60)

An Enquiry can be launched in relation to a self-certificate nine months after the date on which the self-certificate is produced.

14.6 POST-TRANSACTION RULINGS

Although HMRC Stamp Taxes has stated that it will give post-transaction rulings, it has restricted the scope of this obligation. Where the application for the ruling is made at the same time as or subsequent to the filing of the land transaction return or self-certificate, it will not give a ruling but will automatically open an Enquiry. Given that there are normally only 30 days for filing of the return and, in practice, even less where the taxpayer is affected by the time limits for the lodging of documents with the Land Registry and requires his certificate, whether SDLT 5 or SDLT 60, in time to comply with the Land Registry timetable, the idea of a speedy post-transaction ruling must be rejected in favour of a slow and expensive Enquiry.

14.7 SCOPE OF ENQUIRIES

A land transaction return or a self-certificate that has been the subject of one Enquiry may not be the subject of another except in the case of a return that has been amended by the taxpayer (FA 2003, Sched. 10, para. 12(3); Sched. 11, para. 7(3)). However, this does not mean that there can be only one Enquiry into the same transaction. The provisional nature of the tax means that several separate returns may be required for the same transaction and the legislation empowers HMRC Stamp Taxes to launch Enquiries into those subsequent returns, notwithstanding that it has already launched an Enquiry into and agreed for the earlier returns. Moreover, the subsequent Enquiry may provide information upon which a discovery assessment can be issued.

An Enquiry extends to anything contained in the return or required to be contained in the return or the self-certificate that relates either to the question of whether the transaction to which the return or certificate relates is chargeable or to the amount of tax chargeable (FA 2003, Sched. 10, para. 13; Sched. 11, para. 8). If the notice of Enquiry is given as a result of an amendment to a land transaction return by the taxpayer and the Enquiry period relevant to that return has expired or after an Enquiry into the return has already been completed, the new Enquiry is limited to matters to which the amendment relates or to matters that are affected by the amendment (FA 2003, Sched. 10, para. 13(2)).

14.8 APPEALS

At any time when an Enquiry into a return or a self-certificate is in progress, any question arising in connection with the subject-matter of the Enquiry may be referred to the Special Commissioners for their determination (FA 2003, Sched. 10, para. 19; Sched. 11, para. 12). The determination of a question is binding on the parties and has to be taken into account by HMRC Stamp Taxes in reaching its conclusions.

14.9 COMPLETION OF ENQUIRY

An Enquiry is completed when HMRC Stamp Taxes delivers a notice informing the purchaser that it has completed its Enquiries and stated its conclusions. Such closure notice must state whether in the opinion of HMRC Stamp Taxes no amendment of the return is required or make such amendments to the return as may be necessary or state that the self-certificate was correct, and if not correct, whether the transaction to which it relates was chargeable or notifiable (FA 2003, Sched. 10, para. 23; Sched. 11, para. 16).

Except where a referral or a question has been made to the Special Commissioners for their determination, the purchaser may apply to the General or Special Commissioners for a direction that HMRC Stamp Taxes gives a closure notice within a specified period. Such notice must be given unless the General or Special Commissioners are satisfied HMRC Stamp Taxes has reasonable grounds for not giving a closure notice within a specified period (FA 2003, Sched. 10, para. 24; Sched. 11, para. 17).

14.10 INFORMATION POWERS

Enquiry

HMRC Stamp Taxes may give notice in writing to the purchaser to produce to it such documents in his possession or power and to allow it such information in such form as it may reasonably require for the purposes of the Enquiry. The notice must specify the time within which the purchaser is to comply. Such compliance may be satisfied by the giving of copies of documents unless HMRC Stamp Taxes requires the original to be produced. There is a right of appeal against a notice requiring the taxpayer to produce documents or provide information to the Commissioners (FA 2003, Sched. 10, para. 15; Sched. 11, para. 10). A person who fails to produce documents or information as required is liable to a penalty of £50. Where the default continues after a penalty is imposed, the person is also liable to a daily penalty of £30 if the penalty is determined by HMRC Stamp Taxes and £150 if the penalty is determined by the court (FA 2003, Sched. 10, para. 16; Sched. 11, para. 11). If during an Enquiry into a return HMRC Stamp Taxes forms the opinion that the amount stated in the self-assessment is insufficient and that unless the assessment is immediately amended there is likely to be a loss of tax, it may by written notice amend the assessment to make good the deficiency (FA 2003, Sched. 10, para. 17).

14.11 OTHER INFORMATION POWERS

In addition to the powers to demand information when conducting an Enquiry into a land transaction return or self-certificate, HMRC Stamp Taxes may give a written notice requiring the taxpayer or third parties including professional advisers to produce such documents in his possession or power and to provide it with such information in such form as it may reasonably require for the purposes of the Enquiry (FA 2003, Sched. 10, para. 14 and Sched. 11, para. 9), which is supported by the imposition of penalties including a daily penalty of up to £150 per day during which the default continues where this penalty is determined by the court (FA 2003, Sched. 10, para. 16; Sched. 11, para. 11.

14.12 RECORD-KEEPING OBLIGATIONS

The scope of the documents and information gathering powers against persons other than the taxpayer means that other parties to the transaction and their advisers must keep comprehensive records.

There is an obligation upon a purchaser to keep such records as may be needed to enable him to deliver a complete and correct land transaction return (FA 2003, Sched. 10, para. 9) or a self-certificate (FA 2003, Sched. 11, para. 4) and these records must be preserved for a period of six years after the effective date and until any later date on which either an Enquiry into the return is completed or if there is no Enquiry, HMRC Stamp Taxes no longer has power to enquire into the return.

This legislation contains a list of records that must be maintained, namely relevant instruments relating to the transaction such as any contract or conveyance and any supporting maps, plans or similar documents and records of relevant payments, receipts and financial arrangements. However, this list is not exhaustive and the general obligation to make a complete return means that much other documentation will be required such as valuations and surveys since these may, *inter alia*, contain information relevant to the allocation of the consideration between the land and chattels. Mortgage reports, offering particulars will be necessary. Moreover, current Enquiry practice seems to be to ask for the commercial background to the transaction such as correspondence so these and expert reports as well as the background to any valuations such as the instructions to the valuers who may be required to act on a different basis from the general principles of fiscal valuations will be essential records. This list will undoubtedly be extensive in commercial transactions but even routine residential transactions will require significant retention of documents such as estate agents' and mortgagees' correspondence. For example, a valuer advising either a mortgagee considering lending money to the purchaser or a seller as to a price for the property is vulnerable to demands from HMRC Stamp Taxes for documentation and information. Records should be preserved.

14.13 POWERS TO CALL FOR INFORMATION

These powers to request 'information' which includes both documentation and oral testimony include:

(i) The taxpayer

In addition to the power to require information from the taxpayer during an Enquiry described above an authorised officer of the Board may, at any time (i.e. apparently not only during an Enquiry thereby effectively enlarging the powers to investigate a chargeable transaction and to issue a discovery assessment), by notice in writing require a person to deliver documents in that person's possession or power which may contain information relevant to any tax liability of that person (FA 2003, Sched. 13, para. 1). There does not appear to be any time limit whatsoever to this power; but the consent of a

General or Special Commissioner is required for the giving of such notice (FA 2003, Sched. 13, para. 2) and a summary of the reasons for applying for such consent must be supplied to the taxpayer (FA 2003, Sched. 13, para. 4).

The power to demand information does not apply to:

- documents that are personal records or journalistic records or any information contained therein (FA 2003, Sched. 13, para. 20; Police and Criminal Evidence Act 1984, ss.12 and 13);
- documents or information relating to the conduct of any pending appeal (FA 2003, Sched. 13, para. 21(1)).

Copies may be delivered rather than the originals (FA 2003, Sched. 13, para. 23).

Where there are reasonable grounds for believing that a taxpayer may have failed or may fail to comply with the provisions relating to SDLT and such failure is likely to have led or to lead to serious prejudice of the proper assessment or collection of the tax, the Board may by notice in writing require a taxpayer to deliver such documents as are in that person's possession or power which contain or may contain in the Board's reasonable opinion information that may be relevant to the tax liability of that person or to supply any relevant information (FA 2003, Sched. 13, para. 28); this power does not apply to documents that are personal or journalistic records (FA 2003, Sched. 13, para. 31; Police and Criminal Evidence Act 1984, ss.12 and 13).

(ii) Third parties

An authorised officer of the Board may for the purpose of an Enquiry[4] into the tax liability of any person require some person other than the taxpayer to deliver such documents as are in that person's possession or power which may contain in the officer's reasonable belief, information relevant to the tax liability (FA 2003, Sched. 13, para. 6). This applies to any person such as vendors, landlords, mortgagees, valuers of either party and their respective advisers including accountants advising upon the accountancy treatment of the transaction in the accounts of the taxpayer or vendor or landlord. It also extends to persons not involved in the ultimate transaction. For example, a person who made an offer for the property which is rejected and his advisers may be called upon to provide information if HMRC Stamp Taxes forms the opinion that this may have some relevance to the background to the actual chargeable transaction. Persons invited to submit tenders for property and

---

4 This is ambiguous. It may refer to the purpose of conducting an Enquiry or merely for the general purposes of enquiring or investigating into the liability of a taxpayer. It is considered notwithstanding the deficiencies in the drafting that the latter wider meaning is the one likely to be adopted in practice.

their advisers may need to consider what records they ought to maintain as a matter of self-preservation.

The consent of a General or Special Commissioner is required before such a notice can be issued (FA 2003, Sched. 13, para. 7). A copy of the notice must be given to the taxpayer to whom it relates (FA 2003, Sched. 13, para. 9) although there is power for a Special Commissioner to give consent to the issue of a notice without naming the taxpayer to whom the notice relates under prescribed circumstances (FA 2003, Sched. 13, para. 11). The taxpayer must be supplied with a written summary of the reasons for applying to the Commissioners for consent to the issue of the notice (FA 2003, Sched. 13, para. 10).

A notice may not require production of:

- documents or information relating to personal records or journalistic material (FA 2003, Sched. 13, para. 20; Police and Criminal Evidence Act 1984, ss.12 and 13);
- documents relating to the conduct of a pending appeal by the taxpayer (FA 2003, Sched. 13, para. 21(2));
- certain documents that may be legally privileged. Notices may be given to Barristers Advocates and Solicitors only by the Board and not by an authorised officer thereof (FA 2003, Sched. 13, para. 21). However, delivery of such a notice does not apply to a Barrister Advocate or Solicitor so as to require him to deliver or make available without the client's consent any document with respect to which a claim to legal privilege (as defined by (FA 2003, Sched. 13, para. 35) could be maintained (FA 2003, Sched. 13, para. 25);
- documents originating more than six years before the date of the notice unless General or Special Commissioners have given consent to the extension of the period which may only be given if the General or Special Commissioners are satisfied that tax has been or may have been lost owing to the fraud of the taxpayer (FA 2003, Sched. 13, para. 24);
- certain documents in the possession of auditors. A person who has been appointed as an auditor cannot be required to deliver or make available documents that are his property and were created by him or on his behalf for or in connection with the performance of his functions under the statutory provisions controlling his appointment as auditor (FA 2003, Sched. 13, para. 26(1)(a));
- certain documents in the possession of tax advisers. A tax adviser, i.e. a person appointed to give advice about the tax affairs of another person (FA 2003, Sched. 13, para. 26(3)) is not obliged to deliver or make available documents that are his property and consist of communications between the tax adviser and the person in relation to whose tax affairs he has been appointed or any other tax adviser of such a person the purpose of which is the giving or obtaining of advice about those tax affairs (FA

2003, Sched. 13, para. 26(1)(b) and (2)). This is now, however, subject to the obligation to disclose details of 'tax schemes', and there may be difficulties in deciding whether the document or information belongs to the professional adviser who instructed the legal adviser or to the lay client.

Where a document relates to activities as auditor or tax adviser and contains information explaining any information, return or other document that the person to whom the notice is given has, as tax accountant, assisted his client in preparing for or delivering to HMRC Stamp Taxes, or information as to the identity of unnamed taxpayers that has not otherwise been made available to HMRC Stamp Taxes, then the person to whom the notice is given must, if he does not deliver the document or make it available for inspection in accordance with the notice, deliver a copy of any parts of the document that contain such information as is referred to and make available for inspection such parts of the original document which contain such information (FA 2003, Sched. 13, para. 27).

(iii) Tax accountants

Where a person who has stood in relation to others as tax accountant is convicted of an offence in relation to tax by or before a court in the UK or has a penalty imposed upon him for assisting in the preparation of an incorrect return (FA 2003, s.96), an officer of the Board may by notice in writing require him to deliver such documents as are in his possession or power which may contain information relevant to the tax liability to which any client of his is or has been or may be subject (FA 2003, Sched. 13, para. 14). No notice may be given for so long as an appeal is pending against the conviction or penalty (FA 2003, Sched. 13, para. 15) and the consent of the appropriate judicial authority is required for the giving of such notice (FA 2003, Sched. 13, para. 16). Copies may be produced rather than originals (FA 2003, Sched. 13, para. 23).

Such a notice may not require the production of documents or documents that:

- contain personal records or journalist material (FA 2003, Sched. 13, para. 20; Police and Criminal Evidence Act 1984, ss.12 and 13);
- relate to the conduct of a pending appeal relating to tax by the taxpayer (FA 2003, Sched. 13, para. 21(3));
- are legally privileged. A notice may not be given to a Barrister Advocate or Solicitor by an authorised officer but only by the Board (FA 2003, Sched. 13, para. 22) and such a notice does not oblige a Barrister Advocate or Solicitor to deliver or make available without his client's consent any document with respect to which a claim to legal privilege could be maintained (FA 2003, Sched. 13, para. 25). Legal privilege is defined as (FA 2003, Sched. 13, para. 25) communications between a professional legal adviser and his client or any person representing his client in connection with

giving legal advice to the client or made in connection with or in contemplation of legal proceedings and for the purposes of such proceedings. It extends to items enclosed with or referred to in such communications made for the purposes of giving legal advice or in connection with legal proceedings when they are in the possession of the person entitled to them. This does not apply to items held for the furthering of a criminal purpose which may include non-payment of SDLT which may be tax evasion or money laundering.

Regulations have been issued to establish a procedure for the purpose of determining whether a document or part of a document is entitled to legal privilege (FA 2003, Sched. 13, para. 36; Stamp Duty Land Tax (Administration) Regulations 2003, SI 2003/2837).

(iv) Taxpayers and other persons and fraud

Where there are reasonable grounds for suspecting that an offence involving serious tax fraud in relation to SDLT has been or is about to be committed, and that documents that may be required as evidence for the purpose of any proceedings in respect of such an offence, are or may be in the possession or power of any person, whether or not the taxpayer, the Board of HMRC may apply to an appropriate judicial authority to make an order requiring that person to produce the documentation (FA 2003, Sched. 13, para. 32). A person who is the object of such an intended notice is entitled to receive a notice of the intention to apply for an order and to be heard at the hearing of the application unless the appropriate judicial authority is satisfied that this would seriously prejudice the investigation of the offence (FA 2003, Sched. 13, para. 33). Persons who have received a notice of intention to apply for such an order must not seek to destroy any such evidence (FA 2003, Sched. 13, para. 34).

If there are reasonable grounds for suspecting an offence involving serious fraud in connection with or in relation to tax, not just SDLT, an officer of the Board may with the approval of the Board in relation to the particular case, apply for an order to the appropriate judicial authority for the issue of a warrant in writing authorising an officer of the Board to enter the premises if necessary by force and search them (FA 2003, Sched. 13, para. 43). Such an application may only be made if there are reasonable grounds for believing that the use of an application for an order for the delivery of documents might seriously prejudice the investigation (FA 2003, Sched. 13, para. 45). Items that are subject to legal privilege may not be seized under this procedure (FA 2003, Sched. 13, para. 48). This is governed by the same principles as those described above.

Failure to comply with an order to produce information is treated as contempt of court (FA 2003, Sched. 13, para. 40).

APPENDIX A

Land areas for investigation

The following is a broad summary of the major areas for title issues, due diligence and the effective performance of obligations owed to others and as professional advisers where the new regime has given rise to a wholly new set of problems to be investigated by the conveyancer. The explanations of the problems are described in more detail at relevant places within the main text. Enquiries are necessary to determine whether the arrangements are required to be notified to HMRC as a tax avoidance scheme.

GENERAL ISSUES FOR CONTRACTS

It has to be acknowledged that as stamp taxes move increasingly from a documentation to a transaction-based tax with an expanding subjective element in relation to attacks upon steps to mitigate the impact of the tax, such as the condition for certain reliefs that the transaction was entered into for bona fide commercial reasons and not for the avoidance of tax, whatever that may mean, particularly as it may include steps taken to reduce other non-stamp tax charges, circumstances become uncertain because of the subjective element in an area such as the commercial justification for the transaction where HMRC generally does not have an impressive reputation. A key area for requests for disclosure by purchasers will be delivery of any clearance applications for previous transactions, particularly significant clearances where there is no clearance procedure or even the safeguard of rapid adjudication of the new tax. Vendors will increasingly be presented with pressure from extended warranties and indemnities where the subjective element in stamp taxes has increased but they have not obtained a clearance for other taxes, especially where the tax risk passes directly or indirectly to the purchaser. In practice, clearances given in relation to capital gains tax[1] tend to prevail.

There will be a significant problem for fiduciaries such as personal representatives, liquidators and receivers. The issue mentioned includes not only questions of whether there is some liability for the tax in any potential transaction such as where the liability is by statute transferred to a third party who must be made aware of the potential problems and related future costs, but also situations where a personal liability is imposed and, further to investigating the history of the overall context, may lead to a nasty shock of obligations to pay another person's tax, including interests and penalties, where, although there may be a statutory indemnity, this may not be adequate to recoup the personal liability.

---

1 Such as pursuant to Taxation of Chargeable Games Act 1992, ss.137–139, which are preferred to income tax clearances pursuant to, e.g., Income and Capital Taxes Act 1984, ss.767 and 788; the latter being particularly important for land transactions.

Purchasers will require full SDLT histories of the chargeable interest including details of the data behind the return. This may involve the disclosure of commercially sensitive information to competitors, meeting the purchaser's reasonable requirements; but failure to obtain such information will not be regarded by HMRC Stamp Taxes as a reason for mitigation of penalties or a defence to any allegations of negligence where the taxpayer submits what turns out to be an incorrect return, or fails to submit a return, or is unaware that a tax charge has arisen, because he does not have access to the necessary information which is controlled by the other parties.[2] This is particularly harsh since, although HMRC Stamp Taxes has power to demand documents and information from persons other than the taxpayer, it has not seen fit to provide the taxpayer with power to require co-operation from other persons as to make available information in their possession such as their new files and records to taxpayers because it insists that the rules of 'taxpayer confidentiality' prevents it from helping other taxpayers.

PURCHASER

Which regime?

- Whether the completion or other arrangement is pursuant to a contract entered into prior to 1 December 2003 when the transaction may be subject to a stamp duty regime. However, there are many statutory provisions which subject pre-1 December 2003 contracts to SDLT.
- Was the lease initially taxed within the stamp duty or the SDLT regime. This affects the basis of the issues but is also important since different rules apply to certain transactions affecting stamp duty leases. For example, there is no tax charge on holding over a stamp duty lease, there is no credit for stamp duty paid in respect of rent when there is a surrender and regrant of a stamp duty lease, payments in respect of variable consideration such as overage and rent reviews under pre-1 December 2003 may not be taxable. Different rules apply for linked transactions such as the exercise of pre-SDLT options and renewals of leases (FA 2003, Sched. 19 as amended, including retrospective amendments). In the case of leases, the charge to stamp duty is usually significantly lower than its equivalent to SDLT. The search for whether the stamp duty regime applies is usually a good investment for the client. There are, however, issues where there is an exercise of an option to renew a stamp duty lease (FA 2003, Sched. 19, para. 9).

Purchase of property

Freeholds (dealings in existing leases are commented upon below)

- Whether the registered owner or the persons appearing as vendor in the contract are beneficially entitled or a nominee or bare trustee. This is relevant for identifying the 'vendor' for completing SDLT 1 and SDLT 2 and whether the vendor is connected with the purchaser for the purpose of reliefs, connected company charges, the special partnership regime and linked transactions.
- Where there are several acquisitions, whether the vendors are connected for the purpose of the linked transaction rules.

---

2 Such persons may, however, be under obligations to disclose such confidential information to HMRC Stamp Taxes to aid it in the pursuit of taxpayers.

APPENDIX A

- Whether any party to a transaction is a fiduciary such as a trustee, personal representative or undisclosed agent.[3] There is a need to investigate the beneficial interests because there is a question whether his status has changed such as to a nominee or bare trustee as a consequence of an assent or appropriation, deed of appointment or a death of the life tenant so that the true vendor or purchaser can be identified for the above purposes. Letters to the Land Registry explaining the differences between the SDLT 5 or SDLT 60 and TR1 may be required.
- Whether there is variable consideration such as an overage or clawback payment affecting the land and whether this is somehow 'charged' upon the land such as by way of a restrictive covenant or ransom strip.[4]
- Whether the vendor's tax position is provisional only and, if so, whether the liability for the outstanding tax passes to the purchaser.
- Whether any estimates such as future value, or rents, or the amount expected to become payable have been prepared upon a proper basis, probably requiring independent professional advice. The original purchaser's or tenant's open tax position may pass to a third party. Failure to obtain proper advice is negligence or fraud.
- So as to avoid allegations of negligent or fraudulent returns, whether the taxpayer has been properly advised as to his future compliance and payment obligations and appropriate machinery has been put in place to ensure that the taxpayer complies with the outstanding obligation in the future where the initial land transaction return is not final in relation to such items as rent review and variable consideration.
- Whether payment of all or any part of the tax upon the variable consideration can be deferred.
- Whether contractual provisions described as 'conditions' are in law consideration within the charge to tax.
- Where the chargeable consideration consists of property other than cash or debt, whether the market value thereof has been prepared on a proper basis.
- Whether the consideration has been apportioned on a just and reasonable basis between the land interests and other property being acquired; failure to do so is easily open to allegations of fraud and criminal sanctions pursuant to FA 2003, s.95. To assist in the preparation of a return in such circumstances could expose the adviser to a £3,000 penalty (FA 2003, s.96).
- Whether there have been prior or might be subsequent linked transactions which might impact upon the purchaser's tax position.

Options and pre-emption rights

Details of the background to the grant of options whether put, call or cross and including options to renew leases are now relevant since the exercise of the option may be a linked transaction with the grant of the option or lease being renewed. This will be important to:

- the original grantee for retrospective taxation of the option when exercised;
- assignees who, depending upon the official view, may be subject to the linked transaction rule;

---

[3] The rules as to nominees mean that, in practice, there can be no undisclosed agency or nominee arrangement. This raises problems in relation to the position of single nominees and LPA 1925, s.27.
[4] The legal validity of many such arrangements has been questioned because of the lack of benefit to dominant land.

- assignees or purchasers whose tax position might be affected by the exercise of an option by other persons.

Completion arrangements

- Whether there has been earlier substantial performance of an agreement which in the view of HMRC Stamp Taxes occurs if the purchaser obtains the key before completion so that a return should already have been filed and tax paid.
- Whether all information concerning the 'vendor' has been obtained for the completion of the land transaction return.
- Whether the registered owner and/or person(s) appearing in contract are the true vendor as required by SDLT 1.
- Whether the 'vendor' is the registered owner of the property; if not, what is the status of his application to register and filing of his SDLT 1. Undertakings may be required as to production of an SDLT 5 to the purchaser so that he may apply to be registered. Covering letters explaining the differences between SDLT 5 or 60 and TR1, etc., to the Land Registry may be required including details of the vendor's position.
- Whether the persons whose names are to appear in the Land Registry document as transferor and transferee or lessor and lessee are the same as those appearing as 'vendor' and 'purchaser' in the SDLT 1 and SDLT 5. If not, an explanatory letter will be required by the Land Registry.
- Whether the vendor is seeking to rely upon sub-sale relief or the relief for leases granted directly to third parties so that he will not be producing an SDLT 5.
- Whether these sub-sale or equivalent reliefs will take the form of a direct transfer from the original seller to the purchaser at the direction of the intermediate vendor or the intermediate vendor does not have power to direct a sub-sale and so will be taking a transfer. In the latter case, the intermediate vendor may be entitled to the relief for sub-sales (but not leases) notwithstanding that he receives a conveyance or Land Registry transfer. This requires the ultimate purchaser to produce two such transfers but only one SDLT 5 since the intermediate vendor will not be filing any SDLT 1. Full details will be required from the intermediate vendor to enable the required covering letter for the Land Registry to be submitted explaining that no SDLT 5 is required because of sub-sale relief.
- Where there is an agreement for lease and the lease is to be granted directly to the taxpayer who is not a party to the agreement for lease but is an 'assignee' of the right to the lease,[5] details will be required from the original tenant of his position including whether he has substantially performed the original agreement for lease since the taxpayer's position is totally dependent upon the original tenant's tax position. The amount of the charge to tax upon the purchaser depends upon whether FA 2003, Sched. 17A, para. 12B, s.45 or neither applies.
- Whether the necessary declarations and prescribed form SDLT 1 and any powers of attorney or board minutes or approval of representative partners have been obtained to permit someone other than the taxpayer to sign the SDLT 1 or SDLT 60 upon which the vendor's or landlord's title depends if the vendor is a company, trustees, club or association or is not the registered owner. Mortgagees will need to be advised where there may be a delay in registration because, *inter alia*, of SDLT delays.

---

5 Who may not be the same as a person to whom the original tenant directs the grant of the lease.

APPENDIX A

- Whether appropriate steps have been taken by the parties and their advisers to produce and preserve the required records of the transaction. These include not merely the transaction documents, but all relevant documents such as valuations, including apportionments, the initial offer such as estate agents' advertising, correspondence with mortgagees and details of negotiations with vendor.
- Whether the taxpayer has been properly advised as to the obligations in relation to any arrangements whereby tax payments have been deferred.
- Details of the original offer price where market value may be an issue and there may be a discount for bulk purchase or a quick completion which discount is not accepted by HMRC Stamp Taxes as being the market value.[6]
- Whether the transaction is linked to other contemporaneous or prior transactions since the taxpayer may be instructing other solicitors on those transactions.
- Whether the transaction may be linked with subsequent transactions since these may require appropriate undertakings by both parties to supply the necessary information.
- Whether the transaction falls within the wide definitions of 'land exchange' when the special rules may apply for computation and reporting; key areas are deeds of variation of leases which may be surrenders and regrants, 'excepting and reserving' and sale and leaseback transactions.

Leases

(a) Purchase of existing leases

- When the lease was actually granted and the agreement for lease was substantially performed because this affects the calculation of the first five years of the term for rent reviews, including the relief for 'backdating' to a term commencement date, and whether two full land transaction returns are required and, if so, whether the first return has been filed. Details of the assessment are required to calculate the rent credit for the formal grant.
- Many tax problems are passed over to purchasers of existing leases[7] so that a full SDLT history will be required[8] to enable the purchaser to know when a tax charge may arise and to deal properly with his liability to pay and to file land transaction returns and to deal with situations such as:
    - variable premiums where payments remain outstanding;
    - variable rents including reviewable rents because of reviews during the first five years and abnormal increases thereafter;
    - whether the lease was exempt when granted in circumstances where the assignment is to be taxed as the grant of a new lease. The assignee may require some form of contribution to the additional tax charge arising;
    - the background to the lease such as whether it is linked with other leases or may be linked with future possible leases or lease renewal and whether the negotiations relating to the option to renew make it vulnerable to the successive linked lease provisions. Undertakings to supply background information to the original transaction may be required;

---

6 This is likely to prove a major problem in practice as HMRC Stamp Taxes is treating 'exceptions and reservations' as being regrants creating new rights and producing a land exchange taxable at market value.
7 Different issues arise in relation to these problem areas where there is the grant of a new lease.
8 There is no statutory power to demand such information; this must be stipulated for in the contract notwithstanding that it might lead to confidentiality issues for the vendor.

- whether there are existing leases or may be future leases or leases renewable that might be linked transactions which may affect the tax position of the assignee such as the amount of nil rate applied to the rent as per that lease to be carried forward and whether additional tax arises in respect of his lease because of the allocation of different amounts of the nil rate for rent to other linked leases;[9]
- turnover and profit-sharing leases: details of the turnover and profits of the prior tenants where there is a turnover or profit-sharing rent, and sums of rent paid where the five-year period has not expired;

- Undertakings are required to supply information where the vendor or his successors in title may enter into transactions that may be linked with the particular lease since this may affect the tax position of the assignees because he takes over the open tax position of the original tenant in relation to the assigned lease which requires retrospective adjustment.
- Indemnities are required to deal with the possibility that the original self-assessment was too low, where the assignor's open tax position is passed to the assignee by statute he is protected against liability.
- Assignors will require indemnities against the assignee's windfall if the initial tax assessment was high and tax is repayable to the assignee.

(b) New leases

- Parties to new leases, as with parties to other transactions, need to consider not only the information they may require for their own tax purposes but what information they may be required to produce to prospective purchasers of their interests in due course as part of the SDLT history.
- Details of tenant's plans and obligations in relation to fitting out, taking possession or subselling or other possible substantial performance.
- Whether items of additional rent such as service charges or VAT are separately reserved.
- Detailed records of negotiations leading to the term of the lease and options to renew for linked transaction purposes.

---

[9] This applies notwithstanding the principle that linked transactions can arise only between the same parties.

APPENDIX B

Particular problems for the vendor

- The vendor will require undertakings and indemnities from the purchaser since subsequent events may affect his tax liability and reporting obligations.
- Whether the transaction is a land exchange since this involves the vendor in a potential tax charge and reporting obligation. This is an area becoming significant in practice because of the approach of HMRC Stamp Taxes to 'excepting and reserving' as involving regrants of new rights.

OPTIONS

- Details of the exercise of the option are required since the exercise of the option may be linked with the grant and other transactions such as renewals of other linked leases granted by the seller who may be contractually bound to supply information to third parties potentially affected by the exercise.

VARIABLE CONSIDERATION

- Whether there are any outstanding taxation liabilities in respect of the previous acquisition of the property which remain with the vendor.
- Whether the proposed transaction requires payment of tax and/or reporting to be made in respect of any prior acquisition of the chargeable interest or the part thereof being disposed of because payments have to be made in respect of tax on a previous acquisition where the payment of part of the tax has been deferred.
- Whether these outstanding tax liabilities are affected by any of the proposals for dealing with any such outstanding consideration and clawback arrangements, or as a novation of the liability.
- Details of later payments made by the purchaser to third parties may be required because these may affect the vendor's open SDLT position for the original payment.
- Indemnities may be required should the initial tax payment on the vendor's acquisition have been overestimated, otherwise the purchaser receives a windfall profit such as on a rent review during the first five years of the lease and other cases where the legislation transfers his liability to the assignee of the lease land.

LINKED TRANSACTIONS

- Undertakings may be required from the purchaser and his successors in title to supply information relating to later transactions such as lease renewals or holding over, which may be linked with other transactions to which the vendor is a party whether previous or subsequent which may affect the liability to tax such as by reducing the amount of the nil rate slice allocated to any lease which he retains or which he may have previously assigned and may be linked with the leases being currently assigned.

MISCELLANEOUS

- When the vendor is asked to assist in or to agree to the apportionment of the consideration, whether the apportionment has been prepared by the purchaser on a proper basis to avoid suggestions of assisting in a conspiracy to defraud HMRC Stamp Taxes (note the width of the comment on conspiracy in *Saunders* v. *Edwards* [1987] 2 All ER 651).

APPENDIX C

Share purchase issues for investigation

Although the sale of shares in companies holding land are subject only to stamp duty or stamp duty reserve tax, SDLT issues arise, albeit indirectly, but they may be vitally important to the value of the company.

- Whether the company is up to date with its filing of SDLT 1 and paying the tax, and whether all land transaction return certificates (SDLT 5) have been received and submitted to the Land Registry.
- Whether there are any Enquiries proceeding and whether the company is potentially vulnerable to an Enquiry in the future since this may produce additional tax liabilities, interest and penalties.
- Whether there are any SDLT 60 issues outstanding, including relevant transactions not notified.
- Whether the company may be vulnerable to the risk of a Notice of Assessment for a discovery over the 21-year period.
- Whether the company has fully provided for all tax in respect of variable payments. This applies not merely to the initial estimated self-assessment but in respect of the tax charge arising in respect of later payment and adjustments. Assurances are required that the initial assessment was prepared on a proper basis, i.e. sufficient tax was paid.
- Whether the company is affected by any open SDLT liability such as variable consideration and reviewable rents during the first five years.
- Whether payment of any part of the tax has been deferred and whether the amount so deferred is sufficient to cover the potential tax liability.
- Whether all payments have been made punctually for deferral arrangements.
- Whether the potential liability either for postponed tax or for tax on variable payments in relation to acquisitions by the company has been recognised in the company's accounts and subsequent dividend policy. It may be necessary for assurances to be given that nothing has subsequently occurred which might affect the amount of consideration expected to be paid which has not been notified to HMRC.
- Details of the costs of any chargeable building works or services being undertaken by the company which are taxable and whether these are consistent with any deferral arrangements agreed with HMRC.
- Whether the company is a tenant of a lease that may be vulnerable to liability in the future pursuant to the abnormal increase in rent rules.
- Whether the company is a tenant of a lease that was exempt when granted but which will be subject to charge upon assignment as if it were the grant of a new lease since the assignee may require a reverse payment as compensation, i.e. the lease may have a negative value.

SHARE PURCHASE ISSUES FOR INVESTIGATION

- Whether the company is the owner of a chargeable interest that may be vulnerable to the linked transaction rules such as leases with options to renew or leases that are linked with other actual or future or renewed leases which may affect the liability of the company in respect of its leases such as the amount of nil rate slice for rent allocated to it from the initial charge, i.e. a potential retrospective liability for future events such as rent reviews and abnormal increases.
- Whether full details of the SDLT history of all chargeable interests are contained in the company's records since these will be vital for future transactions and calculating liability and meeting its obligations to preserve proper records.
- Whether the company has prepared correct accounts for capital allowances and VAT taking proper account of the potential SDLT.
- Whether the company has been a party to a chargeable transaction which was exempt but is vulnerable to clawback as a consequence of either the current transaction or future transactions.
- Whether the company has a residual liability for clawback in respect of other companies with which it has been associated should those other companies fail to pay the tax relief clawed back even though it was not a party to those transactions.
- Whether the company has been a party to a transaction where its acquisition was treated as a transfer of a going concern for the purposes of VAT and full details of how the SDLT issues were dealt with.
- Whether the company has participated in a notifiable tax scheme and whether HMRC has been notified.

APPENDIX D

Completing the tax return

GENERAL

HMRC Stamp Taxes has published guidance notes on its views as to the completion of the land transaction return (SDLT 6) which also contains relevant code numbers and certain comments on substantive tax issues. Certain of these forms are now available on CD-ROM (Tax Bulletin 75 (March 2005)). However, these views are not comprehensive and it is uncertain how far it is safe for a taxpayer to rely upon the Notes, particularly as they are somewhat selective and lacking in detail. The following is intended to provide assistance in certain aspects where the official guidance is less than clear or non-existent, or possibly incorrect. On this last point, there are significant doubts as to whether HMRC Stamp Taxes will necessarily regard itself as bound by any guidance which it has given. The so-called 'helpline' which appears to be primarily intended to deal with compliance issues rather than substantive matters is not intended to bind HMRC Stamp Taxes and it has been judicially stated that reliance upon a telephone discussion such as with the helpline or other persons will not bind HMRC (*J Rothschild (Holdings) Ltd* v. *IRC* [1988] STC 645 (an appeal on other grounds [1989] STC 435)). It also seems that such reliance on the helpline will not be taken into account in deciding whether there is fraud or negligence and is not a matter to be taken into account in relation to the possible mitigation of penalties. It will in consequence provide no protection for the practitioner where there is a claim based upon breach of duty.

The land transaction return is not the only official document. It must also be noted that many communications with HMRC Stamp Taxes such as amendments to the form are supposed to be in the form and contain such information as it may require.[1] In many cases prescribed forms have not been issued.

It must be recognised that much of the information required by the forms has no direct bearing on the tax, and much information that is appropriate to the tax cannot be disclosed on the form.[2] This is because the forms are simply collecting information for the Treasury and District Valuers. This appreciation of the underlying policy may help to clarify some of the questions on the form.

---

[1] See the procedure for amending returns during the first 12 months (FA 2003, Sched. 10, para. 6), and the making of claims such as for repayments of tax pursuant to an error or mistake (FA 2003, Sched. 10, para. 34 and Sched. 11A).

[2] Hence the ease with which discovery assessments can be issued as in *Langham* v. *Veltema* [2004] STC 544. Covering letters are of no real benefit in this context.

COMPLETING THE TAX RETURN

Identifying the form

The basic forms are submitted, i.e. only the appropriate form may be utilised. The initial forms in Scheds. 1 and 2 to Stamp Duty Land Tax (Administration) Regulations 2003, SI 2003/2837 have been modified. The current list includes:

Land transaction return (SDLT 1)

This is the basic return and self-assessment. Note that the amendments permitting agents to sign the return (FA 2003, Sched. 10, para. 1A) require a special version of SDLT 1 to be utilised because this has to contain the modified declaration required by the regulations. Declarations in the new form include reference to 'agent' as the person confirming the effective date. It seems the purchaser's signature confirming that everything except the effective date is correct can be on a copy of the form.

Additional vendor/purchaser details (SDLT 2)

This is required where there are two or more vendors or purchasers; particularly important where nominees are involved. Since the vendor and purchaser are not necessarily the legal owners of the property or even the parties to the contract, it is necessary to investigate these issues since the identity of the parties is important for a whole range of reasons including the assessment of the tax and the linked transaction rules. This may pose an acute issue for partnerships should, notwithstanding the rule permitting representative partners to carry out certain functions, HMRC Stamp Taxes require details of all of the partners regardless of the numbers involved. However, SDLT 6 suggests that a partnership is to be treated as one vendor or a single purchaser so that only the firm's name is required in Box 36 in SDLT 1. This indicates, but not conclusively, that the names of all of the partners are not required to be disclosed.

Trustees of unincorporated associations such as clubs which may be a body corporate so that their individual identities are not important and the form may not be necessary. It is unclear how many trustees of charities may have to be identified. The rules limiting registration of legal title to the first four trustees does not limit the disclosure if there are other trustees, although one trustee can sign the form.

Additional details of the land (SDLT 3)

As the taxpayer may, in order to save costs, include more than one property in the main SDLT 1 (SDLT 1, Box 26) this form will be required. The inclusion of several properties in one return will reduce the need for duplication of much of the information and possibly avoid the need for apportioning a global consideration for several properties. However, obstacles exist to the utilisation of this facility; namely:

- the structure of the form SDLT 1 is such that only transactions having the same effective date can be entered upon the form;
- SDLT 6 suggests that the facility should be utilised for linked transactions but this requires not only the same effective date but also the same parties. In consequence, where the linked transactions involved connected persons, whether as 'vendors' or 'purchasers', separate returns will be required;
- SDLT 6 in the preface to Box 16 indicates that only one lease can be included in the SDLT 1, because it specifically excludes linked leases; and
- where the properties are in different land registries there will be a need to request separate land transaction return certificates (SDLT 5) for each property (SDLT 1, Box 27).

APPENDIX D

It seems that SDLT 6 requires this return in cases where a freehold is acquired subject to pre-existing leases or a new headlease subject to leases or underleases is granted. For some far from obvious reason, HMRC Stamp Taxes requires full details of all such pre-existing leases to be disclosed (see SDLT 6 in relation to SDLT 1 Boxes 16–22). Further information on all new leases is required by SDLT 4.

Additional details about the transactions (SDLT 4 (as amended))[3]

This form is designed for disposal of land as part of a business sale and, in effect, replaces with amendment the old Stamps Form 22 and Companies Form 88.[4] However, although no separate guidance is provided as to when HMRC Stamp Taxes expects to receive this form, it is probably prudent to assume that this return is required in every case other than routine domestic conveyancing and investigate whether any of the questions are relevant.

Notwithstanding the references to 'chattels', it is not necessary to submit this form where there is a sale of property without a business, such as a sale of a house and chattels unless the purchaser is a company where SDLT 4 may be required in any event because SDLT 1 does not require disclosure of the purchasing company's number.

Looking to the information required by SDLT 4, it seems that it will be required where:

- the property is subject to a lease or tenancy;
- the land transaction is part of a sale of a business;
- the land is commercial property;
- the purchaser is a company;
- the consideration is contingent or uncertain, but not perhaps 'unascertained'. There is, however, an ambiguity because the form, but not SDLT 6, refers to dependence upon future events. It is thought that the reference to 'future events' is to factors that change the calculation rather than merely referring to agreements between the parties which determine the facts upon which the calculation is based such as the square footage of an existing building or market value as at the effective date. However, it has to be noted that the test for the 'certainty' of the consideration has to be applied as at the effective date which is not necessarily the same as formal completion and the pricing mechanism may be fixed by reference to the later date so that when filing the return for the effective date the consideration will be dependent upon future events. Thus at the effective date the building may be only half constructed, at completion it may be constructed but unmeasured. In the former case, SDLT 4 will be required because the consideration is uncertain, and in the latter case because the building is commercial;
- mineral rights have been reserved;
- a post-transaction ruling has been received. This will be an unlikely event in practice since to apply for a post-transaction ruling together with or subsequent to the filing of the land transaction return means that there cannot be such a ruling. This will be regarded by HMRC Stamp Taxes as initiating a full Enquiry. SDLT 4 is only required if the application has been made and the ruling has been received prior to filing SDLT 1 which, in practice, is likely to mean that the taxpayer is out of time for filing both the land transaction return and any Land Registry application;

---

3 Stamp Duty Land Tax (Administration) (Amendment) Regulations 2004, SI 2004/3124.
4 Which has been separately amended by regulations (Stamp Duty and Stamp Duty Land Tax (Consequential Amendment) Regulations 2003, SI 2003/2868.

- arrangements have already been agreed for the postponement of the payment of tax. It seems that SDLT 4 is not required merely if an application for postponement has been made, notwithstanding that tax in respect of which an application to postpone has been made is not due and payable until the application has been refused (Stamp Duty Land Tax (Administration) Regulations 2003, SI 2003/2837, reg. 15(3)) but it will be necessary to file the form because the consideration will be uncertain.

Self-certification (SDLT 60)

At some risk to accuracy this form may be regarded as the equivalent of the certificate required by the Stamp Duty (Exempt Instrument) Regulations 1987, SI 1987/516 where the relief from the former fixed duty applies. Many of the transactions in these lists are exempt from SDLT, but there is not a total identity so that, because certain of those transactions are now fully taxable and if not taxable are nevertheless notifiable by SDLT 1, the precise circumstances for the utilisation have to be regularly checked because from time to time these circumstances are changed. However, in practice, SDLT 60 is required only where the parties need to effect a change in the Land Register. Transactions not notifiable and not involving the Land Registry do not require an SDLT 60, such as sub-sales qualifying for relief.

Payslip

SDLT 1 must be accompanied by payment with details contained in the prescribed payslip. This is attached to the hard copy of the return and should, hopefully, bear the same bar code transaction number as the SDLT 1 page 2. Where the payslip is separate because, for example, the taxpayer is utilising electronic forms, it is necessary to ensure that the bar code is entered on the payslip. It is also necessary to write the bar code number on the cheque so that in the not unlikely event of the cheque and the return becoming separated, HMRC Stamp Taxes may be able to rematch the various documents and payment.

Alterations of the form

There are penalties imposed for ill-treating Revenue forms (FA 2003, s.82) so that alterations to the forms are not encouraged.[5] Three main areas require consideration, namely:

(1) AMENDMENTS

Certain adjustments in the tax position are required to be dealt with by way of amendment such as repayments of tax paid on substantial performance of a contract where the contract is later rescinded or annulled (FA 2003, s.44(9)), or claims for overpaid tax within 12 months after the 30-day filing period which must be accompanied by the documents.[6] Such corrections may also be required where the transaction documentation is rectified in the correct sense of the term. The correction of the drafting errors is likely to mean that incorrect details were entered in the original return. There

---

5 This extends to folding the returns which is prohibited at several places in the return.
6 For claims after this date see FA 2003, Sched. 11A.

APPENDIX D

may also be 'corrections' from HMRC Stamp Taxes where there have been minor errors, such as arithmetic or obvious omissions, in completing the form. Such corrections to the return may only be made within nine months after the return was filed by written notice which can be challenged by the taxpayer (FA 2003, Sched. 10, para. 7).

Such 'amendments' can be made only within 12 months after the expiration of the 30-day filing period, and must be by notice in such form and contain such information as HMRC Stamp Taxes may require (FA 2003, Sched. 10, para. 6). No standard form for such amendments has yet been presented by regulations.

(2) ALTERATIONS TO RETURN

Errors may creep in during the preparation of the land transaction return and, whilst it may in many respects be easier to scrap that return, if being prepared manually it may be tedious and time consuming (and presumably non-chargeable) to repeat the exercise if the form has been virtually completed since masking fluids are prohibited and will result in the form being returned as invalid. Notwithstanding that the forms are ultimately to be scanned electronically and the choice of ink is prescribed by SDLT 1 itself and HMRC Stamp Taxes are accordingly not anxious to encourage physical alterations to the form, it is permitted to cross out the erroneous entry and put the correct figures underneath the boxes. However, there are problems with amending returns prepared on screen after printing. Manual amendments may not be recognised by HMRC Stamp Taxes processes. If such an amendment is required, it is recommended that the on-screen version is amended and the earlier version deleted.

(3) SUBSEQUENT ADJUSTMENTS/CONTINGENT TAX

As described in the main text there are many situations where, notwithstanding the filing of a land transaction return (SDLT 1) and the receipt of the land transaction return certificate (SDLT 5), the taxation position is not final and further full returns with signed declarations are required, with fresh self-assessments retrospectively adjusting the initial tax calculation and, where appropriate, any subsequent intermediate revisions thereof. The adjustment has to be made on a totally new return form. Although the particular return relates to the adjustment of a previous return, it cannot be dealt with as an amendment of the original return even when it is filed within the first 12 months after the initial filing. There will be a separate 'transaction number', i.e. bar code which suggests a separate transaction, but there is no provision for a cross-reference to the earlier land transaction return. The point will emerge to the attention of HMRC Stamp Taxes because of the discrepancies between Boxes 10, 14 and 15, i.e. the relevant consideration, the total tax and the tax currently being paid. The last of these will take into account tax paid with the filing of the prior return and will not be 4 per cent of the chargeable consideration, etc.

It will also be noted that no provision is made on the land transaction return form for negative tax, i.e. where at the time of the filing of the later return there is a claim for repayment of previously overpaid tax such as where the effect of a rent review was overestimated. This presumably has to be dealt with by way of amendment to the original return if within the relevant 12-month period, or pursuant to the claims procedure prescribed in FA 2003, Sched. 11A. The requirement for a notice in the required form will be dealt with, initially, by filing the required form showing nil tax payable and an accompanying letter setting out the previous overpayment with a reference to the relevant bar code number which will, hopefully, be accepted by HMRC Stamp Taxes as a notice in the prescribed form but there will, doubtless, be investigation of the details taking time and adding to the cost.[7] Although this might be regarded as an 'amendment' of the original return by bringing it up to date, it has to be treated as a separate return and, although it may involve a claim for repayment of tax previously overpaid, it is not affected by the restrictions upon error and mistake claims, because although there may have been a mistake in the previous reasonable estimate the current context involves not the correction of errors but the revision of guestimates in the light of subsequent events.

PARTICULAR POINTS ON THE FORMS

Moving on from the requirements to use black ink, capital letters and not folding the form in case the scanners misread the crease as an entry:

SDLT 1

Box 2 refers to the grant of a lease. It is important to note HMRC Stamp Taxes's view that the effect of FA 2003, Sched. 17A, para. 12A is that there are two separate chargeable transactions as at substantial performance of the agreement and as at grant of the lease. Two totally separate returns with two different effective dates will be required. SDLT 4 will also be required.

Box 3 Although it might be thought that this part of the form is concerned with sales of existing interests, such as freeholds or existing leases, the codes to be inserted in Box 3 refer to transfers of interests that are subject to leases or underleases. Although these are not newly created leases, SDLT 6 indicates in the notes between Boxes 15 and 16 that the return must disclose those leases subject to which the interest is being transferred although this has no bearing upon the tax charge. It seems that where the interest transferred is the reversion on several leases, a separate SDLT form for each lease will be required, although much of the information on that form is inappropriate to dealings with leases granted long ago. There is some uncertainty as to whether the notes are correct. In dealing with transfers of freehold interests subject to leases, it seems that SDLT 6 would require the disclosure not merely of the details of the headlease but also of 'each additional sub-lease'. The fact that there is a separate note dealing with the grant of leases subject to existing tenancies requiring details of those tenancies which are accurately described as 'sub-leases' indicates that the sale and purchase of a freehold reversion requires the purchaser to disclose details of all existing leases subject to which he acquires the interest and any sub-leases previously granted out of those leases. This will constitute a significant problem where, for example, there is an acquisition of a freehold interest of a large block of flats by a management company controlled by the tenants. Details of every lease in the block will be required, plus details of any sublettings that the tenants may have entered into, whether on a short-term or a long-term basis.

In addition to details of the leases subject to which the interest is acquired, SDLT 4, Box 2 requires details of the actual use of the premises, such as office or warehouse.

Box 4. Apart from the special case of leases and FA 2003, Sched. 17A, para. 12A there is only one effective date for the transaction and although each subsequent return bears a different transaction number or bar code they have to refer to the date entered into Box 4 on the initial SDLT 1.

Box 5 presents a problem both as to what has to be disclosed and as to the amount of detail required. The former practice for PD forms of inserting 'the usual covenants'

---

[7] Fortunately, interest may be payable on repaid tax.

is probably no longer acceptable. Initially HMRC Stamp Taxes was contending that a full disclosure of all covenants and restrictions is required, including planning restrictions and both historic and current conditions including those created by the transaction.

The width of disclosure of conditions and restrictions including past and newly created circumstances is supposed to be limited by the need for restrictions to affect the value of the land but there is a different explanation in SDLT 6. Since virtually every covenant and restriction and easement may have some effect upon value of the land, it is difficult to see any limitation upon the width of disclosure. However, it is, in practice, rare for the initially agreed price to be adjusted after investigation of title. It can be said that pre-existing restrictions do not affect the value since these will possibly have been taken into account in fixing the offer price, at least where they are fairly standard in content; but HMRC Stamp Taxes draws a distinction between value and price and might argue that although the price was not adjusted it was originally fixed by the seller taking those conditions into account, i.e. their existence affected the value because the asking price was fixed taking them into account. Long-standing restrictions will affect the 'value' because they may inhibit the use of the land; but being in place before the transactions they will not affect the 'price' because the seller will probably have taken these issues into account. It seems that virtually everything is likely to require disclosure. The position is not helped by the fact that the form refers to 'value' whereas SDLT 6 refers to the chargeable consideration. Essentially, the notes for guidance are incorrect since the chargeable consideration is not necessarily linked to the value of the property and the 'value' may be affected by the covenants even though historic. Thus a transaction may be at a deliberately low price or one where the actual consideration is ignored for the purposes of the tax. Since the form has statutory authority, unlike the guidance notes which have no authority, the criterion has to be the possible effect on 'value' which will often have no relationship to the price.

As regards the depth of the disclosure, it seems that all that is required is 'a description'. However, it seems that, in practice, inserting 'see attached photocopy documents' and enclosing copies of the conveyances, leases or other documents has not hitherto been the subject of an attack or Enquiry by HMRC Stamp Taxes.

Box 6 requires the date of the contract. For option arrangements this will be the date of the exercise of the option. For conditional contracts it is the date when the contract is executed not when it becomes unconditional. This date is important for transitional provisions but has little, if any, other practical effect since, apart from options and pre-emption rights, the entering into a contract is not as such taxable. The date will, however, be important in determining whether the taxpayer has taken possession pursuant to the contract. This can be a significant issue where the taxpayer is already in occupation under an earlier arrangement of the land such as a tenant renewing a lease already being in possession prior to the contract date should not constitute substantial performance.

Box 7 refers to land exchanges. It has to be noted that current practices indicate that in the official view 'land exchange' as defined by FA 2003, s.47 (see Chapter 7) includes 'excepting and reserving interests' because this involves a regrant, i.e. a land exchange. Where the box is relevant the transaction may be taxed upon market value, not the contract price, when completing Box 10.

Box 8 goes to the question of whether the grant of the option and its exercise are linked transactions so that the tax upon the option has to be retrospectively recalculated and any option premium has to be included in determining the rate on the main contract. It will include an option to renew or extend or terminate leases (but not necessarily the implementation of break clauses which may not give rise to a chargeable transaction).

Each subsequent linked transaction, whether relating to the same or other property, will require submission of new SDLT 1s because the total premium shown in the original return will be generally retrospectively incorrect. A full return is required, not an amendment to the form, unless perhaps the linked transaction occurs within the 12-month period during which the taxpayer is permitted to correct a return.

Box 10 is particularly unclear and the official advice fluctuates between setting out the actual consideration and the chargeable consideration. As this seems to be required as a *prima facie* check upon the consideration for calculating the tax, it is generally regarded as being appropriate to insert the chargeable consideration and this appears to be consistent with the general drafting policy that the word 'consideration' when unqualified by any adjective is, *prima facie*, 'chargeable consideration'. This makes the treatment of exemptions particularly important. Thus intra-group transactions have to incur the cost of a valuation notwithstanding that no tax is payable. This means that if there is variable consideration the appropriate maximum contingent sum or reasonable estimate as required by FA 2003, s.51 has to be inserted. It will also include the Value Added Tax that is potentially payable if the transaction is not a transfer of a going concern on the current official practice.

Box 10 is also relevant for leases. Although the basic computation and provisions for leases appear later in the return, it will be necessary to include in Box 10 the aggregate of the chargeable premium and net present value of the rent for leases produced from later entries.

Box 11. Although Box 10 would seem to require disclosure of the VAT possibly payable if the transaction is not a transfer of a going concern this is officially regarded as unascertained consideration and has to be included in the chargeable consideration and tax computation and requires delivery of SDLT 4, Box 11 by referring to 'payable' would seem to require this sum to be disclosed. However, SDLT 6 refers to VAT actually paid which may well be a very different amount if the parties are treating the transaction as a transfer of a going concern. Upon this view the entry here is 'nil' if the parties are approaching the transaction as a transfer of a going concern so that no tax is 'paid'. However, as discussed in the main text, there are disputes in practice as to how this should be treated for computation and Box 10 purposes.

Box 12 has an inadequate list of codes in SDLT 6. In particular, contingent consideration does not include unascertained or uncertain consideration but may include potential VAT in relation to transfers as a going concern on the official view, clawback and overage payments and payments for building works and services. These will have to be included under 'other' (34) but further information will be required in Box 4 on SDLT 4, as will details of any deferral arrangements (FA 2003, s.90 and Stamp Duty Land Tax (Administration) Regulations 2003, SI 2003/2837, Part 4).

Box 13 will initially be completed on a provisional basis because there may not be another transaction with which it is linked at that stage such as the grant of a lease with an option to renew. A later transaction may be linked so that retrospectively this entry becomes incorrect and requires 'amendment' which will probably form part of the necessary new complete return retrospectively recalculating the tax (FA 2003, s.81A, which may affect third parties, Sched. 17A, para. 12). The retrospective effect of linked transactions is a key factor in completing and submitting multiple returns.

Linked transactions can be included in the same return (Box 26) only if they have the same effective date, and are between the same parties and not connected persons.

Boxes 14 and 15 The notes for guidance (SDLT 6) are less than helpful and potentially misleading. Box 14 requires disclosure of the total tax, Box 15 requires only the tax paid, which will include the relevant amounts in respect of leases dealt with in later parts of the return, which will have to be 'carried back'. Frequently the amounts shown in these two boxes will differ and not be a precise percentage of the aggregate amount in Box 10 because the land transaction return may be an amending or

APPENDIX D

further return for the same transaction,[8] where a return has been previously submitted. The amount of tax payable with the second or subsequent return will usually be less than the total amount of the tax such as where an instalment of an overage payment or a rent review during the first five years of the term has to be notified. Box 14 may contain a different figure from its predecessors as the reasonable estimates become replaced by facts. Box 15 deals only with the extra tax but cannot cope with tax refunds. The reference in SDLT 6 to the total amount due must mean the extra tax payable at that stage not the overall total amount. Note that if tax payments have been deferred this must be referred to in SDLT 4, Box 5.

Box 17 requires the disclosure of the term commencement date. The practical significance of this is whether the first review falls within the last quarter of the five-year period because of the practice of backdating the term commencement date to the previous quarter day (FA 2003, Sched. 17A, para. 1A). Unfortunately, the double charge upon leases introduced by FA 2003, Sched. 17A, para. 12A means that if there is any significant delay between the substantial performance of the agreement for lease and the grant of the lease, the first review date will inevitably fall within the first five years because the backdating will be more than the three months before the actual grant of the lease excluded from the charge. There may also be issues as to whether any backdated rent is taxable as a premium (FA 2003, Sched. 5, para. 1A).

Box 18 refers to the end of the lease. For periodic tenancies it seems that HMRC Stamp Taxes is expecting a date at the end of the first period. This has to be noted since a periodic tenancy, such as a weekly or monthly tenancy, is treated as being a tenancy for one year. Therefore, although the calculation of the tax and reporting obligations are dealt with by reference to a one-year period or longer for a tenancy for a fixed period and thereafter from period to period until determined by notice, this will be treated for these purposes as a tenancy up until the end of the fixed period. There is, therefore, in many cases a potential discrepancy between the date or period used for the calculation of the tax and the date required on the return.

Box 18 ignores break clauses and options to renew but SDLT 4, Boxes 10, 11 and 12 require details of break clauses and options to renew.

Box 19 requires details of rent-free periods but these will usually be linked to some form of rent review and details of these are required in SDLT 4, Boxes 12, 13, 14 and 15.

Box 20 requires details of the initial rent, including any actual VAT. If, as is likely, the rent is reviewable, details of the review date are required under the reference to the first review or adjustment date and further details are required on SDLT 4, Boxes 12, 13, 14 and 15. It seems that details of other variable rents such as turnover and profit-related rents are not required unless HMRC Stamp Taxes takes the view that these represent uncertain consideration within SDLT 4. SDLT 6 provides no guidance as to variable rents payable in arrears. For example, there may be a lease where the rent may include a base figure plus a turnover element which is payable in arrears once the figures for the relevant year have been agreed. The calculation of the tax will be upon the basis of a reasonable estimate of the rent payable which will include a 'guestimate' of the turnover for the first five years. No guidance is provided as to whether the estimated rent is to be included rather than the base rent. It would be prudent to include the estimated figure for the first rent period so as to avoid any suggestion of attempts to mislead HMRC Stamp Taxes by suggesting that the transaction is smaller than it actually is. Since one of the criteria for initiating an Enquiry is the size of the trans-

---

8 It will be noted that the bar code refers to the return not the transaction so that there will be several returns with different bar codes but no means of cross-referring is provided in the forms.

action, it is likely that an aggressive response will be obtained if a low figure was inserted, although this would be potentially justifiable because of the lack of guidance. Unfortunately, it seems that attempts to rely upon the notes in SDLT 6 will not be regarded as a reason for mitigating penalties for incorrect returns.

In *Box 20* it has to be noted that sums described as rent but paid in respect of periods prior to the grant of the lease are taxed as a premium and should be included in Box 22 (FA 2003, Sched. 5, para. 1A (as amended)). Although rents indexed to RPI are treated as fixed rents for the purpose of calculating the tax, they will not be included as rents where the amount is known. This, like so many other aspects of the various returns, requires the actual information and data rather than any deemed arrangements pursuant to the legislation and regulations.

Box 21 is ambiguous. It refers to the amount of VAT but without specifying the appropriate period. It would seem from the context that this is the actual amount of VAT payable upon the initial rent on an annual basis and not the amount of VAT payable over the period of the lease. It would also seem to require the details of the amount of VAT included in the reasonable estimate of the initial rent.

Box 22 refers to the total premium. This includes all items within the charge to tax other than rent. It would also include rent paid in respect of periods prior to the grant of the lease (see above). It will include payments for building works, services, land exchanges including surrenders and regrants (details of which are required in SDLT 4, Box 9). Details of other consideration such as consideration in kind or periodical premiums (but not premiums payable by instalments) are required to be disclosed in SDLT 4, Box 18. The total premium requires inclusion of any premium, whether in cash or in kind, for the grant of linked leases. This will apply where there is an option to renew a lease which is a linked transaction as well as the grant of other leases as part of the original commercial transaction. The reference to other consideration (Code 04) would seem to include items such as 'additional rents' in the form of insurance premium contributions.

The reference to contingent consideration (Code 09) is limited and does not include uncertain or unascertained consideration. A lease granted for a premium that contains some form of overage or clawback arrangement will not be a contingent consideration and should, presumably, be entered as 'other' under Code 04. SDLT 4, Box 19 requires disclosure of reverse premium payments by the landlord to the tenant and any other consideration being supplied by the landlord to the tenant. This requires disclosure of surrenders and regrants but entries to this effect have already been made on SDLT 1, Box 7 by indicating that the transaction is part of a land exchange.

Box 23, dealing with the net present value of the rent, will because of the prevalence of rent reviews in many cases be prepared on the basis of reasonable estimates. Rent reviews, turnover rents and other matters will require to be disclosed on SDLT 4. A subsequent return SDLT 1, in full, will be required as and when the estimates unwind and the actual data as required by the legislation emerges. It must be noted that a completely new return will be required, including the appropriate entries on SDLT 4. It is not possible to correct or amend the original return to take account of subsequent chargeable rent reviews.

Boxes 24 and 25 deal with the calculation of the tax. But it has to be noted that the entries made in Boxes 22–25 have to be carried back to Boxes 10, 14 and 15.

Box 26 provides a useful facility for avoiding the duplication of forms where they merely repeat the same information from other forms relating to the same transaction other than details of the land and possibly avoiding the need to apportion global consideration to some extent. Although this is not immediately obvious, the benefit of this facility is limited. The impact of Box 4, dealing with the effective date, is that the form can effectively be used for several properties only where these have the same effective date. It is not sufficient that they are all acquired under a single contract since the arrangement may be such that there are different effective dates for various properties. This facility also avoids the need for having to file many subsequent land transaction returns where there are later linked transactions or other events such as payments of instalments in respect of overage payments for certain of the properties but not all of them where the uncertainties have yet to be resolved. In all of these cases where several properties have been acquired under linked or simultaneous arrangements, then all of the forms would require amendment because of the need to include the total consideration for all of the related transactions. Where a single return has been submitted for numerous properties, then only one subsequent form will be required in respect of all of them. It is, therefore, important to try to organise matters in such a way that there is only one effective date, although this could be a problem where leases are concerned because the tenant may go into occupation of some of the premises, but not all, for fitting out or other matters or they may be delayed in certain aspects of the construction works. There may also be difficulties where there is a delay between substantial performance and the date of grant now that these are two separate chargeable events pursuant to the official view of FA 2003, Sched. 17A, para. 12A (as amended).

Box 27 represents a necessary facility if advantage is taken of Box 26. A single land transaction return certificate (SDLT 5) could be seriously inconvenient where the properties are in separate Land Registries. One certificate would not necessarily be the best way of dealing with the registrations, particularly if there have been some delays in the turnaround by HMRC Stamp Taxes and the parties are under pressure to meet Land Registry deadlines. It is usually appropriate to ask for a separate certificate for each property in order to facilitate Land Registry dealings.

Where numerous properties are included, then it will be necessary to complete a separate SDLT 3 for each of the properties. SDLT 1 and SDLT 3 both require details of the local authority in Box 29 and Box 2 respectively. Details of the appropriate codes are contained in SDLT 6.

Box 33 requires a plan if boundaries need to be defined. The bar code reference has to be included on the reverse of the form including details as to the scale of the plan.

SDLT 4 will be required even where there is only one property involved in the transaction if mineral rights are reserved from the transaction (Box 7). A separate SDLT 1 will be required for the particular land if dealing solely with the mineral rights if more than one property is included in the transaction return. Fortunately, HMRC Stamp Taxes does not presently regard the reservation of mineral rights as a regrant producing a land exchange with a market value charge upon the seller of the land and the need to file a separate SDLT 1.

Box 34 requires details of the number of vendors. It must be noted that the vendor is not necessarily the owner of the registered title being transferred, or even a person whose name appears on the contract itself. It is, essentially, the beneficial owner of the property. This is an acute problem where nominees are involved or the property is held upon trust by the first full name for others. This can be a problem where the seller is a body of trustees or a partnership. However, SDLT 6 suggests relaxation of this requirement by stating that a partnership is a single purchaser. Presumably, rather than having to file numerous SDLT 2s for each partner, entry of the partnership name will be sufficient identification of both vendors and purchasers. The fact that the partnership has representative partners who are entitled to act in relation to SDLT on behalf of the firm is not a relevant consideration. These persons are only authorised to act in relation to the role of purchaser but they are not the substitute for the vendor or the purchaser. HMRC Stamp Taxes has not indicated that there is to be any relaxation of these disclosure requirements for other bodies of persons not within the definition of 'company' having numerous members. In some situations the body of persons may be treated as a body corporate, in which case it seems that the name of the association can be inserted as the name of the vendor.

There are difficulties in complying with these requirements since there is no statutory obligation for the person acting as the seller to disclose information. This has to be obtained by request and contractual stipulation. The purchaser is required to exercise his own due diligence in these matters.

Box 38 relating to the vendor's address is a particular illustration of the problems facing purchasers. It is not unknown for vendors to refuse to divulge their address, particularly if they wish to avoid being stalked by a disgruntled purchaser. In such a situation it is not acceptable to HMRC Stamp Taxes for the purchaser to indicate that this information cannot be obtained and an attempt to submit a return on this basis will lead to its rejection. The advice from the so-called helpline is to insert the address of the premises being acquired. This advice is potentially dangerous because, as the parties to the transaction will be fully aware, by the time of completion which will usually be the effective date in this type of case, the vendor will usually have vacated the premises and moved on. Nevertheless, it seems that HMRC Stamp Taxes may not take too aggressive a line in relation to penalties if the purchaser has used reasonable endeavours to obtain the information, although this may create difficulties for it when conducting an Enquiry on a proper basis rather than, at present, as if it were an adjudication for stamp duty.

For companies the address is the registered office of the company even though this may not be the principal place of business. Where a company is incorporated abroad and does not have premises in the UK, it may be that any address for service contained in particulars registered under Companies Act 1985, Part 24 will be sufficient to avoid a penalty.

Box 49, dealing with the number of purchasers, requires an accurate analysis as to who is or are the purchasers. This may require the disclosure of details of numerous persons who are beneficially entitled although not appearing on the Land Register or as parties to the contract. However, as with vendors, there appears to be a relaxation so far as partnerships are concerned. The partnership counts as a single purchaser and an entry of the partnership name would appear to be sufficient in Box 52.

Box 52. Where the purchaser is a company, it is obligatory to file SDLT 4, especially where the company is incorporated abroad.

Box 55 deals with settlements. Where the person appearing on the contract or receiving the transfer is a nominee this box will not be appropriate. In such a case the purchaser disclosed on the form will be the beneficial owner. In consequence, this can only be of relevance where there is not a bare trust or nominee or agency relationship in place.

Box 57 requires details of whether the parties are connected. Various illustrations are given in SDLT 6 but it must be noted that companies within the same group are also connected. This means that such transactions will be dealt with pursuant to the connected company charge or the special regime for partnerships so that the figure to be included in Box 10 will be the market value of the property or the reduced amount for partnerships, not the consideration being paid. This requirement will apply even where the transaction is exempt by reason of intra-group relief or, *prima facie*, qualifies for relief as some form of distribution; but note the reliefs possibly available from the connected company charge in relation to dividends and distributions by and out of companies contained in s.54, FA 2003.

Box 58 is of key practical importance. Given that in England and Wales, but not in Scotland where special practices apply, there will inevitably be several days' delay in

APPENDIX D

the turnaround of the form before the land transaction return certificate (SDLT 5) is produced, and as this is essential for the purpose of obtaining any changes in the Land Register, it is important to ensure that the SDLT 5 certificate is delivered to the person who has the carriage of the registration process. It is, probably, inappropriate for this to be sent to the purchaser's address or to the premises. It is appropriate that the form is sent to the appropriate professional adviser. This may be the person who is acting for the mortgagee who has the greatest incentive in ensuring that the title is registered. Delays in transmitting the form may result in delays in submitting documentation to the Land Registry with consequent problems.

Box 59 raises certain issues consequent upon the entries raised in Box 58, where the form is to be received by an agent. The notes for guidance (SDLT 6) state that this is to deal with correspondence 'arising from the submission of the return'. Whilst, in general, in order to ensure that matters are dealt with expeditiously, it is probably appropriate for the correspondence dealing with the initial submission of the return to be dealt with by professionals, there is a longer-term issue. It is not clear whether HMRC Stamp Taxes will use the entry in Box 59 as a letterbox for initiating an Enquiry. It is, at present, unclear whether this is its intention, but there is a risk that this may be the case. This can be something of a problem since, after the transaction is completed, the lay client and the professional may cease to deal with each other on a regular basis. Moreover, given that there may be a significant delay before the Enquiry is launched, the professional may be unable to contact the taxpayer. Until this matter is clarified there may, therefore, be certain difficulties in completing Box 59 on the basis that the professional is to deal with all correspondence.

Box 69, dealing with trustees, refers to trustees of settlements. Nominees, bare trustees and other fiduciaries will be required to answer 'no' because they will not be the 'purchaser'. Indeed, such persons should have no involvement with the form whatsoever since the person identified as purchaser and the person to sign the declaration must be the beneficial owner, subject to the special rules for signatures.

Box 71 is a key box and its completion is fundamental. The rules as to who is required or, within certain limited circumstances, permitted to sign Box 71 is a matter of considerable complexity, as is now the form of the declaration because of the powers of agents to sign in relation to matters relating to the effective date (FA 2003, Sched. 10, para. 1A (as amended)).

Index

Accountability for tax 275–6
Accountants
    powers to call for information from 292–3
Acquisitions 38–41
    by companies 243–6
    from connected persons 231–2
    not exempt 41
    process of 40–1
    types 39–40
Administrators
    liability for tax 270
Advancement powers 214–215
Agents
    liability for tax 267–8
Aggregating transactions 67–8
Agreements for lease
    effective date 58
    substantial performance 143–6
Allocation of price 43
Alternative financing 123–4
Annuities 93–5
Anti-avoidance rules 112
    intra-group transactions 255
    partnerships 240–1
Appeals 287
Appointment powers 214–5
Apportionment
    computation of tax 77–81
    trusts 210
Arrangements 256
Assessments 283–5
    determinations 283–4
    discovery assessments 284–5
Assignment
    chargeable interests 69–70
    leases 16–7, 141–2, 176–9
        exempt leases 178–9
        liability for tax of assignees 274–5

    problem areas 177–8
Associations
    liability for tax 269–70
Avoidance of tax 32–6, 111
    anti-avoidance rules 112
    form and substance 34–6
    forward planning 35–6
    sham transactions 34

Back dated rent 153
Bare trusts 199, 200–1, 202
    exemptions from connected company charge 244–5
Break clauses 38, 166, 179–80
Building works *see* Works

Calculation of tax *see* Computation of tax
Cancellation of transactions 57
Certificates 279–80, 307
Chargeable consideration 72–5, 79–81, 188–90
Chargeable interests
    acquisitions of chargeable interest from connected persons 231–2
    assignment 69–70
    land 42–3, 44–6
Chargeable transactions
    basic charging provisions 37–41
    goodwill 44
    specific transactions 41–3
Charities 182
Children and young people
    liability for tax of representatives 273
Choses-in-action
    interest in trust funds as 211
Claiming exemptions 114–5
Clawback arrangements 15, 22, 45
    company reliefs 253–4, 256–7

INDEX

Clubs
 liability for tax 269–70
Companies 242–3
 acquisitions by 243–6
 compliance 258–9, 269
 connected companies 243–4
 deemed premiums 171
 deferred or provisional tax 259–60
 distribution by 245
 due diligence 247–8, 258
 exemptions from connected company charge 244–5
 intra-group transactions 183, 254–5
 liability for tax 268–9
 liquidation 245
 liability for tax of liquidators 270
 purchases from 246
 receivership 246
 liability for tax of receivers 272
 reliefs 248–51
  arrangements 256
  clawback arrangements 253–4, 256–7
  intra-group transactions 254–5
  reduced rate for partitions and reorganisations of companies 251–4
 reorganisations/reconstructions 183, 247–8, 249–51
 share sales 258, 302–3
 'time bombs' 246–7
 warranties 258
Completion 10–2, 22, 48, 297–8
 as effective date 50–1
 phased 56
Compliance 30
 companies 258–9, 269
 leases 142–3
 options and pre-emption rights 129
Compulsory purchasers
 reliefs 122
Computation of tax
 carrying out works 99–100
 chargeable consideration 72–5, 79–81
 consideration in kind 82–6
 costs 86–7
 debts, liabilities and mortgages 95–9
 disadvantaged land 61, 65
 foreign currency 99
 global consideration and apportionment 77–81
 initial calculation 104–5

 lease premiums and rents 70
 linked transactions 66–72
 market value 82–6
 mixed property 64–5
 multiple occupancy 63–4
 options and pre-emption rights 70–1
 periodical payments and annuities 93–5
 postponed consideration and instalments 92–3
 provisional tax 75–6
 rates of SDLT 59–61
  nil rate for premiums 181
  reduced rate for partitions and reorganisations of companies 251–4
 residential property 61–3
 reverse payments 109–10
 services 100
 six or more properties 65
 subsequent notification 105–7
 subsequent sales of property 107–9
 theory and practice 87–9
 value added tax 89–92
 variable consideration 101–7
 works 194–5
Conditional arrangements 56–7
 conditional contracts 128
 conditional gifts 74
Consideration *see* Payment (consideration)
Construction works *see* Works
Constructive trusts 19, 198, 206
Contingent consideration 101–2
Contracts 294–5
 conditional 128
 routine *see* Routine contracts
Corporate transactions *see* Companies
Costs 86–7
 value added tax and 92
Covenants 172–4
 estate covenants 39
Cross-options 126

Date *see* Effective date
Debts 95–9
Deceased persons
 estates of 216–8, 220–2
 variation 119–20, 183
 liabilities 217–8
 representatives liability for tax 273–4
Deemed leases 141–2, 154

318

Deemed linked transactions 72
Deemed premiums 171
Deemed rent 153–4
Deferred tax 259–60
Deposits 53–4
Derivative trusts 212–3
Determinations 283–4
Disadvantaged land
  computation of tax 61, 65
Disclaimers 38
Discovery assessments 284–5
Discretionary trusts 211–2
Dividends 245
Domestic arrangements 100
Double charge
  leases 143–6
Drafting issues 20–2
Due diligence 13–4
  companies 247–8, 258
  options and pre-emption rights 128–9

Effective date
  actions not documents 48–50
  agreements for lease 58
  basic position 50–1
  leases 143
  number of effective dates 48–50
  options and pre-emption rights 57–8, 126
  routine contracts 51–7
Employment
  deemed rent and 153–4
Enforcement 282
  appeals 287
  assessments 283–5
  enquiries 282–3, 286–7, 288
  post-transaction rulings 286
  powers to call for information 288, 289–93
  record-keeping obligations 288–9
Enquiries 282–3, 286–7
  appeals 287
  completion 287
  land transaction returns 286
  powers to call for information 288, 289–93
  scope 286–7
Estate covenants 39
Estates of deceased persons 216–8, 220–2
  variation 119–20, 183

Evasion of tax 111
Exchanges 130–4
  leases and 170–1
  major interest for major interest 133
  major interest for minor interest 133–4
  non-major interest for minor interest 134
  trusts 210–1
Exemptions 41, 44, 111–5
  claiming 114–5
  connected company charge 244–5
  exempt property 116
  leases 178–9, 181–5
    reliefs not available 185
  non-notifiable transactions 117–20
  requiring notification 120–4
  transfer of partnership interests 240
  works 190–1
  see also Reliefs

Fitting-out arrangements 20
Fixtures 43, 45
Foreign currency payments 99
Foreign transactions 31–2
Foreign trusts 207, 218
Fraud 293
Future values and rents 85

Gifts
  conditional gifts 74
  exemption for leases 182
  subgifts 215
Going concerns
  value added tax and transfer of 89–91
Goodwill 44

Historical hangovers 124
Holding over
  leases 165–6
  rent 161–2
Hostels 63
Housing authorities
  exemptions for 118, 120–1, 184
  right-to-buy 120, 184

Implied trusts 19, 198–9, 206
Incapacity
  liability for tax of representatives 273
Indemnities 15, 258
  given by tenants 172

INDEX

Index-linked payment (consideration) 94–5
Informal arrangements 18–20
Information
 powers to call for information 288, 289–93
Instalments 92–3
 premiums 169
Intestacies 218
Intra-group transactions 183, 254–5
Investigation of title 7, 8–9, 13–4

Joint purchasers
 liability for tax 267
Joint tenancies
 severance 208–9
Jurisdiction 31–2

Kind
 payment (consideration) in 54–5, 82–6, 132

Land
 chargeable interests in 42–3, 44–6
 exchanges 130–4
  leases and 170–1
 removal of land from partnerships 234–7
 trusts 203
Land Registry 265–6, 276–8
Land transaction return certificate 279
Land transaction returns 286, 305
Leases 136–8, 298–9
 agreements for lease 58
  substantial performance 143–6
 assignment 16–7, 141–2, 176–9
  exempt leases 178–9
  liability for tax of assignees 274–5
  problem areas 177–8
 builders and 187
 charge to tax 147–8
 compliance and 142–3
 covenants and obligations under 172–4
 deemed 141–2, 154
 definition 140–1
 double charge 143–6
 effective date 143
 exemptions 178–9, 181–5
  reliefs not available 185
 grant of 137

 regrant 175–6
 to third parties 146–7
 indefinite term 166–7
 land exchanges involving 170–1
 leaseback arrangements 123–4, 183–4
 licence compared with 139–40
 linked transactions and renewals of 163–4
 merger 180–1
 nominees 138–9
 renewals 165
 reversionary interest 181
 substantial performance 143
 successive leases 17, 71
 surrender 19, 175–6, 180
 term of 164–7
 termination 179–81
 variation 174–6
 see also Premiums; Rent
Legislation 30–1
Liability for tax 251
 accountability for tax 275–6
 certificates 279–80, 307
 connected parties 266–75
 issues 262–5
 Land Registry issues 265–6
 notifiable transactions 278–9
 registration of title 276–8
 taxable person (purchaser) 251–62, 263–5
 vendor 265
Licences 44, 47
 leases compared with 139–40
Life tenants 131
Linked transactions 36, 127–8, 300–1
 aggregating transactions 67–8
 computation of tax 66–72
 deemed 72
 renewals of leases and 163–4
 same parties 68–9
 side effects for assignees 69–70
 successive leases 17, 71, 163–4
Liquidation 245
 liability for tax of liquidators 270

Matrimonial breakdown 119, 182
Mergers of interests 39
 leases 180–1
Mixed property
 computation of tax 64–5
Mortgages 44

computation of tax 95–9
rent-to-mortgage 184
security arrangements 6–7
Multiple occupancy
computation of tax 63–4
Mutual options 126

Negligence
self-assessment and 28, 29
Nominees
exemptions from connected company charge 244–5
leases 138–9
liability for tax 268
Non-documentary arrangements 18–20
Non-notifiable transactions 117–20
Non-residential property
rates of SDLT 61
Notice to quit 38, 166, 179–80
Notifiable transactions 278–9

Old people's homes 63
Operation of law
surrender of leases by 19
Options 45, 50, 125, 126, 296–7, 300
compliance issue 129
computation of tax 70–1
due diligence 128–9
effective date 57–8, 126
exercise 127
linked transactions 127–8
oral exercise 19
provisional tax and 23
sale 128
Oral arrangements 18–20
creation of trusts 196–7
Overage payments 15, 22, 45

Parliamentary constituencies
reorganisation of 122
Partition 134–5
Partnerships 46, 223–4
acquisitions of chargeable interest from connected persons 231–2
actual consideration 232–3
anti-avoidance rules 240–1
deemed premiums 171
interests 228–9
transfers 229–31, 237–41
liability for tax 270–2
ordinary transactions 225–6
profits 228

property 230–1
removal of land from partnerships 234–7
shares 228
special transactions 226–7
stamp duty 224–5
sum of the lower proportions 233–4
terminology 227–31
Payment (consideration)
annuities 93–5
chargeable consideration 72–5, 79–81, 188–90
computation of tax 72–5
global consideration and apportionment 77–81
contingent 101–2
definition of consideration 73–5
deposits/stage payments 53–4
foreign currency 99
index-linked 94–5
instalments 92–3
in kind 54–5, 82–6, 132
no chargeable consideration 118
partnerships 232–3
periodical payments 93–5
postponed consideration 92–3
reverse payments 75, 109–10
substantial 53
unascertained 103, 109
uncertain 103
variable consideration 54–5, 101–7, 300
Payment of tax
enforcement 283
incorrect amount 11
title issues and 7–8
works 194–5
Payslips 307
Personal representatives
assents and appropriation by 120
liability for tax 273–4
purchasers of land from 222
PFI projects 185
Phased completion 56
Planning for tax 35–6
Planning obligations
reliefs 122
Possession 55–6
Post-transaction rulings 286
Pre-emption rights 45, 50, 125–6, 296–7
compliance issue 129
computation of tax 70–1

INDEX

Pre-emption rights (*cont.*)
  due diligence 128–9
  effective date 57–8, 126
Premiums 152, 167–71
  computation of tax 70
  deemed 171
  exclusions from charge on premiums 172–4
  instalments and periodical payments 169
  nil rate 181
  reverse 172
  variable 168–9
  works 169–70
Private finance (PFI) projects 185
Profits 45
Property 295–6
  mixed property 64–5
  non-residential property 61
  partnerships 230–1
    removal of land from partnerships 234–7
  residential property 61–3
  subsequent sales of property 107–9
  trusts 203
    dispositions 206
  see also Land
Provisional tax 22–4, 75–6, 259–60
  rent 149
Public bodies
  reliefs 122, 123
Purchase and resale 124
Purchaser *see* Taxable person (purchaser)

Rates of SDLT 59–61
  nil rate for premiums 181
  reduced rate for partitions and reorganisations of companies 251–4
Receivership 246
  liability for tax of receivers 272
Reconstructions/reorganisations of companies 183, 247–8, 249–51
Record-keeping obligations 288–9
Registered social landlords
  exemptions 118, 120–1, 184
Registration of title 7, 8–9, 276–8
Reliefs 111–2
  assents and appropriation by personal representatives 120
  companies 248–51

  arrangements 256
  clawback arrangements 253–4, 256–7
  intra-group transactions 254–5
  reduced rate for partitions and reorganisations of companies 251–4
  exempt property 116
  grant of leases to third parties 146–7
  premiums 182
  relieved transactions 117–20
  requiring notification 120–4
  restricted sub-sale relief 192–3
  small transactions 116
  sub-sales 116–7
Relocation relief 121–2
Rent 148–62
  abnormal increase risk 159–60
  back dated 153
  commutation 161
  computation of tax 70
  credit 154, 182
  deemed 153–4
  definition 151
  future 85
  holding over 161–2
  increase of 142, 160
  net present value 149–51
  provisional tax 149
  rates of SDLT 61
  reasonable estimates 160
  receipt of 55
  reductions 158, 161
  rent-to-mortgage 184
  reviews 156–8, 159–60
  taxable amount 149–51
  uncertain 155–6
  value added tax and 91–2, 152
  variable 154–6
Renunciations 38
Reorganisations/reconstructions of companies 183, 247–8, 249–51
Representatives
  assents and appropriation by 120
  liability for tax 273–274
  purchasers of land from 222
Resale 124
Rescission 57
Residential property 61–3
  actual use – not intentions 62–3
  definition 62
  not in use at effective date 63

INDEX

rates of SDLT 60
reliefs 121
Resulting trusts 19, 198–9, 206
Retrospection 48–50
Return
completion of 304–16
Revenue enforcement *see* Enforcement
Reverse payments 75, 109–10
Reverse premiums 172
Reversionary interest 181
Right-to-buy 120, 184
Routine contracts
effective date 51–7
substantial performance 52–3

Sale and lease arrangements 123–4, 183–4
Security arrangements 6–7
Self-assessment 27–30, 281
compliance 30
negligence 28, 29
post-transaction rulings 29–30
Self-certificate 279–80, 307
Service charges 151–2, 152
Services
computation of tax 100
Settlements 199, 200–1
Severance of joint tenancies 208–9
Sham transactions 34
Share sales 258, 302–3
Shares 46
Small transactions
reliefs 116
Social landlords *see* Registered social landlords
Societies
liability for tax 269–70
Sources of law 30–1
Spouses
matrimonial breakdown 119, 182
Stage payments 53–4
Stamp duty 1
differences from SDLT 2–3
partnerships 224–5
Stamp duty land tax (SDLT) 1–5
differences from stamp duty 2–3
see also individual topics
Stamp duty reserve tax 1
Subgifts 215
Sub-sales 12
reliefs 116–7
restricted sub-sale relief 192–3

Subsequent sales of property 107–9
Substantial payment 53
Substantial performance 52–3
agreements for lease 143–6
leases 143
Subtrusts (derivative trusts) 212–3
Successive leases 17, 71, 163–4
Surrender of leases 19, 175–6, 180

Tax accountants
powers to call for information from 292–3
Tax return
completion of 304–16
Taxable person (purchaser) 295–9
fraud and 293
liability for tax 251–62, 263–5
powers to call for information from 289–90
Temporary accommodation 63
Testamentary trusts 219
Third parties
grant of leases to 146–7
powers to call for information from 290–2
title issues and payment of tax 7–8
Title issues 5–17
completion 10–2
due diligence 13–4
investigation of title 7, 8–9, 13–4
investigations and requisitions 15–7
payment of tax and 7–8
registration of title 7, 8–9, 276–8
security arrangements 6–7
timetable 10–2
transitional titles 13
warranties and indemnities 15
Transaction basis of SDLT 5, 17–22, 33, 37, 48
drafting issues 20–2
multiple reporting 22
non-documentary arrangements 18–20
Transitional provisions 1
Transitional titles 13
Trusts 19, 45
appointment and advancement powers 214–215
appointment and retirement of trustees 205
apportionment 210
assents and appropriations 219–20

323

INDEX

bare trusts 199, 200–1, 202
  exemptions from connected company charge 244–5
beneficiaries' interests 207–8
constructive trusts 19, 198, 206
creation 196–8
dealings in equitable interests 206
derivative 212–3
discretionary 211–2
estates of deceased persons 216–8, 220–2
  variation 119–20, 183
exchanges 210–1
exemptions from connected company charge 244
implied trusts 19, 198–9, 206
initial vesting of assets 203–4
interest in trust funds 211
internal rearrangement of beneficial interests 213–4
liability for tax of trustees 272–3
life tenants 131
powers of appointment and advancement 214–215
property 203
  dispositions 206
purchase of land 203
purchases of land
  from personal representatives 222
reservation of benefit 215–6
resulting trusts 19, 198–9, 206
SDLT and 202–3
settlements 199, 200–1
severance of joint tenancies 208–9
subgifts 215
subtrusts 212–3
terminology 199–200
testamentary 219
variation 208, 220–2
wills and intestacies 218, 219

Unascertained consideration 103, 109
Uncertain consideration 103
Unwritten transactions 18–20

Value added tax 89
  costs and 92
  rent and 91–2, 152
  transfer of going concerns and 89–91
Variable consideration 54–5, 101–7, 300
Variable premiums 168–9
Variable rent 154–6
Vendor 265
  particular problems for 300–1

Wait-and-see 24–7
  no finality 24–6
  side effects 26–7
Waivers 38
Warranties 15, 258
  corporate reorganisations 248
Will
  tenancies at 47
Wills 218
  testamentary trusts 219
Works 99–100, 186–7
  to be carried out by purchaser/tenant 187–8
  calculation and payment of SDLT 194–5
  exclusion from charge 190–1
  on land being acquired 189–90
  on land not being acquired 188
  phased development 193–4
  premiums and 169–70
  restricted sub-sale relief 192–3
  site assembly 191–4